Praise for Open Days

What the Press is Saying

"For serious garden lovers, a whole vacation could be mapped around the list, which grows every year to include more locations in more states. The majority of visitors put together a day trip or weekend outing; a stop at a garden is also a pleasant distraction from a long-distance drive."

—*Martha Stewart Living*

"The Open Days Program is like a summer-long tour that stretches across the country...Imagine a tool that opens hundreds of garden gates, allowing you to see some of the best gardens in the United States... This program is really a win-win situation for all gardeners."

—*Garden Gate*

"We can never gush enough about *The Garden Conservancy's Open Days Directory*...This guide to visiting America's best private gardens is so informative and organized you won't believe it."

—*California Homes*

What Our Garden Hosts are Saying

"It was a joy to share with people who really care about gardening. I was surprised at the number of people who traveled a great distance to get here."

—*Weston, CT*

"Loads of fun."

—*Los Angeles, CA*

"A great day, giving immense pleasure to so many people."
—*Nantucket, MA*

"This year was the best ever... I look forward to participating next year."
—*Colonia, NJ*

THE GARDEN CONSERVANCY'S
OPEN DAYS DIRECTORY

The Guide to Visiting America's Best Private Gardens

THE GARDEN CONSERVANCY'S
OPEN DAYS DIRECTORY

The Guide to Visiting America's Best Private Gardens

Foreword by Richard G. Turner Jr.

2003
EDITION

Published by The Garden Conservancy, Inc.
Distributed by Harry N. Abrams, Inc.

Distributed by Harry N. Abrams, Inc., New York
Book design by Richard Deon Graphic Art

Publisher's Cataloging-in-Publication
(provided by Quality Books, Inc.)
The Garden Conservancy's open days directory: the guide to visiting hundreds of America's best private gardens, 2003 ed., 9th ed.

      p. cm.
      Includes index.
      ISSN: 1087-7738
      ISBN: 0-8109-9086-5
1. Gardens—United States—Directories.
2. Botanical gardens—United States—Directories.
3. Arboretums—United States—Directories.
     I. Garden Conservancy.
     II. Title: Open days directory
     SB466.U65G37 2001   712'.07473
                    QBI00-836

This book is printed on recycled paper
Manufactured in the United States of America

Cover photo: Peter & Theodora Berg's Garden, Walpole, New Hampshire. Photo by Peter Mauss/Esto

Contents

SPONSORS

. . . .

G*fine*ardening

The Garden Conservancy gratefully acknowledges
Fine Gardening magazine as the National Media
Sponsor of the 2003 Open Days Program.

We also extend our appreciation to the fine
garden businesses and public gardens that have
supported this publication through their advertising.
Please consult these pages for all your gardening
needs and tell our advertisers you saw them in
The Garden Conservancy's Open Days Directory.

Acknowledgments

· ·

Since our inception in 1995, 138 Regional Representatives have volunteered their time and energy to the development of the Garden Conservancy's Open Days Program. We are grateful for their ongoing commitment and efforts.

Alabama

Birmingham
Mrs. A. Jack Allison (1998-2000, 2002)
Mrs. John N. Wrinkle (1998-2000, 2002)

Arizona

Phoenix
Mrs. Scott Crozier (2000-2002)
Mary Irish (2002-2003)
Carolyn O'Malley (2000-2001)
Nancy Swanson (1999)
Gregory S. Trutza (2000-2001)
Mrs. Donald C. Williams (1998-1999)

California

Carmel
Mrs. Lee Meneice (1997-1998)
Los Angeles
Judy Horton (2001-2003)
Pasadena
Judy Horton (2003)
Mrs. Donivee Nash (1999-2000, 2002)
San Diego
Susi Torre-Bueno (2003)
San Francisco Bay Area
Sonny Garcia (1998-2000)
Charmain Giuliani (1998-2000)
Laurie Jake (2000-2003)
Richard G. Turner, Jr. (1998-2000)
Tom Valva (1998-2000)
San Francisco Peninsula
Mrs. Harvey D. Hinman (1998-2003)
Joan Sanders (2000-2003)

Colorado

Colorado Springs
Mrs. Terence Lilly (2000-2003)
Mrs. Gene Moore (1998-2003)
Denver
Mrs. William B. Harvey (2001, 2003)
Mrs. Moses Taylor (1998, 1999, 2001, 2003)

Connecticut

Page Dickey (co-founder)
Penelope Maynard (co-founder)
Jane Havemeyer (1995-2003)
Sara M. Knight (1995-2003)
Enid Munroe (1995-2003)
Melissa Orme (1995-2003)
Pam Peck (1995-2003)

Delaware

Wilmington
Mrs. George P. Bissell, Jr. (1998-1999)
Mrs. Sidney Scott, Jr. (1998-1999)

District of Columbia

Mrs. John Macomber (1997-2001)
Joanne Seale Wilson (1997-2000)

Florida

Jacksonville
Carolyn Marsh Lindsay (1998)
Vero Beach
Mrs. Thomas S. Morse (1998, 1999, 2001)
Mrs. Bruce Roberts (2002-2003)
Mrs. Henry N. Tifft (1998, 1999, 2001)
Mrs. Stephen Wyer (2002-2003)

GEORGIA

Atlanta
Virginia Almand (1998)
George E.N. de Man (2000)
Mrs. William Huger (1999-2000)

HAWAII

Honolulu
Mrs. E. Chipman Higgins (1997-1998)

ILLINOIS

Barrington Hills
Mrs. David C. Earl (2003)
Chicago
Brooks Hartley-Leonard (2001-2003)
Mrs. Charles E. Schroeder (1997-2000, 2003)
Melissa Shennan (2001-2003)
Hinsdale
Susan Beard (2000-2003)
Rockford
Mrs. David C. Earl (2000-2002)
St. Charles & Naperville
Mrs. David C. Earl (2000-2003)
Western Chicago
Mrs. David C. Earl (2003)

INDIANA

Indianapolis
Dr. Gilbert S. Daniels (1997, 1998)

LOUISIANA

New Orleans
Ann Hobson Haack (1998-2001)

MAINE

York Harbor
Mrs. Calvin Hosmer III (2001-2003)

MARYLAND

Annapolis
Mrs. John A. Baldwin (2000-2001)
Baltimore
Mrs. Frances Huber (1998)
Mrs. Clark MacKenzie (1999)
Mrs. Thomas G. McCausland (2000)
Nan Paternotte (1997)
Chestertown
Mrs. Adrian P. Reed (1999)

MASSACHUSETTS

Boston
Diane Dalton (2001-2002)
Kevin Doyle (2003)
Elizabeth Moore (2003)
Mrs. Henry S. Streeter (1997-2000)
Linda Wolcott (2003)
Chatham
Mrs. Prescott Dunbar (2001-2002)
Nantucket
Mrs. Coleman Burke (2002-2003)
Osterville
Mrs. David Cole (2001)
South Dartmouth
Mrs. Helen Goddard (2002)
Mrs. Thomas S. Morse (1998)
Mrs. Robert G. Walker (1999-2000, 2002)
Worcester
John W. Trexler (1998-1999, 2002)

MICHIGAN

Ann Arbor
Marie Cochrane (1999)
George Papadalos (1998)
Bloomfield Hills
Virginia Berberian (2001)
Norm Bodine (2001-2002)
Lynne Clippert (2000)
Mary Sue Ewing (2001-2002)
Starr Foster (1998-1999)
Lois Gamble (2000)
Judy Knutson (2000-2002)
Suzanne Krueger (2003)
Grosse Pointe
Mrs. John Ford (1997-1998)
Mrs. Bragaw Vanderzee (1999)
Harbor Springs
Mrs. John Ford (1998)
Mrs. Frank Hightower (2000)

MINNESOTA

Minneapolis
Mrs. Henry L. Sweatt (1997, 1999)
Mrs. John Winsor (1997)

MISSOURI

Kansas City
Mrs. George Powell III (1997)
Mrs. Dwight Sutherland (1997)
St. Louis
Mrs. William H. T. Bush (1998, 2001)

New Hampshire

Monadnock
Mrs. Story Wright (2000, 2002, 2003)
New London
Mrs. Gusta Teach (2000)
Sea Coast
Ms. Beth Hume (2002)
Squam Lake
George Carr (2000)

New Jersey

Joan Kram (2001-2003)
Mrs. J. Duncan Pitney (1997-2003)

New York

Albany & Schenectady
Mrs. Henry Ferguson (1999-2000)
Joanne Lenden (1998-2001)
Cooperstown
Mrs. H. Rodney Hartman (1998)
Patricia Thorpe (1998, 2002)
Eastern Long Island
Lalitte Scott (1996-2003)
Lake Champlain
Mrs. James T. Flynn (1999-2002)
Mountain Top/Greene County
Mr. & Mrs. Alan T. Wenzell (2002)
Oneonta
Heleen Heyning (2002)
Saratoga Springs
Mrs. Robert Ducas (2000, 2002)
Mr. Bruce Solenski (2000, 2002)
Westchester, Putnam, Dutchess,
& Ulster Counties
Page Dickey (co-founder)
Penelope Maynard (co-founder)
Jane Havemeyer (1995-2003)
Sara M. Knight (1995-2003)
Enid Munroe (1995-2003)
Melissa Orme (1995-2003)

North Carolina

Asheville
Hunter Stubbs (2001-2003)
Chapel Hill & Hillsborough
Taimie Anderson (2001)
Stepheny Houghtlin (2002)
Charlotte
Mary Lindeman Wilson (2002)

Ohio

Akron
Mrs. W. Stuver Parry (1998-1999)
Cincinnati
Ms. Julie Mahlin (2002)
Mrs. William R. Seaman (1999-2002)
Columbus
Mrs. Roger Blair (2000)
Mrs. Robert F. Hoffman, Jr. (2000)
Karen K. Meyer (1999)
Connie Page (1998)
Dayton
Barbara Rion (1997-2002)
Mrs. James Woodhull (1997-2002)
Granville
Mrs. James Murr (2001, 2003)
Janet Oberleissen (1998)

Oklahoma

Tulsa
Breniss O'Neal (2002)

Oregon

Portland
Jill Schatz (2002-2003)
Patricia B. Walker (2002-2003)
Salem
Bobbie Dolp (2002-2003)

Pennsylvania

Bucks County
Jack Staub (2000-2003)
Renny Reynolds (2000-2003)
Philadelphia
Mrs. Frank H. Goodyear (1998-1999)
Mrs. Morris Lloyd, Jr. (2000-2003)
Mrs. Edward Starr III (1998-1999)
Pittsburgh
Bernita Buncher Duber (2000)
Mrs. Joshua C. Whetzel, Jr. (1998, 2000)
State College
Rae Chambers (2001-2002)
Dr. Richard Morgan (2000)
Swarthmore
Mrs. Benjamin H. Heckscher (2001)

South Carolina

Greenville
Mrs. Nelson B. Arrington (1997-1998, 2001)
Mrs. Samuel M. Beattie (1997-1998, 2001)

TENNESSEE

Chattanooga/Lookout Mountain
>   Mrs. Halbert Law (1999-2000, 2002)
>   Mrs. Edward Mitchell (2002)
>   Mrs. John Stout (1999-2000)

Memphis
>   Mrs. Albert M. Austin III (1999)
>   Barbara Keathley, ASLA (2001, 2003)
>   Mrs. David B. Martin (1999)

Nashville
>   Mr. Bob Brackman (2000-2003)
>   Mrs. Robert C. H. Mathews, Jr. (2000-2003)
>   Mr. Ben Page (2000-2003)

TEXAS

Austin
>   James DeGrey David (1998-1999)
>   Deborah Hornickel (2000, 2002-2003)
>   Jennifer Staub Meyers (1998-2000)
>   Dr. Gordon L. White (1998-2000)

Dallas
>   Peter Schaar (2002-2003)

Houston
>   Mrs. J. Taft Symonds (1998-2002)
>   Mrs. Sellers J. Thomas, Jr. (1998-2002)
>   Mrs. Joanne Wilson (2002)

VERMONT

Lake Champlain
>   Mrs. James T. Flynn (1999-2001)
>   Marcia Pierce (2002-2003)

Manchester
>   Mrs. A. V. S. Olcott (1998-2003)

VIRGINIA

Arlington
>   Tom Mannion (2002-2003)

Charlottesville
>   Mrs. Mario di Valmarana (1997)

Middleburg
>   Mrs. Charles H. Seilheimer, Jr. (1997)

Richmond
>   Mrs. Robert A. Bristow II (1997)

WASHINGTON

Seattle
>   Barbara Flynn (1999)
>   Keith Geller (2002-2003)
>   Mrs. Bruce McIvor (1999-2000, 2003)
>   Karla Waterman (2003)

WEST VIRGINIA

Charleston
>   Mrs. Herbert Jones (1997)
>   Mr. & Mrs. James Rufus Thomas II (1998-2000, 2002-2003)

WISCONSIN

Lake Country
>   Mrs. Anthony Meyer (2000)
>   Mrs. Henry Quadracci (2000)

Milwaukee
>   Mrs. William Allis (1998, 1999, 2002)
>   Mrs. Robert W. Braeger (1998, 1999, 2002)

Foreword

. . . .

What greater pleasure could there be for garden enthusiasts than to spend a day visiting the gardens of others?

In the past couple of decades, I've had the good fortune to travel extensively in North America and overseas in pursuit of gardens. Traveling with groups of fellow garden lovers, we visited some of the grandest estate gardens in England, Europe, South Africa, and Australia. I've enjoyed sharing my love for gardens, exploring the history of garden design, and reveling in the plants that have changed the face of our gardens.

The highlight of each trip, however, has been the opportunity to visit smaller private gardens. Sometimes the gardens have been artistic tours de force, other times horticultural extravaganzas. But, invariably, the people who created or maintained the gardens have proven to be the most memorable aspect of the visit: people like ourselves who have chosen to put their creative energies into their gardens and who, in turn, enjoy sharing their creations with total strangers.

To find those private gardens on trips to England, I depended on the *Yellow Book* with its listings of private gardens in virtually all corners of the British Isles open to the public on one or two days each year. I always wished that such a guide could be developed for the United States and nine years ago, one did—the *Open Days Directory*. Since then, the *Directory* has opened the gates of thousands of private gardens.

Of the Conservancy's many projects and programs, the Open Days provides the greatest opportunity for Americans to explore, enjoy, and learn from their garden heritage. Take this copy of the *Directory*, gather up some friends and set out on your own garden excursion to celebrate America's garden heritage.

Richard G. *Turner Jr.*
Editor, Pacific Horticulture
San Francisco, California

From the Chairman

. . . .

The success of the Open Days Program becomes stronger each year. In 2002, we had the pleasure and privilege of realizing our largest season ever with the addition of 242 new gardens, nine new areas, twenty-six additional dates, and three more states—a total of 454 innovative and glorious gardens, enjoyed by more than 60,000 appreciative visitors.

As always, we enjoy outstanding and welcome support from our national and local press, our extraordinary Regional Representatives, our devoted garden visitors, and advertisers and sponsors of the program. Our generous Garden Hosts are the backbone of this unique program and we are abundantly grateful for their talents, expertise, and gracious hospitality.

Each passing year deepens our respect, admiration, and appreciation for the remarkable vision of the Garden Conservancy's founder, Frank Cabot. Without his foresight, tenacity, and selfless generosity, the only organization in the United States dedicated to preserving our invaluable gardening heritage would not exist. In the past thirteen years, the Garden Conservancy has indeed made a difference. Gardens have been restored to their pristine condition and precious land has been preserved so that the bounties of nature can flourish. Our eyes have been reopened to the need to conserve finite plant resources before it is too late.

We are proud to present, once again, this unique opportunity to enter an unprecedented dimension of horticultural delights. Be prepared to be surprised, captivated, fascinated, enlightened, and inspired as you stroll through the beckoning garden gates into the diverse world of stimulating beauty that awaits.

Janet Meakin Poor
Chairman, Open Days Program

Welcome to the Open Days Program

. . . .

The Garden Conservancy's Open Days Program is the only national program that invites the public to visit America's very best private gardens. Modeled after similar programs abroad, including England's popular *Yellow Book* and Australia's Open Garden Scheme, the Open Days Program began in 1995 with 110 gardens in New York and Connecticut. Since then the program has grown to include more than 375 private gardens nationwide in 2003.

The Garden Conservancy's Open Days Program is designed to introduce the public to gardens, provide easy access to outstanding examples of design and horticultural practice, and prove that extraordinary American gardens are still being created. By inviting people into America's private gardens, the Garden Conservancy emphasizes the importance of preserving fine gardens for future generations and building a constituency of committed individuals willing to act on behalf of gardens.

How is the Program Organized?

Each Open Day area has at least one Regional Representative who recruits private gardens in his or her area and assists with the promotion and advancement of the program. Over the years, this roster of volunteers has grown to include more than 150 men and women. You'll find a list of Regional Representatives in the Acknowledgments, beginning on page 9.

If you are interested in learning more about the organization of Open Days throughout the United States, please contact The Garden Conservancy, Open Days Program, P.O. Box 219, Cold Spring, NY 10516. You can call us at (845) 265-5384, fax us at (845) 265-5392, or email us at opendays@gardenconservancy.org.

Admission

A $5 admission fee is collected at each garden. Cash may be paid at the gate or visitors may purchase admission coupons through the Garden Conservancy at a discounted price (see the order form on the last page of the *Directory*). By purchasing a copy of the *Directory*, you receive a free coupon offer, good for entrance to one private garden. Admission coupons remain valid from year to year. Proceeds from the Open Days Program support the national preservation work of the Garden Conservancy, as well as local not-for-profit organizations designated by individual garden hosts.

Admission to the public gardens listed in the *Directory* is set by each public garden. Please see the individual listings for their admission fees. Open Days coupons may not be used at public gardens.

How to Use the Directory

· ·

To make the *Directory* user-friendly, to minimize page flipping, and to maximize its use as a travel planner, we've arranged the garden listings as follows:

- Alphabetically by state (see the table of contents for page numbers)
- Within each state, chronologically by Open Day
- For each Open Day, by county, then alphabetically by town
- Within each town, alphabetically by garden name.

At the end of each chapter, after the private gardens, there is a listing and description of public gardens in that state to add to your garden-visiting itinerary, organized alphabetically by county and town.

Also, starting on page 25, you will find the Open Days by Date index, which lists every Open Day chronologically and every garden across the country that is open that day. That's followed by the Open Days by Location index, starting on page 44, which lists all the gardens alphabetically by state, then by county, then town, with the dates they are open.

To help you locate a specific garden, we've also indexed them by garden name in the back of the *Directory*. For quick reference, at the beginning of each state chapter there is a listing of the Open Days in that state.

An area map is provided for each Open Day, with the locations of the towns that will have gardens open that day. Where appropriate, you will find a note under a particular Open Day referring to other nearby gardens just across state lines that are also open on that day.

The Garden Entries

Each private garden listing includes the name of the garden and its location, the garden host's description of his or her garden, the hours the garden is open, and driving instructions. The instructions assume you will be traveling from the nearest major highway. Please travel with a local map. For information about wheelchair accessibility and the difficulty of the terrain, please contact the Open Days Program.

Public garden listings include the garden name, street address, a telephone number and website, a brief description of the garden, hours of operation, admission fee, and driving instructions. We encourage you to contact the site directly for more information.

The information that appears in this *Directory* was, to the best of our knowledge, correct at the time the *Directory* went to press. Since its publication, however, some changes may have occurred. When possible, the Garden Conservancy will notify you of changes in advance; otherwise, please take note of the schedule changes posted at admissions tables or check the Garden Conservancy's website prior to your visit at www.gardenconservancy.org.

Etiquette in the Garden

The Garden Conservancy's Open Days Program is made possible only through our Garden Hosts' hospitality. We ask you to please reward their generosity by following these simple guidelines:

- Do not pick any plant or remove any part of a plant from the garden. If you require help identifying a plant, please ask the Garden Host.
- Do not leave litter in the garden.
- Stay on the paths.
- Follow any signs or directions provided at the garden.
- Respect the privacy of the owners.
- Please leave all pets at home.
- Children must be supervised at all times.
- Park your car so that others can enter and leave the parking area.
- Please remember to check with the owner before taking photographs; tripods are not permitted.
- Respect the dates and times each garden is open as listed in the *Directory*. Do not contact the garden host directly. Please contact the Open Days Program office at (845) 265-5384 to pursue special visiting arrangements or to bring a group to a garden.

Our Counterparts Around the Globe

While the Garden Conservancy's Open Days Program is the only national garden-visiting program of its kind in the United States, it joins similar programs around the world encouraging people to garden and visit gardens every day.

England's National Gardens Scheme

Certainly the most well known is England's National Gardens Scheme and its publication *Gardens of England and Wales Open for Charity*, more familiarly known as the *Yellow Book*. The National Gardens Scheme, a registered charity, was founded in 1927. Around 3,500 gardens of quality and interest will open for the Scheme 2003. Proceeds from the entry fees support ten nursing, caring, and educational charities. For more information, you may contact Miss Beryl Evans, Chief Executive, Hatchlands Park, East Clandon, Guildford, Surrey GU4 7RT ENGLAND, 44-0-1483-211535, FAX 44-0-1483-211537, website www.ngs.org.uk.

Australia's Open Garden Scheme

Originating in 1987 to promote the knowledge and pleasures of gardens and gardening across Australia, the Open Garden Scheme began with 63 gardens in one state. Today the program includes more than 700 private gardens in all states of Australia and welcomes more than one quarter of a million visitors per year. For more information, contact Neil Robertson, National Executive Officer, Australia's Open Garden Scheme, Westport, New Gisborne, Victoria 3438 AUSTRALIA, 61-3-5428-4557, FAX 61-3-5428-4558, website www.opengarden.abc.net.au.

The information presented in the *Open Days Directory* is collected by Garden Conservancy staff and Regional Representatives around the country. We rely on Garden Hosts to provide information for their listings. Information for public garden listings is likewise gathered from the sites' staff. The Garden Conservancy is not responsible for the accuracy of the information published within these listings.

Nominations to include gardens in *The Garden Conservancy's Open Days Directory* are accepted. Please call or write for a survey form and nomination criteria. For these and any other inquiries regarding the *Open Days Directory*, please contact:

Open Days Program
The Garden Conservancy
P.O. Box 219
Cold Spring, NY 10516
Telephone: (845) 265-5384
FAX: (845) 265-5392
Email: opendays@gardenconservancy.org

What is the Garden Conservancy?

The Garden Conservancy is a national nonprofit organization founded in 1989 to preserve exceptional American gardens for the public's education and enjoyment.

In 1988, Ruth Bancroft's garden, a magnificent collection of cacti, succulents, and native California plants, first captivated the imagination of Frank Cabot. His keen interest in the prospects for the future of this important garden prompted swift action, and history was made on two fronts: he established the Garden Conservancy, the first national organization dedicated to the preservation of exceptional gardens; and the Garden Conservancy obtained the first conservation easement for a garden, thereby ensuring its preservation. Not long after legal custodianship was guaranteed for the Bancroft garden, the Conservancy began mapping out the steps involved in transforming this garden, which had thrived under the constant care and vision of its creator, into a vital public facility. A dedicated group of area residents and garden lovers was enlisted to help oversee the preservation and operation of the garden and, with the continued assistance and support of the Conservancy, a strong master plan was developed. Today, Ruth Bancroft, at 93, can be found working in her garden every day. Meanwhile, the Ruth Bancroft Garden supports a full calendar of tours and educational outreach programs that welcomes the public throughout the season.

Anyone who gardens knows the fragile nature of the gardener's creation: subject to the ravages of climate, weeds, erosion, pests, and other problems, even the most carefully designed gardens can vanish within just a few years when untended. When we lose an exceptional gardens, we lose its beauty, but we also lose the lessons it can teach us about the gardener's era—its values, horticultural science, and aesthetic standards. We conserve gardens because they are a vital part of our nation's cultural heritage.

Over the past twelve years, the Garden Conservancy has worked in partnership with garden owners, community groups, and public agencies to advocate the preservation of hundreds of gardens.

Saving a fine garden requires expertise, funding, and community support—resources the Garden Conservancy brings to bear in preserving great American gardens and opening them to the public. Our work is greatly facilitated by a network of committed volunteers—from our Open Days Garden Hosts and Regional Representatives to neighborhood advocates to the many professionals who offer invaluable advice and expertise. But perhaps the Conservancy's most important preservation resource is a growing membership consisting of thousands of individuals, corporations, and foundations nationwide that provides generous financial support. We thank all who have made the success of the Garden Conservancy possible.

Antonia F. Adezio
President, The Garden Conservancy

THE PRESERVATION PROJECTS OF THE GARDEN CONSERVANCY

. . . .

The Garden Conservancy takes a lead role in the preservation of a garden by helping it make the transition from private to nonprofit ownership and guiding the development of a sound financial and organizational plan. The demands for our preservation services increase each year. Below are three new additions to our growing list of preservation projects.

In addition to their regular visiting schedule, the Preservation Projects of the Garden Conservancy are open this year through our Open Days Program (see page numbers on page 23) and admission is free to Garden Conservancy members.

NEW PRESERVATION PROJECTS

Greenwood Gardens
Short Hills, New Jersey

Greenwood Gardens is a twenty-two acre Italianate garden about twenty miles west of New York City. Surrounded by allées, wildflower meadows, ponds, and cultivated woodlands, the gardens adjoin 2,100 acres of publicly owned parkland. The once residential land-scape was built by the Day family in the early twentieth century, revealing a formal design of strict vistas, allées, terraces, and pools. The garden also incorporates Arts & Crafts materials such as rough stone walls, pavilions, and grottos linked by pebbled walks. A colorful collection of Rookwood pottery, from the famous Midwest studio, graces the garden structures.

WILLIAM NOBLE

Yew Dell Farm
Crestwood, Kentucky

In Yew Dell, horticulturist and world traveler Theodore Klein created a work of art. Inspired by trips abroad and the Kentucky landscape, Klein used his intimate knowledge of plants to design a garden that would motivate others to grow the best. The impressive collection of plants at Yew Dell and the vision of the people behind the saving of this important landscape present a remarkable opportunity to continue Klein's legacy of design and horticulture.

WILLIAM NOBLE

Montrose
Hillsborough, North Carolina

Montrose is a sixty-one-acre property listed on the National Register of Historic Places with gardens begun in the nineteenth century. The grounds contain several nineteenth-century buildings, a rock garden, scree garden, several acres of woodland plantings, and large areas of sunny gardens with unique color and planting schemes. Mass plantings of bulbs, including rain lilies, cyclamen, galanthus, and crocus species, for bloom throughout the year. Unusual trees and shrubs, and trellises, fences, and arbors provide structure in winter, while large urns planted with spectacular color combinations brighten the summer gardens.

Montrose is available for visits; please see listing and directions on page 328.

The following is a complete list of the preservation projects of the Garden Conservancy. Those with page numbers after their listing are open for public visitation and and free to Garden Conservancy members.

The Chase Garden, Orting, WA *(page 400)*

The Fells at the John Hay National Wildlife Refuge, Newbury, NH *(page 241)*

Greenwood Gardens, Short Hills, NJ

The John P. Humes Japanese Stroll Garden, Mill Neck, NY *(page 314)*

Montrose, Hillsborough, NC *(page 328)*

Peckerwood Garden, Hempstead, TX *(page 382)*

Rocky Hills—The Gardens of Henriette Suhr, Mount Kisco, NY *(page 279)*

The Ruth Bancroft Garden, Walnut Creek, CA *(page 127)*

Among the many other gardens the Conservancy has assisted are:

Abkhazi Garden, Victoria, BC, Canada

Arthur Erickson House & Garden, Vancouver, BC, Canada

Ashintully, Tyringham, MA

Aullwood Garden, Dayton, OH

Bellamy-Ferriday Garden, Bethlehem, CT

Blithewold, Bristol, RI

Brookwood Garden, Cooperstown, NY

Cohen-Bray House and Garden, Oakland, CA

Corbin & Moore—Turner Heritage Gardens, Spokane, WA

Cross Estate, Bernardsville, NJ

Dumbarton Oaks Park, Washington, DC

Elizabeth Lawrence Garden, Charlotte, NC

Elk Rock, The Garden at the Bishop's Close, Portland, OR *(page 349)*

Eudora Welty Garden, Jackson, MS

Gibraltar, Wilmington, DE

Hakone Gardens, Saratoga, CA

Historic Deepwood and the Lord & Schryver Conservancy, Salem, OR

Historic Morven, Princeton, NJ *(page 262)*

The James Rose Center, Ridgewood, NJ *(page 260)*

Justin Smith Morrill Homestead, Strafford, VT

The Madoo Conservancy, Sagaponack, NY *(page 320)*

Maudslay State Park, Newburyport, MA

McKee Botanical Garden, Vero Beach, FL *(page 192)*

The McLaughlin Garden & Horticultural Center, South Paris, ME *(page 216)*

Mukai Farm and Garden, Vashon Island, WA

Palm Cottage Gardens, Gotha, FL

Pavilion Gardens at the University of Virginia, Charlottesville, VA

Sonnenberg Gardens, Canandaigua, NY

Springside Landscape Restoration, Poughkeepsie, NY *(page 314)*

Val Verde, Montecito, CA

Van Vleck House & Gardens, Montclair, NJ *(page 261)*

Yew Dell Farm, Crestwood, KY

ADDITIONAL PROGRAMS
OF THE GARDEN CONSERVANCY

· ·

The Garden Conservancy is pleased to offer a range of new programs and tools designed to help the garden enthusiast become more closely connected with preservation efforts taking place across the country.

CAREER OPPORTUNITY

One of the biggest challenges facing garden preservation projects across the country is finding appropriately skilled staff. **The Marco Polo Stufano Garden Conservancy Fellowship** was established to introduce experienced horticulturists and landscape designers to the rewards of this new field and to identify and place such talent in a nine-month assignment at one of our Preservation Projects. Over the past few years, fellows have made lasting contributions at Peckerwood Garden in Hempstead, TX; The Fells in Newbury, NH; The Chase Garden in Orting, WA, and The Ruth Bancroft Garden in Walnut, Creek, CA. Applications for the 2004 fellowship are now available.

BOOK SERIES

Is there a garden in your life? Is it in danger of being lost—to developers, dwindling care, or lack of proper leadership? *Taking a Garden Public: First in a Series of Issues and Case Studies in Garden Preservation* is designed to introduce you to the steps involved in saving America's gardens—steps that you can take to determine whether it is feasible for your project to become a public garden and, if so, how to proceed. Experts in the field of garden preservation have contributed more than 100 pages of advice and a wide selection of case studies of Conservancy Preservation Projects tell the stories of successful grassroots efforts. The second volume of *Taking a Garden Public* will illuminate the ins and outs of fund raising.

Taking a Garden Public is in loose-leaf format and is available at $25 (plus shipping and handling). Look for sample chapters and a printable order form on our website or contact the Preservation Projects Department of the Garden Conservancy at (845) 265-9396.

A VIDEO PRESENTATION

Preserving an American Legacy: An Introduction to the Garden Conservancy is a fifteen-minute video about how the Garden Conservancy came to be and where we are going, as told by the garden conservators helping to fulfill our mission. Since the video's premiere at our Tenth Anniversary Celebration in Charleston, SC, Conservancy members have asked how they could share *Preserving an American Legacy* with their own garden clubs and organizations. We are now pleased to offer a presentation kit that includes the video, an introductory script, and Garden Conservancy materials, all for a special price of $15.

For information on these programs or any of our Preservation Projects, please contact the Garden Conservancy at (845) 265-2029 or log on to our website at www.gardenconservancy.org.

Open Days by Date

· ·

Saturday & Sunday, March 29 & 30

ARIZONA

Maricopa County

Paradise Valley   The DeMore Garden, 10 a.m. to 4 p.m.
Piedras Rojas, 10 a.m. to 4 p.m.
Tranquilo—Dennis & Char Silver, 10 a.m. to 2 p.m.
Ventana Park, 10 a.m. to 4 p.m.

Phoenix   The Dennis & Julie Hopper Residence, 10 a.m. to 4 p.m.
The Onofryton Residence, 10 a.m. to 4 p.m.

Saturday, April 5

FLORIDA

Indian River County

Vero Beach   A Caribbean Courtyard by the Sea, 10 a.m. to 4 p.m.
Garden of Patricia & Robert Hubner, 10 a.m. to 4 p.m.
Mangrove Garden at Carwill Oaks, 10 a.m. to 2 p.m.
Sandy's Garden, 10 a.m. to 4 p.m.

Saturday, April 12

OREGON

Marion County

Salem   Richard & Deanna Iltis, 10 a.m. to 4 p.m.
Rockhaven, 10 a.m. to 4 p.m.

Saturday, April 19

CALIFORNIA

San Diego County

Del Mar The Addisons' Garden, 12 to 4 p.m.

Lynne & Vernon Blackman's Garden, 10 a.m. to 4 p.m.

Jamison Garden, 10 a.m. to 4 p.m.

The Teague Garden, 9 a.m. to 4 p.m.

Pat Welsh's "Pergola Paradise," 10 a.m. to 1 p.m.

Solana Beach Golich's Garden, 12 to 4 p.m.

The Garden of Erik & Irina Gronborg, 12 to 4 p.m.

The Tacktill-Wanerka Garden, 12 to 4 p.m.

The Thirloway Cottage Garden, 12 to 4 p.m.

San Mateo County

Atherton The Larry & Susy Calof Garden, 10 a.m. to 4 p.m.

Lynnie & Rich Dewey's Garden, 10 a.m. to 4 p.m.

Woodside Lurline R. Coonan, 10 a.m. to 4 p.m.

The Jaunich Garden, 10 a.m. to 4 p.m.

Santa Clara County

Palo Alto Mack Garden, 10 a.m. to 2 p.m.

NEW YORK

Westchester County

Bedford Phillis Warden, 10 a.m. to 4 p.m.

Lewisboro The White Garden, 10 a.m. to 4 p.m.

Sunday, April 27

CALIFORNIA

Los Angeles County

Los Angeles Ronnie Allumbaugh Gardens at Getty House, the Official
Residence of the Mayor of Los Angeles, 9:30 a.m. to 3 p.m.

Boeck Garden, 10 a.m. to 4 p.m.

Bungalow Estrada Gardens, 10 a.m. to 4 p.m.

Dar Meyer, 10 a.m. to 4 p.m.

Pepper-Macias Garden, 10 a.m. to 4 p.m.

Yusts' Garden, 10 a.m. to 4 p.m.

West Adams Jennifer Charnofsky's Garden at the Furlong House, 2 to 6 p.m.

Hutchinson Family Garden, 2 to 6 p.m.

Le Parc Sans Soleil, 2 to 6 p.m.

Marais Garden, 2 to 6 p.m.

Peace Awareness Labyrinth & Gardens at the Guasti Villa,
2 to 6 p.m.

Trosper-Raposa Garden, 2 to 6 p.m.

Saturday, May 3

CALIFORNIA
San Diego County

El Cajon Steve & Susie Dentt's Garden, 10 a.m. to 2 p.m.
La Mesa Bill & Pat Allen Garden, 9 a.m. to 2 p.m.
Nugent Garden, 10 a.m. to 4 p.m.
Perennial Adventure—Christine S. Wotruba, 10 a.m. to 4 p.m.
Lemon Grove The Hartung Garden, 1 to 5 p.m.

MASSACHUSETTS
Essex County

Needham Ellen Lathi's Garden, 9 a.m. to 5 p.m.
Taylor Garden, 10 a.m. to 4 p.m.

Norfolk County

Boston Captain Daniel Draper House, 10 a.m. to 4 p.m.
Kelly Wingo's Garden, 10 a.m. to 4 p.m.
Dover The Halligan Garden, 10 a.m. to 4 p.m.
Kevin J. Doyle & Michael Radoslovich—Cairn Croft,
10 a.m. to 4 p.m.
Wellesley Hunnewell Garden, 10 a.m. to 4 p.m.

NEW YORK
Suffolk County

Cutchogue Manfred & Roberta Lee, 10 a.m. to 4 p.m.
East Hampton Mrs. Donald Bruckmann, 10 a.m. to 2 p.m.
Margaret Kerr & Robert Richenburg, 10 a.m. to 2 p.m.
Montauk Richard Kahn & Elaine Peterson, 10 a.m. to 4 p.m.

Sunday, May 4

CALIFORNIA
Marin County

Kentfield Geraniaceae Gardens, 10 a.m. to 4 p.m.
John & Glennis Jones Garden, 10 a.m. to 2 p.m.
Ross Tom Jackson & Kathy Grant's Garden, 10 a.m. to 4 p.m.
Kreitzberg Family Garden, 10 a.m. to 2 p.m.

NEW YORK
Westchester County

Mount Kisco Judy & Michael Steinhardt, 10 a.m. to 4 p.m.

Saturday, May 10

CALIFORNIA
Los Angeles County

Beverly Hills	The Anderson Garden, 10 a.m. to 4 p.m.
Los Angeles	Flower to the People, 9:30 a.m. to 4 p.m.
	Miller/Engel Garden, 10 a.m. to 4 p.m.
	Novick Garden, 10 a.m. to 4 p.m.
Pacific Palisades	Eglee-Dalton Garden, 10 a.m. to 4 p.m.
	Meyer Garden, 10 a.m. to 4 p.m.
	Rapoport Canyon Garden, 10 a.m. to 4 p.m.
Santa Monica	447 11th Street, 10 a.m. to 2 p.m.
	Nancy Goslee Power Garden, 10 a.m. to 4 p.m.

San Diego County

Escondido	Lievers' Garden, 12 to 4 p.m.
Poway	Arnold Garden, 10 a.m. to 4 p.m.
	Betty's Garden, 12 to 4 p.m.
	Casterline Garden, 10 a.m. to 4 p.m.
	Cattolico Garden, 9 a.m. to 1 p.m.
	Les Belles Fleurs—Laurie Connable's Garden, 9 a.m. to 3 p.m.
	Wits End West, 9 a.m. to 1 p.m.

San Mateo County

Atherton	The Larry & Susy Calof Garden, 10 a.m. to 4 p.m.
	Toni & Mike Heren, 10 a.m. to 2 p.m.

CONNECTICUT
Fairfield County

Stamford	Ruth & Jim Levitan, 10 a.m. to 4 p.m.
Westport	Paul Held & Jane Sherman, 10 a.m. to 4 p.m.

NEW YORK
Rockland County

Palisades	The Captain John House Garden, 10 a.m. to 4 p.m.
	Judy Tomkins Gardens, 10 a.m. to 4 p.m.
Upper Nyack	Cornuscopia, 2 to 6 p.m.
Upper Nyack	South Cottage—The Moorings, 10 a.m. to 4 p.m.
Valley Cottage	Hiroshi & Maria Nakazawa, 10 a.m. to 4 p.m.

Saturday, May 17

NEW JERSEY
Essex County
Short Hills Garden of Dr. & Mrs. George E. Staehle, 10 a.m. to 2 p.m.
Winter's Garden, 10 a.m. to 4 p.m.

Morris County
Morris Plains Watnong Gardens, 10 a.m. to 4 p.m.

TENNESSEE
Shelby County
Collierville Kitty P. Taylor, 10 a.m. to 2 p.m.
Memphis Hughes Garden, 10 a.m. to 2 p.m.
Alex & Karen Wellford's Garden, 10 a.m. to 4 p.m.
Gina & John White's Garden, 10 a.m. to 4 p.m.

VIRGINIA
Arlington County
Arlington Palmer Aldrich Garden, 10 a.m. to 4 p.m.
The Craig-Cool Garden, 10 a.m. to 4 p.m.
Garden of William A. Grillo, 10 a.m. to 4 p.m.
The Weeks Garden, 10 a.m. to 4 p.m.
McLean Ridder Garden, 10 a.m. to 4 p.m.

Sunday, May 18

CALIFORNIA
Alameda County

Alameda Watts/Coup Garden, 10 a.m. to 4 p.m.
Berkeley Our Own Stuff Gallery Garden, 10 a.m. to 4 p.m.
Suzanne Porter's Garden, 10 a.m. to 4 p.m.
Oakland Ann Nichols' Garden, 10 a.m. to 4 p.m.
Osmond Garden, 10 a.m. to 4 p.m.

Los Angeles County

Arcadia Sunset Magazine's Demonstration Garden, 9:30 a.m. to 3:30 p.m.
Pasadena Holley Frank's Garden, 10 a.m. to 2 p.m.
Goodan Garden, 10 a.m. to 4 p.m.
Martin-Watterson, 10 a.m. to 2 p.m.
Mead Garden, 10 a.m. to 2 p.m.
Garden of Arnold & Gretl Mulder, 10 a.m. to 4 p.m.
The White Garden, 10 a.m. to 2 p.m.
Yariv Residence, 10 a.m. to 4 p.m.

CONNECTICUT
Fairfield County

Redding Highstead Arboretum, guided walks at 10 a.m., 12 p.m. & 2 p.m.

NEW JERSEY
Bergen County

Englewood Peggy & Walter Jones, 10 a.m. to 4 p.m.
Wyckoff Tall Trees—Garden of Janet Schulz, 10 a.m. to 4 p.m.

NEW YORK
Dutchess County

Amenia Broccoli Hall—Maxine Paetro, 10 a.m. to 4 p.m.
Wappingers Falls Anne Spiegel, 10 a.m. to 4 p.m.

Orange County

Mountainville Cedar House—Garden of Margaret Johns & Peter Stern, 10 a.m. to 6 p.m.

Westchester County

Armonk Cobamong Pond, 10 a.m. to 4 p.m.
Bedford Penelope & John Maynard, 10 a.m. to 4 p.m.
Bedford Hills Phillis Warden, 10 a.m. to 4 p.m.
Hastings-on-Hudson Midge & Dave Riggs, 10 a.m. to 4 p.m.

WASHINGTON
Pierce County

Orting The Chase Garden, 10 a.m. to 3 p.m.
Puyallup Ernie & Julia Graham Garden, 10 a.m. to 2 p.m.

Saturday, May 24

NEW YORK
Westchester County
Mount Kisco　Rocky Hills–The Gardens of Henriette Suhr, 2 to 6 p.m.

Saturday, May 31

CALIFORNIA
San Diego County
Fallbrook　The Anderson/Olson Garden, 10 a.m. to 2 p.m.

Herlihy Farms, 9 a.m. to 1 p.m.

Carol Popet & Mark Benussi, 9 a.m. to 4 p.m.

Scott & Susan Spencer's Garden, 10 a.m. to 4 p.m.

Vista　Barbara's Garden, 12 to 4 p.m.

Felter Jungle Garden, 12 to 4 p.m.

Don Walker's Garden, 12 to 4 p.m.

OREGON
Washington County
Aloha　The Garden of Vickie Braman, 10 a.m. to 4 p.m.

Guinther Garden, 10 a.m. to 4 p.m.

Helvetia　Elizabeth Furse Garden, 10 a.m. to 4 p.m.

Goodwin Gardens, 10 a.m. to 4 p.m.

Hillsboro　Cartwheels—The Garden of Laura M. Crockett,
10 a.m. to 4 p.m.

Hilltop—The Virginia Larson Garden, 10 a.m. to 4 p.m.

WASHINGTON
King County
Kenmore　The Ridge Garden, 10 a.m. to 4 p.m.

Seattle　Noel Angell & Emory Bundy, 10 a.m. to 3 p.m.

The Gannon Garden, 10 a.m. to 4 p.m.

Geller-Irvine Garden, 10 a.m. to 3 p.m.

Lakeside Garden, 10 a.m. to 4 p.m.

Lee & John Neff, 10 a.m. to 4 p.m.

Phil Wood & Judy Mahoney, 10 a.m. to 4 p.m.

Sunday, June 1

CALIFORNIA
Contra Costa County

Orinda   Cummings Garden, 10 a.m. to 4 p.m.
The Garden at 518 Miner Road, 10 a.m. to 4 p.m.
The Garden at 520 Miner Road, 10 a.m. to 4 p.m.
Giardino de Ruscelletto, 10 a.m. to 4 p.m.
Rosemary Merlo's Garden, 10 a.m. to 4 p.m.
Dr. & Mrs. Robert N. Nelson, 10 a.m. to 2 p.m.
Swanson/Thomas Garden, 10 a.m. to 4 p.m.

Walnut Creek   The Ruth Bancroft Garden, 1 to 5 p.m.

CONNECTICUT
Fairfield County

Redding   Highstead Arboretum, guided walks at 10 a.m.,
12 p.m. & 2 p.m.

Westport   Judie & Charlie Kiernan, 2 to 6 p.m.
Susan Lloyd, 10 a.m. to 4 p.m.

NEW YORK
Westchester County

Cortlandt Manor   Vivian & Ed Merrin, 10 a.m. to 2 p.m.

Croton-on-Hudson   The Gardens of Dianna & Howard Smith, 10 a.m. to 4 p.m.

Ossining   Paul & Sarah Matlock, 10 a.m. to 4 p.m.

TENNESSEE
Davidson County

Brentwood   Reynolds Garden, 1 to 5 p.m.

Franklin   Callicótt Garden—Back of Beyond, 1 to 5 p.m.
Hewitt Garden, 1 to 5 p.m.
Stewart Garden, 1 to 5 p.m.

WASHINGTON
Kitsap County

Bainbridge Island   Richard & Joan Kinsman, 10 a.m. to 4 p.m.
Little and Lewis, 10 a.m. to 4 p.m.
Waterman Garden, 10 a.m. to 4 p.m.

Saturday, June 7

CONNECTICUT
Tolland County
Coventry — David & Julia Hayes, 10 a.m. to 4 p.m.

Windham County
Canterbury — Westminster Gardens—Eleanor B. Cote & Adrian P. Hart, 12 to 4 p.m.

MASSACHUSETTS
Essex County
Beverly Farms — Sea Meadow, 10 a.m. to 4 p.m.

Manchester — Grafton, 10 a.m. to 4 p.m.

Manchester-by-the-Sea — The Garden at 9 Friend Street—Frederick Rice, 10 a.m. to 4 p.m.

Marblehead — Gerald & Rose Anne Levinson, 10 a.m. to 4 p.m.

The Parable—Ellen Cool's Garden, 10 a.m. to 4 p.m.

Gardens of Donald & Beverly Seamans, 10 a.m. to 4 p.m.

Swampscott — Wilkinson Garden—Blythswood, 10 a.m. to 4 p.m.

NEW JERSEY
Essex County
Short Hills — Winter's Garden, 10 a.m. to 4 p.m.

Morris County
Chatham — Jack Lagos, 10 a.m. to 4 p.m.

Morris Plains — Watnong Gardens, 10 a.m. to 4 p.m.

Randolph — Jones Garden, 10 a.m. to 4 p.m.

NEW YORK
Columbia County
Copake Falls — Margaret Roach, 10 a.m. to 4 p.m.

Germantown — An Artist's Garden, 10 a.m. to 4 p.m.

Tailings—Robert Montgomery, 10 a.m. to 2 p.m.

Linlithgo — Mark A. McDonald—Runningwater, 10 a.m. to 4 p.m.

Livingston — Starr Ockenga & Donald Forst, 10 a.m. to 2 p.m.

WASHINGTON
Kitsap County
Bainbridge Island — Carol & Gene Johanson, 10 a.m. to 4 p.m.

Just a Garden, 10 a.m. to 2 p.m.

Kingston — Heronswood, 9 a.m. to 3 p.m.

WEST VIRGINIA
Kanawha County
Charleston Container Gardening with Otis Laury, 10 a.m. to 4 p.m.
Garden with Views, 10 a.m. to 4 p.m.
Mr. & Mrs. Herbert E. Jones, Jr., 10 a.m. to 4 p.m.
Laughinghouse—The Giltinans' Garden, 10 a.m. to 4 p.m.
Malden Kanawha Salines—Garden of Mrs. Turner Ratrie,
10 a.m. to 4 p.m.

Sunday, June 8

CALIFORNIA
San Francisco County
San Francisco 104 Wonderful Laidley, 10 a.m. to 4 p.m.
The Garden at 537 Chenery Street, 10 a.m. to 4 p.m.
Garden of Torre San Gimignano, 10 a.m. to 4 p.m.
Miland-Sonenberg Garden, 10 a.m. to 2 p.m.
Muther/Aftergut Garden, 10 a.m. to 4 p.m.
Stephen Suzman Garden, 10 a.m. to 4 p.m.
Pat Wipf's Garden, 10 a.m. to 4 p.m.

CONNECTICUT
Hartford County
Plantsville The Kaminski Garden, 10 a.m. to 4 p.m.

New Haven County
Guilford Angelwood—Mary Anne & Dale Athanas, 10 a.m. to 4 p.m.
Meriden Jardin des Brabant, 1 to 5 p.m.
George Trecina, 1 to 5 p.m.
Middlebury John N. Spain, 10 a.m. to 4 p.m.

NEW YORK
Westchester County
Katonah Cross River House, 10 a.m. to 2 p.m.
Susan & Carmine L. Labriola, 10 a.m. to 4 p.m.
North Salem Artemis Farm—Carol & Jesse Goldberg, 10 a.m. to 4 p.m.
Keeler Hill Farm, 10 a.m. to 4 p.m.

OHIO
Licking County
Alexandria Spring Hill Farm, 10 a.m. to 4 p.m.
Granville Maplewood, 10 a.m. to 4 p.m.
The Gardens at Pau Hana Farm, 1 to 6 p.m.
The Reiner Ross Garden, 10 a.m. to 4 p.m.
Reynolds English Cottage Garden, 10 a.m. to 2 p.m.

PENNSYLVANIA
Montgomery County

Ambler	Cynthia & Morris Cheston, 11 a.m. to 4 p.m.
Dresher	Tollhouse Garden, 11 a.m. to 4 p.m.
Horsham	Brickman's Garden, 11 a.m. to 4 p.m.
Wyndmoor	English Village, 11 a.m. to 4 p.m.

Philadelphia County

Philadelphia	Cleve Gate, 11 a.m. to 4 p.m.
	Peter Hedrick's Garden, 11 a.m. to 4 p.m.
	Old Orchard, 11 a.m. to 4 p.m.

Saturday, June 14
CONNECTICUT
Hartford County

Burlington	The Salsedo Family Garden, 10 a.m. to 4 p.m.
East Windsor Hill	Pat & George Porter, 10 a.m. to 4 p.m.
Simsbury	The Garden of Betty & Dick Holden, 10 a.m. to 4 p.m.

Litchfield County

Litchfield	Dan & Joyce Lake, 2 to 6 p.m.

ILLINOIS
Will County

Naperville	Lynn Dowd's Garden, 10 a.m. to 4 p.m.
	Ron & Linda Henry, 10 a.m. to 4 p.m.
	Debra Doud Stone, 10 a.m. to 4 p.m.

NEW YORK
Dutchess County

Amenia	Broccoli Hall—Maxine Paetro, 10 a.m. to 4 p.m.
Rhinebeck	Cedar Heights Orchard—William & Arvia Morris, 10 a.m. to 4 p.m.

OREGON
Marion County

Salem	Keith & Madge Bauer, 10 a.m. to 4 p.m.
	Alan & Sharon McKee, 10 a.m. to 4 p.m.
	Savicki Garden, 10 a.m. to 4 p.m.

Sunday, June 15

CONNECTICUT
Fairfield County
Greenwich   Stonybrooke, 10 a.m. to 4 p.m.

New London County
Old Lyme   Ruth Perry, 10 a.m. to 4 p.m.
Stonington   Mr. & Mrs. Howard A. Fromson, 10 a.m. to 2 p.m.
Mrs. Frederic C. Paffard, Jr., 10 a.m. to 2 p.m.

NEW YORK
Putnam County
Cold Spring   Stonecrop Gardens, 10 a.m. to 4 p.m.
Garrison   Manitoga, 10 a.m. to 2 p.m.
Ross Gardens, 10 a.m. to 4 p.m.

Westchester County
Bedford   Ann Catchpole-Howell, 10 a.m. to 4 p.m.
Lulu Farm, 10 a.m. to 4 p.m.
North Salem   Jane & Bill Bird, 10 a.m. to 4 p.m.

Saturday, June 21

COLORADO
El Paso County

Colorado Springs   The Bradleys' Garden, 10 a.m. to 3 p.m.
Casa Contenta Garden, 10 a.m. to 3 p.m.
Joleen Dentan's Dwarf Conifers, 10 a.m. 3 p.m.
Our Secret Garden—Florence & Ron Richey, 10 a.m. to 3 p.m.
A Personal Garden, 10 a.m. to 3 p.m.
tawto'ma Gardens, 10 a.m. to 3 p.m.

CONNECTICUT
Litchfield County

Washington   Mr. & Mrs. J. Winston Fowlkes III, 2 to 6 p.m.
Charles Raskob Robinson & Barbara Paul Robinson,
2 to 6 p.m.
George Schoellkopf, 3 to 6 p.m.
Washington Depot   Gael Hammer, 10 a.m. to 4 p.m.

ILLINOIS
Du Page County

West Chicago   Swan Oaks & Gardens, 10 a.m. to 4 p.m.

NEW JERSEY
Bergen County

Maywood   Dail & Tony's Garden, 10 a.m. to 4 p.m.
Ridgewood   The Zusy/Ortiz Garden, 10 a.m. to 4 p.m.
River Edge   Anthony "Bud" & Virginia Korteweg, 10 a.m. to 4 p.m.
River Vale   Cupid's Garden—Audrey Linstrom Maihack, 10 a.m. to 4 p.m.
Tenafly   Linda Singer, 10 a.m. to 4 p.m.

Middlesex County

Colonia   Babbling Brook, 10 a.m. to 2 p.m.

NEW YORK
Suffolk County

Bridgehampton   Mrs. Dinwiddie Smith, 10 a.m. to 2 p.m.
East Hampton   Margaret Kerr & Robert Richenburg, 10 a.m. to 2 p.m.
Carol Mercer, 10 a.m. to 4 p.m.
Southampton   Kim White & Kurt Wolfgruber—Secret Garden,
10 a.m. to 4 p.m.

VERMONT
Chittenden County

Charlotte   Converse Bay Farm, 10 a.m. to 4 p.m.
The Gardens at Golden Apple Orchard, 10 a.m. to 4 p.m.
The Gardens of William & Nancy Heaslip, 10 a.m. to 4 p.m.
Hinesburg   The Hidden Garden of Lewis Creek Road, 10 a.m. to 4 p.m.
Paul Wieczoreck's Garden, 10 a.m. to 4 p.m.

Sunday, June 22

CONNECTICUT
Fairfield County

Fairfield — On the Harbor, 10 a.m. to 4 p.m.
Redding — Gardens at Horsefeathers, 12 to 4 p.m
Ridgefield — Garden of Ideas, 10 a.m. to 4 p.m.
Weston — Birgit Rasmussen Diforio, 10 a.m. to 4 p.m.
West Redding — Hughes-Sonnenfroh Gardens, 10 a.m. to 4 p.m.

ILLINOIS
Cook County

Winnetka — Beauty Without Boundaries, 10 a.m. to 4 p.m.
Dorothy & John Gardner, 10 a.m. to 4 p.m.

Lake County

Highland Park — Markus Collection and Garden, 10 a.m. to 4 p.m.
Kenilworth — Louellen & Tim Murray's Garden, 10 a.m. to 2 p.m.

NEW JERSEY
Monmouth County

Atlantic Highlands — Mrs. Sverre Sorensen, 10 a.m. to 4 p.m.
Rumson — Beliza Ann Furman, 10 a.m. to 4 p.m.
King & Leigh Sorensen, 10 a.m. to 2 p.m.

NEW YORK
Columbia County

Craryville — Susan Anthony & Richard Galef, 10 a.m. to 4 p.m.
East Taghkanic — Grant & Alice Platt, 10 a.m. to 4 p.m.

OREGON
Clackamas County

Oak Grove — Cerf-Treyve Garden, 10 a.m. to 4 p.m.
Paradise Creek, 10 a.m. to 4 p.m.
Quercus Terra, 10 a.m. to 4 p.m.
Survival of the Fittest, 10 a.m. to 4 p.m.
Portland — The Kalbfleisch/Matteucci Garden, 10 a.m. to 4 p.m.

Thursday, June 26

MASSACHUSETTS
Nantucket County

Nantucket — Blueberry Hill—Douglass & Caroline Ellis, 10 a.m. to 4 p.m.
Dr. & Mrs. John W. Espy, 10 a.m. to 4 p.m.
Inishfree—Coleman & Susan Burke, 10 a.m. to 4 p.m.
Kate's Folly, 10 a.m. to 4 p.m.
Nindethana, 10 a.m. to 2 p.m.
Townhouse Garden, 10 a.m. to 4 p.m.
Constance Umberger, 10 a.m. to 2 p.m.
Whitney Garden, 10 a.m. to 4 p.m.

Siasconset — Hedged About—Charlotte & Macdonald Mathey,
10 a.m. to 4 p.m.

Saturday, June 28

COLORADO
Arapahoe County

Cherry Hills Village — MacKenzie Family Garden, 10 a.m. to 4 p.m.
David & Brenda Schrier, 10 a.m. to 4 p.m.

Englewood — Rosemont, 10 a.m. to 4 p.m.

CONNECTICUT
Litchfield County

Colebrook — Marveen & Michael Pakalik, 10 a.m. to 4 p.m.
Falls Village — Bunny Williams, 10 a.m. to 4 p.m.
Sharon — Lee Link, 12 to 4 p.m.
West Cornwall — Doug Mayhew—Jurutungo Viejo, 10 a.m. to 4 p.m.
Michael Trapp, 10 a.m. to 4 p.m.

ILLINOIS
Lake County

Barrington — The Gardens at Wandering Tree—The "Glorée & Tryumfant"
Garden Railway, 10 a.m. to 4 p.m.

PENNSYLVANIA
Bucks County

New Hope — Kevin Hasney's Garden, 10 a.m. to 4 p.m.
Jericho Mountain Orchards, 10 a.m. to 4 p.m.
Pineville — Emilie & Walter Cullerton—Oxford Gardens, 10 a.m. to 4 p.m.
Silverdale — Carol A. Pierce, 12 to 6 p.m.
Wrightstown — Hortulus Farm, 10 a.m. to 4 p.m.

Saturday, June 28
VERMONT
Bennington County
Dorset   Nissen Garden, 10 a.m. to 4 p.m.
    Westerly, 10 a.m. to 4 p.m.
Manchester   Glebelands, 10 a.m. to 4 p.m.
    White Tree Farm, 10 a.m. to 4 p.m.
Manchester Center   Edwards' Garden, 10 a.m. to 4 p.m.
    Joan & Lee Fegelman's Garden, 10 a.m. to 4 p.m.

Sunday, June 29
CONNECTICUT
Litchfield County
Bridgewater   Maywood Gardens, 10 a.m. to 2 p.m.

Sunday, July 6
CONNECTICUT
New Haven County
Meriden   Jardin des Brabant, 1 to 5 p.m.
    George Trecina, 1 to 5 p.m.

NEW YORK
Dutchess County
Amenia   Jade Hill—Paul Arcario & Don Walker, 10 a.m. to 4 p.m.
Millbrook   Far A-Field—John Whitworth, 10 a.m. to 4 p.m.
Salt Point   Ely Garden, 10 a.m. to 4 p.m.
Stanfordville   Zibby & Jim Tozer, 10 a.m. to 2 p.m.

Saturday, July 12

ILLINOIS
Kane County
St. Charles   Charles & Patricia Bell, 10 a.m. to 4 p.m.
The Haggas Garden, 10 a.m. to 2 p.m.

MAINE
York County
York   Braveboat Harbor Farm—Calvin & Cynthia Hosmer,
10 a.m. to 4 p.m.
Godfrey Pond Garden, 10 a.m. to 4 p.m.
Johnson Garden, 10 a.m. to 4 p.m.
Radochia Gardens & Neighbors, 10 a.m. to 4 p.m.
Sea Spray—Georgia & Dan McGurl, 10 a.m. to 4 p.m.

NEW YORK
Suffolk County
Mattituck   Maurice Isaac & Ellen Coster Isaac, 10 a.m. to 4 p.m.
Dennis Schrader & Bill Smith, 10 a.m. to 4 p.m.
Sagaponack   Susan & Louis Meisel, 10 a.m. to 2 p.m.

Ulster County
Olivebridge   James Dinsmore Garden, 10 a.m. to 4 p.m.
Phoenicia   The Garden of Jane & Alfred Peavy, 10 a.m. to 4 p.m.
Saugerties   The Donald Elder & Richard Suma Garden, 10 a.m. to 4 p.m.
Willow   Suzanne Pierot's "Garden by the Stream," 10 a.m. to 4 p.m.
Woodstock   Joanne & Richard Anthony, 10 a.m. to 4 p.m.

NORTH CAROLINA
Buncombe County
Asheville   Garry-Doll Garden, 10 a.m. to 4 p.m.
Knowe Manor, 10 a.m. to 4 p.m.
The Richmond Hill Inn, 10 a.m. to 4 p.m.
Sanders' Garden, 10 a.m. to 4 p.m.

Sunday, July 13

MICHIGAN
Oakland County
Beverly Hills   Yvonne's Garden, 10 a.m. to 4 p.m.
Birmingham   The Dr. Alice R. McCarthy Garden, 10 a.m. to 4 p.m.
Bloomfield Hills   Virginia Fox, 10 a.m. to 4 p.m.
Judy & Jim's Garden, 10 a.m. to 4 p.m.
Franklin   Hickory Hill, 10 a.m. to 4 p.m.

Saturday, July 19

ILLINOIS
Cook County

Hinsdale	Musso Garden, 10 a.m. to 4 p.m.
	The Gardens of Kellie & Barry O'Brien, 10 a.m. to 4 p.m.
La Grange	Catherine & Francis Donovan, 10 a.m. to 4 p.m.
Oak Brook	Susan & Ken Beard, 10 a.m. to 4 p.m.
	Shady Oaks—Joe & Barbara McGoldrick, 10 a.m. to 4 p.m.

NEW HAMPSHIRE
Cheshire County

Alstead	Mountain View—Gordon & Helene Moodie, 10 a.m. to 4 p.m.
Alstead Center	Bill & Judy Moran's Garden, 10 a.m. to 4 p.m.
Walpole	Peter & Theodora Berg's Garden, 10 a.m. to 4 p.m.

Hillsborough County

Hancock	Schaefer Gardens, 10 a.m. to 4 p.m.

Sullivan County

Acworth	The Gardens on Grout Hill, 10 a.m. to 4 p.m.

Sunday, July 20

CONNECTICUT
Hartford County

Avon	Green Dreams—Garden of Jan Nickel, 10 a.m. to 4 p.m.
Glastonbury	Ferrante Garden, 10 a.m. to 4 p.m.
	The Murray Gardens, 10 a.m. to 4 p.m.
Wethersfield	Gary Berquist, 10 a.m. to 4 p.m.

NEW YORK
Westchester County

Bedford Hills	Phillis Warden, 10 a.m. to 4 p.m.

OREGON
Multnomah County

Portland	Bates-McDonald Garden, 10 a.m. to 4 p.m.
	High Hatch—Garden of Susan Stevenson, 10 a.m. to 4 p.m.
	O'Bannon's Garden, 10 a.m. to 4 p.m.
	Alice & Wayne Plummer Garden, 10 a.m. to 4 p.m.
	Wat Pho? Pan-Asian Garden, 10 a.m. to 4 p.m.

Sunday, July 27

ILLINOIS

Du Page County

West Chicago The Ball Horticultural Trial Garden, 10 a.m. to 4 p.m.

Lake County

Highland Park Magic Garden, 10 a.m. to 2 p.m.
Lake Forest Camp Rosemary, 10 a.m. to 4 p.m.
Carr Garden, 10 a.m. to 4 p.m.
Old Mill Farm, 10 a.m. to 4 p.m.
Mettawa Mettawa Manor, 10 a.m. to 4 p.m.

Sunday, August 10

CONNECTICUT

Fairfield County

Redding Highstead Arboretum, guided walks at 10 a.m.,
12 p.m. & 2 p.m.
West Redding Hughes-Sonnenfroh Gardens, 10 a.m. to 4 p.m.

Hartford County

Plantsville The Kaminski Garden, 10 a.m. to 4 p.m.

New Haven County

Meriden Jardin des Brabant, 1 to 5 p.m.
George Trecina, 1 to 5 p.m.

Saturday, August 16

NEW JERSEY

Essex County

Nutley Graeme Hardie, 10 a.m. to 4 p.m.
Silas Mountsier, 10 a.m. to 4 p.m.

Saturday, September 6

NEW JERSEY

Bergen County

Maywood Dail & Tony's Garden, 10 a.m. to 4 p.m.
Somerset County
Far Hills Kennelston Cottage, 10 a.m. to 4 p.m.

NEW YORK

Columbia County

Copake Falls Margaret Roach, 10 a.m. to 4 p.m.
Millerton Helen Bodian's Garden, 2 to 6 p.m.

Sunday, September 7
CONNECTICUT
Hartford County
Avon   Green Dreams—Garden of Jan Nickel, 10 a.m. to 4 p.m.
Burlington   The Salsedo Family Garden, 10 a.m. to 4 p.m.

Saturday, September 13
NEW YORK
Putnam County
Patterson   The Farmstead Garden, 12 to 6 p.m.

TEXAS
Dallas/Collin County
Dallas   Michael Cheever's Garden, 10 a.m. to 4 p.m.
Judy Fender's Garden, 10 a.m. to 4 p.m.
Dave & Tracey Mason's Garden, 10 a.m. to 4 p.m.
Doyle Terry & Donna Ohland-Terry, 10 a.m. to 4 p.m.
Richeson Garden, 10 a.m. to 4 p.m.
Peter & Julie Schaar, 10 a.m. to 4 p.m.
Sewell Garden, 10 a.m. to 4 p.m.

Sunday, September 14
CONNECTICUT
Fairfield County
Greenwich   Stonybrooke, 10 a.m. to 4 p.m.

NEW YORK
Rockland County
Palisades   The Captain John House Garden, 10 a.m. to 4 p.m.
Judy Tomkins Gardens, 10 a.m. to 4 p.m.

Westchester County
Lewisboro   The White Garden, 10 a.m. to 4 p.m.
Waccabuc   James & Susan Henry, 10 a.m. to 5 p.m.

Sunday, October 5
TEXAS
Burnet County
Spicewood   Jackson Garden, 11 a.m. to 6 p.m.

Travis/Williamson County
Austin   The Anderson Garden, 11 a.m. to 6 p.m.
Martha & Cliff Ernst, 11 a.m. to 6 p.m.
The Green Residence, 11 a.m. to 6 p.m.
Nokes Family Garden, 11 a.m. to 6 p.m.
Reissig Garden, 11 a.m. to 6 p.m.

OPEN DAYS BY LOCATION

· ·

ARIZONA
Maricopa County

Paradise Valley	The DeMore Garden, Saturday & Sunday, March 29 & 30
	Piedras Rojas, Saturday & Sunday, March 29 & 30
	Tranquilo—Dennis & Char Silver, Saturday & Sunday, March 29 & 30
	Ventana Park, Saturday & Sunday, March 29 & 30
Phoenix	The Dennis & Julie Hopper Residence, Saturday & Sunday, March 29 & 30
	The Onofryton Residence, Saturday & Sunday, March 29 & 30

CALIFORNIA
Alameda County

Alameda	Watts/Coup Garden, Sunday, May 18
Berkeley	Our Own Stuff Gallery Garden, Sunday, May 18
	Suzanne Porter's Garden, Sunday, May 18
Oakland	Ann Nichols' Garden, Sunday, May 18
	Osmond Garden, Sunday, May 18

Contra Costa County

Orinda	Cummings Garden, Sunday, June 1
	The Garden at 518 Miner Road, Sunday, June 1
	The Garden at 520 Miner Road, Sunday, June 1
	Giardino de Ruscelletto, Sunday, June 1
	Rosemary Merlo's Garden, Sunday, June 1
	Dr. & Mrs. Robert N. Nelson, Sunday, June 1
	Swanson/Thomas Garden, Sunday, June 1
Walnut Creek	The Ruth Bancroft Garden, Sunday, June 1

Los Angeles County

Arcadia	Sunset Magazine's Demonstration Garden, Sunday, May 18
Beverly Hills	The Anderson Garden, Saturday, May 10
Los Angeles	Ronnie Allumbaugh Gardens at Getty House, the Official Residence of the Mayor of Los Angeles, Sunday, April 27;
	Boeck Garden, Sunday, April 27
	Bungalow Estrada Gardens, Sunday, April 27
	Dar Meyer, Sunday, April 27
	Flower to the People, Saturday, May 10
	Miller/Engel Garden, Saturday, May 10
	Novick Garden, Saturday, May 10
	Pepper-Macias Garden, Sunday, April 27
	Yusts' Garden, Sunday, April 27

Pacific Palisades	Eglee-Dalton Garden, Saturday, May 10
	Meyer Garden, Saturday, May 10
	Rapoport Canyon Garden, Saturday, May 10
Pasadena	Holley Frank's Garden, Sunday, May 18
	Goodan Garden, Sunday, May 18
	Martin-Watterson, Sunday, May 18
	Mead Garden, Sunday, May 18
	Garden of Arnold & Gretl Mulder, Sunday, May 18
	The White Garden, Sunday, May 18
	Yariv Residence, Sunday, May 18
Santa Monica	447 11th Street, Saturday, May 10
	Nancy Goslee Power Garden, Saturday, May 10
West Adams	Jennifer Charnofsky's Garden at the Furlong House, Sunday, April 27
	Hutchinson Family Garden, Sunday, April 27
	Le Parc Sans Soleil, Sunday, April 27
	Marais Garden, Sunday, April 27
	Peace Awareness Labyrinth & Gardens at the Guasti Villa, Sunday, April 27
	Trosper-Raposa Garden, Sunday, April 27

Marin County

Kentfield	Geraniaceae Gardens, Sunday, May 4
	John & Glennis Jones Garden, Sunday, May 4
Ross	Kreitzberg Family Garden, May 4
	Tom Jackson & Kathy Grant's Garden, Sunday, May 4

San Diego County

Del Mar	The Addisons' Garden, Saturday, April 19
	Lynne & Vernon Blackman's Garden, Saturday, April 19
	Jamison Garden, Saturday, April 19
	The Teague Garden, Saturday, April 19
	Pat Welsh's "Pergola Paradise," Saturday, April 19
El Cajon	Steve & Susie Dentt's Garden, Saturday, May 3
Escondido	Lievers' Garden, Saturday, May 10
Fallbrook	The Anderson/Olson Garden, Saturday, May 31
	Herlihy Farms, Saturday, May 31
	Carol Popet & Mark Benussi, Saturday, May 31
	Scott & Susan Spencer's Garden, Saturday, May 31
La Mesa	Bill & Pat Allen Garden, Saturday, May 3
	Nugent Garden, Saturday, May 3
	Perennial Adventure—Christine S. Wotruba, Saturday, May 3
Lemon Grove	The Hartung Garden, Saturday, May 3
Poway	Arnold Garden, Saturday, May 10
	Betty's Garden, Saturday, May 10
	Casterline Garden, Saturday, May 10
	Cattolico Garden, Saturday, May 10

Les Belles Fleurs—Laurie Connable's Garden, Saturday, May 10

Wits End West, Saturday, May 10

Solana Beach Golich's Garden, Saturday, April 19

The Garden of Erik & Irina Gronborg, Saturday, April 19

The Tacktill-Wanerka Garden, Saturday, April 19

The Thirloway Cottage Garden, Saturday, April 19

Vista Barbara's Garden, Saturday, May 31

Felter Jungle Garden, Saturday, May 31

Don Walker's Garden, Saturday, May 31

San Francisco County

San Francisco 104 Wonderful Laidley, Sunday, June 8

The Garden at 537 Chenery Street, Sunday, June 8

Garden of Torre San Gimignano, Sunday, June 8

Miland-Sonnenberg Garden, Sunday, June 8

Muther/Aftergut Garden, Sunday, June 8

Stephen Suzman Garden, Sunday, June 8

Pat Wipf's Garden, Sunday, June 8

San Mateo County

Atherton The Larry & Susy Calof Garden, Saturday, April 19;
Saturday, May 10

Lynnie & Rich Dewey's Garden, Saturday, April 19

Toni & Mike Heren, Saturday, May 10

Woodside Lurline R. Coonan, Saturday, April 19

The Jaunich Garden, Saturday, April 19

Santa Clara County

Palo Alto Mack Garden, Saturday, April 19

COLORADO

Arapahoe County

Cherry Hills Village MacKenzie Family Garden, Saturday, June 28

David & Brenda Schrier, Saturday, June 28

Englewood Rosemont, Saturday, June 28

El Paso County

Colorado Springs The Bradleys' Garden, Saturday, June 21

Casa Contenta Garden, Saturday, June 21

Joleen Dentan's Dwarf Conifers, Saturday, June 21

Our Secret Garden—Florence & Ron Richey, Saturday, June 21

A Personal Garden, Saturday, June 21

tawto'ma Gardens, Saturday, June 21

CONNECTICUT

Fairfield County

Fairfield	On the Harbor, Sunday, June 22
Greenwich	Stonybrooke, Sunday, June 15; Sunday, September 14
Redding	Gardens at Horsefeathers, Sunday, June 22
	Highstead Arboretum, Sunday, May 18; Sunday, June 1; Sunday, August 10
Ridgefield	Garden of Ideas, Sunday, June 22
Stamford	Ruth & Jim Levitan, Saturday, May 10
Weston	Birgit Rasmussen Diforio, Sunday, June 22
Westport	Paul Held & Jane Sherman, Saturday, May 10
	Judie & Charlie Kiernan, June 1
	Susan Lloyd, Sunday, June 1
West Redding	Hughes-Sonnenfroh Gardens, Sunday, June 22; Sunday, August 10

Hartford County

Avon	Green Dreams—Garden of Jan Nickel, Sunday, July 20; Sunday, September 7
Burlington	The Salsedo Family Garden, Saturday, June 14; Sunday, September 7
East Windsor Hill	Pat & George Porter, Saturday, June 14
Glastonbury	Ferrante Garden, Sunday, July 20
	The Murray Gardens, Sunday, July 20
Plantsville	The Kaminski Garden, Sunday, June 8; Sunday, August 10
Simsbury	The Garden of Betty & Dick Holden, Saturday, June 14
Wethersfield	Gary Berquist, Sunday, July 20

Litchfield County

Bridgewater	Maywood Gardens, Sunday, June 29
Colebrook	Marveen & Michael Pakalik, Saturday, June 28
Falls Village	Bunny Williams, Saturday, June 28
Litchfield	Dan & Joyce Lake, Saturday, June 14
Sharon	Lee Link, Saturday, June 28
Washington	Mr. & Mrs. J. Winston Fowlkes III, Saturday, June 21
	Charles Raskob Robinson & Barbara Paul Robinson, Saturday, June 21
	George Schoellkopf, Saturday, June 21
Washington Depot	Gael Hammer, Saturday, June 21
West Cornwall	Doug Mayhew—Jurutungo Viejo, Saturday, June 28
	Michael Trapp, Saturday, June 28

New Haven County

Guilford	Angelwood—Mary Anne & Dale Athanas, Sunday, June 8
Meriden	Jardin des Brabant, Sunday, June 8; Sunday, July 6; Sunday, August 10
	George Trecina, Sunday, June 8; Sunday, July 6; Sunday, August 10
Middlebury	John N. Spain, Sunday, June 8

New London County

Old Lyme	Ruth Perry, Sunday, June 15
Stonington	Mr. & Mrs. Howard A. Fromson, Sunday, June 15
	Mrs. Frederic C. Paffard, Jr., Sunday, June 15

Tolland County

Coventry	David & Julia Hayes, Saturday, June 7

Windham County

Canterbury	Eleanor B. Cote & Adrian P. Hart, Saturday, June 7

FLORIDA
Indian River County

Vero Beach	A Caribbean Courtyard by the Sea, Saturday, April 5
	Garden of Patricia & Robert Hubner, Saturday, April 5
	Mangrove Garden at Carwill Oaks, Saturday, April 5
	Sandy's Garden, Saturday, April 5

ILLINOIS
Cook County

Hinsdale	Musso Garden, Saturday, July 19
	The Gardens of Kellie & Barry O'Brien, July 19
La Grange	Catherine & Francis Donovan, Saturday, July 19
Oak Brook	Susan & Ken Beard, Saturday, July 19
	Shady Oaks—Joe & Barbara McGoldrick, Saturday, July 19
Winnetka	Beauty Without Boundaries, Sunday, June 22

Du Page County

West Chicago	The Ball Horticultural Trial Garden, Sunday, July 27
	Swan Oaks & Gardens, Saturday, June 21

Kane County

St. Charles	Charles & Patricia Bell, Saturday, July 12
	The Haggas Garden, Saturday, July 12

Lake County

Barrington	The Gardens at Wandering Tree—The "Glorée & Tryumfant" Garden Railway, Saturday, June 28
Highland Park	Magic Garden, Sunday, July 27
	Markus Collection & Garden, Sunday, June 22
Kenilworth	Louellen & Tim Murray, Sunday, June 22
Lake Forest	Camp Rosemary, Sunday, July 27
	Carr Garden, Sunday, July 27
	Old Mill Farm, Sunday, July 27
Mettawa	Mettawa Manor, Sunday, July 27
Winnetka	Dorothy & John Gardner, Sunday, June 22

Will County

Naperville	Lynn Dowd's Garden, Saturday, June 14
	Ron & Linda Henry, Saturday, June 14
	Debra Doud Stone, Saturday, June 14

MAINE
York County

York Braveboat Harbor Farm—Calvin & Cynthia Hosmer,
Saturday, July 12
Godfrey Pond Garden, Saturday, July 12
Johnson Garden, Saturday, July 12
Radochia Gardens & Neighbors, Saturday, July 12
Sea Spray—Georgia & Dan McGurl, Saturday, July 12

MASSACHUSETTS
Essex County

Beverly Farms Sea Meadow, Saturday, June 7
Manchester Grafton, Saturday, June 7
Manchester-by-the-Sea The Garden at 9 Friend Street—Frederick Rice,
Saturday, June 7
Marblehead Gerald & Rose Anne Levinson, Saturday, June 7
The Parable—Ellen Cool's Garden, Saturday, June 7
Gardens of Donald & Beverly Seamans, Saturday, June 7
Swampscott Wilkinson Garden—Blythswood, Saturday, June 7

Nantucket County

Nantucket Blueberry Hill—Douglass & Caroline Ellis, Thursday, June 26
Dr. & Mrs. John W. Espy, Thursday, June 26
Inishfree—Coleman & Susan Burke, Thursday, June 26
Kate's Folly, Thursday, June 26
Nindethana, Thursday, June 26
Townhouse Garden, Thursday, June 26
Constance Umberger, Thursday, June 26
Whitney Garden, Thursday, June 26
Siasconset Hedged About—Charlotte & Macdonald Mathey,
Thursday, June 26

Norfolk County

Dover Kevin J. Doyle & Michael Radoslovich—Cairn Croft,
Saturday, May 3
The Halligan Garden, Saturday, May 3
Needham Ellen Lathi's Garden, Saturday, May 3
Taylor Garden, Saturday, May 3
Kelly Wingo's Garden, Saturday, May 3
Wellesley Hunnewell Garden, Saturday, May 3
Westwood Captain Daniel Draper House, Saturday, May 3

MICHIGAN
Oakland County

Beverly Hills Yvonne's Garden, Sunday, July 13
Birmingham The Dr. Alice R. McCarthy Garden, Sunday, July 13

Bloomfield Hills	Virginia Fox, Sunday, July 13
	Judy & Jim's Garden, Sunday, July 13
Franklin	Hickory Hill, Sunday, July 13

NEW HAMPSHIRE
Cheshire County

Alstead	Mountain View—Gordon & Helene Moodie, Saturday, July 19
Alstead Center	Bill & Judy Moran's Garden, Saturday, July 19
Walpole	Peter & Theodora Berg's Garden, Saturday, July 19

Hillsborough County
Hancock	Schaefer Gardens, Saturday, July 19

Sullivan County
Acworth	The Gardens on Grout Hill, Saturday, July 19

NEW JERSEY
Bergen County

Englewood	Peggy & Walter Jones, Sunday, May 18
Maywood	Dail & Tony's Garden, Saturday, June 21; Saturday, September 6
Ridgewood	The Zusy/Ortiz Garden, Saturday, June 21
River Edge	Anthony "Bud" & Virginia Korteweg, Saturday, June 21
River Vale	Cupid's Garden—Audrey Linstrom Maihack, Saturday, June 21
Tenafly	Linda Singer, Saturday, June 21
Wyckoff	Tall Trees—Garden of Janet Schulz, Sunday, May 18

Essex County
Nutley	Graeme Hardie, Saturday, August 16
	Silas Mountsier, Saturday, August 16
Short Hills	Garden of Dr. & Mrs. George E. Staehle, Saturday, May 17
	Winter's Garden, Saturday, May 17; Saturday, June 7

Middlesex County
Colonia	Babbling Brook, Sunday, June 22

Monmouth County
Atlantic Highlands	Mrs. Sverre Sorensen, Sunday, June 22
Rumson	Beliza Ann Furman, Sunday, June 22
	King & Leigh Sorensen, Sunday, June 22

Morris County
Chatham	Jack Lagos, Saturday, June 7
Morris Plains	Watnong Gardens, Saturday, May 17; Saturday, June 7
Randolph	Jones Garden, Saturday, June 7

Somerset County
Far Hills	Kennelston Cottage, Saturday, September 6

NEW YORK
Columbia County

Copake Falls	Margaret Roach, Saturday, June 7; Saturday, September 6
Craryville	Susan Anthony & Richard Galef, Sunday, June 22
East Taghkanic	Grant & Alice Platt, Sunday, June 22
Germantown	An Artist's Garden, Sunday, June 7
	Tailings—Robert Montgomery, Saturday, June 7
Linlithgo	Mark A. McDonald—Runningwater, Saturday, June 7
Livingston	Starr Ockenga & Donald Forst, Saturday, June 7
Millerton	Helen Bodian's Garden, Saturday, September 6

Dutchess County

Amenia	Broccoli Hall—Maxine Paetro, Sunday, May 18; Saturday, June 14
	Jade Hill—Paul Arcario & Don Walker, Sunday, July 6
Millbrook	Far A-Field—John Whitworth, Sunday, July 6
Rhinebeck	Cedar Heights Orchard—William & Arvia Morris, Saturday, June 14
Salt Point	Ely Garden, Sunday, July 6
Stanfordville	Zibby & Jim Tozer, Sunday, July 6
Wappingers Falls	Anne Spiegel, Sunday, May 18

Orange County

Mountainville	Cedar House—Garden of Margaret Johns & Peter Stern, Sunday, May 18

Putnam County

Putnam	Stonecrop Gardens, Sunday, June 15
Garrison	Manitoga, Sunday, June 15
	Ross Gardens, Sunday, June 15
Patterson	The Farmstead Garden, Saturday, September 13

Rockland County

Palisades	The Captain John House Garden, Saturday, May 10; Sunday, September 14
	Judy Tomkins Gardens, Saturday, May 10; Sunday, September 14
Upper Nyack	Cornuscopia, Saturday, May 10
	South Cottage—The Moorings, Saturday, May 10
Valley Cottage	Hiroshi & Maria Nakazawa, Saturday, May 10

Suffolk County

Bridgehampton	Mrs. Dinwiddie Smith, Saturday, June 21
Cutchogue	Manfred & Roberta Lee, Saturday, May 3
East Hampton	Mrs. Donald Bruckmann, Saturday, May 3
	Margaret Kerr & Robert Richenburg, Saturday, May 3; Saturday, June 21
	Carol Mercer, Saturday, June 21
Mattituck	Maurice Isaac & Ellen Coster Isaac, Saturday, July 12
	Dennis Schrader & Bill Smith, Saturday, July 12
Montauk	Richard Kahn & Elaine Peterson, Saturday, May 3

Sagaponack	Susan & Louis Meisel, Saturday, July 12
Southampton	Kim White & Kurt Wolfgruber—Secret Garden, Saturday, June 21

Ulster County

Olivebridge	James Dinsmore Garden, Saturday, July 12
Phoenicia	The Garden of Jane & Alfred Peavy, Saturday, July 12
Saugerties	The Donald Elder & Richard Suma Garden, Saturday, July 12
Willow	Suzanne Pierot's "Garden by the Stream," Saturday, July 12
Woodstock	Joanne & Richard Anthony, Saturday, July 12

Westchester County

Armonk	Cobamong Pond, Sunday, May 18
Bedford	Ann Catchpole-Howell, Sunday, June 15
	Lulu Farm, Sunday, June 15
	Penelope & John Maynard, Sunday, May 18
Bedford Hills	Phillis Warden, Saturday, April 19; Sunday, May 18; Sunday, July 20
Cortlandt Manor	Vivian & Ed Merrin, Sunday, June 1
Croton-on-Hudson	The Gardens of Dianna & Howard Smith, Sunday, June 1
Hastings-on-Hudson	Midge & Dave Riggs, Sunday, May 18
Katonah	Cross River House, Sunday, June 8
	Susan & Carmine L. Labriola, Sunday, June 8
Lewisboro	The White Garden, Saturday, April 19; Sunday, September 14
Mount Kisco	Judy & Michael Steinhardt, Sunday, May 4
	Rocky Hills—The Gardens of Henriette Suhr, Saturday, May 24
North Salem	Artemis Farm—Carol & Jesse Goldberg, Sunday, June 8
	Jane & Bill Bird, Sunday, June 15
	Keeler Hill Farm, Sunday, June 8
Ossining	Paul & Sarah Matlock, Sunday, June 1
Waccabuc	James & Susan Henry, Sunday, September 14

NORTH CAROLINA
Buncombe County

Asheville	Garry-Doll Garden, Saturday, July 12
	Knowe Manor, Saturday, July 12
	The Richmond Hill Inn, Saturday, July 12
	Sanders' Garden, Saturday, July 12

OHIO
Licking County

Alexandria	Spring Hill Farm, Sunday, June 8
Granville	Maplewood, Sunday, June 8
	The Gardens at Pau Hana Farm, Sunday, June 8
	The Reiner Ross Garden, Sunday, June 8
	Reynolds English Cottage Garden, Sunday, June 8

OREGON

Clackamas County

Oak Grove	Cerf-Treyve Garden, Sunday, June 22
	Paradise Creek, Sunday, June 22
	Quercus Terra, Sunday, June 22
	Survival of the Fittest, Sunday, June 22
Portland	The Kalbfleisch/Matteucci Garden, Sunday, June 22

Marion County

Salem	Keith & Madge Bauer, Saturday, June 14
	Richard & Deanna Iltis, Saturday, April 12
	Rockhaven, Saturday, April 12
	Savicki Garden, Saturday, June 14

Multnomah County

Portland	Bates-McDonald Garden, Sunday, July 20
	High Hatch—Garden of Susan Stevenson, Sunday, July 20
	O'Bannon's Garden, Sunday, July 20
	Alice & Wayne Plummer Garden, Sunday, July 20
	Wat Pho? Pan-Asian Garden, Sunday, July 20

Polk County

Salem	Alan & Sharon McKee, Saturday, June 14

Washington County

Aloha	The Garden of Vickie Braman, Saturday, May 31
	Guinther Garden, Saturday, May 31
Helvetia	Elizabeth Furse Garden, Saturday, May 31
	Goodwin Gardens, Saturday, May 31
Hillsboro	Cartwheels—The Garden of Laura M. Crockett, Saturday, May 31
	Hilltop—The Virginia Larson Garden, Saturday, May 31

PENNSYLVANIA

Bucks County

New Hope	Kevin Hasney's Garden, Saturday, June 28
	Jericho Mountain Orchards, Saturday, June 28
Pineville	Emilie & Walter Cullerton—Oxford Gardens, Saturday, June 28
Silverdale	Carol A. Pierce, Saturday, June 28
Wrightstown	Hortulus Farm, Saturday, June 28

Montgomery County

Ambler	Cynthia & Morris Cheston, Sunday, June 8
Dresher	Tollhouse Garden, Sunday, June 8
Horsham	Brickman's Garden, Sunday, June 8
Wyndmoor	English Village, Sunday, June 8

Philadelphia County

Philadelphia　Cleve Gate, Sunday, June 8
Peter Hedrick's Garden, Sunday, June 8
Old Orchard, Sunday, June 8

TENNESSEE
Davidson County

Brentwood　Reynolds Garden, Sunday, June 1
Franklin　Callicott Garden—Back of Beyond, Sunday, June 1
Hewitt Garden, Sunday, June 1
Stewart Garden, Sunday, June 1

Shelby County

Collierville　Kitty P. Taylor, Saturday, May 17
Memphis　Hughes Garden, Saturday, May 17
Alex & Karen Wellford's Garden, Saturday, May 17
Gina & John White's Garden, Saturday, May 17

TEXAS
Burnet County

Spicewood　Jackson Garden, Sunday, October 5

Dallas/Collins County

Dallas　Michael Cheever's Garden, Saturday, September 13
Judy Fender's Garden, Saturday, September 13
Dave & Tracey Mason's Garden, Saturday, September 13
Richeson Garden, Saturday, September 13
Peter & Julie Schaar, Saturday, September 13
Sewell Garden, Saturday, September 13
Doyle Terry & Donna Ohland-Terry, Saturday, September 13

Travis/Williamson County

Austin　The Anderson Garden, Sunday, October 5
Martha & Cliff Ernst, Sunday, October 5
The Green Residence, Sunday, October 5
Nokes Family Garden, Sunday, October 5
Reissig Garden, Sunday, October 5

VERMONT
Bennington County

Dorset　Nissen, Saturday, June 28
Westerly, Saturday, June 28
Manchester　Glebelands, Saturday, June 28
White Tree Farm, Saturday, June 28
Manchester Center　Edwards' Garden, Saturday, June 28
Joan & Lee Fegelman's Garden, Saturday, June 28

Chittenden County

Charlotte   Converse Bay Farm, Saturday, June 21
The Gardens at Golden Apple Orchard, Saturday, June 21
The Gardens of William & Nancy Heaslip, Saturday, June 21
Hinesburg   The Hidden Garden of Lewis Creek Road, Saturday, June 21
Paul Wieczoreck's Garden, Saturday, June 21

VIRGINIA
Arlington County

Arlington   Palmer Aldrich Garden, Saturday, May 17
The Craig-Cool Garden, Saturday, May 17
Garden of William A. Grillo, Saturday, May 17
The Weeks Garden, Saturday, May 17
McLean   Ridder Garden, Saturday, May 17

WASHINGTON
King County

Kenmore   The Ridge Garden, Saturday, May 31
Seattle   Noel Angell & Emory Bundy, Saturday, May 31
The Gannon Garden, Saturday, May 31
Geller-Irvine Garden, Saturday, May 31
Lakeside Garden, Saturday, May 31
Lee & John Neff, Saturday, May 31
Phil Wood & Judy Mahoney, Saturday, May 31

Kitsap County

Bainbridge Island   Carol & Gene Johanson, Saturday, June 7
Just a Garden, Saturday, June 7
Richard & Joan Kinsman, Sunday, June 1
Little and Lewis, Sunday, June 1
Waterman Garden, Sunday, June 1
Kingston   Heronswood, Saturday, June 7

Pierce County

Orting   The Chase Garden, Sunday, May 18
Puyallup   Ernie & Julia Graham Garden, Sunday, May 18

WEST VIRGINIA
Kanawha County

Charleston   Container Gardening with Otis Laury, Saturday, June 7
Gardens with Views, Saturday, June 7
Mr. & Mrs. Herbert E. Jones, Jr., Saturday, June 7
Laughinghouse—the Giltinans' Garden, Saturday, June 7
Malden   Kanawha Salines—Garden of Mrs. Turner Ratrie,
Saturday, June 7

Open Days visitors admire the Washington, Connecticut, garden of Charles Raskob Robinson & Barbara Paul Robinson. Photo by Laura Palmer.

Private Garden Visiting through the Open Days Program

Any gardener will agree that whether it's their own garden or someone else's, spending time in a garden is the best way to learn and to be inspired. All of the private gardens participating in the Open Days Program have something special to offer. They encompass a wide range of landscape styles, plant materials, and design ideas. Don't miss a single chance to visit gardens in your area or around the country. For those you cannot see this season, here are sixteen pages of color photographs from Open Days gardens around the country. Enjoy!

Open Days

The Northwest

Salem and Portland, Oregon,
join Seattle, Washington,
to bring you the best of this
horticultural destination.
See gardens that boast
magnificent views of snow-
capped mountains, tranquil
Japanese-inspired retreats, or
woodland gardens of quiet
serenity. Visit April through
July and don't forget the
nurseries and public gardens
galore!

Alan & Sharon McKee Garden,
Salem, Oregon. Photo by Chris Greenwood.

Paradise Creek, Oak Grove, Oregon

Little and Lewis, Bainbridge Island, Washington

The Northeast

This region of great gardening diversity will take you from seacoast to mountain top with the fullest garden-visiting calendar in the program. You can begin the season viewing the pastel display of spring bulbs and keep going until the hot colors of late summer.

Charles Raskob Robinson & Barbara Paul Robinson Garden, Washington, Connecticut. Photo by Laura Palmer.

Richard Kahn & Elaine Peterson Garden, Montauk, New York (Eastern Long Island). Photo by Betsy Pinover Schiff.

Gardens of Donald & Beverly Seamans,
Marblehead, Massachusetts.

Peter & Theodora Berg's Garden, Walpole,
New Hampshire. Photo by Gordon Hayward.

Hortulus Farm, Wrightstown, Pennsylvania (Bucks County). Photo by Laura Palmer.

California

From San Francisco to San
Diego, we've got this state
covered. Experience art in the
garden like nowhere else as well
as an astonishing variety of plant
material from around the world.
Beginning in April, dozens of
gardens await your visit.

Yusts' Garden, Los Angeles, California.
Photo by Laura Palmer

Don Walker's Garden, Vista, California.

John & Glennis Jones Garden, Kentfield, California. Photo by Noel Gieleghem.

Midwest

Illinois, Michigan, and Ohio offer magnificent estate gardens, a collector's obsession, and numerous shady paths ending in lake views and hidden gardens.

The Gardens at Pau Hana Farm, Granville, Ohio.

Markus Collection & Garden. Highland Park, Illinois. Photo by Linda Oyama Bryan.

The Dr. Alice R. McCarthy Garden, Bloomfield Hills
Michigan. Photo by Bridge Communications, Inc.

The South

In this region, you can visit the lush mangrove gardens of Florida, the wildflowers of Tennessee and North Carolina, and Virginia's shady gardens nestled under mature trees. Every state is worth the trip.

Laughinghouse — The Giltinan's Garden, Charleston, West Virginia

Knowe Manor, Asheville, North Carolina

A Caribbean Courtyard by the Sea,
Vero Beach, Florida.
Photo by Mark Schumann.

The West and Southwest

Native plants abound in this region. Texas bluebells, the columbines of Colorado, and Arizona's agaves and cacti are set amid magnificent views. Don't be surprised to find English- and Asian-inspired gardens as well. Arizona kicks off the Open Days season in late March and Austin, Texas, wraps it up in early October.

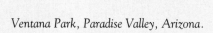
Ventana Park, Paradise Valley, Arizona.

Richeson Garden, Dallas, Texas.

tawto'nta Gardens, Colorado Springs, Colorado.

Preservation Projects

In 2002, the Garden Conservancy designated three new preservation projects as Sponsored Gardens, joining the ranks of such greats as the Ruth Bancroft Garden, Chase Garden, and Peckerwood Gardens, all pictured here. You can read about these new projects beginning on page 21. They join a long list of spectacular private gardens that are now some of the most popular public destinations in the United States. You will find descriptions and visiting information for these gardens within their corresponding Open Days areas.

Peckerwood Garden, Hempstead, Texas. Photo by Elsie Kersten.

Thank you! Through your participation in the Open Days Program, you are helping to make our preservation work possible. If you are not already a Garden Conservancy member, we encourage you to join us. Complete information is included on the last page of this *Directory*.

The Chase Garden, Orting, Washington.

The Ruth Bancroft Garden, Walnut Creek, California. Photo by Mick Hales.

Public Garden Visiting through the Open Days Program

The Open Days Program is pleased to include information on hundreds of public gardens across the country and we encourage you to visit them. Check the listing for public gardens in your area.

The Open Days Program provides additional opportunities to visit public gardens across the country that have limited visiting hours or events to coincide with area Open Days. These gardens are included in the Open Days by Date and Open Days by Location indexes at the beginning of the *Directory*.

Stonecrop Gardens is the former garden of Frank and Anne Cabot, now a public garden under the direction of Caroline Burgess and affiliated with the Garden Conservancy. (See page 3 1 6 for details.)

ARIZONA

Ventana Park, Paradise Valley

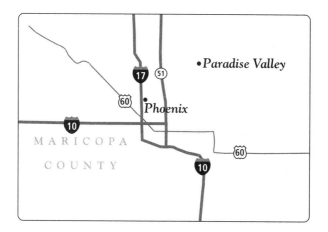

Saturday & Sunday, March 29 & 30
MARICOPA COUNTY

PARADISE VALLEY
The DeMore Garden
3300 East Berridge Lane, Paradise Valley

This is an exquisite and lavish collection of agaves, succulents, perennials, trees, and shrubs. Designed and installed over a number of years, this garden incorporates both the owners' sense of desert plantings and the designer's exuberance for plants. This large garden has many different aspects, from native plantings to lush, colorful areas full of seasonal plants.

Hours: 10 a.m. to 4 p.m.

Go north on 32nd Street past Camelback Road. Turn right onto Calle Sin Nombre. At "T" intersection, turn left. At next "T" intersection, turn right. Berridge Lane is cul-de-sac almost immediately on left. Please park on street.

Proceeds shared with Desert Botanical Garden

Piedras Rojas
5802 North Harding, Paradise Valley

When working with the landscape architect, we agreed that we wanted the pool to feel like an irrigation holding pond in the desert, reminiscent of irrigation troughs found on old ranches and farms in Arizona. Surrounded by a wild garden of paloverdes, bottlebrush, creosote, and wildflowers, our garden attracts all manner of wildlife—hummingbirds, quail, lizards, an owl, and even an exuberant boy or two!

Hours: 10 a.m. to 4 p.m.

Take Camelback Road to 32nd Street. Go north and turn east onto Stanford, then north onto Homestead to Harding. Turn right and go to #5802. *Please park on street.*

Proceeds shared with Desert Botanical Garden

Tranquilo—Dennis & Char Siler
6030 North 51st Place, Paradise Valley

The swimming pool with views of Camelback Mountain serves as a water feature, continually providing soothing sounds of water to desert ears. Experience an Arizona desert landscape and enjoy the intimate seating areas with fireplaces and chimineas featured in this design by landscape architect Christy Ten Eyck. The house is of mortar-washed adobe and was the first house in the Phoenix area by architect George Christensen.

Hours: 10 a.m. to 2 p.m.

From Route 51, take Glendale Avenue exit onto Lincoln Drive. Go to 51st Place. Turn right and go to #6030.

From Scottsdale, take Scottsdale Road to McDonald Drive. Go west to 51st Place; turn right. House is third on left.

Proceeds shared with Desert Botanical Garden.

Ventana Park
8101 North Mummy Mountain Road, Paradise Valley

A plethora of paths await your arrival. Meandering brick paths take you through five acres of once rocky desert to a lush green landscape made tranquil by the ever-present sound of falling water. With imagination in hand, I set out to create a variety of garden niches. From this concept evolved a koi waterlily pond, herb and vegetable gardens, a citrus grove, a butterfly and hummingbird garden, cactus gardens, a rose garden combined with topiaries, a formal reflective pool, and a Santa Fe garden with wildflowers scattered throughout. Pieces of contemporary steel sculpture share space with whimsical stone animals. Additional structures, including a sunken tennis court, greenhouse, a labyrinth garden shaded by elm trees giving harmony and peace, and playground, complete the space for family, friends, and nature.

Hours: 10 a.m. to 4 p.m.

From Route 51, take Glendale Avenue exit onto Lincoln Drive. Take east to Tatum Boulevard (4800 E.) and go north 2.5 miles to Doubletree Road. Go east 1 mile to 56th Street. Turn south .6 mile to Mockingbird Lane east (past stop sign at Mockingbird Lane west). Turn left, then right at next street (Mummy Mountain Road). Proceed to end of road; entrance to #8101 is on left.

Proceeds shared with Desert Botanical Garden

The Dennis & Julie Hopper Residence
5901 East Jean Avenue, Phoenix

This is a landscape for art and gatherings to inspire artists and guests while strolling through the grounds. The vision was to create a space for new artists to display their creations. Since the garden has been created, the owner has sponsored salons for artists and architects to converse. The garden's hardscape and fountains were designed by Greg Trutza. The site has magnificent paloverdes, mesquites, and cactus that had formerly been allowed to merge visually with the surrounding desert. Most of the exciting cacti and agaves were kept in place. The masses of paloverdes were thinned to enhance their framework and allow passages. The most striking feature in the landscape is the meandering desert aqueduct, which symbolically brings the waters of life to this desert again. It splashes down on cubistic pedestals of antique noche stone, which also serve as seat platforms to cool off in the chlorinated water. The terraces are covered in stained travertine mosaics. After one passes through any of the aqueduct portals, they encounter granite paths, which lead to other art locations. A tall meandering wall with art windows blocks the view to the neighbor's auto court. The desert landscape was planted with masses of Xeriscape specimens to create another level of texture and structural quality in the landscape. New retaining walls were added to create terraced gardens. A forty-foot-long serpent sculpture provides extra seating and a division to other cactus collections.

Hours: 10 a.m. to 4 p.m.

From Camelback Road, turn north into the Phoenician Resort. Immediately after contemporary entry water features, turn left onto Elsie Avenue. There is a residential empty lot for parking. From parking area, Jean Avenue is a short walk north and then west. *Please park in lot.*

Proceeds shared with Desert Botanical Garden

The Onofryton Residence
2244 East Vogel Avenue, Phoenix

This magnificent Tuscan-style house is situated on the edge of the Phoenix Preserve with breathtaking mountain views rising from the backyard. The homeowner is an avid gardener who also enjoys water gardening. The landscape plantings, hardscape patios, and water features were designed by Greg Trutza, who nestled the two-story house into a rich palette of desert trees and divert the guests across a bridge to enter the inner courtyard. Both streams in front and rear, as well as the retaining walls, are made of local rock surrounding the house. Visitors will enjoy the examples of how to landscape a hillside lot, as well as the drought-tolerant, native plant compositions.

Hours: 10 a.m. to 4 p.m.

Take Route 51 to Shea exit. Go west to 26th Street. Turn south, then go west on Mountain View Road. Turn south onto 23rd Street, then turn right onto East Vogel Avenue.

Proceeds shared with Desert Botanical Garden

Public Gardens
MARICOPA COUNTY

PHOENIX
Desert Botanical Garden
1201 North Galvin Parkway, Phoenix (480) 941-1225 www.dbg.org

Surrounded by rugged red buttes and home to more than 20,000 plants, Desert Botanical Garden's 145 acres comprise one of the most complete collections of desert flora in the world. Spring is an especially beautiful time to visit the Harriet K. Maxwell Desert Wildflower Trail, when hundreds of varieties of wildflowers burst into bloom.

Hours: October through April, daily, 8 a.m. to 8 p.m.; May through September, 7 a.m. to 8 p.m.; closed Christmas and July 4

Admission: $7.50 adults, $6.50 senior citizens, $3.50 children 5 to 12, children under 5 free

Take McDowell Road east to Galvin Parkway and turn south. Garden is on Galvin Parkway/64th Street just south of McDowell Road; entrance is clearly marked on east side of Galvin, just north of Phoenix Zoo, in Papago Park.

SCOTTSDALE
The Cactus Garden at The Phoenician
6000 East Camelback Road, Scottsdale (480) 423-2657 www.thephoenician.com

Up the steps, across from the main entrance to The Phoenician resort, the Cactus Garden is a small gem nestled against the base of Camelback Mountain. Flagstone pathways wind through a wide variety of well-marked cacti and succulents, punctuated by pieces of bronze statuary.

Hours: year round, daily, dawn to dusk

Admission: free

Entrance to The Phoenician is on Camelback Road. Garden is directly across from lobby and up steps. The Phoenician is located at base of Camelback Mountain in the Valley of the Sun.

SUPERIOR
Boyce Thompson Arboretum State Park
37615 Highway 60, Superior (520) 689-2811 arboretum.ag.arizona.edu

Boyce Thompson Arboretum is Arizona's oldest and largest botanical garden, featuring plants of the world's deserts. Encompassing 323 acres, it includes the Cactus Garden, Taylor Family Desert Legume Garden, Curandero Trail of Medicinal Plants, Wing Memorial Herb Garden, and Hummingbird/Butterfly Garden.

Hours: year round, daily, 8 a.m. to 5 p.m.; closed Christmas

Admission: $6 adults, $3 children 5 to 12, children under 5 free

Take Route 60/Superstition Freeway east from Phoenix. Entrance located on south side of highway, just west of Superior.

CALIFORNIA

The Hartung Garden, Lemon Grove.
Photo by William Gullette.

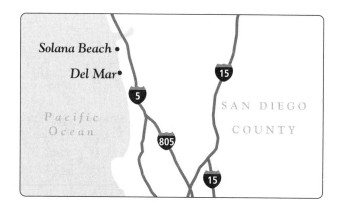

Saturday April 19
SAN DIEGO COUNTY

Del Mar
The Addisons' Garden
1175 Solana Drive, Del Mar

Enter into a private courtyard with an outdoor fireplace surrounded by palm trees and potted flowering plants. Our half-acre garden has a little bit of everything. As you wander through, you'll see exotic fruit trees, raised-bed vegetable gardens, and an unusual collection of flowering shrubs and plants collected from around the world. That gentle movement you see could be the thirty-plus box turtles in a lovely outdoor enclosure or the "resident" scrub jay ready to eat a peanut out of your hand. This garden has been featured in several books and magazines, including *Sunset, Better Homes & Gardens,* and *Garden.*

Hours: 12 to 4 p.m.

From I-5, take Lomas Santa Fe exit and go east. Turn right at Marine View (first right), then left onto Solana Drive. We are #1175, a large Spanish-style house on right side of street. *Please park on Highland Drive as there is no parking allowed on Solana.*

Proceeds shared with San Diego Horticultural Society

Lynne & Vernon Blackman's Garden

13591 Nogales Drive, Del Mar

Salsipuedes! Spanish for: "Leave if you can." Here you will find a splash of whimsy, color, and horticultural diversity as well as a hint of Giverny, of an urban farm, and the soul made calm by an herb-planted walking meditation labyrinth and moon-viewing mirror on a bluff near the Pacific Ocean. This exquisite one-and-one-third-acre garden set among rare native Torrey pine trees is filled with art, places to rest, masses of heritage and modern roses, arbors, butterflies, and surprises that beckon you to tarry. Lynne is an author and plantsperson who imagines, then creates her garden with a balance of form, foliage, shadow, and insight. Be careful, you may fall under its spell.

Hours: 10 a.m. to 4 p.m. Also open by appointment only from April through August. Call (858) 755-1048.

From I-5, take Del Mar Heights Road exit. Turn west towards ocean. Continue about .6 mile to Mar Scenic Drive. Turn left and go 1 block to Cordero Road. Turn right and go 1 block to Nogales Drive. Turn left and go 1 block to end of street. There are 4 beige stucco gateposts with house numbers which read, "Torrey Point, Private Drive." Garden is at house on left within gates. Enter at southernmost iron gate. *Please park on adjacent city streets or within gateposts along sides of private road. Do not block private road that continues beyond Blackman's residence.*

Jamison Garden

1209 Crest Road, Del Mar

This garden reflects our continuing passion for stone, Asiatic plants, and Japanese design and aesthetics. The foundation of the garden is the unique blue-and-black granite boulders that we found local quarries for the last decade. The architectural elements of the garden, the fencing, front gate entryway, and pergola evoke both Japanese and Craftsman detailing. The hardscape is comprised of Chinese slate walls, stone paths, and a Japanese water basin, which flows into a koi pond. Because a traditional Japanese garden would not be practical in this arid climate, we have tried to include more drought-tolerant plants along with our maples, camellias, azaleas, and bamboo. A "secret garden" comprised of vegetables, herbs, and old roses is tucked away on the south side of the garden.

Hours: 10 a.m. to 4 p.m.

From San Diego, take I-5 north to Del Mar Heights Road exit. Turn left (west) at first traffic light and proceed west toward ocean through 2 more lights. Turn right at third light onto Crest Road, a winding road with a canyon to the east. Go to Kalamath Street. House is on right.

From north San Diego County, take I-5 to Via de la Valle/Del Mar exit. Turn right at first light and turn left onto Jimmy Durante Boulevard. Del Mar fairgrounds and racetrack will be on right. Follow as it merges into Camino Del Mar. In Del Mar, turn left onto 15th Street (at second light). Proceed up hill, turn right at top. House is on left, between Via Alta and Kalamath. *Please park on street.*

Proceeds shared with San Dieguito River Valley Land Conservancy

The Teague Garden
1244 Umatilla Drive, Del Mar

Our garden is a more natural, free-flowing garden, like a walk in the woods, with meandering rock paths lined with South African bulbs—most flowering in April. We are plant collectors, so expect the unusual. We are surrounded by many rare clumping bamboos. One of our features is the use of purple to maroon foliage plants. We have many unusual trees and Australian plants, as well as Japanese plants.

Hours: 9 a.m. to 4 p.m.

From I-5, take Via de la Valle exit in Del Mar. Go west 1 block and make immediate left onto Jimmy Durante Boulevard south, around Del Mar racetrack. Continue south to merge onto Camino del Mar, less than .5 mile. Turn left at 15th Street and continue uphill 3 blocks to stop sign at Via Alta; turn right. Turn right at Umatilla Drive, only 1 block long. *Please park on Umatilla and walk down alley, past 1 house. Alley is heavily planted with flowers. There is some parking down alley for handicapped.*

Proceeds shared with San Diego Horticultural Society

Pat Welsh's "Pergola Paradise"
1825 Zapo Street, Del Mar

My garden nestles on a hillside above the sea and is designed in the Mediterranean style for entertaining, outdoor living, and *plein air* painting. Old trees and shrubs, fountains, pathways, trellises, and arbors give the garden character and romance. Vines, roses, and wildflowers make it brilliantly colorful in spring. Two patios are separated by an earth berm accented with Greek urns and drought-resistant plants. Pergolas drip with Chinese and Japanese wisteria. Dry stone walls support terraces for vegetables and wildflowers. A small grove of Australian tea trees underplanted with ferns, clivias, and hanging baskets shelters the house, designed by John Lloyd Wright and built by my husband and me in 1996. The brick and stone "rugs," brick planters, and mixed-media mosaic representing ocean, California sun, and the art of gardening are recent additions.

Hours: 10 a.m. to 1 p.m.

From I-5, take Via de la Valle exit in Del Mar. Go west 1 block to Jimmy Durante Boulevard and turn left (south). Follow for less than 1 mile, past Del Mar racetrack and fairgrounds, across a bridge over San Dieguito River, and under a railway bridge next to the railroad tracks. Merge onto Camino del Mar south. Get into left lane and go 1 block to first traffic light and entrance to Del Mar Plaza underground parking. Make a U-turn to head north again. Drive 1 short block and turn right at first corner, which is Seaview. At top of hill, turn right at stop sign onto Bellaire Street. Follow Bellaire, which is a winding road, 1 long block to next corner. Turn left onto Zapo Street; #1825 is first garden on right. *Please park on wide drive or on street.*

Proceeds shared with Quail Botanical Gardens

SOLANA BEACH
Golich's Garden
750 Barbara Avenue, Solana Beach

Our house is on three different levels about three blocks from the ocean. The front and upper backyard have a variety of roses, perennials, trees, and flowering shrubs. The upper backyard has a dry stream bed meandering through the flowers. The lower backyard has an outdoor garden railway, which runs from one side of the yard to the other. With several bonsai bushes and miniature buildings, the railway looks right at home on the hillside. Ocean breezes are both a delight and a challenge for the variety of perennials as well as the citrus and apple trees.

Hours: 12 to 4 p.m.

From I-5, take Lomas Santa Fe (do not confuse with Santa Fe Drive) exit west. Go 5 blocks, 1 block past Solana Beach Fire Station, and make a sharp right onto Granados (you are now traveling north). Go about 8 blocks where street will make a U-turn and start going south. At turn, street changes to Barbara Avenue. We are about 5 houses after turn in a 2-story redwood house on east side of street. *Please park on street.*

Proceeds shared with the San Dieguito Garden Club

The Garden of Erik & Irina Gronborg
424 Dell Court, Solana Beach

We have lived in and developed our small garden in a suburban neighborhood near the ocean for more than twenty-five years. We wanted to create our own beautiful, private space, screened from the outside world. We are both artists and the garden is an expression of our art and philosophy. Irina is a painter and botanical artist, Erik a sculptor and ceramicist. Using color, ceramics, wooden structures, rocks and walls, and plants appropriate to our dry climate, we have created a series of unique spaces: a cactus and succulent garden, bromeliad garden, formal vegetable garden, and raised pool with waterlilies and a fountain. Palms, flowers, vines, and fruit trees make a safe habitat for birds and butterflies.

Hours: 12 to 4 p.m.

From I-5, take Lomas Santa Fe exit, go west to Solana Hills Drive (first street that has a traffic light), and turn right. Make first left onto Dell Street. Turn right onto Dell Court. *Please park on street.*

The Tacktill-Wanerka Garden
465 Glencrest Drive, Solana Beach

This garden is a culmination of Phil and Janet's years of experiences applied to this young California garden, incorporating existing coastal chaparral and large trees on one terraced acre. The garden expresses the owners' concept of adventure with new discoveries at every turn. As you enter through the Japanese-style gate, you encounter a Zen and Japanese garden to reach the front door to the Asian-influenced house. With the multi-level garden, you will find a succulent garden; a cascading dry-stream bed; some small ponds; a young citrus grove; an orchid and carnivorous plant greenhouse; an orchid, fern, and bromeliad retreat; a tri-level deck with hot tub; stands of exciting bamboo; a tropical garden; a nursery area; assorted fruit trees; bonsai and kusamono-bonsai viewing areas; entertainment patio; and stone sculpture accented with styled succulent plantings and a classroom area. There is something to delight everyone.

Hours: 12 to 4 p.m.

Take I-5 to Lomas Santa Fe exit. Go west about 2 blocks; second block is Glencrest Drive. Turn right at traffic light. After first stop sign, go past several houses. There will be a series of 4 mailboxes with a paved road just before them. Turn left up hill to first house on right. *There is limited parking on this small street, but ample parking on Glencrest Drive. There are four small parking areas up hillside, with room for two or three cars in each.*

Proceeds shared with Quail Botanical Gardens

The Thirloway Cottage Garden
1105 Santa Madera Court, Solana Beach

I created this English cottage garden seven years ago so that my wife and I could have our wedding reception in the backyard. It has a dense privacy hedge of ornamental pear trees separated by wall-mounted planters spilling over with lush flowers. Curving beds filled with many varieties of azaleas, camellias, begonias, fuchsias, and perennials guarantee something blooming almost year around. Clematis, a rarity on the coast in San Diego, spread colors up into arbors and trees. There are unique handcrafted birdhouses and rose arbors in the garden, which I made. I am also a hands-on gardener. Additionally, there is a small Japanese garden off the master bedroom.

Hours: 12 to 4 p.m.

From I-5, take Lomas Santa Fe exit east to Santa Helena (left) to Santa Victoria (left) to Santa Alicia (right) to Santa Rufina Drive (left) to Santa Madera Court (left) to #1105 at end of street on left. It is about 1 mile from I-5 to garden. *Please park on street.*

Proceeds shared with San Dieguito Garden Club

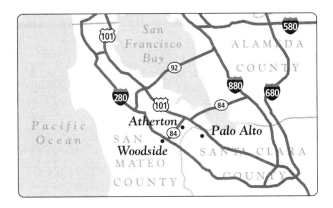

SAN MATEO COUNTY

ATHERTON

The Larry & Susy Calof Garden
126 Stockbridge Avenue, Atherton

In April, come walk under drifts of cherry, crab apple, dogwood, and wisteria blossoms; return in May for the scent of 150 lavishly underplanted roses. Designed by the owners, with particular attention to foliage, color, and texture, this garden is filled with unexpected nooks and the owners' collection of frog figures and fountains, a lovely pool, a raised orchard of dwarf fruit trees, a charming potting shed, brick patios, stands of beautiful old redwoods, a cat run for Bibbity, Bobbity and Boo, as well as benches that invite you to stay awhile and enjoy the beauty of each season.

Hours: 10 a.m. to 4 p.m.

From I-280, take Highway 84/Woodside Road east down to El Camino Real. From Highway 101, take Highway 84/Woodside Road west to El Camino Real. Take Highway 82/El Camino Real south 1 mile to Stockbridge Avenue, which is just past traffic light at Fifth Avenue. Turn right and go .7 mile to #126 on right. *Please park along street.*

Lynnie & Rich Dewey's Garden
97 Hawthorn Drive, Atherton

For me, our garden is the greatest gift. As I wander through the many rock-lined pathways bordered by raised perennial beds, I am constantly astonished by the dazzling and subtle array of colors and textures orchestrated to create such an amazing place of peacefulness. I am immediately filled with an incredible sense of calmness, well-being, and contentment. There are beautiful views from every vantage point as you walk from one end to the other. My favorite spot is the fishpond with its steppingstone bridge, gentle waterfalls, and fire-colored dragonflies.

Hours: 10 a.m. to 4 p.m.

From Highway 101, take Marsh Road/Atherton exit. Go west on Marsh Road to end at Middlefield Road. Turn left and go to James Avenue. Turn left through iron gate, go 2 blocks to Hawthorn Drive, and turn left. Garden is at first house on right. *Please park along road.*

Lurline R. Coonan
176 Harcross Road, Woodside

My property of thirty-two acres was originally part of Rancho las Pulgas, an old Spanish land grant. The Pennsylvania colonial-style house is surrounded by a New England garden, featuring California plants that suit our climate. Annuals and perennials bloom along the paths and I have made areas for shrubs, cutting flowers, vegetables, and fruit trees. The patterned entrance garden and rose garden are appropriate to the architecture of the house.

Hours: 10 a.m. to 4 p.m.

From I-280, take Woodside Road exit and go east. Turn left onto Alamedase Las Pulgas. Turn left again onto Fernside and left a final time onto Harcross Road.

The Jaunich Garden
384 Mountain Home Road, Woodside

Kathy and Bob's tranquil five-acre garden was designed three years ago to capture their favorite view of the western hills. What was mostly California scrub is today an award-winning garden. Rain is captured in a natural creek bed and flows into a small pond lined with willows and blackberries. Paths meander through the vegetable garden, past greenhouses filled with orchids, through the rose garden, and alongside mature olive trees. Garden beds are filled with grasses, lavender, and other Mediterranean plants. Brilliant red Meidiland shrub roses make a show along the western fence.

Hours: 10 a.m. to 4 p.m.

Take I-280 to Woodside Road and turn west. Go uphill to town. At first traffic light at Robert's Market, turn left onto Mountain Home Road. Go about 1 mile to #384. *Please park outside gate along street.*

SANTA CLARA COUNTY
Mack Garden
1116 Hamilton Avenue, Palo Alto

This is a garden of rooms. You are welcomed by a pair of cobblestone pillars leading into a courtyard of random pavers framed by a three-tiered arbor on one side and the house on the other. Continue on down a shady path onto a crescent-shaped brick terrace which faces the lawn with beds of flowers, shrubs, and trees on either side. An apron of old brick bordered by two very old crape myrtles leads your eye through the pergola to the focal point, an eighteenth-century French fountain centered on two raised brick planters. Surrounding the pool area on three sides is a trellis on which various flowering vines grow. The plantings in the garden include fruit trees, flowering trees and shrubs, perennials, roses, and fragrant vines.

Hours: 10 a.m. to 2 p.m.

From San Francisco, go south on Highway 101 approximately 39 miles to University Avenue turn-off (just beyond Willow Road, Menlo Park), being sure to go towards Palo Alto rather than East Palo Alto. Head west on University a few blocks to Lincoln Avenue (a traffic light). Turn left, then right onto very next street, Hamilton Avenue. Number 1116 is about halfway down block on left. *Please park on street.*

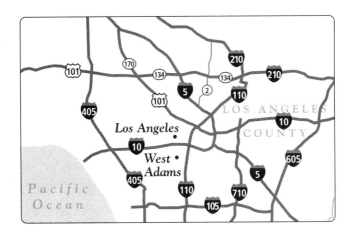

Sunday, April 27

*Maps, admission tickets, and Garden Conservancy information will be available
at the Ronnie Allumbaugh Gardens at Getty House from 9:30 a.m. to 3 p.m.,
and at the Peace Awareness Labyrinth & Gardens from 2 to 6 p.m.*

LOS ANGELES COUNTY

LOS ANGELES

Ronnie Allumbaugh Gardens at Getty House, the Official Residence of the Mayor of Los Angeles

605 South Irving Boulevard, Los Angeles

This historic Windsor Square garden was sensitively restored in 1995 by Kennedy Landscape
Design Associates. The original Tudor Revival-style garden was designed in 1928 by the renowned garden maker A.E. Hanson, but, over the years, the garden had deteriorated. The
garden today is interpreted creatively for use as the official Mayor's residence, including a
large rear lawn that can be fully tented. Paths lead visitors to the wisteria-covered pergola, the
ivy house, and the sunken garden with fountain and tennis court. Historic features that were
lost over the years have been restored, including the flagstone walk, sunken garden, and
several interior walls.

Hours: 9:30 a.m. to 3 p.m.

From I-10, exit at La Brea Avenue north and proceed to Sixth Street. Turn right;
Irving Boulevard is about 1 mile east of La Brea Avenue.

From I-110, exit at Sixth Street and proceed west about 4 miles to Irving Boulevard.
Getty House is on southwest corner of Irving and Sixth. *Please park on street.*

Boeck Garden
949 South Longwood Avenue, Los Angeles

Survey the gardens from the seventy-five-foot-long bridge high above El Rio del Jardin de las Flores, a stream that is host to wild birds, crawfish, and mosquito fish. Beyond the pool at the end of the bridge are the lawn and arbor levels. Descend the brick steps to the lower bridge. Ahead you will see two former dog runs converted to an herb garden in whimsical containers reflecting the owners' musical and literary interests.

Hours: 10 a.m. to 4 p.m.

From Highway 101 South, take Highland Avenue/Hollywood Bowl exit and go south on Highland. Cross Wilshire Boulevard, go 2 blocks and turn left onto Ninth Street. Take first right onto Longwood Avenue.

From I-10, take La Brea Exit north to Olympic Boulevard. Turn right, then pass 2 traffic lights (second is Highland Avenue), and go 1 block to Longwood. Turn left.

Bungalow Estrada Gardens
379 North Wilton Place, Los Angeles

This urban cottage garden was created with loving care and an eye to distract us from the stressful pace of Wilton Place. The front yard's rescued picket fence encloses this garden from the street. Our jacaranda tree, with fern-like leaves and blue flowers, shades our front yard. Perennials provide enough flowers for outside and inside our home most of the year. The large brick columns flanking our porch are covered with drooping purple-red fuchsia, reminding us of ballerinas. The rear yard is our sanctuary. The twisted willow tree, large ficus hedge, and charming garden accessories make our garden intimate. The hand-painted door and the old wooden-ladder arbor are worth the price of admission. Our proudest accomplishment: the pond and waterfall brings the whole garden together.

Hours: 10 a.m. to 4 p.m.

From Highway 101 south, exit at Sunset Boulevard, onto Van Ness Avenue south. Continue, crossing Sunset and Santa Monica Boulevards and cross Melrose Avenue to fourth left at Elmwood Avenue. Go 2 blocks to Wilton Place.

From Highway 101 north, exit at Sunset Boulevard. Take Sunset West offramp, turn right onto Sunset, then left at first traffic light onto Van Ness. Proceed as directed above.

From I-10, exit at La Brea Avenue north and go to Beverly Boulevard. Turn right, pass Highland Avenue, Rossmore, and Larchmont Boulevard. Turn left onto Wilton Place.

From I-110, exit at Third Street west and go about 4 miles to Wilton Place, west of Western Avenue. Turn right and go north across Beverly Boulevard. Number 379 is on southeast corner of Wilton and Elmwood, 1 block north of Beverly Boulevard. *Please park on street.*

Proceeds shared with Pet Pride and Temple Israel of Hollywood Nursery School

Dar Meyer
146 South Larchmont Boulevard, Los Angeles

This five-year-old urban oasis features a series of symmetrically arranged outdoor rooms embracing a restored 1921 Moroccan-style villa. Gone are ho-hum grass lawns and a cracked concrete driveway. We added gravel entry courtyards graced by queen palms, enclosure walls with a wooden gate, Mediterranean herbs, an oleander allée, and a gravel drive. We restored a shaded glass-roofed interior atrium with a traditional fountain and rearranged access to the back garden where vintage tangerines hold court over a gravel-paved dining area.

Hours: 10 a.m. to 4 p.m.

From Highway 101, take Highland Boulevard south, go east (left) on Beverly Road, and south (right) onto Larchmont Boulevard one half block south of village to #146.

From I-10, take La Brea Boulevard north, go east (right) on Third, go north (left) on Larchmont to #146. *Please park on Larchmont Boulevard.*

Pepper-Macias Garden
384 North Ridgewood Place, Los Angeles

A woodsy Pacific Northwest theme was used to harmonize with our 1914 Craftsman bungalow house. Our guests are welcomed by a small grove of liquidambar trees and Canary Island pines. We've taken advantage of our corner lot with a 150-foot parkway to plant a vast cutting garden, which includes dozens of rosebushes, along with other perennials and annuals. The original clinker-brick Craftsman-style pergola covered with bougainvillea and wisteria serves as a backdrop for the recently installed pool and spa. A unique mix of flagstone, brick, and concrete was used to create new patios and pathways that appear as though they were original to the house. The landscape includes a mature California sycamore, a collection of Japanese maples, splashes of bright colors, and an electric mix of perennials with multicolored and variegated foliage. Vintage containers are used throughout, some original to the house.

Hours: 10 a.m. to 2 p.m.

From Highway 101 south, exit at Sunset Boulevard, you will be on Van Ness Avenue south. Continue, crossing Sunset and Santa Monica Boulevards and cross Melrose Avenue to fourth left at Elmwood Avenue. Go 1 block to Ridgewood Place.

From Highway 101 north, exit at Sunset Boulevard. Take Sunset West off ramp and turn right onto Sunset and left at first signal onto Van Ness. Proceed as directed above.

From I-10, exit at La Brea Avenue north and go to Beverly Boulevard. Turn right and pass Highland Avenue, Rossmore and Larchmont Boulevards and turn left onto Ridgewood Place which is 1 block past the signal at Van Ness.

From I-110, exit at Third Street west and go about 4 miles to Wilton Place. Turn right onto Wilton Place and go north to Beverly Boulevard. Turn left and go 1 block west to Ridgewood Place and turn right. Number 382 is on the southeast corner of Ridgewood and Elmwood, 1 block north of Beverly Boulevard and 1 block east of Wilton Place. *Please park on street.*

Yusts' Garden
500 South Rossmore Boulevard, Los Angeles

This garden is designed in the Italian style, divided into four sections—the formal garden, the hidden garden, the woods, and the orchard.

Hours: 10 a.m. to 4 p.m.

The garden is located 3 miles south of Hollywood and Vine at southeast corner of Rossmore Boulevard and Fifth Street. Note that Vine becomes Rossmore south of Melrose Avenue.

Jennifer Charnofsky's Garden at the Furlong House
2657 Van Buren Place, West Adams

My organic garden uses primarily drought-tolerant Mediterranean and California native plants suited to our climate. The English cottage-style front garden reflects the plum color of the 1910 Craftsman house (Los Angeles Historic-Cultural Monument #678). The rear vegetable garden, interspersed with flowers, uses the French intensive method (raised beds, double digging, close planting). There will be a speaker on the method. The original fountain and wisteria-covered pergola create a relaxing garden room. The house is a gateway to a National Register District street, one of several such districts in historic West Adams.

Hours: 2 to 6 p.m.

From I-10, exit at Normandie Avenue south to Adams Boulevard. Pass Adams and turn left onto 27th Street. Go 3 blocks and turn left onto Van Buren Place. Number 2657 is on northwest corner of 27th and Van Buren. Normandie is about 1 mile east of Arlington on Adams Boulevard. _Please park on street._

Proceeds shared with West Adams Heritage Association

Hutchinson Family Garden
2176 West 24th Street, West Adams

Our garden was designed by Thomas Batcheller Cox to be an extension of our 1910 West Adams Craftsman house, both in design and plant choice. Over a period of ten years, a barren, dusty yard with one great old tree (and plenty of rusting appliances) was transformed into a series of garden rooms including: an open air dining room with a citrus perimeter; a secret garden path with trellised walls and perennial borders; a miniature terrace defined by a porch and brick wall fountain; a grassy area shaded by a Chinese elm for romping and swinging; and a swimming pool surrounded by plants that is a cross between a reflecting pool and swimming hole. The resulting gardens create a peaceful retreat to balance the urban setting.

Hours: 2 to 6 p.m.

From I-10, exit at Arlington Avenue and go south to Adams Boulevard. Turn left, then left again onto Gramercy Place. Turn left onto 24th Street. _Please park on street._

Proceeds shared with West Adams Heritage Association

Le Parc Sans Soleil
2455 Gramercy Park Place, West Adams

A former home of Los Angeles's park director in the 1920s, this West Adams garden was rediscovered by its current owners. After removing thirty trees, they unearthed an original concrete fountain beneath two giant deodar cedar trees. The oasis features a collection of rare ferns complemented by many California specimen plants. A columned garden pergola acentuates the Colonial Revival home. The property is also home to a _Palais des Poulets, des Lapins, et des Tortues_ and to a family of wild parrots.

Hours: 2 to 6 p.m.

From I-10, exit at Arlington Avenue south to West Adams Boulevard. Turn left, then left again onto Gramercy Place. Turn right onto Gramercy Park Place. _Park on street._

Proceeds shared with West Adams Heritage Association

Marais Garden
2534 Ninth Avenue, West Adams

This West Adams garden is wild looking, with the multiplicity of textures that comes when trees, flowers, succulents, spiky plants, tall and wispy grasses, shrubs, and ground covers are jumbled together. It is a gray-green, dry climate garden in which drought-adapted plants from Africa, Australia, the Mediterranean, and the Americas provide the background to the few more colorful accent plants gleaned from various film shoots. In the reclaimed alley at the back is a kitchen garden with raised beds, which supplies enough of many kinds of vegetables to make the supermarket almost superfluous.

Hours: 2 to 6 p.m.

From I-10, exit Arlington Avenue south to West Adams Boulevard. Turn right, then right again onto Ninth Avenue. *Please park on street.*

Proceeds shared with West Adams Heritage Association

Peace Awareness Labyrinth & Gardens at the Guasti Villa
3500 West Adams Boulevard, West Adams

The spectacular facade of a 1910 Beaux Arts Italian Renaissance villa (Los Angeles Historic-Cultural Monument #478) can be seen from the sycamore-lined front walk. The villa was built by Secundo Guasti, an Italian immigrant who established the largest winery in the world at the turn of the twentieth century. Fountains and marble lions stand guard. Monumental plantings flank the east and west wings. Visitors will walk through the entry court, grand ballroom, and out to the rotunda, where the two-level flagstone courtyard comes into view with reflecting pools, fountains, flowering plants, a rose-covered pergola, and a hand-cut stone labyrinth fashioned after the Chartres Cathedral Labyrinth. On the lowest levels there is a Bali-inspired meditation garden with water features and places to sit and soak in the peaceful beauty of nature right in the middle of West Adams.

Hours: 2 to 6 p.m.

From I-10, exit at Arlington Avenue south to Adams Boulevard. Turn right and proceed to #3500. *Please park on street.*

Proceeds shared West Adams Heritage Association and Peace Theological Seminary

Trosper-Raposa Garden
2515 Fourth Avenue, West Adams

An Arts & Crafts garden updated: a symphony of textures forms the framework for the red-and-white perennial arc (both colors of Stanford and Harvard, the owners' alma maters) next to the public sidewalk. Behind the 1909 Craftsman house (the Blanche and Lucien Gray House, Los Angeles Historic-Cultural Monument #600) is a koi pond, hybrid roses, and a pergola covered with the original wisteria. The sweet peas should be in bloom.

Hours: 2 to 6 p.m.

From I-10, exit at Arlington Avenue south to West Adams Boulevard. Turn right and right again onto Fourth Avenue. *Please park on street.*

Proceeds shared with West Adams Heritage Association

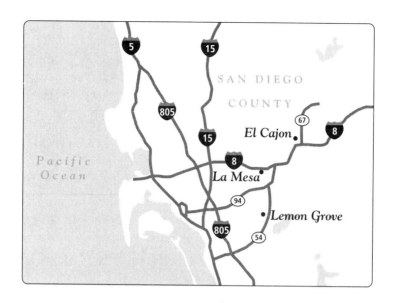

Saturday, May 3

SAN DIEGO COUNTY

EL CAJON

Steve & Susie Dentt's Garden

1470 Grove Road, El Cajon

Our garden has evolved from a beautiful traditional landscape to a garden full of wit and whimsy. It has been said, "It is a little bit country, a little bit English, a little bit rustic, and a whole lot charming." We love to combine plants with whimsical and interesting objects such as our birdhouse collection with more than seventy to date. Our garden is a broad, flat acre where as you meander through its rooms and vignettes. We hope that one will be overcome with a feeling of delight.

Hours: 10 a.m. to 2 p.m.

From Los Angeles, take I-5 south to I-805 south to I-8 east. Go about 15 miles and take El Cajon Boulevard. Veer right onto Chase Avenue and go about 3.5 miles. Turn left onto Grove Road.

From I-15 south, take I-8 east and proceed as directed above. *Please park on Coco Palms Drive.*

Proceeds shared with the Susan G. Komen Breast Cancer Foundation

LA MESA

Bill & Pat Allen Garden

9840 Grosalia Avenue, La Mesa

You may think that you are in the midst of the Cotswolds when you enter the front gate of the Allens' English-style cottage garden. The quaint granite French Normandy hand-hewn stone cottage built in 1929 with its high pitched slate roof evokes images of a bygone era. A pastel color palette of mostly pinks, blues, whites, and yellows is displayed among the more than 100 rosebushes, hollyhocks, foxgloves, delphiniums, verbascums, heathers, primroses, lavenders, and buddleia, to name a few. Through the 'Iceberg' rose archway and down the stairs, one enters into a secret garden not visible from the street. Meandering flagstone paths lead the way to the birdhouse village, the birdbath, and armillary. Various seating areas invite you to sit and watch the hummingbirds or listen to the bright yellow finches sing as they feed on thistle seed pouches.

Hours: 9 a.m. to 2 p.m.

From I-8 east, take Severin/Fuerte exit. Veer right onto Fuerte (1 block), turn left onto Grossmont Boulevard (1 long block), turn right onto Grossmont Summit (1 block), and turn right onto Grosalia Avenue. Ours is the gray stone house on left.

From I-8 west, take Severin/Fuerte exit. Turn right onto Severin, take immediate right onto Murray Drive (1 block), turn right onto Grossmont Boulevard (cross over I-8), take immediate left onto Grossmont Summit (1 block), and turn right onto Grosalia Avenue. *Please park along street.*

Proceeds shared with the San Diego Museum of Art

Nugent Garden

4705 Maple Avenue, La Mesa

Inspired by several trips to the United Kingdom during the past eight years, our goal was to design and build an English cottage garden for our late 1940s-era Southern California home. Featuring a large rose collection and hundreds of colorful annuals and perennials, this fully landscaped, one-third-acre property provides a haven for butterflies, hummingbirds, and gardening enthusiasts alike. In addition to impressive hardscape and structural elements, our garden includes an eclectic blend of exotic bamboo, tropical vines, and Asiatic, Australian, Mediterranean, and South American trees and shrubs.

Hours: 10 a.m. to 4 p.m.

From I-8, take 70th Street/Lake Murray Boulevard exit. Head south on 70th Street about .25 mile to El Cajon Boulevard. Turn left and head east 1 mile. Turn right onto Maple Avenue (located just before entrance to Auto Zone parking lot) and follow south 3 blocks. House is on left with street number painted on curb. *Please park along street and enter garden through redwood arbor located in center of front yard.*

Proceeds shared with the San Diego Horticultural Society

Perennial Adventure—Christine S. Wotruba
10548 Anaheim Drive, La Mesa

This garden is an adventure for the plant collector or "junkie." Unusual bulbs, flowers from seeds, and shrubs of all sizes are planted in a series of gardens surrounding my hillside home. Inspired by English cottage gardens, paths direct the visitor through beds and borders abundant with color. Interesting combinations show off a manzanita under a redbud tree surrounded by South African bulbs and roses, and a yarrow lawn overlooking a color border that includes New Zealand carex, Australian grevillea, and sages. This collector's garden has another aspect and that is a small retail nursery known for its variety.

Hours: 10 a.m. to 4 p.m.

From San Diego on I-8, go east to La Mesa. On left is Grossmont Shopping Center. Take off ramp to Fuerte Drive, turn right, and go up hill. Continue about 2.5 miles through 1 traffic light to Avocado Boulevard, which is second light. Turn right and go 4 short blocks. Turn right onto Anaheim Drive. Street is only 2 blocks long. Number 10548 is in second block on right.

From downtown San Diego on Highway 94, take G Street, which becomes Highway 94 just east of 16th Street. Continue to Avocado Boulevard exit. Turn left past Rancho San Diego Shopping Center, continue through 2 lights, and go up hill about 8 blocks. Turn left onto Anaheim Drive. Number 10548 is on second block. *Please park on street in front of garden and all along right side of street.*

Lemon Grove
The Hartung Garden
8450 Adams Street, Lemon Grove

Tropicals, including palms, philodendrons, and bromeliads, create the structural bones of this garden with extensive plantings of camellias and azaleas. A collection of plants, natives of Africa, Latin America, and Asia, lends an international touch. This half-acre urban garden, once a part of a citrus grove, was designed twenty-six years ago by the late San Diego horticulturist W. F. Sinjen, with meandering brick paths, seating areas, and four fishponds to create a restful hideaway.

Hours: 12 to 4 p.m.

From Highway 94, take Lemon Grove Avenue exit. Turn south to Broadway. Turn left (east) and continue to Kempf (2 traffic lights). Turn right (south) and continue 1 short block to Golden Avenue. Turn left (east), continue to Adams Street, and turn right (west). We are fourth house on right.

Proceeds shared with Quail Botanical Gardens

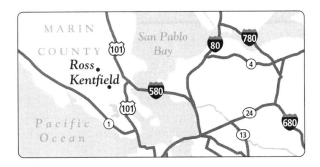

Sunday, May 4

MARIN COUNTY

KENTFIELD

Geraniaceae Gardens

122-124 Hillcrest Avenue, Kentfield

These tranquil gardens were developed as living praise to hardy geraniums, and other rare and unusual shrubs and hardy perennials. The one-acre site began as a small, flat area and long, steep slopes of bright yellow clay. It was a challenge to carve out areas for cultivation. There are two sunny perennial and shrub borders in the upper garden for hot- and cool-colored plants, and linking staircases to a lower woodland garden. A small nursery displays plants in the geranium family. The garden has a number of sculptures by Bay Area artists and there are many seats and a small *casita* for resting and talking.

Hours: 10 a.m. to 4 p.m.

From junction of Highway 101, take Sir Francis Drake Boulevard west 2 miles. At traffic lights, turn left onto College Avenue. Kentfield fire station is at light. Pass a second pedestrian light and 2 stop signs. At second stop sign, turn right onto Estelle Avenue (West America Bank is on right). Go to stop sign and turn right onto Hillcrest Avenue to 2nd house on right. Do not block driveway. There are 2 gardens next to each other, at #122 and #124. Arrows will indicate a path through them, with exit at beginning of driveway. *Please park on right side of Hillcrest Avenue.*

From the East Bay, take I-580 across Richmond-San Rafael Bridge. Take second exit, Sir Francis Drake Boulevard/San Anselmo/Kentfield. Road passes San Quentin Prison and, after several miles, goes underneath Highway 101. Proceed as directed above.

John & Glennis Jones Garden

229 Upper Toyon, Kentfield

Favored by this temperate Kentfield microclimate, John and Glennis Jones' garden has been described by Barbara Hopper of the California Horticultural Society as "a horticulturist's and landscape designer's treasure chest, an artful blend of flower and foliage colors." For this garden, designer Brandon Tyson's goal has been to create a sense of maturity and the impression that the garden has been in place since the California Mediterranean-style home was built in the 1930s. Complementing this outstanding collection of plants gathered from around the world are equally exotic garden features, including jimbanang urns from central Java and a waterspout for the koi pond cast from the finial once used to decorate an antique palanquin from the Malabar coast.

Hours: 10 a.m. to 2 p.m.

From Highway 101, take San Anselmo/Richmond Bridge exit onto Sir Francis Drake Boulevard west, under freeway. Go 1.5 miles; immediately after Sloat Garden Center on right, turn right onto Laurel Grove. Go .6 mile to third stop sign. Turn right onto Makin Grade. Climb to top of hill; then bear right onto Upper Toyon (from Laurel Grove, it is about .6 mile). Number 229 is third property.

From the East Bay, take I-580 over Richmond-San Rafael Bridge. Take Sir Francis Drake Boulevard/San Anselmo/Kentfield exit (shortly after crossing bridge). Follow East Sir Francis Drake Boulevard past Larkspur Ferry Terminal to West Sir Francis Drake Boulevard. Go under train trestle. Proceed as directed above. *Please park on Upper Toyon.*

Ross

Tom Jackson & Kathy Grant's Garden

16 Brookwood, Ross

Twenty years ago, this shady, sloping site in the lee of Mount Tamalpais with winter rain, warm days, and cool nights seemed perfect for a Himalayan foothill garden. Now there is a canopy of *Trachycarpus* and other palms, magnolias, and camphor, with a middle story of rhododendron and bamboo. A spring forms the focus of the Zen rock garden. The art collection has grown with the garden. It has works by Viola Frey, Magdalena Abakamowitz, and others under the arbor and in the brick courtyard. The glasshouse, with its granite spa, potted palms, and sculpture, forms the jewel in this complex but intimate garden.

Hours: 10 a.m. to 4 p.m.

From Highway 101, take San Anselmo/Richmond Bridge exit. Follow San Anselmo signs under freeway to Sir Francis Drake Boulevard west. Go 2.5 miles, past College of Marin. At traffic light opposite Marin Art and Garden Center, turn left onto Lagunitas. Cross bridge and turn left onto Ross Common. At next corner, turn right onto Redwood, then take first right onto Brookwood. Last house on right is #16.

Kreitzberg Family Garden

Spring Road, Ross

Our hillside garden is surrounded by five acres of oaks, dogwoods, redwoods, rhododendrons, and azaleas. A cedar staircase climbs under a terraced pergola draped with gnarled ropes of wisteria and clematis. Guests ascend to the sound of waterfalls. With a vie of the Ross Valley, the paths wind upward past a giant redwood standing sentinel over magnolia, tree fern lilac, hawthorne, and fuchsia. At the third koi pond are iris and wild strawberry. Among daphne, isotoma, Japanese maple, and anemone, stands a weathered-copper heron. Ivy, laurel, and honeysuckle flourish near the vine-covered cistern which provides water from five spring-fed wells. Hordes of hummingbirds visit us year round.

Hours: 10 a.m. to 2 p.m.

From Highway 101, take Sir Francis Drake Boulevard west. Go 2.25 miles to Ross. Turn left at traffic light onto Lagunitas Road. Go to 2nd stop sign and turn left onto Willow. Go 1 block and turn right onto Madrona, past horse corral. Take first left onto Spring Road. *Please park on street.*

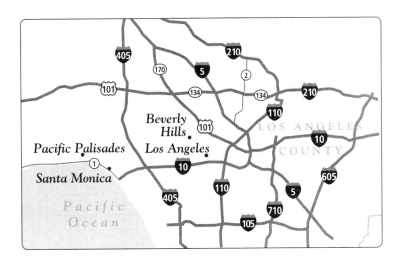

Saturday, May 10

Maps, admission tickets, and Garden Conservancy information will be available at
Flower to the People from 9:30 a.m. to 4 p.m.

LOS ANGELES COUNTY

BEVERLY HILLS
The Anderson Garden
604 North Arden Drive, Beverly Hills

With dahlias, bearded irises, camellias, bamboos, wisteria bonsai, water cannas, hydrangeas, fuchsias, giant hibiscus, a grafted five-color hibiscus tree, antique roses, and an eloquent assortment of potted cymbidiums flourishing under a carrot tree, the Anderson Garden combines the quaint charm of a traditional cottage garden with the exotic lushness of a cool and serene tropical retreat. It welcomes visitors with a towering angel trumpet tree that showers pale peach flowers over a water garden and an array of rare and colorful begonias. The subtle, sweet fragrances of rare gingers and plumeria make this garden a feast for the senses. Many plants bear the names of relatives and friends, sentimental reminders that honor important life transitions and celebrate special events.

Hours: 10 a.m. to 4 p.m.

From Highway 101, exit at Highland Avenue and take south to Santa Monica Boulevard. Turn right and head west into Beverly Hills.

From I-10, take La Cienega Boulevard exit, head north, and turn left onto Santa Monica Boulevard. Arden Drive is fourth right after Doheny Drive. Number 604 is in second block above Santa Monica Boulevard. *Please park on street.*

Los Angeles
Flower to the People
2816 Burkshire Avenue, Los Angeles

The Flower to the People garden is a truly urban garden experience. We have endeavored to create a symbiotic relationship between our residence and our landscape, so that you are immersed in our home once you leave the street. The front yard, enclosed by voluptuous perennials, serves as a "living foyer," welcoming you into our open and airy residence. Vibrantly colored stucco walls evoke visions of St. Martin or Provence as you stroll down side pathways to reach our design studio and backyard "secret garden." Something will grab and hold your attention. Maybe it is the *Bambusa vulgaris* 'Vittata' with its golden-and-green stripes, or maybe it's the red posts covered in climbing *Rosa* 'Dublin Bay'. In any event, you'll want to pull up a chair and take it all in. Alternatively, climb the stairs to the roofdeck dining room and appreciate a bird's-eye view of our urban oasis.

Hours: 9:30 a.m. to 4 p.m.

From points east, exit I-10 at Bundy south and continue to National Boulevard. Turn left. We are 1 block north (left) of National Boulevard between Bundy and Barrington. east side of Burkshire Avenue.

From points north and south, take I-405 to I-10 west and proceed as directed above.

From points west, exit I-10 at Centinela and turn left off exit onto Pico Boulevard. Turn right onto Bundy from Pico. Proceed as directed above. *Please park on street.*

Marek/Bernatz Garden
2252 25th Street, Santa Monica

A stone path leads you to our entry courtyard with a sandstone checkerboard "carpet" and a bubbling fountain made from old Spanish tiles. The front yard, inspired by the gardens of Old California and the south of France, is filled with aloes, agaves, lavenders, and yellow roses. A mighty Chinese elm dominates the back garden and outdoor living spaces. Inspired by gardens in Mexico and the tropics, brightly colored walls and lush plantings of hot-colored cannas, birds of paradise, gingers, salvias, and orange and red roses fill this garden. A vegetable, rose, and cutting garden completes the tour at the back of the garden.

Hours: 10 a.m. to 4 p.m.

From I-10 west, take Cloverfield Exit. At top of ramp, turn left onto Cloverfield Boulevard. At traffic light, turn left onto Pico Boulevard. Go 2 blocks to 25th Street and turn right. House is fifth on right. From I-10 east, take 20th Street Exit. Turn right onto 20th Street. Turn left onto Pico Boulevard. Go to 25th Street and turn right. House is fifth on right. *Please park on street.*

Miller/Engel Garden

1553 South Livonia Avenue, Los Angeles

Our garden grew gradually out of my efforts with designer Katherine Glascock to realize more fully the classic architecture and interior of our 1934 Spanish Revival-style home. It has an enclosed front courtyard with antique brick and a large covered porch. An old fountain commands center stage and is surrounded by potted plants and a diverse mix of plants, i.e., rosemary, black-eyed Susan, dwarf citrus. The rear garden, an outdoor living/dining room, is surrounded by vividly colored walls. Within the intimacy of the small space, the dramatic *Phormium*, ornamental grasses, succulents, cacti, *Datura*, and *Abutilon* provide color and foliar contrast. An integral part of the charm of this garden is the abundant use of collectibles, including Bauer pottery, vintage painted Mexican pots, found ironwork, and quirky 1950s garden décor, all of which unites the interior and exterior spaces.

Hours: 10 a.m. to 4 p.m.

Located in the Beverlywood area of West Los Angeles. North of I-10, 1 block west of Robertson Boulevard and 3 small blocks south of Pico Boulevard on corner of Livonia Avenue and Pickford. Look for old Spanish home on northwest corner. *Please park on street.*

Novick Garden

3127 Cardiff Avenue, Los Angeles

Landscape designer Katherine Glascock has created privacy and serenity in the small front and rear corner gardens. Crape myrtles border the street edge and *Camellia sasanqua* frame the entry steps, flanked by a rose garden. Weaver's bamboo and a canopied overhead shade the house and deck of the rear garden. Bougainvillea scrambles over a rustic structure surrounded by roses and frames a contemporary sculpture by Betty Gold. Italian buckthorns form a tall privacy screen. Fruit trees will mature to create further privacy. Bearded irises sweep from the garden entry to the fruit trees.

Hours: 10 a.m. to 4 p.m.

Located 6 blocks west of Robertson Boulevard, 1 block north of National Boulevard. Near the Robertson off-ramp of I-10.

Eglee-Dalton Garden
920 Iliff Street, Pacific Palisades

Spun around a beautifully restored and enhanced 1920s Spanish Revival-style house, this is a quintessentially eclectic California garden. Every inch of the fifty- by 125-foot lot is developed in a series of garden rooms and halls distinguished by dramatic and diverse plantings, classic and outlandish ornaments, and an array of water features. Fifteen years in the making, the garden has evolved not only in response to architectural change, but in lockstep with the clients' deepening appreciation of classic Californian and Hawaiian crafts. Serene but stunningly vital, the garden was designed by landscape architect Rob Steiner.

Hours: 10 a.m. to 4 p.m.

Take Pacific Coast Highway to Chautauqua Boulevard. Go north to Sunset Boulevard. Turn left, then take first right onto Hartzell. Proceed to Carey Street, turn right and go 1 block to Iliff. Turn left; #920 is a high-hedged red stucco house in middle of block. *Please park along street.*

Meyer Garden
17568 Camino de Yatasto, Pacific Palisades

Nestled next to the Santa Monica Mountains' wilderness, the Meyer Garden contains towering rock outcroppings, rare and endangered native plants, and an intermittent stream. As a visual foil to the native hillside, the interior gardens exude hot colors, bold succulent forms, oversized pots, and exceptional trees. The garden was designed by Stephanie Wilson Blanc and has been featured in national magazines. Connected by stone and gravel walkways are six well-defined rooms. One room has a fireplace, another a potting bench with a natural rock basin; farthest out is a seating area cloistered by the stream and towering boulders.

Hours: 10 a.m. to 4 p.m.

From I-405, take I-10 west. This will end going into McClure Tunnel and you will exit onto Pacific Coast Highway north. Pass California Incline, Chautauqua Boulevard/ West Channel, and Temescal Canyon. Turn right onto Sunset Boulevard, 4 miles from McClure Tunnel. Go .5 mile, passing Self Realization Center Lake Shrine on right, and turn left onto Palisades Drive. Go 2.2 miles, passing Hidden Café on left and turn left onto Vereda de la Montera. After .2 mile, turn into guard gate. It is .3 mile to Meyer house, a white 2-story Greek-style house with Aegean blue roof and shutters and olive trees in front. *Please park on street.*

Rapoport Canyon Garden
539 Muskingum Avenue, Pacific Palisades

It began with a pond and grew as a collaboration between the owners, designer Judy Horton and contractor Joan Brooke into four landscaped levels facing west on Las Pulgas Canyon. This garden is reminiscent of New England, with its descending stairway, which passes a hydrangea garden and leads to a Chinese elm shading a cluster of oakleaf hydrangeas, abutilon, and eleagnus. A knoll, feeding the pond, features an 'Erfurt' rose and a Sangu Kaku Japanese maple. The natural-style koi pond is surrounded by cattails and papyrus. A shrub area combines 'Dapple Dawn', 'Penelope', 'Lordly Oberon', and 'Mutabilis' roses with a pomegranate, euphorbia, and buddleia. Below them are a gravel Petanque court and grape arbor, which frames a stairway to the vegetable garden on the lowest level. All this is watched over by a lavender-bordered fruit orchard and weeping mulberry.

Hours: 10 a.m. to 4 p.m.

From I-405, take Sunset Boulevard exit, drive about 12 minutes through Palisades Village, past Temescal Cyn (Pali High School on left) and El Medio. Turn left onto Muskingum (Temple Kehillat Israel on right) and go 3 blocks south to house on right with lavender trim.

From I-10, go west to PCH, north to Temescal Cyn, and turn right. Ocean is on left. Go up hill to Sunset Boulevard, turn left, and proceed as above.

Santa Monica
447 11th Street
447 11th Street, Santa Monica

Six years ago, the homeowner and designer Susanne Jett began a garden design which evolved to include an expansion and restoration of the classic Spanish Revival period bungalow house. The front entry flows up through a dry wash of hot colors and muted greens into an intimate courtyard of wildflowers and bubbling water. Hummingbirds and butterflies are lovers and frequent visitors of this garden. The backyard offers a private, lush extension to interior living space. Bamboo, fruit trees, flowering shrubs, and vines are part of the rich, fragrant environment surrounding a flagstone and ground cover patio with sunken spa. Personally designed wrought iron trellises, fencing, and gates provide architectural elements of beauty as well as security for the dogs.

Hours: 10 a.m. to 2 p.m.

From Los Angeles, take I-10 west/Lincoln Boulevard exit. Turn right onto Lincoln Boulevard to Marguerita Avenue. Turn left onto 11th Street. House is just around corner on east side of street.

From the Valley, take I-405 south; exit onto Sunset Boulevard west to Bundy Drive. Turn left onto Bundy and go to San Vicente Boulevard, turn right. Go to 11th Street and turn left (south). Go about 2.5 blocks. House is on left. *Please park on street.*

Nancy Goslee Power Garden
1015 Pier Avenue, Santa Monica

This is a tiny garden near the beach in Santa Monica. The courtyard is stuffed with plants and very colorful, with bright walls and fountains. This is a difficult zone to garden in because of the damp climate and fog, so I change potted plants for added color and amusement. A rare Kashmir cypress hangs over a wall fountain, while a giant Burmese honeysuckle drapes down the house. A huge *Dracaena draco* guards the front gate. I even left a bottlebrush from the original planting because the hummingbirds love it and it stands for perserverance (it lasted during the construction).

Hours: 10 a.m. to 4 p.m.

Take I-10 west to Lincoln Boulevard. Turn left, pass Ocean Park Boulevard, and continue to Pier Street. Turn left and go to end of block. House is on left. *Please park on street.*

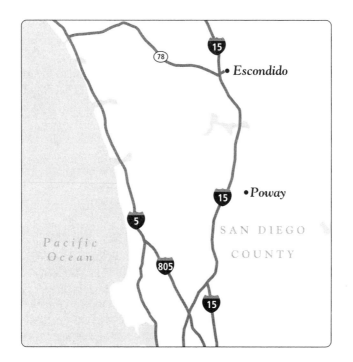

SAN DIEGO COUNTY

Escondido
Lievers' Garden
1564 Pedregal Drive, Escondido

Our challenge was to take a dying avocado grove on a steep, boulder-strewn hillside and create a natural garden with plants native to a Mediterranean-type climate. Forty years later, it's still a work in progress. Two distinct gardens developed. In the upper garden, rock paths guide the visitor around native granite boulders to the tree-shaded gathering spots. The second garden, spilling down the sloping hillside, hosts a meadow of yarrow, narcissus, and South African bulbs. Wildlife-friendly trees, shrubs, ornamental grasses, and succulents surround the meadow. Secret gardens invite you to leave the main path and enjoy the show.

Hours: 12 to 4 p.m.

From I-15, take South Escondido exit at Via Rancho Parkway and turn right (changes name to Bear Valley Parkway at San Pasqual High School). Go 4.1 miles to Idaho Street, turn left and go .8 mile to Pedregal Drive. Turn left and go to end of cul-de-sac. *Please park on Pedregal Drive.*

Poway
Arnold Garden
15638 Boulder Mountain Road, Poway

Our nineteen-acre, boulder-strewn, hilltop property is a combination botanical garden and nature preserve. The overall theme of the garden and property is, "In balance with nature," and careful attention has been paid to the use of massive boulders, natural slopes, and native plants. The botanical portion of the property is an extensive collection of hundreds of tropical and subtropical plants from around the world, including more than eighty palm and fifty cycad species, as well as flowering trees, aloes, proteas, orchids, bromeliads, and ferns. More than fifteen acres of our property is highly diverse, undisturbed coastal chaparral, which will be in peak bloom in April and May.

Hours: 10 a.m. to 4 p.m.

From I-15, go east on Rancho Bernardo Road 1.75 miles (it becomes Espola Road after .81 mile). Turn right onto Martincoit Road and go 1.27 miles. Turn right onto Orchard Gate Road and go .32 mile. Turn left onto Lime Grove Road and go .25 mile. Turn right onto Arroya Vista Road for .14 mile. Turn left onto Boulder Mountain Road and go straight up through gate for .53 mile. *Please park along wide road on property and walk or take shuttle up narrow driveway to house, gardens, and trails.*

Betty's Garden
15063 Huntington Gate Drive, Poway

Enter our garden and feel a mother's embrace. The gardens were a collaboration between the owners and Mrs. Elkus's mother, Betty, who helped design them to reflect the Mediterranean surroundings of Poway. The gardens meander as a series of outdoor rooms that beckon with their blend of fragrant plants, pottery, and garden statuary. The courtyard invites with lemon trees, bougainvillea, jasmine, lavender, and a bubbling fountain. Betty's house overlooks her rock garden and pool pavilion, planted with butterflies and birds in mind. The gardens attract local fauna, including the occasional bobcat.

Hours: 12 to 4 p.m.

From I-15, take Ted Williams exit and go east about 3 miles. Turn right at fourth traffic light onto Twin Peaks and follow about 2 miles. Turn left at fourth light onto Espola Road, proceed up hill, and turn left at Del Poniente. Take first left into Huntington Gate and onto Huntington Gate Drive. We are behind fourth set of gates on left. *Please park only on south side of Huntington Gate Drive and walk up drive to first house on left.*

Proceeds shared with San Diego Hospice

Casterline Garden
16291 Martincoit Road, Poway

Our long, steep driveway includes an island of boulders and interesting plant material. One side features a huge orange pincushion protea, a bush poppy, and naked coral tree. My husband, Paul, tends his roses at the top. Ahead is a rustic gate to the Santa Fe-style garden room. Formerly the garage, it has been pictured in national magazines. Flower beds inside the fence frame a pool with a vanishing edge facing a big view of nearby mountains. Continue on the wandering paths and you will pass by an incredible variety of trees and shrubs, eventually reaching a secluded garden on the other side of the house.

Hours: 10 a.m. to 4 p.m.

From I-15, take Rancho Bernardo Road exit and go east about 3 miles (name will change to Espola Road). Continue to Martincoit Road, where you must turn right. About .75 mile will bring you to #16291 on left. *Please park on right shoulder and walk up driveway. If driveway looks too strenuous, you may walk or drop off from next driveway up hill and enter through arch.*

Proceeds shared with the San Dieguito River Valley Land Conservancy

Cattolico Garden
15706 Boulder Mountain Road, Poway

Four years ago, our challenge was to fashion a garden that complemented steep slopes and narrow terrain. Hence, retaining walls, paths, arbors, and decks became the building blocks that gave birth to its unique character. A kaleidoscope of shrubs, vines, perennials, and annuals grows along meandering paths leading to a rock garden, a shady retreat, a cottage-style garden, roses, and a woodland area, which opens out to the native flora. Bird baths, whimsical ornaments, and a birdhouse collection add to the charm. The pathways culminate at our upper patio, which encompasses a bird's-eye view of the surrounding mountains.

Hours: 9 a.m. to 1 p.m.

Take I-15 to Rancho Bernardo Road exit and go east. Rancho Bernardo Road turns into Espola Road. Turn right at traffic light onto Martincoit Road (Stoneridge Country Club is on left and Prudential Realty on right). The preceding road is Valle Verde. Go 1 mile to top of hill. Turn right onto Orchard Gate. Turn left onto Lime Grove (preceding road is Ranch Hallow). Turn right onto Arroya Vista and left onto Boulder Mountain Road. Distance from I-15 to Boulder Mountain Road is 4 miles. House is third on right, white colonial style. *Please park on either side of street.*

Proceeds shared with the San Dieguito River Valley Land Conservancy

Les Belles Fleurs—Laurie Connable's Garden

13003 Avenida la Valencia, Poway

My home and garden occupy an acre of fertile soil adjacent to a creek and equestrian trail. The garden has attracted visitors from all over the world, many of whom comment on the profusion of color and the aura of peace that prevails. Emerald grass outlines perennials beds, three large rose beds, and a delightful lily pond with waterfall. Whimsical aspects include Ladybug Lane, the chicken condo, and a critter-proof organic potager. My garden has been featured in several publications, including *Better Homes & Gardens* and *Sunset* magazines.

Hours: 9 a.m. to 3 p.m.

From I-15 south, take Rancho Bernardo Road exit. Turn right onto Pomerado Road, then left onto Avenida La Valencia at second traffic light. After you pass stop sign, go to ninth house on right.

From I-15 north, take Bernardo Center Drive east. Turn right onto Bernardo Heights Parkway, then left onto Pomerado. Proceed as directed above.

Proceeds shared with the San Diego Horticultural Society

Wits End West

13639 Jackrabbit Road, Poway

Wits End West is a riparian, woodland garden that uses native and non-native trees, shrubs, and flowers to offer respite from the Southern California heat. The natural stone outcrops in the garden and its surroundings lend the area great charm and character. Ours is a woodland garden that relies on the varying natural vertical aspects of large native oaks and ornamental flowering trees and shrubs to provide four different canopy habitat levels as well as a series of smaller compartmentalized spaces that offer intimacy and privacy. A variety of plants from around the world has helped to create this woodland paradise, which is enjoyed by us and a large number of the local fauna.

Hours: 9 a.m. to 1 p.m.

From I-15, take Rancho Bernardo Road east for about 2 miles. (Just after crossing Pomerado Road, the name changes to Espola Road.) Turn right (south) onto Orchard Bend about .25 mile after Martincoit Road traffic light. Third street on right is Jackrabbit Road. Wits End West is at #13639, second house on left with red mailbox. *Please park on street, leaving driveways clear.*

Proceeds shared with the San Diego Horticultural Society

SAN MATEO COUNTY

ATHERTON
The Larry & Susy Calof Garden
126 Stockbridge Avenue, Atherton

In April, come walk under drifts of cherry, crab apple, dogwood, and wisteria blossoms; return in May for the scent of 150 lavishly underplanted roses. Designed by the owner, with particular attention to foliage color and texture, this garden is filled with unexpected nooks and the owners' collection of frog figures and fountains, a lovely pool, the raised orchard of dwarf fruit trees, a charming potting shed, brick patios, stands of beautiful old redwoods, a cat run for Bibbity, Bobbity, and Boo, as well as benches that invite you to stay awhile and enjoy the beauty of each season.

Hours: 10 a.m. to 4 p.m.

From Highway 101, take Woodside Road/Highway 84 west to El Camino Real. Take El Camino Real/Highway 82 south 1 mile to Stockbridge, just past traffic light at Fifth Avenue. Turn right onto Stockbridge and go .7 mile to #126 on right. *Please park along street.*

From I-280, take Woodside Road/Highway 84 east down to El Camino Real. Proceed as directed above.

Toni & Mike Heren
37 Deodora Drive, Atherton

When the current owners moved to the property in 1980, the back garden was ivy with a patch of lawn. A pool and brick patios were put in, as well as subsequent perennial borders, a woodland area, and a rose garden. The front garden was renovated in June 2001, eliminating a juniper hedge and horseshoe asphalt driveway, replacing them with a large formal rose garden with perennials, trees, and other woody plants.

Hours: 10 a.m. to 2 p.m.

From Highway 101, take Marsh Road/Atherton exit west. Travel west on Marsh Road until it ends at Middlefield Road. Turn left and continue for .2 mile to James Avenue (large double gates to Lindenwood). Continue for .8 mile and turn right onto Greenoaks Drive. First left (about .2 mile) is Deodora Drive. Number 37 is on left, first house on Deodora.

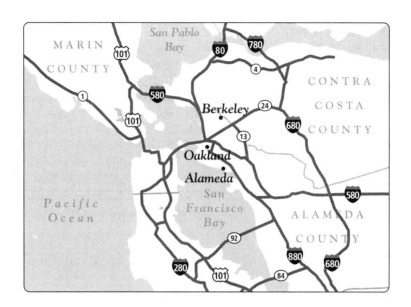

Sunday, May 18

ALAMEDA COUNTY

ALAMEDA
Watts/Coup Garden
1000 Park Street, Alameda

Ours is a small urban garden with a wisteria-covered pergola (circa 1911), magnolia, camellias, and roses. Planting beds have been enlarged to contain an unusual mix of antique and the avant-garde, hot plants and old standbys, where we enjoy pushing the limits of the expected, the intentional, and the happy accident. The garden serves as a playground for our design business and now contains two small water features, entomological silkscreens, an area of recycled glass mulch, and various lighting experiments, including Frankenstein lamps and Atomic Brocco lights.

Hours: 10 a.m. to 4 p.m.

From San Francisco and Berkeley, take I-880 south to 23rd Avenue exit in Oakland. Cross Park Street Bridge and proceed through 9 traffic lights; #1000 is on left.

From San Jose and south, take I-880 north to 29th Avenue exit in Oakland. Turn right onto Fruitvale and go under freeway. Cross Fruitvale Bridge and go straight on Tilden Way to Park Street. Turn left and go 6 blocks to Clinton Street. *Please park on street.*

Our Own Stuff Gallery Garden
3017 Wheeler Street, Berkeley

My small urban garden has, over the past twenty-four years, become mature—that is to say, way over my head, an oasis, and a world of its and our own. Unusual subtropical plants still intermingle with sculptures in steel, stone, and ceramic, which Mark Bulwinkle, Sara Floor, and I have made. I have added a "beach," a faux eroded landfill of pebbles and shard. The ex-driveway is now The Big Beauty Garden, where strong colors and bold foliage embrace a ten-foot-tall ceramic, beatific female figure. The national collection of Bambusa Ceramica continues to increase in size and varieties. The garden never holds still. We invite new and returning visitors every Sunday afternoon.

Hours: 10 a.m. to 4 p.m.

From I-80/I-580 by San Francisco Bay, take Ashby Avenue/Berkeley exit. After 1.5 miles, look for Shattuck Avenue. There are 2 gas stations at that intersection. Cross Shattuck and turn right onto Wheeler Street. Look for fourth house on left, #3017. *Please park on Wheeler or Emerson Street.*

Proceeds shared with Strybing Arboretum

Suzanne Porter's Garden
2810 Webster Street, Berkeley

The one constant element in my garden is its urban setting. The long, narrow lot with its southern orientation is host to unusual, sometimes rare plants that place an emphasis on foliage color and texture. Within the bounds of this setting I have created small areas for sitting; one of these has a column of water that flows down its edges, bringing the soothing sound of water. Focal points in the garden change from season to season, depending on the blooms of ornamental grasses and other perennials.

Hours: 10 a.m. to 4 p.m.

From I-80/I-580 by San Francisco Bay, take Ashby Avenue/Berkeley exit. Go about 2.5 miles to College Avenue. Cross College Avenue and turn right at second street onto Piedmont Avenue. Go 1 block to Webster Street and turn right. Garden is third house on right, #2810. *Please park on street.*

Ann Nichols' Garden
486 Boulevard Way, Oakland

This is a garden of many levels, each devised, with the help of landscape designer Bob Clark, as an outdoor room. Along the side, one meanders past gurgling water, which passes through salvage pipes, onto shells, and into three ponds connected by a mini-canal. Inside the gate is the "entry parlor" filled with foliage of black and silver. The walkway continues through the white garden into the mid-level lawn, bordered by beds of red and orange. Higher on the hill is the rose garden, defined by rows of weeping sequoia and underplanted in blue.

Hours: 10 a.m. to 4 p.m.

From I-580, take Grand Avenue exit. Continue .5 mile and turn right onto Boulevard Way. House is about 1.25 blocks on left. *Please park on street.*

Osmond Garden
5548 Lawton Avenue, Oakland

Mine is a small, shady garden located in the urban heart of Rockridge. It is intensively planted and intensely personal, serene, and private within the reaching walls of foliage that enclose it. For me, gardening here is a journey in search of memory. It is a slow discovery of what I've lost, a gradual remembrance of a buried past. My effort to discover what is hidden is serious and I have tried to mitigate the rigor of the effort with touches of whimsy throughout the garden. There are mannequins here and crocodiles, mirrors, and freestanding windows, pools and baths for birds, and the garden is (at least for me) a place of quiet beauty at all times of the year.

Hours: 10 a.m. to 4 p.m.

Located in Rockridge area of Oakland, just 2 blocks from Rockridge BART station, our house is at 5548 Lawton Avenue. Take College Avenue to Lawton Avenue, then turn east onto Lawton.

Proceeds shared with the Ruth Bancroft Garden

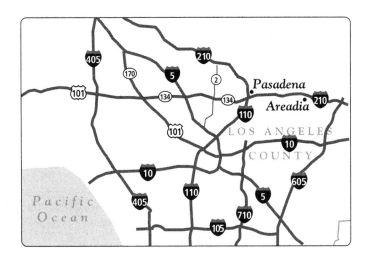

Maps, admission tickets, and Garden Conservancy information will be available at Sunset Magazine's Demonstration Garden at the LA County Botanic Garden from 9:30 a.m. to 3 p.m.

LOS ANGELES COUNTY

ARCADIA

Sunset Magazine's Demonstration Garden at the LA County Botanic Garden

301 North Baldwin Avenue, Arcadia

This one-and-one-half-acre space contains eight small gardens, each designed by a Southern California landscape architect or garden designer. The purpose of each garden is to inspire and educate home gardeners by presenting themes that translate into residential situations, such as: gardening under oak trees, outdoor entertaining areas, California native plant gardens, courtyard gardens, and water gardens. Along with a large variety of plant material, you will see the latest products for landscaping, including wooden decks, pavers, and wall treatments. The master plan and entry were designed by Laguna Beach landscape architect Ann Christoph.

Hours: 9:30 a.m. to 3:30 p.m.

From I-210, exit onto Baldwin Avenue. Continue south. Turn right into the arboretum. Entrance to Sunset Demonstration Garden is in middle of east-side parking area and will be open for Open Days Program on this day only.

Holley Frank's Garden
270 South Arroyo Boulevard, Pasadena

After four years of work renovating this garden, originally designed by Katherine Bashford, I am starting to see the light at the end of the tunnel. I had rounded concrete borders built to contain the large flower beds. Perched on the edge of the arroyo, this garden has an eclectic feel. Plantings of roses and fruit/citrus trees blend with dogwoods and hostas. A huge wisteria vine, planted when the house was completed in 1926, envelops both the front and the back of the house. The back garden is brighter and more private, with a greenhouse and vegetable beds hidden behind the garage.

Hours: 10 a.m. to 2 p.m.

From Highway 134, exit onto Orange Grove Boulevard. Turn south for .7 mile and turn right (west) onto California Boulevard. Follow to dead end at Arroyo Boulevard. Turn right (north) and go .4 mile to #270.

From Pasadena Freeway, exit onto Orange Grove Boulevard north. Go 1.2 miles to California Boulevard and proceed as directed above. *Please park on street.*

Goodan Garden
546 La Loma Road, Pasadena

This garden was designed in 1991 by Robert Cornell. Many of the plants have changed, but his hardscape provides a wonderful canvas to experiment with drought-tolerant plants. This garden is watered once a week, yet it looks as lush as traditional borders. Broken concrete paths thread through the beds surrounding an oval lawn. Plant profile, leaf color, and texture guide the plant choices. The front garden is deep and narrow, which makes scale a challenge. It has a Dr. Seuss theme, played out in the unusual shapes and colors of leaves and flowers. Old olive trees dominate the front lawn, which is filled with many types of sage and lavender, *Iris* 'Goodan's Peach', kangaroo paws, euphorbias, phormium, agapanthus, buddleias, *Melianthus major*, heuchera, Douglas iris, ribes, alstroemeria, blue oat grass, penstemon, westringia, daylilies, echium, and bird of paradise. Cobalt blue pots accent the entry. The back garden is shallow and narrow, terraced down the slope. Citrus trees and staghorn ferns stand out, as do the variegated hydrangeas and hellebores. More lavender, rosemary, and sage grow next to the rose bed. A narrow black lap pool lies on the eastern edge at the top of the slope. Two white Lady Banks' roses grow on the trellis over the patio, giving full shade coverage. A path along the eastern side of the house leads to a small shaded succulent garden with some unusual specimens.

Hours: 10 a.m. to 4 p.m.

From Highway-134, get on Orange Grove Boulevard south; from I-110, get on Orange Grove north. Go 1 mile to California Boulevard and turn west. La Loma Road comes off California just west of intersection with Orange Grove, about 1 short block to south side. Turn left onto La Loma. It curves to become parallel with California. Garden has an orange pilaster next to driveway on south side of street with old olives lining driveway. *Please park on street.*

Martin-Watterson
808 South San Rafael Avenue, Pasadena

Sited on one and one-third acres, the house is one of five Montecito architect George Washington Smith designed in greater Los Angeles in the Andalusian style. The garden, originally designed in 1927 by A.E. Hanson, was restored by the present owners. It features a rose garden with more than 250 roses; a wisteria pergola; cactus/aloe garden; Mediterranean drought-tolerant garden; a hillside of shaped shrubs; a grass garden; and a tented pool pavilion with original tile benches. The garden has been photographed and featured in *Los Angeles Times Magazine*, *House & Garden*, *Martha Stewart Living*, and *Sunset*.

Hours: 10 a.m. to 2 p.m.

From Highway 134/I-210, take San Rafael Avenue exit. From I-110, take Orange Grove Boulevard exit, go north to California, and turn left onto Arroyo Boulevard. Turn left onto La Loma, then right onto La Loma across bridge, uphill to San Rafael, and veer left twice to #808. *Please park on street.*

Proceeds shared with LA County Botanic Garden and the California Arboretum Foundation

Mead Garden
945 Ellington Lane, Pasadena

The Mead Garden provides a park-like surround for a 1920s Palladian structure originally designed as an entertainment pavilion. The three-quarter acre garden features diverse formal elements within a setting of California live oaks. One of these shades the patio area, in combination with an Eastern red oak and a Chinese fringe tree. Nearby, a stand of timber bamboo provides an interesting counterpoint. There is also a pool area and a small garden featuring drought-tolerant plants.

Hours: 10 a.m. to 2 p.m.

From I-210, exit at San Rafael; from Colorado, which parallels freeway to south, turn left onto San Rafael. Follow to intersection with La Loma, then turn right and go 2 blocks to Laguna Road. Turn left; Ellington Lane is 2nd street on right.

From I-110 Pasadena Freeway, exit at Avenue 64. Follow into Pasadena and just past Church of the Angels bear right onto Burleigh Drive. At stop sign, turn right onto Laguna Road and proceed 1 block to Ellington on right. *Please park on street.*

Garden of Arnold & Gretl Mulder
1150 Laurel Street, Pasadena

This is a sixty-plus-year-old California garden on the site of an old olive garden. It overlooks the arroyo seco and San Gabriel mountains. The planting is primarily in the Mediterranean style. It is made of several separate open "rooms" and the interior of the house opens to these areas.

Hours: 10 a.m. to 4 p.m.

Located off Linda Vista Avenue in West Pasadena 1.6 miles north of the Holly Street and Linda Vista traffic light. Follow signs "To Rose Bowl" to corner. Laurel Street is east of Linda Vista Avenue. *Please park on street.*

The White Garden

630 Prospect Boulevard, Pasadena

This garden is located in the historical district of Prospect Park, well known for its camphor-tree-lined streets. The landscaping is new, as the house and garden were in desperate need of attention. We created an overall theme of strong formal hedging and 'Iceberg' roses as an anchor. We added to this many English roses and informal plantings such as delphinium, clematis, foxglove, verbascum, and lavender. The landscaping provides textures, colors, and a place for friends and family to gather in an outdoor kitchen, where we enjoy vegetables grown in our own ever-changing vegetable garden. Additional features include various arbors wrapped in roses, a koi pond, obelisks, shaped topiaries, wisteria, a hillside knot garden, and outdoor fireplace.

Hours: 10 a.m. to 2 p.m.

From Highway 134, take Orange Grove Boulevard exit. Go north to Prospect Boulevard on left and continue to #630.

From I-110/Pasadena Freeway, take Orange Grove Boulevard. Go north to Prospect Boulevard and continue to #630. *Please park on street.*

Yariv Residence

1000 South San Rafael Avenue, Pasadena

Creating a garden for her parents' Spanish Colonial Revival-style home was a once-in-a-lifetime opportunity for garden designer Gabriela Yariv. The exterior architectural bones of this garden are classical Italian and simply breathtaking. The garden's three levels are connected by an existing elaborate system of balustraded walls and terraces, dotted with numerous fountains. While the estate captured the Mediterranean spirit, the gardens evoked no special sense of place. Yariv's goal was to create a horticulturally diverse garden featuring iconic Mediterranean plants. For inspiration, she looked to the villas of Tuscany and the wonderful Montecito gardens created in the early part of the twentieth century. Mature cypresses and melaleucas were brought in to give instant structure to the garden, while mature olive trees were craned in to replace carotwood trees by the pool. The garden features a large formal lawn surrounded by clipped boxwood hedges and blooming white 'Iceberg' roses, a circular orangerie, rose garden, contemporary cactus/succulent garden, and a pool garden planted with olives and numerous other drought-tolerant perennials such as pampas grass, Jerusalem sage, lavenders, succulents, rosemary, and verbenas. The garden was featured in the *Los Angeles Times Magazine* 2002 annual garden issue.

Hours: 10 a.m. to 4 p.m.

From the valley, take Highway 101 east to Highway 134 east. Exit at San Rafael and turn right off exit ramp. Turn right onto Colorado. Make first left onto South San Rafael to #1000.

From West Los Angeles, take I-10 to I-110 north/Pasadena Freeway to end. Continue straight onto Arroyo Parkway. Turn left onto California Boulevard to end. Turn left onto Arroyo Avenue and right onto La Loma (across from bridge). Make first left onto Hillside. Turn left onto San Rafael and continue to #1000 on left.

From the east, take I-210 west, which becomes Highway 134 west. Take first exit for San Rafael and turn left off exit ramp. Turn right onto Colorado. Make immediate left onto South San Rafael. Go 1 mile to #1000 on left. *Please park on street.*

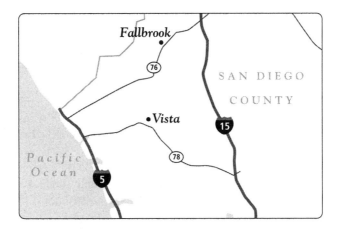

Saturday, May 31

SAN DIEGO COUNTY

FALLBROOK

The Anderson/Olson Garden

805 Tumbleweed Lane, Fallbrook

Southern California's unique Mediterranean climate inspired us to create a garden that, for the most part, gets by on very little supplemental water. The most notable feature of the property is the half-acre hillside in front of the house, where we have created a "desert garden" to showcase my collection of succulents and other arid-climate plants. Meandering paths lead through an otherworldly landscape of aloes, cacti, and euphorbias of every imaginable size and form, accented with unique artworks. At the top of the hill is a grand tile-roofed pavilion, from which you can enjoy a stunning view of the garden and the distant mountains. Other features include the tile-paved entry courtyard with a huge vine-draped pergola and the gracious rear terrace with its more tropical poolside plantings.

Hours: 10 a.m. to 2 p.m.

From Highway 76, take Olive Hill Road (at Arco gas station) 2.7 miles to Del Valle and turn left. From Mission Road in Fallbrook, take Olive Hill Road (at high school) about 3 miles to Del Valle and turn right. Once on Del Valle, go .5 mile to fork. Take right fork onto Tumbleweed Lane. Go through stop sign at Sleeping Indian Road and #805 will be next house on right, at wrought-iron gates. *Please park on left side of street only and walk in.*

Proceeds shared with the Fraternity House, Inc.

Herlihy Farms

4417 Brodea Lane, Fallbrook

Herlihy Farms is a commercial flower farm specializing in "filler" flowers for the wholesale flower trade. We are located in the lovely rolling hills of Fallbrook in northern San Diego County. This beautiful setting, which many have likened to Tuscany, is the backdrop for private gardens arranged around the house. There is an intimate secret garden of roses and perennials, a flagstone raised-bed vegetable garden, a formal rose garden with box hedges and gravel paths, an herb garden filled with iris, roses, fruit trees, and herbs, and a charming citrus garden with a fountain, dwarf citrus, and a rustic pergola.

Hours: 9 a.m. to 1 p.m.

Take Highway 76 to Sage Road and turn north. Go .5 mile and look for a white rail fence. Turn right onto Brodea Lane immediately after passing fence. We are located at #4417. *Please park on street; do not block driveway.*

Carol Popet & Mark Benussi

220 Rancho Camino, Fallbrook

We made our downward sloping one-acre wild garden look much larger than it really is by the clever planting of more than 200 trees and bamboos beneath which a huge variety of shrubs, vines, and ground covers grows. We enjoy walking along nearly 1,000 feet of meandering paths, which are dotted with eye-catching metal animal sculptures and blooming perennials year round. Along the way we have added garden structures, dry creeks, wine bottle walkways, a redwood-and-glass greenhouse, and a rustic waterlily pond with a waterfall, together with many scattered seating areas where we relax in a secluded and serene setting and watch our three Airedale terriers play.

Hours: 9 a.m. to 4 p.m.

From I-15, take Highway 76/Pala Road west to Bonsall. Turn right at traffic light onto Olive Hill Road, which follows light at Mission Road/S13. Go 2.5 miles to Rancho Camino, which follows Saddle Creek Road on right. Turn right and continue to #220, which is on right just beyond Via Aquaviva.

From I-5, take Highway 76/Mission Road east to Bonsall. Turn left at light onto Olive Hill Road, which follows light at North River Road. Proceed as directed above. *Please park on street.*

Proceeds shared with the Art & Cultural Center at Fallbrook

Scott & Susan Spencer's Garden
2778 Los Alisos Lane North, Fallbrook

Our garden sits on a frost-free hilltop and features a large collection of temperate, tropical, and subtropical plants from all over the world. Created as a showroom for Scott's garden design business, it is an eclectic mix of formal structure and naturalistic plant groupings art-fully assembled to demonstrate the wide range of garden styles possible in a Zone 9-10 climate. Beautiful dry-stone walls and paths form a strong geometry of interlocking circles to contrast with the lavish abundance of perennials, grasses, and shrub roses spilling out of the raised beds. Bark-lined paths invite you to wander through naturalistic beds of woodland plants under redwood and cypress trees. This is a young garden but with both a mature feel and sense of style.

Hours: 10 a.m. to 4 p.m.

From I-15, take Highway 76. Travel west about 2 miles to Gird Road. Turn right and continue to "T" intersection at Reche Road, about 3 miles. Turn left and proceed about .25 mile to Live Oak Park Road. Turn right and go 200 yards to Los Alisos Lane. Turn right and proceed 100 yards to Los Alisos North. Turn left and proceed about .25 mile to street sign post "Los Alisos North, 2700 Block." Turn right and proceed to top of hill to last driveway on left, #2778. *Please park on street.*

From I-5, take Highway 76 east to Gird Road. Turn left and proceed as directed above.

Proceeds shared with the Nature Conservancy

VISTA

Barbara's Garden
1905 Warmlands Avenue, Vista

This twenty-year-old garden was started on a little more than half an acre of poor soil formerly used as a motorcycle track. It has evolved over the years into a tranquil refuge described by some as a contemplative place. Perennials and annuals surround a sunken garden, pond, wa-terfall, garden sculpture, fountain, herb garden, fruit trees, and a children's vegetable garden. It has been designated as a National Backyard Wildlife Habitat Program and has been fea-tured in three gardening magazines and on HGTV.

Hours: 12 to 4 p.m.

From I-5, go east on Highway 76 for 9.7 miles to Vista/Bonsall exit. Go right 1.8 miles to Warmlands Avenue. Turn left and go .4 mile to fork in road. Bear right and go .6 mile to #1905. Look for a two-story home with slanted wooden siding on left.

From I-15, take Gopher Canyon exit west. Go through canyon (about 15 minutes, no stops) to traffic light at East Vista Way. Turn left and go 2 lights to Warmlands Avenue. Proceed as directed above. *Please park on upper driveway, or side of road.*

Felter Jungle Garden
920 Quails Trail, Vista

I invite you to tour my one-acre rain forest, started in 1976 and located on a hill with many trails meandering through the jungle. Three wooden bridges with bamboo railings connect the trails as they cross a lush tropical canyon. There are seating areas of rock and wooden benches and two different picnic areas. You will see fourteen varieties of fig trees, including a huge banyon tree and the very rare *Ficus dammarapsis kingiana* with leaves up to two feet long. The jungle has a wide assortment of flowering tropical trees, plus many varieties of palm trees, bananas, heliconias, cannas, and gingers. Of special interest to me are aroids, including climbing philodendrons, monsteras, the big-leaf syngonium, alocasias, colocasias, and xanthosoma. I hope you will enjoy my recreation of a natural jungle.

Hours: 12 to 4 p.m.

From I-5, take Highway 78 east 7.46 miles to Mar Vista Drive exit and turn right. Make an immediate left onto Thibodo Road. Turn right at "Quail Ranch" gate. Call from gate, "Felter" residence. Follow Rolling Hills to Quails Trail and turn right. We are second house on left. *Please park along street.*

Proceeds shared with the San Diego Horticultural Society

Don Walker's Garden
1781 Sunrise Drive, Vista

Around the perimeter of my triangular-shaped half-acre garden, I'm growing drought-tolerant California natives and Proteaceae material in well-draining decomposed granite soil. The garden is on a steep slope and by using mortared broken concrete retaining walls, I have created some usable bricked flat spaces for leisure enjoyment. In each of these flat areas are goldfish ponds, which I share with the marauding raccoons. The interior of the garden receives the necessary water to maintain nineteen genera of palms, seven genera of cycads, and many hybrid plumerias. The understory plantings are mostly bromeliads, ferns, geraniums, and assorted plants of many genera growing next to meandering brick paths. Placed in the trees are orchids, bromeliads, and staghorn ferns. Spanish moss is growing on everything above eye level.

Hours: 12 to 4 p.m.

From Highway 78, take Mar Vista exit and go north. Turn left at traffic light onto Santa Fe. At first traffic light, turn right onto Monte Vista, follow to second stop sign, and turn left onto Valley. Valley dead ends at Sunrise Drive. Turn right and make another right into my driveway. My house is on corner.

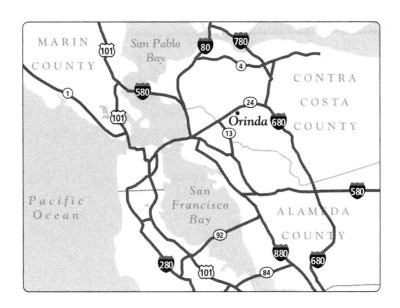

Sunday, June 1

Note: The Ruth Bancroft Garden in Walnut Creek will also be open on this date.
Please consult their listing in the Public Garden section at the end of
this chapter for directions and hours.

CONTRA COSTA COUNTY

ORINDA

Cummings Garden

513 Miner Road, Orinda

This forty-year-old garden is also an amateur rhododendron hybridizer's nursery. Most rhododendrons will be through blooming by June, but the new foliage on them and on the Japanese maples is elegant and, on some, extraordinarily beautiful and arguably more suited to the Japanese-style architecture of the house than the gaudy blooms. The garden has a large collection of "big-leaf" (*falconeri* and *grande*) species and hybrid rhododendrons. Some Japanese iris (*kaempferi*) may be in bloom and there will surely be clematis, roses, and fuchsias. In the center of the garden is a pair of naturalistic pools connected by a small stream, with goldfish and koi.

Hours: 10 a.m. to 4 p.m.

Follow Camino Pablo (Orinda exit) northwest 1 mile from Highway 24. Turn right onto Miner Road and follow about 1.5 miles to Valley View Road on right. *This cul-de-sac has ample parking and is within walking distance of two gardens on Valley View Lane, three gardens on Miner Road, and one on Brookbank Road.*

The Garden at 518 Miner Road
518 Miner Road, Orinda

The stone columns and rolling gate along the road are the first indication of the creative, colorful garden within. Garden designer Suzanne Porter reoriented the landscape by taking out a huge lawn and circular drive to create a perennial border anchored with Japanese maples. A gentle slope dotted with oaks is the setting for the back garden. Here Porter introduced perennials, which thread through the woods and cascade over a rocky outcropping at the edge of a swimming pool for a tranquil, natural setting.

Hours: 10 a.m. to 4 p.m.

Follow Camino Pablo (Orinda exit) west 1 mile from Highway 24. Turn right onto Miner Road and follow about 1.5 miles to Valley View Road on right. *This cul-de-sac has ample parking and is within walking distance of two gardens on Valley View Lane, three gardens on Miner Road, and one on Brookbank.*

The Garden at 520 Miner Road
520 Miner Road, Orinda

This hillside garden has two moods. The lower, more formal garden, with its boxwood spheres and gently arching pergola, was originally laid out by Ron Lutsko to showcase the owner's sculpture collection. Each of these rooms has its own mood and flower color. Garden designer Suzanne Porter has updated the plantings throughout and created a continuous garden up to and beyond the house. Shade-loving perennials hug the path toward the private terrace near the kitchen. From this point the upper garden, bedecked with ornamental grasses, many perennials, and fruit trees, reveals its wild beauty.

Hours: 10 a.m. to 4 p.m.

Follow Camino Pablo (Orinda exit) west 1 mile from Highway 24. Turn right onto Miner Road and follow about 1.5 miles to Valley View Road on right. *This cul-de-sac has ample parking and is within walking distance of two gardens on Valley View Lane, three gardens on Miner Road, and one on Brookbank.*

Giardino de Ruscelletto
16 Brookbank Road, Orinda

Giardino de Ruscelletto or "Garden of the Little Brook" is a formal garden sculpted from an unimproved area on both sides of a small stream bed. Granite-lined paths lead the visitor throughout the garden accented with well over 100 species of plants and abundant groupings of roses, azaleas, camellias, hydrangeas, dahlias, rhododendrons, as well as many beds of smaller plants. Large architectural lattice panels provide additional structure to the garden's design. Not to be missed is a less formal garden in the rear of the house which covers a large hillside area with more paths and a major display of flowering plants and shrubs. The front garden was designed by Magic Gardens; rear garden by Bob Clark.

Hours: 10 a.m. to 4 p.m.

Follow Camino Pablo (Orinda exit) west 1 mile from Highway 24. Turn right onto Miner Road and follow about 1.5 miles to Valley View Road on right. *This cul-de-sac has ample parking and is within walking distance of the garden, as well as two gardens on Valley View Lane and three gardens on Miner Road.*

Rosemary Merlo's Garden
17 Valley View Lane, Orinda

Large boulders, seemingly placed by a giant in irregular clumps, act as a natural retaining wall for the driveway of this hillside garden. Serenity was the top request of this garden owner when she worked with the designer, Suzanne Porter. Taupe-colored stucco walls create a secluded area near the house, carving out the garden, which sits in a natural oak woodland. Mahonias, loropetalum, Western sword fern, and rubus are repeated throughout the garden and wind through the oaks to the adjoining area where a terrace extends the house to the views of the hills beyond.

Hours: 10 a.m. to 4 p.m.

Follow Camino Pablo (Orinda exit) west 1 mile from Highway 24. Turn right onto Miner Road and follow about 1.5 miles to Valley View Road on right. *This cul-de-sac has ample parking and is within walking distance of two gardens on Valley View Lane, three gardens on Miner Road, and one on Brookbank.*

Dr. & Mrs. Robert N. Nelson
112 Camino Sobrante, Orinda

From the street, our garden is entered through carved wooden gates. The original garden was put in by Aerin Moore of Magic Gardens, but we have changed and added our plant material, which we have collected over the years. The site is rather hilly, with a lot of different levels and several patios that connect via stone walkways. The flower beds are a series of rock gardens filled with annuals, perennials, roses, hydrangeas, azaleas, rhododendrons, dogwoods, bulbs, and ferns. Garden art by Mark Bullwinkle and Keeyla Meadows is right at home in this setting and complemented by many containers filled with flowers. Over much of the garden mature oak trees provide a leafy canopy.

Hours: 10 a.m. to 2 p.m.

Follow Camino Pablo (Orinda exit) west from Highway 24 to second traffic light. Turn right at Camino Sobrante (Safeway market on corner) and follow up hill. Garden is less than 1 mile from village.

Swanson/Thomas Garden
16 Valley View Lane, Orinda

Repeating the theme of the boulder retaining walls on the drive to the Merlo garden, designer Suzanne Porter uses a similar approach to the hillside here. The curved retaining wall embraces the hill in a combination of smooth, dry-stacked surfaces periodically broken by boulders in more random arrangements, which creates a sculptural tension and the backbone to the garden below. The owners requested a spot for their hammock and a koi pond; Porter has included these elements while creating an understory near the house that includes dogwoods, ferns, hellebores, and spring-flowering shrubs, enhancing the oak woodland.

Hours: 10 a.m. to 4 p.m.

Follow Camino Pablo (Orinda exit) west 1 mile from Highway 24. Turn right onto Miner Road and follow about 1.5 miles to Valley View Road on right. *This cul-de-sac has ample parking and is within walking distance of two gardens on Valley View Lane, three gardens on Miner Road, and one on Brookbank.*

Sunday, June 8

SAN FRANCISCO COUNTY

SAN FRANCISCO

104 Wonderful Laidley

104 Laidley Street, San Francisco

We were honored to be featured in Page Dickey's book *Inside Out: Relating Garden to House.* Our garden was terraced by the original owner/builder using local red rock circa 1910. The current "design" is to have the longest possible amble to reach the best view (and hot tub). Plants are a mixed collection of what we like and what does well on our hill. A silver tree, king protea, and pincushions from South Africa are doing very well. Our pond is now four feet deep, finally solving the "raccoon eat koi" problem. Come enjoy!

Hours: 10 a.m. to 4 p.m.

From Highway 101, take Army/Cesar Chavez exit and go west to Noe Street, traveling about 10 blocks. Turn left; street dead ends on Laidley. We are 3 houses to left of intersection of Laidley and Noe. House is dark green.

From I-280 north, follow signs to Bay Bridge but exit at San Jose Avenue. After first traffic light on San Jose, turn left onto Dolores and immediately left onto 30th Street. Turn left onto Noe Street and proceed as directed above. We are #104. *Please park along street.*

Proceeds shared with the Friends of the Urban Forest

The Garden at 537 Chenery Street

537 Chenery Street, San Francisco

The garden has been created to take advantage of its inherent strengths—excellent soil, sunny position, gentle slope, and mild climate. Our love of English gardens is reflected in the design and choice of plants. A central flagstone path is flanked by broad borders of new and old roses, flowering shrubs, and as many different and unusual perennials as we could pack in. The color and fragrance in June are overwhelming. The path terminates onto a broad patio with a small pond on one side stocked with water plants and fish. We've also integrated a kitchen garden into the design and have tried to combine foliage and flower colors uniquely while creating a harmonious overall effect.

Hours: 10 a.m. to 4 p.m.

From San Francisco, take Dolores Street south to 30th Street. Turn right, then immediately turn left onto Chenery Street. Go 5 blocks to #537.

From Marin or East Bay, take I-280 towards Daly City. Exit at Monterey Boulevard. Turn right at end of exit ramp, then take first left at traffic light onto Diamond Street. Pass BART station on right, go through light, and turn right at first stop sign onto Chenery Street. Go 2 blocks to #537.

From I-280 north, take San Jose Avenue exit. Turn left onto Dolores Street. Turn left again onto 30th Street and left once more onto Chenery Street. Go 5 blocks to #537. *Please park on street.*

Proceeds shared with the Glen Park Garden Club

Garden of Torre San Gimignano

140 Laidley Street, San Francisco

The Torre, designed by architects Jeremy Kotas, Skip Shaffer, and Christina Francavillese, was built in 1990 to be an integral part of its terraced garden. It is located on the primary street of the historic Fairmount Tract, laid out in 1864 to be the city's first suburb for country homes. Situated on the north-facing slope of Miguel Hill, the site provides a panoramic view of the skyline of downtown San Francisco. As the Torre is on the sheltered side of the city's hilly spine, the setting provides a haven for subtropical plants. After entering the portal from Laidley Street, one mounts three flights of stairs through a rock garden to enter the foyer. One continues up a helical stairway, through the atrium with a side garden, to the living room and dining room, to the back garden with a serpentine stairway leading to the top patio terrace with its unobstructed view of downtown. The garden's informal layout is based on a design created by Roger Scharmer but modified and executed by the owners of the Torre, William Gregory and Richard L. Ingraham.

Hours: 10 a.m. to 4 p.m.

From Market Street, travel south to Noe Street, turn left, then left again onto Laidley Street.

From I-280, proceed into city, exiting onto San Jose. Proceed to 30th Street, turn left, and proceed to Noe Street. Turn left and left again onto Laidley Street. *Please park on street.*

Proceeds shared with Strybing Arboretum

Miland-Sonenberg Garden
117 Fair Oaks Street, San Francisco

In what was a solid concrete patio, nearly surrounded by three-story residential buildings, this thirty-by-thirty foot garden is an oasis of dense, highly diverse foliage and flowering plants. Once the original concrete was removed, the owners put back irregularly shaped pieces in a circle within the rectangle of the garden's perimeter, thus creating a mandala form. Full of art, real and kitsch, the garden is centered on a sculptural fountain adorned with skull-shaped rocks. The garden's verticality is emphasized by dozens of flowering vines that climb the neighboring walls, as well as a tree house-like porch worked into the vine-covered stairwell. Cantilevered out from the porch floor is a massive bronze hand of Buddha.

Hours: 10 a.m. to 2 p.m.

Located in San Francisco's sunny Mission District, the garden is at the eastern edge of the Noe Valley neighborhood. Fair Oaks is a small street running parallel to and between Dolores and Guererro, two north-south arterials. Number 117 is just off intersection of 22nd Street and Fair Oaks.

From Bay Bridge or Highway 101, take Duboce Street off-ramp to Guererro. Turn left and go south to 22nd Street. Turn right and look for parking.

Proceeds shared with Strybing Arboretum

Muther/Aftergut Garden
153 Upper Terrace, San Francisco

This august Edwardian Italianate house formerly belonged to a mayor of San Francisco. Built on a woody knoll above the city, the original garden was large and sunny, but windy and poorly connected to the house. Stephen Suzman extended the entry porch over a new loggia built around the southwest side of the house to a terrace off the dining room. Limestone balustrades, keystones, molding, and coping were added to echo similar elements on the side of the house. Large ceramic urns were placed on the balustrade and filled with *Trachycarpus fortunei* palms, white iberis, and burgundy trailing pelargoniums. The main garden is divided into two levels by retaining walls. The upper level consists of an oval lawn surrounded by a mixed perennial shrub border. Semi-pleached purple-leaf plums screen the neighboring houses. 'Niobe' clematis enlivens the trees after the plum blossoms have faded. Purple smokebush echoes the color for the plums. On the lower level is a terrace of pink Chinese sandstone terminated by an arbor. The old concrete walkway along the east side of the garden was transformed into a fruit tunnel of espaliered apples, pears, Asian pears, crab apples, and figs trained onto an elegant metal pergola. The client and designer selected a rich and subtle palette of pink, rose, maroon, burgundy, deep purple, and campanula blues, which plays off the pink sandstone paving. Perennials and bulbs are varied to provide color throughout the year.

Hours: 10 a.m. to 4 p.m.

From Golden Gate Bridge, take Route 1 to Park Presidio, go left onto Fulton (to turn left onto Fulton, turn right onto Cabrillo, left on 14th Street, and left onto Fulton. Turn right onto Stanyon, left onto Frederick, turn right onto Masonic, then right onto Upper Terrace to #153. *Please park on street.*

From Highway 101 south, take Fell Street exit. Turn left onto Masonic. Proceed up past crest of hill and turn right onto Upper Terrace to #153.

Stephen Suzman Garden
233 Douglass Street, San Francisco

The garden behind my Victorian cottage isn't large, but it can be a magical place, with its dense foliage and multiple layers of flowers, shrubs, vines, and trees. It is divided into garden rooms, with rhododendrons, azaleas, and ferns lining the path to the lawn, which leads to an octagonal gazebo displaying climbing roses, clematis, and honeysuckle. Some plants recall my childhood in South Africa, others I discovered at Oxford in England. In the midst of a city neighborhood, it offers gratification for all the senses, with something blooming fragrantly year round.

Hours: 10 a.m. to 4 p.m.

Located between 18th and 19th Streets, drive west on Market Street past Castro Street. Turn left onto Douglass Street and drive 2 blocks. *Best parking is found on streets west of house.*

Pat Wipf's Garden
3500 21st Street, San Francisco

A very large Siberian elm influences my south-facing garden. It is a romantic, lush, scent-filled place with three water features and a small patio. I am an artist (pastels) and my interest in texture and color is apparent with my plant choices. I have tried to create vistas within the garden as well as from inside the house. There is a small lawn, which provides a visual rest from the borders and space for entertaining (including my daughter's wedding last year). There are many vines on trellises and fences that help to enclose the space and create a sanctuary. Also, please note I volunteer at Strybing Arboretum's nursery and have become a plantaholic.

Hours: 10 a.m. to 4 p.m.

House and garden are located on corner of Dolores and 21st Street. Nearest BART is at 24th Street. "J" streetcar stops at 21st Street, which is 1 block away.

Proceeds shared with Strybing Arboretum Society

Public Gardens

ALAMEDA COUNTY

BERKELEY

University of California Botanical Garden

200 Centennial Drive, Berkeley (510) 642-0849 www.mip.berkeley.edu/garden

This is one of the world's richest collections of living plants, with more than 13,000 plant species from five continents, arranged geographically, as well as the Chinese Medicinal Herb Garden, Redwood Grove, and a tropical rain forest exhibit.

Hours: Labor Day through Memorial Day, daily, 9 a.m. to 4:45 p.m.; Memorial Day through Labor Day, daily, 9 a.m. to 7 p.m.; closed Christmas Day

Admission: $3 adults, $2 senior citizens, $1 children 3 to 18, children under 3 free

From San Jose, San Francisco, or Sacramento, take I-80 to Berkeley. Exit at University Avenue, follow east, and turn left onto Oxford Street. Turn right onto Hearst. Turn right onto Gayley Road (second traffic light). At first stop sign, turn left onto Stadium Rim Way. At first stop sign, turn left onto Centennial Drive. Garden is .75 mile up hill on right.

OAKLAND

Dunsmuir Historic Estate

2960 Peralta Oaks Court, Oakland (510) 615-5555 www.dunsmuir.org

John McLaren, designer of Golden Gate Park in San Francisco, is said to have assisted in designing the gardens at the Dunsmuir Estate for the Hellman family, who owned it from 1906 until the late 1950s. Today, its fifty acres are still graced with a wide variety of trees that surround the turn-of-the-century Neoclassical Revival-style mansion.

Hours: February through October, Tuesday through Friday, 10 a.m. to 4 p.m., also open the first Sunday of each month, May through September, 10 a.m. to 3 p.m.

Admission: grounds are free

From I-580 east, take 106th Avenue exit. Make 3 quick left turns to cross freeway, then turn right onto Peralta Oaks Drive. Follow signs to Dunsmuir.

From I-580 west, exit at Foothill/MacArthur Boulevard and veer to right onto Foothill Boulevard. Turn right onto 106th Avenue and turn right again onto Peralta Oaks Drive. Follow signs to Dunsmuir.

Kaiser Center Roof Garden
300 Lakeside Drive, Oakland

Kaiser Center Roof Garden is a three-and-one-half-acre park located four floors above street level on top of the Kaiser Center garage. Despite its urban setting, boundary hedges, winding paths, bermed plantings, and a reflecting pond give the garden a quiet, oasis-like quality. Specimen trees, shrubs, perennials, and annuals provide year-round horticultural interest.

Hours: year round, weekdays, 7 a.m. to 7 p.m.

From San Francisco, take Bay Bridge to I-580 south (towards Hayward). One mile past bridge, take Harrison Street exit and turn right onto Harrison. Go through 3 traffic lights. Lake Merritt is on left and Kaiser Building is ahead on right. Continue straight on Harrison and get into right lane. Turn right onto 20th Street and make immediate right into parking garage. There is also street parking. Take garage elevator to Roof Garden level.

CONTRA COSTA COUNTY

KENSINGTON

The Blake Garden of the University of California
2 Norwood Place, Kensington (510) 524-2449

This 10.5-acre garden was given to the university in the early 1960s by the Blake family. The garden was established when the house was designed and built in the 1920s. It has a large display of plants ranging from drought-tolerant to more moisture-loving plants from places such as Asia.

Hours: year round, weekdays, 8 a.m. to 4:30 p.m.; closed on university holidays

Admission: free

From I-80, take Buchanan Street off-ramp east. Follow Buchanan, which turns into Marin Avenue, to a traffic circle with a fountain. Take fourth exit off circle onto Arlington Avenue. Travel 1.8 miles to Rincon Road on left. Blake Garden is #70.

WALNUT CREEK

The Ruth Bancroft Garden
1500 Bancroft Road, Walnut Creek (925) 210-9663
www.ruthbancroftgarden.org

A PROJECT OF
THE GARDEN
CONSERVANCY

The Ruth Bancroft Garden rises above the status of a collection to an exceptional demonstration of the art of garden design. Working primarily with the dramatic forms of her beloved succulents, Mrs. Bancroft has created bold and varied compositions in which the colors, textures, and patterns of foliage provide a setting for the sparkle of floral color.

Hours: Open Day event June 1, 1 to 5 p.m.; otherwise, open by appointment only

Admission: $5

Located just north of Highway 24, exit I-680 onto Ygnacio Valley Road. Turn right and follow approximately 3 miles to Bancroft Road. Turn left and pass Stratton. At end of wooden fence, turn right into #1500 Bancroft Road.

ARCADIA
The LA County Botanic Garden
301 North Baldwin Avenue, Arcadia (626) 821-3222 www.arboretum.org

The arboretum is a 127-acre horticultural and botanical museum with plants from around the world blooming in every season. The arboretum staff has introduced more than 100 flowering plants to the California landscape and boasts tree collections from many countries.

Hours: year round, daily, 9 a.m. to 4:30 p.m.

Admission: $5 adults, $3 students/senior citizens, $1 children 5 to 12, children under 5 free

Off I-210 exit on Baldwin Avenue. Arboretum is in San Gabriel Valley, freeway close to downtown Los Angeles, and next to Pasadena.

BEVERLY HILLS
Virginia Robinson Garden
Elden Way North, Beverly Hills (310) 276-5367

You will find more than six acres of display gardens, including a terrace rose garden, Italian terrace garden, the formal mall, and an extensive palm garden.

Hours: Tours by appointment only, Tuesday through Friday. Docent-led tours by reservation only.

Admission: $10 adults, $5 students/senior citizens

Take Sunset Boulevard to Crescent Drive North to Elden Way North. Parking available on property; no street parking available.

LA CANADA FLINTRIDGE
Descanso Gardens
1418 Descanso Drive, La Canada Flintridge (818) 949-4200 www.DescansoGardens.org

Descanso Gardens are a rare find—a woodland garden in the midst of California chaparral and Los Angeles urban sprawl, including a twenty-acre California live oak forest containing 39,000 camellia plants, the five-acre International Rosarium with more than 3,100 antique and modern roses, North America's largest clematis collection, and a one-acre lilac grove where lilacs for warm-winter climates originated.

Hours: year round, daily, 9 a.m. to 5 p.m.; ticket sales end at 4:30. Closed Christmas Day

Admission: $5 adults, $3 senior citizens/students, $1 children 5 to 10, children under 5 free

From I-210, exit onto Angeles Crest Highway. Turn south. Turn right onto Foothill Boulevard, left onto Verdugo Boulevard, and left onto Descanso Drive.

Los Angeles
Exposition Park Rose Garden
Exposition Boulevard & Fugueroga Street, Los Angeles (213) 763-3115 www.laparks.org/exporosegarden/rosegarden.html

This is a beautiful place to experience nature and a respite from urban activities which showcases roses. Opened in 1928, it is considered the first municipally operated public rose garden in the United States. Designated as a Los Angeles County point of historical interest in 1987, this seven-acre garden contains approximately 10,000 rosebushes of more than 100 varieties. All-American Rose Selections donates its new, award-winning rose cultivars each year. In addition to the Rose Garden, Exposition Park is the site of the Los Angeles Memorial Coliseum and swim stadium which hosted the Olympics in 1932 and 1984, the Natural History Museum of Los Angeles, the California Science Center, and the California African-American Museum.

Hours: March 16 through December 31, daily, 10 a.m. to dusk; January 1 to March 15, closed for maintenance

Admission: free

Take I-110 south to Exposition Boulevard exit. Exposition Park site is just west of I-110 between Exposition Park Boulevard and University of Southern California on the north, Figueroa Street on the east, Martin Luther King Jr. Boulevard on the south, and Vermont Avenue on the west. Rose Garden faces Exposition Boulevard. A decorative brick wall screens garden from street. Parking is available inside Exposition Park or on street.

The Getty Center
1200 Getty Center Drive, Los Angeles (310) 440-7300 www.getty.edu

The Getty Center offers tranquil gardens and water features amid dramatic architecture, breathtaking hillside views, and outdoor spaces. Lush plantings and trees provide color, texture, and shade in counterpoint to the architecture of Richard Meier. The Central Garden is conceived by Robert Irwin as a "sculpture in the form of a garden aspiring to be art."

Hours: year round, Tuesday, Wednesday, Thursday and Sunday, 10 a.m. to 6 p.m., Friday and Saturday, 10 a.m. to 9 p.m.; closed Monday and major holidays.

Admission: free

From I-405, exit at Getty Center Drive. Take Sepulveda to Getty Center Drive.

La Casita del Arroyo Garden
177 South Arroyo Boulevard, Pasadena (626) 449-9505

La Casa del Arroyo Garden is a water demonstration garden designed by Isabelle Green in the late 1980s. The small garden is divided into sections illustrating plants with different water requirements and includes a butterfly sanctuary. Owned by the City of Pasadena, it is maintained by the La Casita Foundation with the help of the Pasadena Garden Club.

Hours: year round, daily, dawn to dusk

Admission: free

From I-210 in Pasadena, exit south onto Orange Grove Boulevard. Turn right onto Arbor Street to Arroyo Boulevard. Turn right and #177 is on left.

From I-110, continue from end of freeway north on Arroyo Parkway. Turn left onto California Boulevard which dead ends at Arroyo Boulevard. Turn right and continue to #177.

Norton Simon Museum Sculpture Garden
411 West Colorado Boulevard, Pasadena (626) 844-6928 www.nortonsimon.org

The Norton Simon Garden was opened in 1997, redesigned by Nancy Goslee Powers & Associates along with a refurbishing of the museum by Frank Gehry. A large pond is the highlight of the garden, filled with water plants, especially waterlilies. Colorful plantings surround the pond, with sculpture carefully placed so as to be viewed alone. It is a striking garden and also has a small café overlooking it.

Hours: year round, daily, dawn to dusk

Admission: free

Located on corner of Orange Grove and Colorado Boulevard. Entrance is on Colorado.

The Huntington Library, Art Collections, and Botanical Gardens
1151 Oxford Road, San Marino (626) 405-2141 www.huntington.org

The former estate of railroad magnate Henry Huntington showcases more than 14,000 plant species in 150 acres of gardens. Highlights include a twelve-acre desert garden, rose garden, Japanese garden, jungle garden, and ten acres of camellias. English tea is served in the Rose Garden Tea Room.

Hours: September through May, Tuesday through Friday, 12 to 4:30 p.m., weekends, 10:30 a.m. to 4:30 p.m.; June through August, Tuesday through Sunday, 10:30 a.m. to 4:30 p.m.

Admission: $10 adults, $8.50 senior citizens, $7 students, $4 children 5 to 11, children under 5 free

Located near Pasadena, about 12 miles northeast of downtown Los Angeles. From downtown, take I-110 until it ends and becomes Arroyo Parkway. Continue north 2 blocks and turn right onto California Boulevard. Go 2 miles, turn right onto Allen Avenue, and go 2 short blocks to Huntington gates. For recorded directions from other freeways, call (626) 405-2100.

The Old Mill "El Molino Viejo"
1120 Old Mill Road, San Marino (626) 449-5458

El Molino Viejo was built during the Mission Days, about 1816. The local Indians built the gristmill for the Mission San Gabriel. The Diggers Garden Club maintains the drought-tolerant gardens appropriate to the period. The grounds have native oaks, citrus orchards, sycamore, bay, and olive trees, pomegranate trees surrounding a patio area, ceanothus, heuchera, many sages, calla lilies, ribes, rosemary, and Douglas iris. Lady Banks' roses grow on the side of the building and cover the pergola.

Hours: year round, Tuesday through Saturday, 1 to 4 p.m.

Admission: free

Take Lake Avenue South until it curves and turns into Oak Knoll Road. Go past Ritz Carlton at bottom of hill. Turn left at Old Mill Road. Garden is located about 1 block east of intersection of Old Mill Road and Oak Knoll Road.

ORANGE COUNTY
LAGUNA BEACH
The Hortense Miller Garden
Hillcrest Drive, Laguna Beach (949) 497-3311

The Hortense Miller Garden, established in 1959, covers two and one-half acres. More than 1,500 species of plants are represented, including exotics from around the world, old-fashioned favorites, and native coastal sage scrub. In her well-designed, sustainable garden, Mrs. Miller uses little fertilizer, almost no pesticides, and a minimum of irrigation.

Hours: year round, Tuesday through Saturday. Closed on major holidays. Visits booked in advance by Laguna Beach Recreation Department at (949) 497-3311, ext. 426.

Admission: free

Garden is located at a private residence in a gated community. Guests are met by docents at Riddle Field on Hillcrest Drive and escorted to garden. Call for reservations.

SAN DIEGO COUNTY
EL CAJON
The Water Conservation Garden
12122 Cuyamaca College Drive West, El Cajon (619) 660-0614 www.thegarden.org

This is a unique demonstration garden dedicated to the seven principles of Xeriscape. The garden presents water-wise, Mediterranean zone plantings in vistas both lush and semi-arid. Meandering paths through gently undulating terrain lead past garden features delightful to both children and adults. This award-winning garden invites self-guided tours. Docent-led tours provided on weekends.

Hours: year round, Tuesday through Sunday, 10 a.m. to 4 p.m.

Admission: free

From I-805, take State Route 94 east. When freeway becomes a surface road, go straight to fourth traffic light at Cuyamaca College Drive West. Turn left; driveway to parking lot is second right.

ENCINITAS
Quail Botanical Gardens
230 Quail Gardens Drive, Encinitas (760) 436-3036 www.qbgardens.org

Quail Botanical Gardens is a thirty-acre oasis in Encinitas. Gardens include nearly 4,000 specimens representing fifteen distinct bio-geographic regions, in three general plant habitat types: desert collections, Mediterranean collections, and subtropical/tropical collections. Ten demonstration gardens focus on conservation education, horticultural themes, or ethno-botanical uses of plants.

Hours: year round, daily, 9 a.m. to 5 p.m.; closed Thanksgiving, Christmas, and New Year's Day.

Admission: $5 adults, $4 senior citizens, $2 children 5 to 12, children under 5 free

Exit I-5 at Encinitas Boulevard. Go east 4 traffic lights and turn left onto Quail Gardens Drive. Follow this small road .25 mile and turn left into Quail Botanical Gardens. Parking is free.

SAN FRANCISCO COUNTY

SAN FRANCISCO
The Japanese Tea Garden
Hagiwara Drive, San Francisco (415) 831-2700

The oldest public Japanese garden in the United States, dating from 1894, it was created for the California Mid-Winter Exposition to represent a Japanese village. The five-acre stroll garden includes a drum bridge, teahouse, pagoda, two gates built for the 1915 Panama Pacific Exposition, and a Temple Belfry Gate. It also has a large bronze Buddha cast in 1790.

Hours: October 1 through February 29, daily, 8:30 a.m. to 5 p.m.; March 1 through September 30, daily, 8:30 a.m. to 6 p.m.

Admission: $3.50 adults, $1.75 children 6 to 12, $1.25 senior citizens, children under 6 free

Located in center of Golden Gate Park near DeYoung Museum and Academy of Sciences on Hagiwara Drive.

Strybing Arboretum & Botanical Gardens
Ninth Avenue at Lincoln Way in Golden Gate Park, San Francisco (415) 661-1316
www.strybing.org

Strybing Arboretum & Botanical Gardens sprawls over fifty-five acres and features 7,000 plant varieties from all over the world. Specialty gardens include the Primitive Plant Garden, Moon-Viewing Garden, Asian Discovery Garden, California Native Plant Garden, and Fragrance Garden. Visit our bookstore, with the west coast's most complete horticultural selection. A wide array of lectures, classes, workshops, and tours in garden design, horticulture, botany, and ecology are offered through our education department.

Hours: year round, weekdays, 8 a.m. to 4:30 p.m., weekends and holidays, 10 a.m. to 5 p.m.

Admission: free, but donations are appreciated

Located in Golden Gate Park, at corner of Ninth Avenue and Lincoln Way.

PALO ALTO
The Elizabeth F. Gamble Garden
1431 Waverley Street, Palo Alto (650) 329-1356 www.gamblegarden.org

This two-and-one-third-acre urban garden, located forty miles south of San Francisco, surrounds a turn-of-the-century house and carriage house. The formal gardens have been restored from the original plans. The working gardens include experimental demonstrations and displays. The formal gardens and buildings may be rented to private parties on weekends.

Hours: year round, daily, dawn to dusk; access to certain areas may be restricted on weekends.

Admission: free

From Highway 101, exit onto Embarcadero West. Turn left onto Waverley Street. Parking lot is on left.

From I-280, exit onto Page Mill Road East, cross El Camino, and continue on Oregon Expressway. Turn left onto Waverley Street. House is on corner of Waverley and Churchill. Parking lot is north of house.

WOODSIDE
Filoli
Canada Road, Woodside (650) 364-8300 www.filoli.org

A 654-acre estate, Filoli is a registered State Historical Landmark and listed on the National Register of Historic Places. Sixteen acres of formal gardens are divided into a number of separate garden rooms.

Hours: Mid-February through October, Tuesday through Saturday, 10:30 a.m. to 2:30 p.m., docent-led tours every Tuesday and Wednesday; please call for information

Admission: $10 adults, $1 children 5 to 12

From I-280, take Edgewood Road exit and follow signs.

San Jose
Emma Prusch Farm Park

647 South King Road, San Jose (408) 926-5555 www.sanjoseparks.org

Emma Prusch Farm Park offers visitors opportunities to learn about San Jose's agricultural past. Its forty-seven acres features San Jose's largest barn; more than 100 community and school garden plots; a rare fruit orchard featuring a strawberry tree, wild pear tree, and a raisin tree; and a grove of international trees.

Hours: year round, daily, 8:30 a.m. to dusk; closed Thanksgiving, Christmas, and New Year's Day,

Admission: free

From Highway 101, take Story Road east exit. Turn left at King Road and left at next traffic light into driveway.

From I-680, take King Road exit and turn left. Turn right at second light into driveway.

From I-280, take King Road exit and turn right. Proceed to next light and turn right into driveway.

Colorado

OPEN DAY:

June 21
June 28

tawto-ma Gardens, Colorado Springs

Saturday, June 21

EL PASO COUNTY

COLORADO SPRINGS

The Bradleys' Garden

3760 Camels View, Colorado Springs

Our garden is located on a mesa overlooking the Garden of the Gods and Pikes Peak. Inspired by the color palette of Matisse, the Xeriscape garden was designed by Fawn Hayes Bell, ASLA, in 2001 to enhance our contemporary house, which responds to Western aesthetics. The semi-public spaces, fronting on the golf course to the rear and the street to the front, contain a blend of native plant materials massed to complement the environment. The private court-yard space is a gallery of color, line, form, and texture that leads the guest through a curved walk to the glassed entryway.

Hours: 10 a.m. to 3 p.m.

From I-25, take Fillmore Street exit west. Turn north onto Mesa Road and stop at the Xeriscape Demonstration Garden on right to purchase tickets. From Xeriscape garden, proceed north on Mesa to Kissing Camels Estates entrance on right. From guard gate, take first left, which is Hill Circle, and follow to Camels View. House is eighth from corner on right, #3760.

Casa Contenta Garden

3220 Camels Ridge Lane, Colorado Springs

This small garden was created to reflect a tranquil feeling, a relaxed formality. It is a garden of long-blooming perennials, roses, formal privet hedges, topiaries, a gravel path with stepping-stones, a smattering of antique statuary, and an enclosed rose garden facing the Kissing Camels Golf Course with an exciting view of Pikes Peak.

Hours: 10 a.m. to 3 p.m.

From I-25, take Fillmore Street exit west. Turn north onto Mesa Road and stop at the Xeriscape Demonstration Garden to purchase a ticket for entry to this gated property. Proceed right to Kissing Camels Estates, directly across from the Garden of the Gods Club. Proceed up hill of Kissing Camels Drive and turn right onto Camels Ridge Lane. We are located at #3220. *Please park on street.*

Joleen Dentan's Dwarf Conifers
1690 Hill Circle, Colorado Springs

My garden was never designed. It just happened. Once a perennial garden until rabbits got the upper hand, in self-defense I began gradually replacing lost perennials with dwarf conifers. It now contains only evergreens. Various sizes, shapes, and textures create the interest, along with a broad range of green hues from blues to yellows. The effect is restful, with the added advantage of being attractive year round. Off my living room is a small enclosed Japanese-inspired garden using material appropriate to our climate and featuring a sixteenth-century Japanese snow-viewing lantern called a *yukimi-gata*.

Hours: 10 a.m. to 3 p.m.

From I-25, take Fillmore exit west. Turn right onto Mesa Road and stop to buy tickets at the Xeriscape Demonstration Garden at water treatment facility on right to entrance to Kissing Camels Estate. After passing gate house, turn right onto Hill Circle and continue for about .5 mile to house on left set back somewhat from road and with sunroom in front. *Please park on street.*

Our Secret Garden—Florence & Ron Richey
5040 Lyda Lane, Colorado Springs

When we purchased our older house in Kissing Camels several years ago, it was the backyard that attracted us the most. We are located on the fairway of a golf course, but have complete privacy from the golfers. We were fortunate enough to have an English gardener who created a festive garden with many varieties of roses, daylilies, moss roses, grasses, and daisies. The backyard has open lawns for dogs to romp, but beautiful gardens on all the outer edges. Some parts are elevated with stonework, plus, we have a pool with a charming waterfall and flowers hidden in the rockwork. There is also a smaller waterfall closer to the terrace, so we and any guests can hear the soft sound of water running over rocks. It is surrounded by large green ferns, impatiens, and other brightly colored plants. The reason we call our garden "secret" is that no one can see it unless they are on our back terrace. Also, the grandchildren enjoy their "secret path" behind the large waterfall.

Hours: 10 a.m. to 3 p.m.

From I-25, take Fillmore Street exit west. Turn right onto Mesa Road and stop at Xeriscape Demonstration Garden on right. Purchase tickets there for admission to this gated neighborhood. Proceed right on Mesa Rod to Kissing Camels Drive and turn right onto Kissing Camels Estates. After gate entry, take second left onto Lyda Lane and proceed to #5040. *Please park on street.*

Proceeds shared with the Humane Society of the Pikes Peak Region

A Personal Garden
5000 Lyda Lane, Colorado Springs

Visitors enter this walled, wheelchair-accessible garden through a wrought-iron gate and follow a path to a spacious lawn, bound on one side by a shaded patio. From the house one looks across the patio and lawn to a long, curved, raised bed and beyond the protecting wall to Pikes Peak. The bed, centered on a fountain, is planted with evergreens and perennials, and pink-and-white annuals provide color. On either side, a sculpture of a child is sheltered from the sun under trees, which cast leafy shadows.

Hours: 10 a.m. to 3 p.m.

From I-25, take Fillmore Street exit west. Turn right onto Mesa Road and stop at Xeriscape Demonstration Garden on right to purchase a ticket for entry to this gated property. Proceed right on Mesa Road to Kissing Camels Drive and turn right into Kissing Camels Estates. After gate entry, take second street to left to #5000, first house on right. *Please park on street.*

tawto'ma Gardens
3450 Mesa Road, Colorado Springs

The tawto'ma gardens are on the west side of Colorado Springs overlooking the Garden of the Gods Park at the foot of Pikes Peak. The gardens surround a house primarily built of the pink sandstone found in the Garden of the Gods. The gardens contain an extensive variety of plant materials, both perennial and annual, with an abundance of roses of all types. The designs include a butterfly garden, cutting garden, herb garden, shaded woodland garden, water features, and a rose court. It is an outstanding horticultural display in breathtaking natural surroundings!

Hours: 10 a.m. to 3 p.m.

From I-25, take Fillmore exit west. Turn north onto Mesa Road and pass Xeriscape Demonstration Garden at water treatment facility. Do not turn right at first gated entrance into Kissing Camels Estates. Instead, pass Garden of the Gods Club on left. Turn right at gated entrance on east side of Mesa Road. *A designated parking area is located just inside entrance. Note: This garden requires considerable walking, steps, and slopes. No handicap assistance is available.*

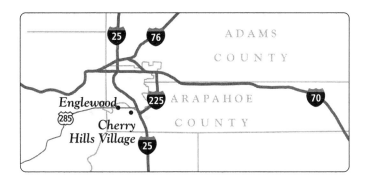

Saturday, June 28

ARAPAHOE COUNTY

CHERRY HILLS VILLAGE

MacKenzie Family Garden

4420 South Franklin Street, Cherry Hills Village

This garden was developed to provide a varied space for a family of five. The focal point is a bi-level pond with a waterfall. The property is bordered on the east by Little Day Creek. There is a nice flat, grassy area for picnicking, plenty of shade from many mature trees, and a large stone terrace overlooking it all. Tucked behind a guest house is a raised-bed vegetable and herb garden and on the southwestern side of the main house is a perennial garden.

Hours: 10 a.m. to 4 p.m.

Go south on University Boulevard. One mile south of Hampden is Quincy. Go west on Quincy to Franklin. Go south on Franklin and watch for #4420 on left. *Please park on street.*

David & Brenda Schrier

21 Viking Drive, Cherry Hills Village

Our garden is a combination of flowers, trees, and shrubs. Shade and sun perennial gardens as well as garden sculpture, a greenhouse, and pond are a special focus of our garden. Gardening is one of our passions, therefore, our garden changes as we try new plants, colors, and textures. Our garden inspires us, comforts us, and provides a great sanctuary for our family and friends.

Hours: 10 a.m. to 4 p.m.

Number 21 Viking Drive is near Belleview and Clarkson. Go north on Clarkson off Belleview and take first right onto Viking. Go left at next 2 stop signs. Number 21 is on left. *Please park on street.*

ENGLEWOOD
Rosemont
4700 South El Camino Drive, Englewood

Rosemont is a new Colorado garden, with an English-style perennial border set off by the warm red of Colorado sandstone. The plantings provide four-season interest, mixing annuals and perennials with evergreens, trees, shrubs, and a wide variety of roses. There are numerous garden rooms, ranging from a contemplative shady woodland to a sweeping sunny meadow of native plants and a formal bowling green with an antique color palette. Multi-level patios allow dining and entertaining, with massed container plantings adding seasonal color and large water features providing a backdrop of sound. The second phase of the garden is approaching completion nearby, and continues in the same design tradition. It will provide additional space for vegetable and cutting gardens, water gardens, formal overlooks, and native wildflowers, all in view of Colorado's magnificent Front Range.

Hours: 10 a.m. to 4 p.m.

From I-25, take Belleview exit west. Go to Holly Street and turn right (north) at traffic light. At first stop sign, at intersection with Charlou, turn right (east). Go to first stop sign and intersection with El Camino. House will be ahead on left, northeast corner of intersection. *Please park along El Camino and walk back to south side of property where entrance is located.*

Public Gardens
ARAPAHOE COUNTY

COLORADO SPRINGS
Cheyenne Mountain Zoo
4250 Cheyenne Mountain Zoo Road, Colorado Springs (719) 633-9925 www.cmzoo.org

Cheyenne Mountain Zoo is located at 7,000 feet above sea level on the side of Cheyenne Mountain. The horticultural efforts are focused on native plants, theme gardens, and naturalized exhibits. Three favorite gardens are the Hummingbird Garden, Butterfly Garden, and Asian Highlands.

Hours: Labor Day through Memorial Day, daily, 9 a.m. to 5 p.m.; rest of year, daily, 9 a.m. to 6 p.m.

Admission: $10 adults, $8 senior citizens, $5 children 3 to 11, children under 3 free

From I-25, take Exit 138/Circle Drive/Lake Avenue and drive west 2.8 miles to Broadmoor Hotel. Turn right at hotel and follow signs.

Colorado Springs Fine Arts Center Gardens
30 West Dale, Colorado Springs (719) 634-5581

Two gardens grace the grounds around the Southwest Deco building, both filled with sculptures. Plantings have been designed by the Broadmoor Garden Club and include many indigenous grasses, shrubs, and trees, all labeled. One garden is a pocket park on a main thoroughfare. The garden, entered through the Fine Arts Center, is an enclosed sculpture courtyard offering a different, more protected climate.

Hours: year round, Tuesday through Saturday, 9 a.m. to 5 p.m., Sunday, 1 to 5 p.m.

Admission: free on Saturday

From I-25, take Exit 143/Uintah Street east. Go about 3 blocks and turn right (south) onto Cascade Avenue. Drive through campus of Colorado College and turn right (west) onto Dale. Corner garden at Cascade Avenue and Dale is entrance to Fine Arts Center property. Please park in lot across from building's entrance.

The Colorado Springs Utilities Xeriscape Demonstration Garden

2855 Mesa Road, Colorado Springs (719) 448-4800

This spectacular garden overlooking the Garden of the Gods was created by Colorado Springs Utilities to show their customers just how beautiful and economical a water-wise landscape can be. Interpretive signs explaining the seven principles of Xeriscape draw visitors through the garden on a self-guided tour. Over 600 plant species, grouped by water use, display the diversity of color, form, and texture sustainable in Colorado's high desert climate, where water is a precious commodity.

Hours: year round, daily, dawn to dusk; garden personnel available Monday through Friday, 9 a.m. to 5 p.m.

Admission: free

From I-25, take Fillmore exit west. Go up hill past Coronado High School to traffic light at junction of Fillmore and Mesa Road. Turn right and drive north about .5 mile. Garden is on east side of road, surrounded by a red sandstone wall.

The Demonstration Garden of the Horticultural Art Society of Colorado Springs

4403 Lyle Circle, Colorado Springs (719) 596-4901

The garden was designed to demonstrate plants and shrubs that will thrive in a sheltered, semi-shaded city garden. Featured are perennial beds, rose beds, a fragrance garden for the handicapped, a children's garden, regional native plant berm, rock garden with a stream and wilding area, ground-cover display, and the All-American Selections display garden.

Hours: year round, daily, dawn to dusk

Admission: free

From I-25, take Exit 143/Uintah Street east and make next right onto Glen Avenue. Proceed past Willow Pond and city greenhouses to garden, at corner of Glen Avenue and Mesa Road in Monument Valley Park.

From the east, turn west off Cascade Avenue onto Cache la Poudre (at Colorado College). Cross bridge west over Monument Creek and garden is on the immediate right with a parking lot to left.

Garden of the Gods Visitor Center

1805 North 30th Street, Colorado Springs (719) 634-6666

Garden of the Gods is a unique biological melting pot where several life zones converge. The grasslands of the Great Plains meet the pinyon-juniper woodlands characteristic of the American Southwest, and merge with the mountain forests skirting 14,100-foot Pikes Peak.

Hours: June 1 through August 31, daily, 8 a.m. to 8 p.m.; September 1 through May 31, daily, 9 a.m. to 5 p.m.

Admission: free

From Denver, take I-25 south. Take Exit 146 onto Garden of the Gods Road. Turn left onto 30th Street and go .25 mile. Visitor center will be on left.

Starsmore Hummingbird Garden
2120 South Cheyenne Canon Road, Colorado Springs (719) 578-6146

The Hummingbird Garden at Starsmore Discovery Center is full of native perennials that attract hummers: penstemon, columbine, bee balm, agastache, Indian paintbrush, and fireweed. A new scree garden has been added to recreate the hot, dry, lean conditions loved by many of the penstemons, scarlet gilia, and others.

Hours: June through August, daily, 9 a.m. to 5 p.m.

Admission: free

Take I-25 to Exit 140B/South Tejon and turn right onto Tejon, which becomes Cheyenne Boulevard. Travel 3 miles west. Follow "Seven Falls" and "Starsmore Discovery" signs to South Cheyenne Canon Road. Please park in lot.

LITTLETON
Chatfield Nature Preserve
8500 Deer Creek Canyon Road, Littleton (303) 973-3705 www.botanicgardens.org

Chatfield Nature Preserve's 700 acres wind along Deer Creek, encompassing several distinct High Plains habitats. Nature trails thread around wetland and prairie ecosystems. Educational stops along the trails explain surrounding vegetation and encourage wildlife watching. A nineteenth-century farmstead has been restored to present an authentic view of pioneer life on the Colorado High Plains. Chatfield Nature Preserve is run by Denver Botanic Gardens.

Hours: year round, daily, 9 a.m. to 5 p.m.

Admission: $2 adults, $1 children 6-15, children under 6 free

Located just southwest of Wadsworth Boulevard and C-470 intersection. Proceed south on Wadsworth Boulevard from this intersection to second traffic light and turn right (west) onto Deer Creek Canyon Road. Chatfield's entrance gate is .4 mile on left.

Hudson Gardens
6115 South Santa Fe Drive, Littleton (303) 797-8565

This thirty-acre Regional Display Garden accents sixteen individual gardens, including a historic rose garden, rock garden canyon, water gardens, demonstration gardens, and a railroad garden. There are also excellent perennial and shrub collections for Zones 4 and 5 climates. Gardens are labeled and individual handouts are available.

Hours: April 1 through October 31, daily, 9 a.m. to 5 p.m.; reduced winter hours

Admission: $4 adults, $3 senior citizens, $2 children 3 to 12

From C-470 north on South Santa Fe Drive 3 miles, on left, across street from Arapahoe Community College; or .5 mile south on South Santa Fe Drive from Bowles Avenue/ Littleton Boulevard junction to South Santa Fe Drive on right.

Denver

Denver Botanic Gardens

909 York Street, Denver (720) 865-3500 www.botanicgardens.org

Denver Botanic Gardens is an urban oasis. Stroll through the world-renowned Rock Alpine Garden or visit the Japanese, Herb, or Water-Smart Gardens, to name a few. The gift shop offers books, gifts, gardening tools, and more. The Helen Fowler Resource Center has an extensive collection of horticultural books and catalogs. Special events and plant shows are planned throughout the year.

Hours: October through April, daily, 9 a.m. to 5 p.m.; May through September, Saturday through Tuesday, 9 a.m. to 8 p.m., Wednesday through Friday, 9 a.m. to 5 p.m.

Admission: $6.50 adults, $4.50 senior citizens, $4 children 6 to 15, children under 4 free; discounted admission from October through April

Located 5 minutes east of the downtown area and accessible by major RTD bus routes. From I-25, exit east onto Sixth Avenue. Proceed east to Josephine Street, and turn north. Parking lot is on the left, between Ninth and Eleventh Avenues.

CONNECTICUT

Angelwood—Garden of Mary Anne & Dale Athanas, Guilford. Photo by Dale P. Athanas.

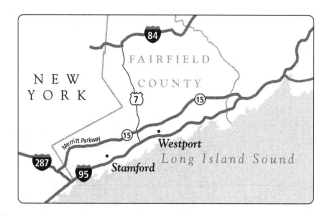

Saturday, May 10

FAIRFIELD COUNTY

Stamford

Ruth & Jim Levitan

26 Wake Robin Lane, Stamford

This unique one-acre woodland garden is covered with dogwoods and azaleas blooming over a carpet of old-fashioned spring perennials and biennials. It was created over a forty-year period by the owners, both dedicated amateur gardeners.

Hours: 10 a.m. to 4 p.m.

From Merritt Parkway/Route 15, take Exit 35/High Ridge Road. Go 50 yards north and turn left onto Wire Mill Road. Continue about .5 mile, crossing a small bridge, and turn right onto Red Fox Road. Go up hill 1 block and turn left onto Wake Robin Lane. *Please park in street.*

Westport

Paul Held & Jane Sherman

195 North Avenue, Westport

Sloping terrain and dappled sunlight make a perfect environment for growing some precious, rare plants. This garden includes a delightful mix of shrubs and ground covers, both alpine and woodland. It is home to the largest collection of *Primula sieboldii* in North America and Europe.

Hours: 10 a.m. to 4 p.m.

From Merritt Parkway/Route 15, take Exit 42. Go under parkway if coming from north; turn left off exit if coming from south. Go to Route 136 and go north to first stop sign, which is North Avenue. Turn right and go .3 mile to #195 on tree or mailbox. *Please park on street on curb.*

Proceeds shared with Unitarian Church in Westport/Coming of Age Group

Sunday, May 18

FAIRFIELD COUNTY

REDDING

Highstead Arboretum

127 Lonetown Road, Redding

The dappled shade provided by five native species of oak on a terrain of wet and dry soil proved perfect shelter and habitat for a collection of deciduous azaleas. Fourteen East Coast native species are now represented at a site where pinxterbloom azalea alone was originally found. This naturalistic setting in the heart of the woodland is also home to ericaceous companion plants and has been fenced for protection from deer. Mid- to late May should find several in bloom, a perfect opportunity to be spoiled by the color and fragrance during a ninety-minute guided tour of the arboretum. Set on fifty acres of geographic extremes, the arboretum is also open weekdays by appointment, and offering two other distinct seasonal walks on June 1 and August 10. Please call weekdays, 8:30 a.m. to 4:30 p.m., for more information, (203) 935-8809.

Hours: Guided walks at 10 a.m., 12 p.m., and 2 p.m.

From I-95 or Merritt Parkway/Route 15, take Route 7 north. Turn right onto Route 107 for 6 miles (be sure to follow signs for 107 as it crosses Route 53). Pass police station, Redding Elementary School, and Redding Country Club. Take second driveway on left after country club, #127. Follow signs into arboretum; driveway is .5 mile long.

Sunday, June 1

FAIRFIELD COUNTY

REDDING
Highstead Arboretum
127 Lonetown Road, Redding

A guided tour of Highstead's *Kalmia* collection in bloom presents the opportunity to compare the characteristics of mountain laurel found in the wild with plants that have been cultivated. A part of the North American Plant Collection Consortium, this collection has over sixty cultivars to admire. This ninety-minute guided walk will also traverse more than 26 acres of native mountain laurel growing in a variety of soils and exposures. Set on fifty acres of geographic extremes, the arboretum is also open weekdays by appointment, and offering two other distinct seasonal walks on May 18 and August 10. Please call weekdays, 8:30 a.m. to 4:30 p.m., for more information, (203) 935-8809.

Hours: Guided walks at 10 a.m., 12 p.m., and 2 p.m.

From I-95 or Merritt Parkway/Route 15, take Route 7 north. Turn right onto Route 107 for 6 miles (be sure to follow signs for 107 as it crosses Route 53). Pass police station, Redding Elementary School, and Redding Country Club. Take second driveway on left after country club, #127. Follow signs into arboretum; driveway is .5 mile long.

Westport
Judie & Charlie Kiernan Garden
196 Long Lots Road, Westport

Boxwoods enclose the circular drive in front of the house, where weeping Katsura trees, co-lumnar purple-leaf beeches, and a group of Nootkatensis (false cyrpess) are taking on solidity aftern nine years. Of interest in the back garden, protected from deer, is a strong color play between weeping purple-leef beeches growing beside a group of gold threadleaf *Chamaecyparis*. Evergreen verticals offer strong influence over the terrace garden's perennial beds. Two broad candelabra-form espalieried apple trees, started from eighteen-inch whips, are now a fruitful ten feet tall.

Hours: 2 to 6 p.m.

From I-95, take Exit 18. From south, turn left onto Sherwood Island Connector; from north, turn right. Follow to end at Post Road and turn left. Make first right onto Long Lots Road. Go about 1.7 miles to #196. Please park on street.

Proceeds shared with Project Inform

Susan Lloyd
59 Center Street, Westport

A stone outcropping alongside the early nineteenth-century house hides the garden beyond. The long, narrow property ends at a brook with astilbe and hosta beds. This is a family garden with a tree house and playground. The large perennial bed (124 by sixteen to twenty feet) is a collection of purples, yellow, white, and some pink and illustrates a love of different foliage shapes and textures.

Hours: 10 a.m. to 4 p.m.

From I-95, take Exit 18. If heading north, turn left at end of exit ramp; if southbound, turn right. Turn right at second traffic light onto Greens Farms Road. First left is Center Street. Number 59 is third house on right, with a white picket fence.

From Merritt Parkway/Route 15, take Exit 42. If southbound, turn left at end of exit ramp; if northbound, turn right onto Weston Road; turn left at the second stop sign onto Cross Highway. Make first right onto Roseville Road and cross Post Road (Route 1). Take first left onto Hillandale. Turn right at stop sign onto West Parish and turn right at "T" in road onto Center Street. Number 59 is on left side. *Please park on house side of street.*

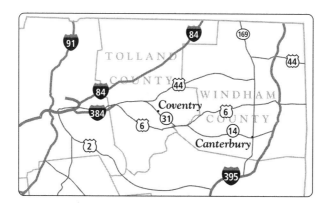

Saturday, June 7
TOLLAND COUNTY

<small>COVENTRY</small>
David & Julia Hayes
905 South Street, Coventry

Sculptor David Hayes, whose work is found in many public and private collections in this country and in Europe, lives and works on this old farm. Hayes displays his completed works in an old orchard, by the pond, in a large hayfield, and behind the house. They are in or near informal gardens of herbs, wildflowers and ferns, roses (mostly old roses), annuals, and vegetables. Wear comfortable shoes as the paths are not all smooth.

Hours: 10 a.m. to 4 p.m.

From Hartford, take I-84 east briefly to I-384 and follow to end, about 8 miles. Continue on Route 44 towards Coventry about 4 miles, to the fourth traffic light. Meadowbrook shopping center is on right. Turn right onto Route 31/Main Street just past shopping center and continue several miles past school, firehouse, lake, another school and fire house, and town hall. Continue halfway down long hill to blinking light at junction of Routes 31 and 275 and Lake Street. Turn right and go 1 mile (name changes from Lake to Cross Street) to "T" intersection at South Street. Turn left and continue a generous .5 mile to #905, on right. *Please park along street. Driveway is available for those with walking difficulties.*

From Norwich and other points southeast, take Route 32 north from Norwich through Willimantic. In Mansfield, on Route 32, you will come to junction of Routes 32 and 31, opposite drive-in theater. Turn left onto Route 31 and go several miles into Coventry Village. Halfway up hill there is a blinking traffic light at junction of Routes 31 and 275 and Lake Street. Turn left onto Lake Street and proceed as directed above.

WINDHAM COUNTY

CANTERBURY

Westminster Gardens—Eleanor B. Cote & Adrian P. Hart

26 Westminster Road, Canterbury

The area surrounding the house has border plantings of dwarf evergreens, rhododendrons, azaleas, other shrubs, and perennials. There is also a stone terrace with a waterfall. The back area is about three acres. It has nearly an acre of woodland gardens with crushed stone walkways, 750 different varieties of hosta, and many astilbes, pulmonarias, ferns, and other shade-loving plants. The remaining area has twenty gardens planted with various ornamental grasses, shrubs, perennials, and annuals, with tall bearded iris and peonies blooming in June, followed by Japanese iris and Siberian iris, with daylilies and Asiatic and Oriental lilies blooming in July. An Oriental garden with a goldfish pond is located next to the woods. Benches have been placed throughout the gardens so visitors may stop to rest. A new feature is a dry rock river complete with bridge.

Hours: 12 to 4 p.m.

From I-395 south, take Exit 89. Turn right at end of exit ramp. Follow Route 14 about 6 miles to stop sign at bottom of hill. Turn right. Go over bridge to a 4-way stop at intersection of Routes 169 and 14. Go straight on Route 14. Number 26 is second house on left after Citgo gas station.

From I-395 north, take Exit 83A. Turn left at end of exit ramp. Follow Route 169 about 10 miles to intersection of Routes 169 and 14. Turn left onto Route 14/Westminster Road. Proceed as directed above. *Please park along road. Handicapped may park in driveway.*

Proceeds shared with Pound Hounds, Inc.

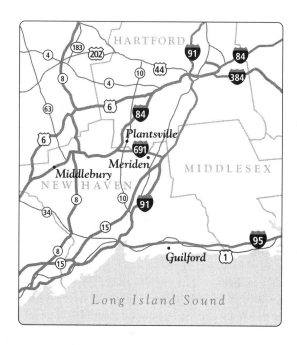

Sunday, June 8
HARTFORD COUNTY

PLANTSVILLE
The Kaminski Garden
513 Marion Avenue, Plantsville

I am always amazed as I pass from the front yard, where grass barely grows, through the gate into the four-year-old garden's hues of green punctuated with flowers. Mature trees anchor the yard; sweeping curves define garden beds where the emphasis is on foliage. The tumbled bluestone used for the patio, raised planting beds surrounding the deck, garden bed edgings, and the pathways to the freeform pool soothes the eye with its consistency. Shade predominates throughout, as do a wide variety of shade-tolerant perennials, shrubs, and Japanese maples. Sun abounds by the pool; specimen evergreens and sweeps of flowers thrive here.

Hours: 10 a.m. to 4 p.m.

From I-84, take Exit 30/Marion Avenue. From Hartford (I-84 west), turn right onto Marion; from Waterbury (I-84 east), turn left onto Marion. Once on Marion, travel about 1 mile, passing Frost Street. Next driveway on right is our house, #513. House is slate blue with detached two-car garage. *Please park in driveway.*

Proceeds shared with Dana-Farber Cancer Institute

GUILFORD

Angelwood—Mary Anne & Dale Athanas
66 Christopher Lane, Guilford

A secret garden—from the front of this well-landscaped southern colonial you would not realize that we have forty gardens, garden rooms, and water features awaiting your enjoyment. Observe from the multi-level deck the amphitheater of plantings and streams surrounded by woodland. Highlights of the garden include a circular garden with its two-tiered fountain, formal perennial gardens, rock garden, ponds, daylily borders, and much more. We designed and planted all of the gardens over a period of nine years. New gardens were added in 2002: an entrance garden called the Azalea Walk includes many types of azaleas, boxwood, hostas, and coral bells, highlighted by a four-foot urn within a raised box surrounded by boxwood, Alberta spruce, begonias, and santolina; the Anniversary Garden, consisting of ornamental grasses, sedum, spirea, and sedge; and a woodland path surrounded by two streams consisting of many varieties of hosta and ferns—this is where the angel of Angelwood can be found.

Hours: 10 a.m. to 4 p.m.

From Hartford, take I-91 south to Exit 15/Route 68/Durham. At end of exit ramp, turn left onto Route 68 and follow until it ends in Durham. Turn right onto Route 17 and follow about 1.5 miles (past Route 79, which will be on left) to Route 77. Turn left and go several miles to a traffic light at a major intersection. Turn right onto Route 80 and travel 1 mile to light. Turn left onto Long Hill Road. Travel 1.3 miles and look for Christopher Lane on left (two stone entrance walls). Turn left and look for #66 on left just before a cul-de-sac. It is a large white colonial with a formal front porch (columns) set back from road.

From New York area, take I-95 north to Exit 57. Turn right at end of exit ramp and go 1 mile (past Bishop's Orchards on left) to first light. Turn left onto Long Hill Road. Go about 3 miles to Christopher Lane, turn right, and look for #66 on left just before a cul-de-sac.

Proceeds shared with Dana Farber Cancer Institute/Women's Cancer Research Center

MERIDEN

Jardin des Brabant
131 Corrigan Avenue, Meriden

This is one woman's enclosed garden retreat on three quarters of an acre since 1972. The upper lawn features a large beech and a perimeter of flowering shrubs, dwarf conifers, shade and sun perennials, *kousa* and *florida* dogwoods, and annuals. A seventy-five-foot dawn redwood dominates the lower gardens of perennials, roses, annuals, and vines. Grass paths lead toward, and past, a stone-and-stucco storage house with hayrack planters. A small potager, an ancient apple tree shading hostas and ferns, a side border with miniature lilac standards and lilies, and a *Viburnum plicatum* hedge complete the secluded rear garden, which dissolves into open lawn.

Hours: 1 to 5 p.m.

From I-84, take I-691 east to Exit 5/Chamberlain Highway. Turn right at end of exit and take an immediate right onto Steuben Street. Steuben becomes Corrigan at top of hill. Go around bend to beginning of cemetery on right. Garden is directly across street.

From I-91, take I-691 west to Exit 6/Lewis Avenue. Turn left at end of exit. Turn left at end of Lewis onto Kensington Avenue. Turn left at the end of Kensington onto Chamberlain Highway. Go past Target store on right and look for Steuben Street immediately after 7-Eleven on left and highway exit on right. Proceed as directed above. *Please park on either side of street. Watch for children in area.*

Proceeds shared with Connecticut Horticultural Society

George Trecina
341 Spring Street, Meriden

This is a professional landscape designer's display and trial gardens, with one third of an acre of continuous mixed borders containing more than 300 varieties of woody plants and perennials, some unusual. The planting schemes are enhanced with an assortment of annuals, tender perennials, and container plantings with a decidedly tropical theme. The sloping front yard—structured with paths, walls, and stairways—features a white garden and a "wild" garden.

Hours: 1 to 5 p.m.

From I-91, take I-691 west to Exit 6/Lewis Avenue. Turn right off exit and follow to end. Turn right onto Hanover Street to first traffic light. Turn left onto Columbus Avenue and go to second stop sign. Turn left onto Prospect Avenue, then turn at first right onto Spring Street to fourth house on right, #341.

From I-84, take I-691 east to Exit 5/Chamberlain Highway. Turn right off exit and follow to end. Turn left onto West Main Street to the first light. Turn right onto Bradley Avenue and go to first stop sign. Turn left onto Winthrop Terrace and past light onto Columbus Avenue. Proceed as directed above. *Please park along Spring Street.*

MIDDLEBURY
John N. Spain
69 Bayberry Road, Middlebury

Garden areas include a rock garden, woodland garden with paths, an outdoor (winter-hardy) cactus garden, planted walls, and troughs. The rock garden combines dwarf conifers with hardy cacti and many unique rock garden plants. There is also a 32-foot-long landscaped greenhouse of cacti and succulents.

Hours: 10 a.m. to 4 p.m.

From I-84 west, take Exit 17. Go straight on Route 64 to second traffic light. Turn right onto Memorial Drive. At end, turn left onto Kelly Road. Go .25 mile and turn onto second street on right, Three Mile Hill Road. Continue to third street on right, Bayberry Road. House, #69, is second on right. *Please park along road.*

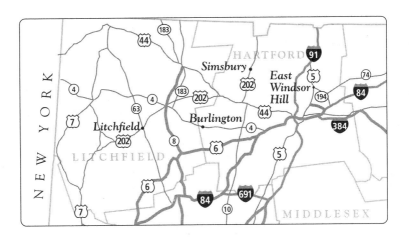

Saturday, June 14

HARTFORD COUNTY

BURLINGTON
The Salsedo Family Garden
15 Half King Drive, Burlington

Our gardens have been created on a unique location, a hilltop with a magnificent view 1,000 feet above sea level bordering on 4,000 acres of watershed and state forest. Begun in 1977, this site has undergone various physical transformations resulting in stonewalled terraces that render this acre-plus location usable. The last big change in 1995 added an expanded backyard terrace with a pool, post-and-beam gardener's toolshed, dwarf conifer collection, vegetable garden, and a collection of hardy chrysanthemums. The front yard features low maintenance lawns punctuated by beds of native and exotic trees, shrubs, and perennials. The emphasis of this landscape is sustainability with a focus on low care and minimal water requirements.

Hours: 10 a.m. to 4 p.m.

Take I-84 to Exit 39, and head west on Route 4 towards Farmington. Go through Farmington about 3 miles to Unionville Center to traffic light. Pass Friendly's on left. At light, bear right onto Route 4 (Old Masonic Hall on right, church on left). Go 1 mile along Farmington River. At light, turn left onto Route 4 and go up hill toward Burlington. Go about 1 mile and turn left onto Belden Road (fish hatchery sign is on left). Go to stop sign. Turn right onto George Washington Turnpike and take next left onto Cornwall. Go up hill and turn right onto Nassahegan, then second left onto Half King Drive. Go to bottom of cul-de-sac to middle gravel drive with granite mailbox post labeled #15 leading to a red cedar house. *Please park in cul-de-sac.*

EAST WINDSOR HILL
Pat & George Porter
1533 Main Street, East Windsor Hill

Surrounding an early nineteenth-century historic house in an historic district and on a scenic road, our gardens are both formal and English country. There are formal English rose beds, an herb garden, moon gardens, and perennial borders backed with yew or hemlock hedges. Plants and ferns swing on long hooks from old maple trees. A spectacular wall of climbing hydrangea backs a border of old roses that faces an espaliered apple tree allée. This leads to horse barns, an English glasshouse, a grape-covered pergola, swimming pool, ornamental grasses, and a rugosa rose border, all overlooking the Connecticut River meadows. In the south yard, a golden hops-covered pergola is surrounded by azaleas and rhododendrons.

Hours: 10 a.m. to 4 p.m.

From I-91, take I-291 east. Cross Connecticut River. Take Exit 4. Stay in left lane. Turn left onto Route 5 north. Go 3 miles. Turn left at traffic light onto Sullivan Avenue. Turn left again onto Main Street and go 1 mile south. Number 1533 is on right.

From I-84, take I-291 west. Turn right on South Windsor exit. Turn left onto Route 5 north and proceed as directed above. *Please park on street.*

SIMSBURY
The Garden of Betty & Dick Holden
7 Crane Place, Simsbury

This garden, begun in 1963, is an effort to establish an Americanized version of an English cottage garden. It is a diverse collection of perennials and vines vying for their place in the sun. A sincere effort has been made to have profuse bloom from early spring to late fall. The garden includes a small water garden, vegetable garden, mini-rose garden, and grape arbor. Emphasis is placed on unusual foliage plants. Beautiful fences, numerous rock walls, and arbors enhance the plantings. A variety of golf and baby shoes planted with sedum are tucked into corners. The birds, bees, and butterflies are ever-present visitors in this certified backyard habitat.

Hours: 10 a.m. to 4 p.m.

From I-84, take Exit 39 into downtown Farmington/Route 4. Turn right onto Route 10 north through Avon into Simsbury. After passing "Welcome to Simsbury" sign, turn left at next traffic light onto Old Meadow Plain Road. Continue to top of hill. Turn left onto Woodcliff Drive. Bear left at fork and take next left onto Crane Place. Garden is on right, #7.

LITCHFIELD COUNTY

LITCHFIELD

Dan & Joyce Lake

258 Beach Street, Litchfield

Litchfield Horticultural Center is a thirty-two-acre private residence with a retail landscape nursery and Christmas tree farm. Viewers can enjoy more than thirty perennial gardens, both sunny and shady, a large locust arbor, rustic pergola, ornamental grass garden, pond-side expressions and woodland shade gardens. We have extensive amounts of native mountain laurel and many large boulders in our landscape. All areas are designed in harmony with nature and the naturalistic setting of ledges and several large ponds. We have fields of growing landscape trees and a landscaped container nursery with an allée and a formal design with tasteful accents. A new classic shade house and Zen gardens have been added.

Hours: 2 to 6 p.m.

In Litchfield, at traffic light on Route 202 by Stop & Shop, turn onto Milton Road. After .25 mile, fork right onto Beach Street. Go 2 miles and Horticultural Center is on right. There are stone columns, stone walls, and large maple trees. We are 2 miles from Milton Road, 2.25 miles from Route 202.

Proceeds shared with Habitat for Humanity of Peconic

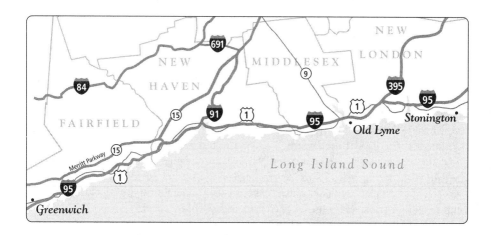

Sunday, June 15
FAIRFIELD COUNTY

GREENWICH

Stonybrooke

29 Taconic Road, Greenwich

About thirty years ago, we fell in love with this rambling old property of waterfalls, rock outcroppings, and open space. It was the site of Caleb Meade's sawmill, which, in the eighteenth and nineteenth centuries, provided lumber and fine paneling for this and many other houses in Greenwich. During the Depression, the house was restored and enlarged by architect Richard Henry Dana for the Carleton Granberrys. The modest gardens enhance the natural landscape. You will see dwarf conifers, old-fashioned perennials, roses, and a long row of seventy-year-old peonies. You may walk along the stony brook, passing the old dam and self-sown foxgloves growing willy-nilly. Or you may just sit and reflect in the old white pine grove, on the hill overlooking the orchard, beside the ponds, or on the lawn with a view.

Hours: 10 a.m. to 4 p.m.

From Merritt Parkway/Route 15, take Exit 31/North Street south towards town. Take third road on left, Taconic Road. Go down hill to Byfield Lane on right and park. Stonybrooke begins just past Byfield. *There are a few spaces to park farther on by mailbox. Those who have difficulty walking may go up drive to park on level.*

Proceeds shared with Green Fingers Garden Club/Garden History & Design

Old Lyme
Ruth Perry
Route 156, Old Lyme

Visit a cottage garden with a sense of humor. There is a rose garden, an herb garden, bog garden, and lots of perennials. A developing formal garden is the most recent addition.

Hours: 10 a.m. to 4 p.m.

From I-95, take Exit 70/Old Lyme. Turn onto Route 156 north. Go about 5 miles to intersection of Route 156 and Nehantic State Forest. Perry garden is on right. *Please park along Park Road.*

Stonington
Mr. & Mrs. Howard A. Fromson
43 Main Street, Stonington

This intimate village garden is a living area "extension" of this early nineteenth-century house. French doors open from several rooms onto brick walks that surround a lap pool. Along the walks are a shady border featuring a wide variety of hosta and ferns, a spreading magnolia, a culinary herb garden, and a Japanese nook. The garden has been a labor of love for both Howard and Sandy and their handiwork can be seen throughout.

Hours: 10 a.m. to 2 p.m.

From I-95, take Exit 91/Stonington Borough Village. At end of exit ramp, if coming from north, turn left; if coming from south, turn right. Go .25 mile and turn left onto North Main Street. Continue about 2 miles across Route 1 to stop sign and turn left onto Trumbull Street. At next stop sign, turn right over bridge (railroad tracks) into village. Follow Water Street to Union Street (Hungry Pallet) and turn left. Go 1 block and turn left onto Main Street. House is on corner of Main and Church Streets.

Mrs. Frederic C. Paffard, Jr.
389 North Main Street, Stonington

A century-old boxwood hedge a quarter of a mile long, rose arbors, and a perennial cutting garden are highlights of this old-fashioned garden. There are interesting old outbuildings, a carriage house, grapery, greenhouse, annual cutting gardens, a ha-ha, and a pond once used for ice—now home for the herons. English boxwood and perennial seedlings grown on site are available for sale with 10% of the proceeds donated to the Garden Conservancy.

Hours: 10 a.m. to 2 p.m.

From I-95, take Exit 91/Stonington Borough Village. Go south to North Main Street, then turn left towards Stonington Borough. Go about 1.5 miles to #389.

From Route 1, turn north onto North Main Street at traffic light. Number 389 is second driveway on right. *Park anywhere.*

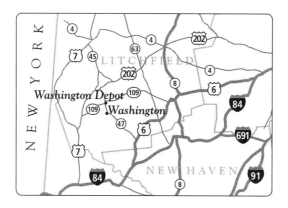

Saturday, June 21

LITCHFIELD COUNTY

WASHINGTON

Mr. & Mrs. J. Winston Fowlkes III

72 Potash Hill Road, Washington

This garden, designed by Nancy McCabe, consists of long perennial borders and a woodland garden. Two terraces are richly planted.

Hours: 2 to 6 p.m.

From Washington Green, take Wykeham Road about 2 miles, bearing right at fork. Turn right onto East Street, passing a complex of barns, and follow 1 mile to end. At stop sign, turn left, then make an immediate right onto Potash Hill Road. Follow to end. House, #72, is a barn with a 3-car garage. *Please park on road.*

Charles Raskob Robinson & Barbara Paul Robinson

88 Clark Road, Washington

Brush Hill includes a series of gardens on varied topography around an eighteenth-century Connecticut farmhouse and barn amidst old stone walls. The garden includes a rose walk featuring old roses and climbers, a fountain garden planted in yellows and purples, herbaceous borders, and a terraced garden planted in hot colors leading up to a garden folly and through an arch to a woodland walk with a series of cascading pools. There is an old Lord & Burnham greenhouse, along with a white wisteria-draped bridge over a half-acre pond with grass borders. The gardens have been featured on HGTV, *A Gardener's Diary,* in Rosemary Verey's book *The Secret Garden,* and in *House & Garden* and numerous other magazines. Visit www.BrushHillGardens.com

Hours: 2 to 6 p.m.

From I-84, take Exit 15/Southbury. Take Route 6 north to Route 47 and turn left. Go 4 miles, passing Woodbury Ski Area on left, and turn right onto Nettleton Hollow Road. Go 4.1 miles, past intersection of Wykeman and Carmel Hill Roads, and *watch for sign to enter parking field on left.*

George Schoellkopf

300 Nettleton Road, Washington

This is an old-fashioned, but unusual, rambling formal garden informally planted with an exuberant abundance of both common and exotic plants in subtle, and sometimes surprising, color combinations. High walls and hedges divide separate "rooms" and open to create interesting vistas out towards the landscape. New areas are currently under construction.

Hours: 3 to 6 p.m.

From I-84, take Exit 15/Southbury. Take Route 6 north through Southbury and Woodbury. Turn left onto Route 47 north. Go 4 miles, past Woodbury Ski Area on left, and turn right onto Nettleton Hollow Road. Go 1.7 miles. House is on right. *Please park along road.*

WASHINGTON DEPOT

Gael Hammer

63 River Road, Washington Depot

This is a cottage garden designed to engulf the house with flowers and shrubs and provide different spaces for outdoor living. Special areas include oversized borders, a grass garden, a white moon garden, an enormous "step" garden, and container gardens on an old-fashioned porch and sunny deck. The garden has been featured in *Martha Stewart Living* and *House Beautiful* magazines.

Hours: 10 a.m. to 4 p.m.

From Route 109, travel to Washington Depot. Take River Road .5 mile from town. *Please park in front of house.*

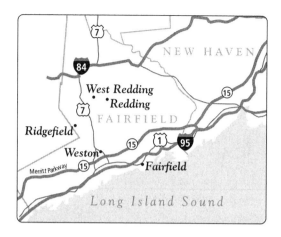

Sunday, June 22

FAIRFIELD COUNTY

FAIRFIELD

On the Harbor

328 Sasco Hill Road, Fairfield

My gardens surround an 1894 Second Empire-style house overlooking Southport Harbor. They were begun in 1996 with the help of Mike Donnally. Boxwood, beech, and arborvitae provide structure and continuity throughout the various gardens. A garden room looks out onto a small parterre, which is separated from the moss garden by antique garden gates. A small stone-and-brick terrace, designed by Agnes Clark in the 1950s, leads to the back terrace, overhung by an eighty-year-old white wisteria. Below the terrace are raised beds containing peonies and iris and below the raised beds are parterres, whose structure provides year-round interest. An organic heirloom vegetable garden transitions the upper gardens to the lower grass meadow.

Hours: 10 a.m. to 4 p.m.

From I-95, take Exit 19 and turn onto Post Road traveling east towards Fairfield. At first traffic light, turn right onto Sasco Hill Road. House, #328, is on right. *Please park along road.*

REDDING

Gardens at Horsefeathers

313 Umpawaug Road, Redding

Horsefeathers is known in Redding as the Aaron Barlow house. Joel Barlow, after whom the Redding high school is named, one of Aaron's brothers, lived here after the French Revolution. Joel, a diplomat and renowned poet, was an attaché at the U. S. embassy in Paris at the time of Thomas Jefferson and was instrumental in the signing of the Purchase of Louisiana from France. While residing in the house, he composed "The Columbiad," his most famous work. Circa 1723, the house is the oldest in Redding. The totally organic gardens are influenced by French and English period gardens and are structured around the "reflecting pool," with French curves of nepeta on the outer borders. Stone walls, boxwood, and a pergola give the garden architectural "bones" in all seasons.

Hours: 12 to 4 p.m

From Route 7 north, take Route 107 at Georgetown 1.7 miles to Umpawaug Road. Continue on Umpawaug 3.5 miles to Horsefeathers sign on left. *Look for parking signs on right.*

Ridgefield
Garden of Ideas
647 North Salem Road, Ridgefield

Fifteen years ago, this spot was covered with Kentucky bluegrass and poison ivy-infested woods. Today a fine collection of both woody and herbaceous ornamental plants grows here, along a stunning natural marsh. A large raised-bed vegetable garden produces a bounty of delicious edibles from April through November. Stroll through shade and sun, ponder poetic verse displayed along the way, and relax in one of many secluded nooks. Other points of interest include hand-built cedar structures, whimsical statuary, water features, unusual annuals, and lots of birds and bugs. A plankway across the marsh allows visitors a close-up look at a lovely crop of wild rice, *Zizania aquatica.*

Hours: 10 a.m. to 4 p.m.

From Route 35 in Ridgefield, take Route 116 for 2.9 miles. Garden is on left.

From Route 121 in North Salem, take Route 116 into Connecticut. House is on right, 1.3 miles from New York border. Please look for driveway with Garden of Ideas sign.

Weston
Birgit Rasmussen Diforio
7 Indian Valley Road, Weston

A steep and dramatic 100-foot-long granite ledge, uncovered and terraced by the owner, dominates this hilly site. It culminates at the rear of the property with a recirculating waterfall and pond. Large, undulating mixed borders emphasize contrasts in the color and texture of foliage. A stone terrace, tucked away at the start of the woodland walk, offers a completely different atmosphere and is a favorite retreat for reading and relaxing.

Hours: 10 a.m. to 4 p.m.

From Merritt Parkway/Route 15, take Exit 42 and go north on Route 57. At blinking traffic light past Weston Center, turn left over river and continue on Route 57 for about 3 miles. Indian Valley Road is on right.

From I-84, take Route 7 south. Turn left at Exxon gas station at Route 107, then right onto Route 57/Georgetown Road. Indian Valley Road is less than 1 mile on left.

Hughes-Sonnenfroh Gardens
54 Chestnut Woods Road, West Redding

Our twenty-two-year battle with the deer is at last over! We could no longer tolerate watching our beloved plants being eaten and last year we fenced in our entire five acres. What a difference a year makes. Our plants have recovered and are thriving in their protected environment. I am a landscape designer and my husband is an arborist, so we share a strong love of plants. We have enjoyed watching the "children" grow and many of the conifers and shrubs have developed into mature specimens. I like big borders—the wider, the deeper, the better I like it. I also believe in placing the right plants in the right places, so they are content and work hard for me, smothering the weeds and blooming their heads off. Concentrating on the long view has always been important to me and I am finally pleased with the garden settings on our property. After our 2002 Open Days, we realized we needed a more proper entrance to the gardens through the arbor. So we hope you'll come and visit and see the new deer-resistant border flanking the arbor. We don't need it now, but as a designer and gardener, I know how very frustrating gardening with deer can be! Look for a keyed garden map to help you identify the ornamental trees, evergreens, conifers, and deciduous shrubs on our property. Hopefully, our gardens will provide a worthwhile stop on the tour and a good dose of continuing education.

Hours: 10 a.m. to 4 p.m.

From I-84, take Exit 3/Route 7 south. Go 3 miles to traffic light at Route 35. Bear left, continue on Route 7 south for 1.5 miles. At third light, turn left onto Topstone Road. Go .25 mile downhill, cross railroad tracks, and bear left uphill for .5 mile. Take second left onto Chestnut Woods Road. House, #54, is third on right. *Please park along driveway or on north side of Chestnut Woods Road.*

From Merritt Parkway north, take Exit 39B onto Route 7 north. Go about 1.5 miles to end. Turn right at light. Go to second light and turn left onto Old Route 7 north, towards Wilton and Danbury. Travel 10 miles and watch for Walpole Woodworkers on right. Go 1 mile and turn right at light onto Topstone Road. Proceed as directed above.

From I-95 north, take Exit 15 to Route 7 north. Go .3 mile to Route 7 extension to end. Turn right at light at end. Take second left onto Old Route 7 north and proceed as directed above.

From Route 35 in Ridgefield, go east to fountain in Ridgefield. Turn left at fountain, proceed .25 mile, and turn right onto Route 102. Go 2 miles to Route 7. Turn left. Go 1.5 miles; look for Walpole Woodworkers on right. Go 1 mile to light at Topstone Road. Turn right and proceed as directed above.

Proceeds shared with the Redding Garden Club

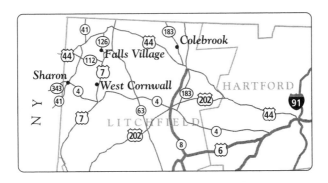

Saturday, June 28
LITCHFIELD COUNTY

COLEBROOK
Marveen & Michael Pakalik
46 Stillman Hill Road, Colebrook

One open, sunny acre with distant views of the Berkshires features three long herbaceous perennial/shrub borders, each devoted to the seasons, and a new evergreen shrub border which keeps mysteriously expanding. A lovely woodland garden blends with native flora. A stone patio features unusual container plantings and some of the funky garden ornaments were featured in the Time-Life book *Decorating Your Garden*.

Hours: 10 a.m. to 4 p.m.

From Route 8 north or Route 44 west, travel to Winsted and take Route 183 north to Colebrook. At intersection of Routes 182 and 183, turn left and go to top of hill. Number 46 is first white house on right.

From Route 44 east to Norfolk, bear left at George's Norfolk Garage and take Route 182 about 4 miles (just past Route 182A) to top of hill. Number 46 is white house on left. *Please park on street.*

FALLS VILLAGE
Bunny Williams
Point of Rocks Road, Falls Village

Interior designer and garden book author Bunny Williams' intensively planted fifteen-acre estate has a sunken garden with twin perennial borders surrounding a fishpond, parterre garden, year-round conservatory filled with tender plants, large vegetable garden with flowers and herbs, and woodland garden with meandering paths and a pond with a waterfall. There are also a working greenhouse and an aviary with unusual chickens and fantail doves. Recent additions include an apple orchard with mature trees, a rustic Greek Revival pool house folly, and a swimming pool with eighteenth-century French coping.

Hours: 10 a.m. to 4 p.m.

From Route 7 north, go to Falls Village. Turn left at blinking traffic light onto Main Street/Route 126. Bear right (still on Route 126). Go to stop sign at Point of Rocks Road. Driveway is directly ahead. *Please park in field adjacent to house.*

Lee Link
99 White Hollow Road, Sharon

Three stone walls cascade down a sunny hillside. The space between each is planted with perennial borders, which bloom with the flowering seasons of spring and summer. One level is set off by a water garden, which reflects a winter conservatory on the hill behind it.

Hours: 12 to 4 p.m.

From junction of Routes 7 and 112, turn onto Route 112. Go about 2 miles to "Entrance to Lime Rock Race Track" sign. Turn left onto White Hollow Road and travel 2.5 miles. House, #99, is on right, opposite a white fence.

From Route 41 in Sharon, turn right onto Calkinstown Road. Take second left onto White Hollow Road. Driveway is on left opposite a white fence.

Doug Mayhew—Jurutungo Viejo
20 Kirk Road, West Cornwall

On the banks of the Housatonic River, the gardens of Jurutungo Viejo offer unmatched vistas, which reflect the gardener's testament to nature and experimentation. Doug Mayhew and his firm, Mayhew Orion Inc., have been described as "an avant-garde voice who creates his own natural wonders." Jurutungo Viejo is an exotic oasis from another world. Gourds and castors pervade the monumental cast-iron temple alongside *Cycas, Araucaria, Cryptomeria, Agave, Dicksonia, Melianthus,* et al. Whether exploring the arboretum or getting lost among the moods of painters and poets, visitors can share in the unusual ecosystem this four-acre garden offers.

Hours: 10 a.m. to 4 p.m.

From West Cornwall, take Route 7 north about 1.5 miles. Turn right onto Kirk Road. Garden is located at #20. Follow signs.

From intersection of Routes 112 and 7, go about 3.5 miles south on Route 7 and turn left onto Kirk Road. *Please park along street*

Michael Trapp
7 River Road, West Cornwall

This Old World-style garden is intimate, with cobbled paths, terraced gardens, raised perennial beds, and reflecting pools. Overlooking the Housatonic River, the property has a distinct French/Italian flavor.

Hours: 10 a.m. to 4 p.m.

From Route 7, take Route 128 east through covered bridge into West Cornwall. Continue on Route 128, taking second left onto River Road. House is yellow with gray trim, first on left, sitting behind Brookside Bistro. *Please park in front or along road.*

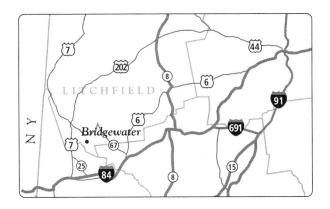

Sunday, June 29

LITCHFIELD COUNTY

BRIDGEWATER

Maywood Gardens

52 Cooper Road, Bridgewater

This private estate features a sunken perennial garden protected by ten-foot stone walls, a gazebo garden planted with butterfly- and hummingbird-attracting flowers and shrubs, a rose garden arranged in a French pattern design surrounded by a circle of hemlocks, a woodland path populated by mature beech and cherry trees as well as viburnums and rhododendrons, a ledge garden on an exposed hillside, a heather bed, a white garden, an herb garden, an ornamental kitchen garden, and a 4,000-square-foot greenhouse.

Hours: 10 a.m. to 2 p.m.

From I-84, take Exit 9 and travel north on Route 25 towards Brookfield Village. Turn right onto Route 133 east towards Bridgewater. Cross Lake Lillinonah Bridge and take first right after bridge onto Wewaka Brook Road. Go .75 mile and turn right onto Beach Hill Road to end. Turn right onto Skyline Ridge. Go .5 mile and turn right onto Cooper Road. *Please park on right across from greenhouse complex.*

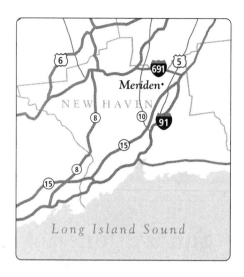

Sunday, July 6
NEW HAVEN COUNTY

MERIDEN
Jardin des Brabant
131 Corrigan Avenue, Meriden

This is one woman's enclosed garden retreat on three quarters of an acre since 1972. The upper lawn features a large beech and a perimeter of flowering shrubs, dwarf conifers, shade and sun perennials, kousa and florida dogwoods, and annuals. A seventy-five-foot dawn redwood dominates the lower gardens of perennials, roses, annuals, and vines. Grass paths lead toward, and past, a stone-and-stucco storage house with hayrack planters. A small potager, an ancient apple tree shading hostas and ferns, a side border with miniature lilac standards and lilies, and a *Viburnum plicatum* hedge complete the secluded rear garden, which dissolves into open lawn.

Hours: 1 to 5 p.m.

From I-84, take I-691 east to Exit 5/Chamberlain Highway. Turn right at end of exit and take an immediate right onto Steuben Street. Steuben becomes Corrigan at top of hill. Go around bend to beginning of cemetery on right. Garden is directly across street. From I-91, take I-691 west to Exit 6/Lewis Avenue. Turn left at end of exit. Turn left at end of Lewis onto Kensington Avenue. Turn left at the end of Kensington onto Chamberlain Highway. Go past Target store on right and look for Steuben Street immediately after 7-Eleven on left and highway exit on right. Proceed as directed above. Please park on either side of street. Watch for children in area.

Proceeds shared with Connecticut Horticultural Society

George Trecina

341 Spring Street, Meriden

This is a professional landscape designer's display and trial gardens, with one third of an acre of continuous mixed borders containing more than 300 varieties of woody plants and perennials, some unusual. The planting schemes are enhanced with an assortment of annuals, tender perennials, and container plantings with a decidedly tropical theme. The sloping front yard—structured with paths, walls, and stairways—features a white garden and a "wild" garden.

Hours: 1 to 5 p.m.

From I-91, take I-691 west to Exit 6/Lewis Avenue. Turn right off exit and follow to end. Turn right onto Hanover Street to first traffic light. Turn left onto Columbus Avenue and go to second stop sign. Turn left onto Prospect Avenue, then turn at first right onto Spring Street to fourth house on right, #341.

From I-84, take I-691 east to Exit 5/Chamberlain Highway. Turn right off exit and follow to end. Turn left onto West Main Street to the first light. Turn right onto Bradley Avenue and go to first stop sign. Turn left onto Winthrop Terrace and past light onto Columbus Avenue. Proceed as directed above. *Please park along Spring Street.*

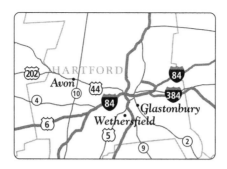

Sunday, July 20

HARTFORD COUNTY

<small>Avon</small>

Green Dreams—Garden of Jan Nickel

71 Country Club Road, Avon

Behind the iron gates of a twenty-year-old established garden, winding paths and secret rooms create a fantasy garden. Contrasting styles feature extravagant use of distinctive perennials, shrubs, and grasses. Vistas abound, offering contemporary and European ideas intertwined with elements of architectural interest. Iron, stone, wood, concrete, and pottery add dramatic flair to the Old World charm of this magnificent garden.

Hours: 10 a.m. to 4 p.m.

From I-84, take Exit 39/Farmington/Route 4. From intersection of Routes 10 and 4, turn right onto Route 10 for 5.7 miles to Route 44. Turn left and follow .7 mile to intersection of Route 10 and Old Farms Road. Turn left and travel 1.3 miles to Country Club Road. Turn right and travel .3 mile to #71. *Please park across street on Tamara Circle.*

Proceeds shared with Animal Friends of Connecticut

<small>Glastonbury</small>

Ferrante Garden

104 Partridge Landing, Glastonbury

Situated in a development of "shy" one-acre building lots, the challenge was to create a landscape that would afford privacy without being claustrophobic. We wanted to create the feeling of a Renaissance garden, with its symmetry and balance, without being overly rigid. A brick walk leading to a small pergola adds a focal point, while trees and shrubs of many different shades and textures define the shapes of the various beds.

Hours: 10 a.m. to 4 p.m.

Take Route 2 to Exit 8/Hebron Avenue/Route 94. Travel east 7 miles. Turn right into Balmoral development on Brentwood Drive. Remain on Brentwood to end (.5 mile). A white house with black shutters and a widow's walk on roof will be directly in front of you. Turn right. Counting "widow's walk" house, we are fifth on left.

The Murray Gardens
576 Thompson Street, Glastonbury

This is a colorful collection of gardens created for new construction, utilizing mature plantings of perennials divided and moved from our previous property, and unusual native trees. The property features three perennial borders planted along old stone walls and fences, a carpet rose bank and herb garden, a woodland path in a naturalized front yard setting, as well as a new sixty-foot hydrangea bed. Our backyard includes sun and shade plantings built into the pool deck and an inviting sunken Japanese garden accessed by a footbridge over a small stream connecting two ponds.

Hours: 10 a.m. to 4 p.m.

From Hartford, take Route 2 east to Exit 10. Turn left off exit ramp onto Route 83. Take first right onto Chimney Sweep Hill. Go uphill 1.5 miles to end. Turn left onto Thompson Street. House is about .25 mile on right, across from farm.

From the east, take Route 2 west to Exit 11. Go left off ramp, then take second right onto Thompson Street. Our house, #576, is 1.5 miles on right. *Please park on street.*

WETHERSFIELD
Gary Berquist
165 Jordan Lane, Wethersfield

This half-acre garden has three ponds, two streams, and nine waterfalls, with koi in one pond and goldfish in the others. Rare trees and plants are found among the steppingstone paths and rock-lined berms. A white Victorian bridge leads into the garden, which is anchored by a screened gazebo. Part shade garden, part butterfly garden, part water garden, and rock work offer something for everyone.

Hours: 10 a.m. to 4 p.m.

Take Exit 28 off I-91. Take immediate right onto Route 99 south exit. Come to traffic light and turn right onto Jordan Lane; #165 is on left before overpass.

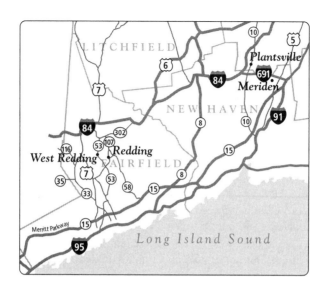

Sunday, August 10
FAIRFIELD COUNTY

REDDING
Highstead Arboretum
127 Lonetown Road, Redding

The sweet smell of swampland? A magnificent natural stand of sweet pepperbush fills the air with its summer scent. Nearly three acres of this unusually late native bloomer is made accessible by boardwalk for a dry-footed discovery of the swamp habitat at Highstead. This habitat is one of several at the arboretum maintained to allow the appreciation of the native plants, birds, and wildlife dwelling there. A one-hour guided walk will lead you to the pond and meadow, where selected cultivars of this shrub have been introduced for comparison. Set on fifty acres of geographic extremes, the arboretum is also open weekdays by appointment, and offering two other distinct seasonal walks on May 18 and June 1. Please call weekdays, 8:30 a.m. to 4:30 p.m., for more information, (203) 938-8809.

Hours: Guided walks at 10 a.m., 12 p.m., and 2 p.m.

From I-95 or Merritt Parkway/Route 15, take Route 7 north. Turn right onto Route 107 for 6 miles (be sure to follow signs for 107 as it crosses Route 53). Pass police station, Redding Elementary School, and Redding Country Club. Take second driveway on left after country club, 127 Lonetown Road. Follow signs into arboretum; driveway is .5 mile long.

WEST REDDING
Hughes-Sonnenfroh Gardens
54 Chestnut Woods Road, West Redding

Our twenty-two-year battle with the deer is at last over! We could no longer tolerate watching our beloved plants being eaten, and last year we fenced in our entire five acres. What a difference a year makes. Our plants have recovered and are thriving in their protected environment. I am a landscape designer and my husband is an arborist, so we share a strong love of plants. We have enjoyed watching the "children" grow and many of the conifers and shrubs have developed into mature specimens. I like big borders—the wider, the deeper, the better I like it. I also believe in placing the right plants in the right places, so they are content and work hard for me, smothering the weeds and blooming their heads off. Concentrating on the long view has always been important to me and I am finally pleased with the garden settings on our property. After our 2002 Open Days, we realized we needed a more proper entrance upon arrival to the gardens through the arbor. So we hope you'll come and visit and see the new deer-resistant border flanking the arbor. We don't need it now, but as a designer and gardener, I know how very frustrating gardening with deer can be! Look for a keyed garden map to help you identify the ornamental trees, evergreens, conifers, and deciduous shrubs on our property. Hopefully, our gardens will provide a worthwhile stop on the tour and a good dose of continuing education.

Hours: 10 a.m. to 4 p.m.

From I-84, take Exit 3/Route 7 south. Go 3 miles to traffic light at Route 35. Bear left, continue on Route 7 south, go 1.5 miles. At third light, turn left onto Topstone Road. Go .25 mile, downhill, cross railroad tracks, and bear left uphill .5 mile. Take second left onto Chestnut Woods Road. House, #54, is third on right. *Please park along driveway or on north side of Chestnut Woods Road.*

From Merritt Parkway/Route 15 north, take Exit 39B onto Route 7 north. Go about 1.5 miles to end. Turn right at light. Go to second light and turn left onto Old Route 7 north, towards Wilton and Danbury. Travel 10 miles and watch for Walpole Woodworkers on right. Go 1 mile and turn right at light onto Topstone Road. Proceed as directed above.

From I-95 north, take Exit 15 to Route 7 north. Go .3 mile to Route 7 extension to end. Turn right at light. Take second left onto Old Route 7 north and proceed as directed above. From Route 35 in Ridgefield, go east to fountain in Ridgefield. Turn left at fountain, proceed .25 mile, and turn right onto Route 102. Go 2 miles to Route 7. Turn left. Go 1.5 miles and look for Walpole Woodworkers on right. Go 1 mile to light at Topstone Road. Turn right and proceed as directed above.

Proceeds shared with the Redding Garden Club

PLANTSVILLE
The Kaminski Garden
513 Marion Avenue, Plantsville

I am always amazed as I pass from the front yard, where grass barely grows, through the gate into the four-year-old garden's hues of green punctuated with flowers. Mature trees anchor the yard; sweeping curves define garden beds where the emphasis is on foliage. The tumbled bluestone used for the patio, raised planting beds surrounding the deck, garden bed edgings, and the pathways to the freeform pool soothes the eye with its consistency. Shade predominates throughout, as do a wide variety of shade-tolerant perennials, shrubs, and Japanese maples. Sun abounds by the pool; specimen evergreens and sweeps of flowers thrive here.

Hours: 10 a.m. to 4 p.m.

From I-84, take Exit 30/Marion Avenue. From Hartford (I-84 west), turn right onto Marion; from Waterbury (I-84 east), turn left onto Marion. Once on Marion, travel about 1 mile, passing Frost Street. Next driveway on right is our house, #513. House is slate blue with detached two-car garage. *Please park in driveway.*

Proceeds shared with Dana Farber Cancer Institute/Womens Cancer Research Center

MERIDEN
Jardin des Brabant
131 Corrigan Avenue, Meriden

This is one woman's enclosed garden retreat on three quarters of an acre since 1972. The upper lawn features a large beech and a perimeter of flowering shrubs, dwarf conifers, shade and sun perennials, kousa and florida dogwoods, and annuals. A seventy-five-foot dawn redwood dominates the lower gardens of perennials, roses, annuals, and vines. Grass paths lead toward, and past, a stone-and-stucco storage house with hayrack planters. A small potager, an ancient apple tree shading hostas and ferns, a side border with miniature lilac standards and lilies, and a Viburnum plicatum hedge complete the secluded rear garden, which dissolves into open lawn.

Hours: 1 to 5 p.m.

From I-84, take I-691 east to Exit 5/Chamberlain Highway. Turn right at end of exit and take an immediate right onto Steuben Street. Steuben becomes Corrigan at top of hill. Go around bend to beginning of cemetery on right. Garden is directly across street.

From I-91, take I-691 west to Exit 6/Lewis Avenue. Turn left at end of exit. Turn left at end of Lewis onto Kensington Avenue. Turn left at the end of Kensington onto Chamberlain Highway. Go past Target store on right and look for Steuben Street immediately after 7-Eleven on left and highway exit on right. Proceed as directed above. Please park on either side of street. Watch for children in area.

Proceeds shared with the Connecticut Horticultural Society

George Trecina
341 Spring Street, Meriden

This is a professional landscape designer's display and trial gardens, with one third of an acre of continuous mixed borders containing more than 300 varieties of woody plants and perennials, some unusual. The planting schemes are enhanced with an assortment of annuals, tender perennials, and container plantings with a decidedly tropical theme. The sloping front yard—structured with paths, walls, and stairways—features a white garden and a "wild" garden.

Hours: 1 to 5 p.m.

From I-91, take I-691 west to Exit 6/Lewis Avenue. Turn right off exit and follow to end. Turn right onto Hanover Street to first traffic light. Turn left onto Columbus Avenue and go to second stop sign. Turn left onto Prospect Avenue, then turn at first right onto Spring Street to fourth house on right, #341.

From I-84, take I-691 east to Exit 5/Chamberlain Highway. Turn right off exit and follow to end. Turn left onto West Main Street to the first light. Turn right onto Bradley Avenue and go to first stop sign. Turn left onto Winthrop Terrace and past light onto Columbus Avenue. Proceed as directed above. *Please park along Spring Street.*

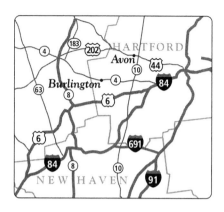

Sunday, September 7
HARTFORD COUNTY

AVON
Green Dreams—Garden of Jan Nickel
71 Country Club Road, Avon

Behind the iron gates of a twenty-year-old established garden, winding paths and secret rooms create a fantasy garden. Contrasting styles feature extravagant use of distinctive perennials, shrubs, and grasses. Vistas abound, offering contemporary and European ideas intertwined with elements of architectural interest. Iron, stone, wood, concrete, and pottery add dramatic flair to the Old World charm of this magnificent garden.

Hours: 10 a.m. to 4 p.m.

From I-84, take Exit 39/Farmington/Route 4. From intersection of Routes 10 and 4, turn right onto Route 10 for 5.7 miles to Route 44. Turn left and follow .7 mile to intersection of Route 10 and Old Farms Road. Turn left and travel 1.3 miles to Country Club Road. Turn right and travel .3 mile to #71. *Please park across street on Tamara Circle.*

Proceeds shared with the Animal Friends of Connecticut

BURLINGTON
The Salsedo Family Garden
15 Half King Drive, Burlington

Our gardens have been created on a unique location, a hilltop with a magnificent view 1,000 feet above sea level bordering on 4,000 acres of watershed and state forest. Begun in 1977, this site has undergone various physical transformations resulting in stonewalled terraces that render this acre-plus location usable. The last big change in 1995 added an expanded back-yard terrace with a pool, post-and-beam gardener's toolshed, dwarf conifer collection, vegetable garden, and a collection of hardy chrysanthemums. The front yard features low maintenance lawns punctuated by beds of native and exotic trees, shrubs, and perennials. The emphasis of this landscape is substainability with a focus on low care and minimal water requirements.

Hours: 10 a.m. to 4 p.m.

Take I-84 to Exit 39, and head west on Route 4 toward Farmington. Go through Farmington about 3 miles to Unionville Center to traffic light. Pass Friendly's on left. At light, bear right onto Route 4 (Old Masonic Hall on right, church on left). Go 1 mile along Farmington River. At light, turn left onto Route 4, and go up hill toward Burlington. Go about 1 mile, and turn left onto Belden Road (fish hatchery sign is on left). Go to stop sign. Turn right onto George Washington Turnpike, take next left onto Cornwall. Go up hill and turn right onto Nassahegan, then second left onto Half King Drive. Go to bottom of cul-de-sac to middle gravel drive with granite mailbox post labeled #15 leading to a red cedar house. *Please park in cul-de-sac.*

Sunday, September 14
FAIRFIELD COUNTY

GREENWICH
Stonybrooke
29 Taconic Road, Greenwich

About thirty years ago, we fell in love with this rambling old property of waterfalls, rock outcroppings, and open space. It was the site of Caleb Meade's sawmill, which, in the eighteenth and nineteenth centuries, provided lumber and fine paneling for this and many other houses in Greenwich. During the Depression, the house was restored and enlarged by architect Richard Henry Dana for the Carleton Granberrys. The modest gardens enhance the natural landscape. You will see dwarf conifers, old-fashioned perennials, roses, and a long row of seventy-year-old peonies. You may walk along the stony brook, passing the old dam and self-sown foxgloves growing willy-nilly. Or you may just sit and reflect in the old white pine grove, on the hill overlooking the orchard, beside the ponds, or on the lawn with a view.

Hours: 10 a.m. to 4 p.m.

From Merritt Parkway/Route 15, take Exit 31/North Street south towards town. Take third road on left, Taconic Road. Go down hill to Byfield Lane on right and park. Stonybrooke begins just past Byfield. *There are a few spaces to park farther on by mailbox. Those who have difficulty walking may go up drive to park on level.*

Proceeds shared with Green Fingers Garden Club

Public Gardens

FAIRFIELD COUNTY

Brookfield

Brookfield Historical Society Museum Garden

165 Whisconier Road, Brookfield (203) 740-8140 www.brookfieldcthistory.org

Designed by Dr. Rudy J. Favretti, this nineteenth-century herb garden complements the 1876 museum it adjoins. The focal point is a sundial surrounded by coral bells and thyme. There is a brick walk throughout the property. The garden was created and is maintained by the Brookfield Garden Club.

Hours: year round, daily, dawn to dusk

Admission: free

Located on corner of Routes 25 and 133 in Brookfield.

Darien

Bates-Scofield House

45 Old King's Highway North, Darien (203) 655-9233 www.darien.lib.ct.us/historical

The herb garden, adjacent to the Bates-Scofield House Museum, was planted and is maintained by the Garden Club of Darien. It contains many varieties of culinary, medical, and strewing herbs known to have been used in Connecticut in the eighteenth century.

Hours: year round, daily, dawn to dusk

Admission: grounds are free

From I-95, take Exit 13. Turn left onto Post Road. At second traffic light, turn left onto Brookside Road. Bear right at curve; house and parking lot are on left.

Fairfield

Connecticut Audubon Birdcraft Museum

314 Unquowa Road, Fairfield (203) 259-0416 www.ctaudubon.org

America's oldest private songbird sanctuary was founded in 1914. The five-acre sanctuary (originally fourteen acres), planted to attract birds with trees and shrubs, was designed by Mabel Osgood Wright (1859-1934), a pioneering American conservationist, photographer, and author. Demonstration plantings to attract birds and butterfly meadow restoration are in progress.

Hours: year round, Tuesday through Friday, 10 a.m. to 5 p.m., weekends, 12 to 5 p.m.

Admission: suggested donation $2 adults, $1 children

From I-95, take Exit 21/Mill Plain Road. Go north on Mill Plain Road .5 mile to stop sign. Turn right onto Unquowa Road and go .5 mile to parking entrance immediately on left after I-95 overpass.

NEW CANAAN
New Canaan Nature Center
144 Oenoke Ridge Road, New Canaan (203) 966-9577 www.newcanaannature.org

Two miles of trails crisscross natural areas of this forty-acre site, providing access to unusual habitat diversity—including wet and dry meadows, two ponds, wet and dry woodlands, dense thickets, an old orchard, and cattail marsh. Highlights include a bird and butterfly garden, a large herb garden, wildflower garden, naturalist's garden, small arboretum, and a 4,000-square-foot solar greenhouse.

Hours: year round, Monday through Saturday, 9 a.m. to 4 p.m.

Admission: free

From Merritt Parkway/Route 15, take Exit 37 and follow Route 124 through town. Located on Route 124, 1 mile north of New Canaan town center.

STAMFORD
The Bartlett Arboretum
151 Brookdale Road, Stamford (203) 322-6971

The arboretum is a 63-acre living museum embracing natural woodlands, perennial borders, meadows, display gardens, and an educational greenhouse. The site includes a trail system and a raised boardwalk through a seven-acre wetland. The arboretum offers a wide variety of educational programs and courses for children, enthusiasts, and serious horticulturists, plant sales, a plant information service, and guided tours and walks.

Hours: year round, daily, dawn to dusk

Admission: free

From Merritt Parkway/Route 15, take Exit 35. Follow High Ridge Road/Route 137 north (left off north- or southbound ramps) for 1.5 miles to Brookdale Road on left.

Stamford Museum & Nature Center
39 Scofieldtown Road, Stamford (203) 322-1646 www.stamfordmuseum.org

The center's 118 acres include woodland trails and a 300-foot boardwalk along a stream for parents with strollers, the elderly, and people in wheelchairs. A garden with plants indigenous to Connecticut is at the boardwalk entrance. The setting for the property includes flowering trees, shrubs, and ground covers, as well as a lake, waterfall, fountain, and sculpture.

Hours: year round, Monday through Saturday and holidays, 9 a.m. to 5 p.m., Sundays, 11 a.m. to 5 p.m.

Admission: $6 adults, $5 senior citizens/children 5 to 13, children under 5 free

From I-95, take Exit 7 to Washington Boulevard/Route 137 north to Merritt Parkway/Route 15. Located .75 mile north of Exit 35 on Merritt Parkway/Route 15 at junction of High Ridge Road/Route 137 and Scofield Road.

STRATFORD
Boothe Memorial Park—Wedding Rose Garden
55 Wild Wood Drive, Stratford (203) 381-2046

A brick pathway lined with perennials, annuals, and shrubs leads to the exuberant Wedding Rose Garden. Separated into two garden rooms, the Wedding Garden has a restored fountain and displays 'Love', 'Honor', and 'Cherish' roses. The Rainbow Room features a colorful explosion of thirty-four varieties. Climbing roses on trellises and an arbor enclose the garden.

Hours: year round, daily, dawn to dusk

Admission: free

From I-95 south, take Exit 38/Merritt Parkway. Continue to Exit 53. Go south on Route 110 to Main Street Putney, which forks to right. Head south on Main Street for .25 mile to park on left.

From I-95 north, take Exit 33. Follow Ferry Boulevard, bear left at fork, and go under thruway. Bear right onto East Main Street/Route 110 to its end (Main Street Putney). Go .7 mile to park on right.

WESTPORT
The Bird & Butterfly Demonstration Garden at Earthplace
10 Woodside Lane, Westport (203) 227-7253

The garden serves as an example of plants that do not threaten the Connecticut environment. Both native and well-behaved non-native plants were selected for their function: to feed and protect birds and butterflies. The promise to promote the balance of nature has been kept. It is a pesticide-free garden. The Native Plant Court at Earthplace features native plants found in southern Fairfield County.

Hours: year round, Monday through Saturday, 9 a.m. to 5 p.m., Sunday, 1 to 4 p.m.

Admission: suggested donation $2 adults, $1 children

From I-95, take Exit 17 and turn left at end of exit ramp onto Route 33 north. Go 1.5 miles and turn left onto Route 1. Go .5 mile and turn right at second traffic light onto King's Highway north. Take first left onto Woodside Avenue (becomes Woodside Lane). Go .9 mile to Earthplace.

WILTON
Weir Farm National Historic Site
735 Nod Hill Road, Wilton (203) 834-1896 www.nps.gov/wefa

From 1882 to 1919, Weir Farm was the summer home of the American Impressionist painter J. Alden Weir. Sixty acres have been preserved of the landscape that inspired Weir and his contemporaries. A Colonial Revival sunken garden, built by Weir's daughter in the 1930s, was rehabilitated in the spring of 1998.

Hours: year round, daily, dawn to dusk

Admission: free

From I-84, take Exit 3/Route 7 south. Follow for 10 miles into Branchville section of Ridgefield and turn right at traffic light onto Route 102 west. Take second left onto Old Branchville Road. Turn left at first stop sign onto Nod Hill Road. Follow for .7 mile; site is on right and parking on left.

HARTFORD COUNTY

BURLINGTON
Harriet Beecher Stowe Gardens
Beach Road, Burlington (860) 673-5782

A lovely example of overflowing, intimate cottage gardening on a domestic scale, the gardens were created by landscape designers Stevenson, Fuoco, and Canning. The main feature is the Blue Cottage Garden, ablaze in mid-June. July and beyond, the Pink and Red Garden, "High Victorian" Texture Garden, and Orange, Yellow, and White Garden take center stage. Enjoy many lovely historic roses in early June.

Hours: year round, daily, dawn to dusk

Admission: free

From I-84, take Exit 46/Sisson Avenue. Turn right onto Sisson Avenue, then right onto Farmington Avenue. Turn right onto Forest Street. Parking lot is on right.

FARMINGTON
Hill-Stead Museum's Sunken Garden
35 Mountain Road, Farmington (860) 677-4787 www.hillstead.org

Designed circa 1920 by landscape designer Beatrix Jones Farrand, this one-acre garden is surrounded by original stone walls and includes thirty-six different flower beds. Nearly ninety varieties of perennials, in combinations of pinks, blues, white, purples, and grays, are represented.

Hours: year round, daily, 7 a.m. to dusk

Admission: free

From I-84, take Exit 39/Route 4 west. Go to second traffic light and turn left onto Route 10 south/Main Street. At next light, turn left onto Mountain Road. Museum entrance is .25 mile on left.

Stanley-Whitman House
37 High Street, Farmington (860) 677-9222 www.stanleywhitman.org

Period herb garden. Public tours available.

Hours: May through October, Wednesday through Saturday 12 to 4 p.m.; November through April, weekends, 12 to 4 p.m.; or by appointment

Admission: $5 adults, $4 seniors, $2 students

From I-84, take Exit 39/Route 4. Proceed straight on Route 4 west .8 mile to traffic light at intersection of Routes 4 and 10. Turn left at light onto Route 10/Main Street, proceed about .2 mile to next light, turn left onto Mountain Road, and proceed .2 mile. Turn left onto High Street and go .1 mile. Look for museum sign on right.

HARTFORD
Elizabeth Park Rose & Perennial Garden
Asylum Avenue, Hartford (860) 231-9443 www.elizabethpark.org

This 15,000-specimen rose garden is the oldest municipal rose garden in the country. Also included are perennials, rock gardens, heritage roses, an herb garden, a wildflower garden, and annual displays. The Lord & Burnham greenhouses offer seasonal displays. The new cafe is open year round.

Hours: year round, daily, 6 a.m. to 10 p.m.; greenhouses, weekdays, 8 a.m. to 3 p.m.

Admission: free

From I-84, take Exit 44/Prospect Avenue. Head north on Prospect Avenue. Park is on corner of Prospect and Asylum Avenues.

WEST HARTFORD
Noah Webster House
227 South Main Street, West Hartford (203) 521-5362 www.ctstateu.edu/noahwebster.html

The Noah Webster House has a raised-bed teaching garden planted with herbs and other plants available to the Websters during the middle of the eighteenth century. A small demonstration plot of vegetables is also grown. Plants are labeled, so visitors may guide themselves through the garden.

Hours: year round, daily, dawn to dusk

Admission: free

Located 1 mile south of I-84 at Exit 41. Follow signs at end of exit ramp and travel for 1 mile. Museum is on left.

Webb House Colonial Revival Garden at the Webb-Deane-Stevens Museum

211 Main Street, Wethersfield (860) 529-0612 www.webb-deane-stevens.org

Designed by landscape architect Amy Cogswell in 1921 and restored in 1999-2000, the garden features stone-dust walkways leading to handmade cedar arbors and Colonial Revival-style geometric beds filled with old-fashioned flowers such as Canterbury bells, larkspur, hollyhocks, perennial foxglove, and twelve rose varieties.

Hours: May through October, Wednesday through Monday, 10 a.m. to 4 p.m.; November through April, weekends only, 10 a.m. to 4 p.m.

Admission: free

From I-91,take Exit 26 and follow signs to Historic District and Webb House and Deane House.

LITCHFIELD COUNTY

BETHLEHEM

Bellamy-Ferriday House & Garden

9 Main Street North, Bethlehem (203) 266-7596 www.hartnet.org/~als

Initially designed circa 1920, the Ferriday Garden is a romantic, nine-acre landscape comprised of interesting woody and herbaceous plants. Since 1992, the Antiquarian and Landmarks Society staff has been restoring the large collections of lilacs, old roses, peonies, and perennials. A formal yew and chamaecyparis parterre connects an orchard and meadow.

Hours: May through October, Wednesday, Friday, and weekends, 11 a.m. to 4 p.m.

Admission: $3 garden, $5 house and garden

From I-84, take Exit 15/Southbury. At end of exit ramp, take Route 6 east 13 miles to Route 61 and turn left. At intersection with Route 132, stay on Route 61 and take first left into driveway.

BRIDGEWATER

Beatrix Farrand Garden at Three Rivers Farm

694 Skyline Ridge Road, Bridgewater (860) 354-1788

This 1921 garden was rediscovered in 1993 and recreated adapting the original Farrand hardscape and design to the present environmental conditions. The garden is located within a beautiful 275-acre property where the Shepaug and Housatonic Rivers converge. A 1931 magazine article described the entire property as a Chinese garden and "arboretum of rare charm," with 105 varieties of Chinese flora.

Hours: May through September, fourth Sunday of the month, or by appointment

Admission: $5

From I-84, take Exit 9 and travel north on Route 25 to Brookfield Center. Turn right onto Route 133 east towards Bridgewater. Cross Lake Lillinonah Bridge and take first right onto Wewaka Brook Road. Go .75 mile and turn right onto Beach Hill Road to end. Turn right onto Skyline Ridge Road. Go to dead end road and take a sharp left. Please park along road between buildings.

Laurel Ridge Foundation
Wigwam Road, Litchfield

The display of the genus *Narcissus* was planted over about ten acres in 1941. The original 10,000 daffodils have naturalized for the past fifty years. The current owners have maintained the display and welcome visitors to drive by and share its splendor.

Hours: April through May, daily, dawn to dusk

Admission: free

Take Route 118 east from Litchfield to Route 254. Turn right and go 3.5 miles. Turn right onto Wigwam Road. Planting is about 1 mile on left.

White Flower Farm
Route 63, Litchfield (860) 567-8789 www.whiteflowerfarm.com

White Flower Farm is best known as a mail-order nursery, but it's also a great place to visit. In addition to the working nursery, the grounds are home to an impressive collection of mature trees and shrubs. There are also numerous display gardens featuring perennials, tender perennials and annuals, bulbs, and roses. Tour maps are available at the visitor center or the store.

Hours: April through October, daily, 9 a.m. to 6 p.m.; November through March, daily, 10 a.m. to 5 p.m.

Admission: free

The garden is located on Route 63; it is .7 mile north of Route 109 and 3.5 miles south of Route 118. Watch for sign and park in lot just north of store.

THOMASTON
Cricket Hill Garden
670 Walnut Hill Road, Thomaston (860) 283-1042 www.treepeony.com

A visit to this garden/nursery has been likened to stepping into a scroll painting of Chinese tree peonies. See more than 200 named varieties of tree peonies in an array of colors, flower forms, and fragrances. Free catalog available.

Hours: May through June, Wednesday through Sunday, 10 a.m. to 4 p.m.; other times by appointment

Admission: free

From I-95 or I-84, take Route 8 north. Take Exit 38/Thomaston, turning left at bottom of exit ramp onto Main Street. Turn left at third traffic light onto Route 254. Go .5 mile on Route 254 to a blinking yellow light. Turn left onto Walnut Hill Road. Go up hill 1 mile and see our sign on right.

WOODBURY
Gertrude Jekyll Garden at the Glebe House Museum
Woodbury (203) 263-2855

In 1926, Gertrude Jekyll was commissioned to plan an "old-fashioned" garden to enhance a new museum dedicated to America's first Episcopal bishop. Although small in comparison to other designs she completed, the garden includes 600 feet of classic English-style mixed border and foundation plantings, a small formal quadrant, and an intimate rose allée.

Hours: House open April through October, Wednesday through Sunday, 1 to 4 p.m., November, weekends only; 1 to 4 p.m. Garden open year round, daily, dawn to dusk

Admission: $2 garden only, $5 house and garden

From I-84, take Exit 15/Southbury. Continue on Route 6 east for 10 minutes to Woodbury. Look for junction with Route 317. Take Route 317 to fork, bear left, and Glebe House Museum is 100 yards ahead.

MIDDLESEX COUNTY

MIDDLETOWN
Shoyoan Teien—The Freeman Family Garden
343 Washington Terrace, Middletown (860) 685-2330 www.wesleyan.edu.east

Shoyoan Teien is a Japanese-style viewing garden designed and built by Stephen Morrell in 1995. Inspired by the "dry landscape" aesthetic, the garden's raked gravel riverbed evokes the prominent bend in the Connecticut River as it flows through wooded hills near Middletown. Japanese tea ceremonies are periodically performed in the adjacent tatami room.

Hours: Open Day event May 17, 10 a.m. to 12 p.m., otherwise open weekends during academic year, noon to 4 p.m.; please call for specific open dates

Admission: free

From the north, take I-91 south to Exit 22 (left exit) to Exit 15/Route 9 and follow signs to Wesleyan.

From the south, take I-95 to Exit 18/I-91 north or take Merritt/Wilbur Cross Parkway/ Route 15 to Route 66 east and follow signs to Wesleyan.

From the Northeast, take Massachusetts Turnpike/I-90 west to I-84 west to Hartford, then I-91 south to Exit 22 south (left exit). Go south on Route 9 and follow signs to Exit 15/Wesleyan.

Take I-95 south through Providence, to Exit 15/Route 9 north and follow signs to Wesleyan.

HAMDEN
Pardee Rose Gardens
180 Park Road, Hamden (203) 946-8142

The Pardee Rose Garden covers about three acres in East Rock Park. The rose beds are laid out geometrically, leading to a three-tiered central brick rose garden, and are planted with 1,500 rosebushes. More than 400 named varieties are currently grown. There are two greenhouses, as well as annual and perennial flower plantings.

Hours: year round, daily, dawn to dusk

Admission: free

From I-95, take I-91 to New Haven. Take Exit 5 and continue north on State Street for 2 miles. Turn left onto Farm Road. Garden is 1 block up hill.

COVENTRY
Caprilands Herb Farm
534 Silver Street, Coventry (860) 742-7244 www.caprilands.com

More than thirty theme gardens designed by Adelma Grenier Simmons illustrate the use of herbaceous plants, shrubs, annuals, vegetables, and herbs in numerous creative and decorative settings. Highlights include a silver garden, Saints' Garden, Shakespeare Garden, butterfly garden, botanic garden, naturalist's garden, and dyer and weaver's garden.

Hours: year round, daily, except holidays, 9 a.m. to 5 p.m.

Admission: free

The farm is on Silver Street in North Coventry, south of Routes 44 and 31. Route 31 is accessed from I-84. Route 44 is accessed from I-384E.

FLORIDA

A Caribbean Courtyard by the Sea, Vero Beach.
Photo by Mark Schumann

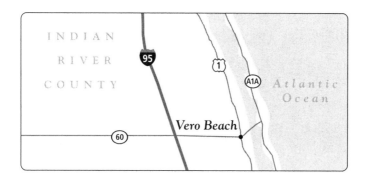

Saturday, April 5
INDIAN RIVER COUNTY

Vᴇʀᴏ Bᴇᴀᴄʜ
A Caribbean Courtyard by the Sea
2255 Windward Way, Vero Beach

My courtyard is typical of Andalusian courtyards in Spain, which were recreated in the Caribbean during the Spanish conquest. Since I was born in Cuba, I wanted a courtyard similar to those. Mine is anchored by a central fountain surrounded by Canary Island palms and masses of multicolored impatiens, birds of paradise, and gardenia bushes. The courtyard leads to a lap pool visible from the courtyard through a jasmine-covered archway. A wide variety of tropical palms, plants, and bushes of red bougainvillea and pink hibiscus surround the pool area.

Hours: 10 a.m. to 4 p.m.

From Palm Beach, take I-95 north to Exit 68/Route 60/Vero Beach. Go east on Route 60 about 8.5 miles to traffic light at Indian River Boulevard. Turn right (south). Go .5 mile to first light at 17th Street. Turn left (east) and go over bridge. At first light, turn right (south) onto Route A1A. Travel about 4 miles and look for The Moorings sales information office on right. Look for American flag flying on mast at Windward Way. Turn left (east) onto Windward Way. Follow to end of street to last house on right.

From Melbourne, travel south on Route 1 to Vero Beach. Once in town, look for 17th Street. There is a light at intersection and a Walgreens on northwest corner. Turn left (east) onto 17th Street and go over bridge. Proceed as directed above. *Please park on street.*

Garden of Patricia & Robert Hubner
911 Greenway Lane, Vero Beach

Experience the serenity of this glorious garden embracing harmonious shades of green and varying textures of leaves, fronds, and branches, all shaded by a canopy of majestic live oaks. Touches of pure white emerging from azaleas and gardenias enhance the cool, calm setting. A unique, bold, blue-green Bismark palm stands as a sentry at the front entry. Stroll around the path to the rear of the house to enjoy views of the verdant golf course in both directions. Enter the screened terrace, dominated by a handsome black rectangular pool and a fountain surrounded by sago and fishtail palms, beautifully enhanced by the owners' expansive, magnificent collection of white orchids. The focal point of the entrance to this tranquil landscape is the replica of Claude Monet's famous Giverny bridge, which spans a trickling black stone pool and myriad lush jungle ferns. Even the artist himself would be inspired to paint in such surroundings.

Hours: 10 a.m. to 4 p.m.

From I-95, take Exit 68/Route 60, proceed east to Indian River Boulevard (about 8 miles), and turn right. Proceed to next traffic light and turn left onto 17th Street Bridge (before power plant on left). Cross over Route A1A and take first immediate left onto Club Drive. At second stop sign, turn right onto Greenway Lane; first driveway on left is #911. After your visit to Hubner garden, proceed east on Greenway Lane to Ocean Drive, where you will find Sandy's Garden at intersection of Ocean and Ladybug Lane.

Mangrove Gardens at Carwill Oaks
455 Coconut Palm Road, Vero Beach

Located on the Indian River Lagoon, our garden encompasses mangroves, wetlands, lagoons, spoil islands, and upland grounds accessible by a series of walkways, bridges, and paths. Enter the mangroves from the drive court and be greeted by the soft gurgling of the freshwater stream as it trips its way through a mini-rain forest. Follow the forest paths north to Serenity Island and stop for a visit in the Thai Orchid House. Proceed along Dendrobium Walk to General's Island and meet our permanent visitor from Xian, China. Continue west along Evelyn's Walk toward the sound of Tibetan wind chimes and find the Kitchen Garden, which is located along the Indian River. Wander the paths through the Kitchen Garden and proceed directly south along River Walk, crossing the southern lawn to a path that leads you to Panther's Lair walkway and island. View a large lagoon containing creatures indigenous to our area. Possibly see various wading birds feeding in the shallows of the lagoon. Return to the southern lawn and proceed along the east side of the house to the lake terrace with its herb garden pots. The drive court where the tour started is a short walk away via a paver path through the potting/growing area used for propagation of some of the plants just seen. It is our hope that our gardens will demonstrate that mankind and mangroves are not mutually exclusive but can co-exist and flourish. Here the mangrove fringes and their tidal lakes provide a place for all marine life to begin—a nursery for the ocean's bounty. Take away with you the thought that, with careful planning, this precious ecosystem, so important to our rivers and oceans, can and should be preserved for the present and for all time.

Hours: 10 a.m. to 2 p.m.

From Route 60, proceed to Route A1A north and go about 2 miles. Turn left (west) onto Fred Tuerk Drive at Indian River Shores Town Hall. Follow road to rear gate of community of John's Island. Register your vehicle with guard, who will issue you a numbered Garden Conservancy sign, which must be prominently displayed on your windshield. Proceed as directed by guard. (Visitors will be admitted at gate only by showing a copy of *The Garden Conservancy's Open Days Directory, 2003 Edition.* No exceptions.)

Proceeds shared with McKee Botanical Garden and the Environmental Learning Center

Sandy's Garden
921 Ladybug Lane, Vero Beach

In creating our new environment, I knew I wanted to be in harmony with the rich history of our neighborhood, Old Riomar, famous for its historic homes and oak-canopied lanes. I had the luxury and challenge of creating something from a clean palette, so I started with a sense that it was more about the land than about a building. I wanted the garden as part of my life, not as a supplement to it. So, one enters the jasmine-covered arched garden space, by auto or on foot, wandering on Chicago brick paths around the south end through my orchid pagoda into the motor court, continuing on between the main house and guest cottage to the north end of the property. This is where I have my own little citrus grove, which thrives on the warm winter salt air and moisture, providing my kitchen with fresh grapefruit, oranges, and limes and their hypnotic aroma during the spring blossom season. Several thunbergia vines run almost wild, adding a kind of riotous look to the north space. Facing the ocean side is my pool garden, bordered by birds of paradise, seagrape, plumbago, and cracker rosebushes. The outdoor loggia is filled with pots of seasonal plants and overlooks the southeast garden, where my little boy bird bath attracts local birds, bees, and butterflies. From this outdoor space one goes through a gate to my kitchen garden, which is filled with herbs, seasonal flowers, topiaries, and architectural garden pieces.

Hours: 10 a.m. to 4 p.m.

From Route 60, go south on Club Drive to Ladybug Lane. House is located on corner of Ladybug and Ocean Drive. *Please park on street.*

Proceeds shared with McKee Botanical Garden

Public Gardens
INDIAN RIVER COUNTY

Vero Beach
McKee Botanical Garden
350 U.S. Highway 1, Vero Beach (772) 794-0601 www.mckeegarden.org

The garden is eighteen acres of what was originally an eighty-acre tropical hammock designed by landscape architect William Lyman Phillips in the 1930s. McKee is on the National Register of Historic Places and received Outstanding Achievement Award for Historic Landscape by the Florida Trust for Historic Preservation.

Hours: Tuesday through Sunday, 10 a.m. to 5 p.m.; closed major holidays

Admission: $6 adults, $5 seniors citizens, $3.50 children

Garden is located at 350 U.S. Highway 1, at southern gateway to Vero Beach, on the mainland. It is 2 hours southeast of Orlando and 1 hour north of West Palm Beach.

ILLINOIS

Markus Collection & Garden, Highland Park.
Photo by Linda Oyama Bryan.

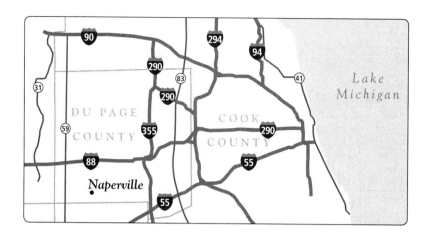

Saturday, June 14
WILL COUNTY

NAPERVILLE
Lynn Dowd's Garden
2504 River Woods Drive, Naperville

I have transformed a soybean field into a private arboretum and botanical garden. My garden includes whimsical characters such as a wizard, lumberjack, Indian, and black bear and provides complete tranquility, in marked contrast to my work as an attorney. I have recently added a historically correct fourteen-foot totem pole to the portion of my garden that I am sculpting into a prairie. From spring through fall, the colors are constantly changing. I truly enjoy what has become a work in progress.

Hours: 10 a.m. to 4 p.m.

From downtown Naperville, take Washington Street south to Naper Boulevard. Turn left and go to first street on right, River Woods Drive. Go to end of street, #2504.

From Naperville Road, travel south and merge into Naper Boulevard south to River Woods Drive. Turn left and go to end of street, #2504. *Please park on street.*

Ron & Linda Henry
28W700 Leverenz, Naperville

The garden, backed by open vistas, is an exuberant combination of flowering beds and borders full of vibrant and unusual annuals and perennials, two ponds, and a variety of shrubs, vines, and grasses. Ablaze with color and awash in interesting shapes and textures, the garden is an outdoor extension of the house. Trellises and arbors hold roses, clematis, and annual vines. In early September, the billowing white sweet clematis running up the custom-made trellises at the side of the house holds center stage in the white garden. A bridge, spanning the faux lake of blue fescue, treats the visitor to one of the many elements of Linda's creativeness in the whimsical touches amidst the blue grass, while the various tender summer bulbs planted throughout the grounds add a tropical feel. The planting schemes are further enhanced by an assortment of container plantings. Many out-of-the-ordinary annuals, a bouquet waiting to be gathered, attest to our interest in the rare, new, and unusual.

Hours: 10 a.m. to 4 p.m.

From I-88, take Naperville Road exit south to 75th Street (Naperville Road becomes Naper Boulevard about .5 mile south of I-88). Turn right onto 75th and proceed about 3.75 miles to Book Road. Turn left, and proceed about 2 miles to Leverenz, and turn left. House is several down on north side (left) of street. *Please park on street.*

Debra Doud Stone
2487 Westbranch Court, Naperville

A river, a creek, a 100-year-old burr oak, and a large pond are the natural "backbones" of our garden, providing both beautiful scenery and panoramic vistas. As striking as these treasures are, when we purchased this barren property approximately ten years ago, they provided only the bare essentials of the basic garden design. Gradually, we have added structure of our own. Six arbors, several stone patios, and strategically placed benches are all tied together by winding grassy pathways, which bid you to explore and see what surprises await around the next corner. One room flows into the next and, over time, they have each acquired their own personalities. A woodland garden has evolved around the hammock, a large rose garden exists in the center of the property, and several gardens exist in both dense, as well as dappled, shade. Framed by a weeping larch, a tropical paradise resides in a hidden corner. The cottage garden beckons butterflies and birds, while the kitchen garden basks in sunlight near the back door. Plantings include the ordinary, but more so the unusual, with many varieties of magnolias, Japanese maples, and tree peonies, as well as an interesting array of hydrangeas scattered throughout the landscape. In addition, a young wisteria vine is making itself at home covering one of the arbors, espaliered apple trees form the backbone of the kitchen garden, and two of the six arbors are literally encased with blooming roses right around the middle of June. Less commonly seen trees, including a tulip tree and dawn redwood, provide shade as well as horticultural and vertical interest. We have attempted to develop a garden that is a relaxing sanctuary, yet full of interest to both the novice and seasoned gardener alike.

Hours: 10 a.m. to 4 p.m.

From I-88, take Naperville Road exit south to 75th Street (Naperville Road becomes Naper Boulevard about .5 mile south of I-88). Turn right and proceed to Washington. Turn left (south) and follow to Ring Road. Turn right, then take first left onto Knoch Knolls. Take first left into Rivermist subdivision, go over bridge, and turn right onto Westbranch Court. Follow to cul-de-sac, which we are in the center of.

Proceeds shared with the DuPage Community Clinic

Saturday, June 21

DU PAGE COUNTY

WEST CHICAGO

Swan Oaks & Gardens

1 N 352 Indian Knoll Road, West Chicago

Swan Oaks & Gardens is a twenty-acre site, heavily wooded with large oak and hickory, with a meadow and two ponds, that are home to two mute swans. The perennial gardens are located over several acres surrounding the house. They consist of a terraced garden, courtyard garden, spring wildflower garden, and an extensive perennial border. The design was accomplished by Anthony Tyznik, former chief landscape architect at the Morton Arboretum in Lisle, Illinois.

Hours: 10 a.m. to 4 p.m.

From the east or west, take I-88 to Winfield Road exit. Continue north about 5 miles to Geneva Road. Turn left and go about 1 mile to Indian Knoll Road. Turn right and proceed .5 mile to #1 N 352 on west side of street. *Please park on street.*

From the north, take Route 59 to Route 64/North Avenue and turn left. Proceed 1.5 miles to Prince Crossing Road and turn right. Go about 2 miles to Geneva Road and turn left. Proceed as directed above.

Sunday, June 22
COOK COUNTY

KENILWORTH
Louellen & Tim Murray Garden
315 Essex Road, Kenilworth

Walls, gates, and pathways invite the visitor to meander, investigate, and discover. The front garden takes its inspiration from the pattern of windows framing the front door. Presiding over the mixed plantings are four standard *Syringa meyeri* 'Paliban' trees. Moving southward, one passes through a secretive "Rhododendron Hell," which harkens back to my Appalachian roots. This thickly planted broadleaf woodland features a seven-foot-tall *Rhododendron* 'Northern Lights'. The patio garden next offers a panoramic vista. Raised flower beds, a tiny fishpond, a "crazy quilt" of pavers, and containers galore nestle around an antique iron gate. Lastly, the courtyard rock garden bids farewell in its cacophony of colorful alpines. It is to Craig Bergmann Landscape Design and to my very supportive husband that this garden owes its existence.

Hours: 10 a.m. to 2 p.m.

From Edens Expressway/I-94, exit east onto Lake Avenue/Old Skokie Highway. Continue east to Greenbay Road. Turn north and proceed to intersection at Kenilworth Avenue. Turn east and go 4 blocks to Essex Road. Turn south. Number 315 is last house on left in first block south of Kenilworth Avenue. *Please park on street.*

WINNETKA
Beauty Without Boundaries
1130 Laurel Avenue, Winnetka

"House in the Garden" is for visitors of any age or ability. The owner worked with Deborah Nevins to create a classical garden without barriers, yet with a sense of intimacy between people and the landscape. The Hicks-yew garden rooms each create a different experience. From the terrace, hide away in the sixteenth-century topiary garden and pergola with Chinese roundels. Gaze at the dappled shade of the Haifa honey-locust allée with tapestry-like plantings. See the sturdy, lowland plants that populate a dell and the amphitheater formed by billowy cushions of boxwood; the gracious ribbon-like garden path is wide enough for two people, one in a wheelchair. The accessible decomposed granite path drains quickly. Benches strategically punctuate the path (distance can also be a barrier). Behind the waterspout, the evergreen path gives the feel of a walk in the forest. The symmetrical, open lawn with waterspout and beech tree is bordered by an eight-foot sandy subsurface that packs hard and is bump- and barrier-free. York stone pavers are set with one-eighth-inch joints in stonedust for fast drainage with enough roughness to grip soles and rubber tires, yet not so much to be bumpy. All house entrance courts slope slightly, avoiding the need for steps and adding access for all guests to the French-styled manor house. If you are interested in learning more about gardens with this type of accessibility, please visit the Enabling Garden at the Chicago Botanic Garden.

Hours: 10 a.m. to 4 p.m.

From Edens Expressway/I-94 south, take Tower Road exit. Proceed east to Burr (1 block before Green Bay Road). Turn right and go 2 blocks. Enter property through 2 pillars across from Hubbard Woods School.

From Edens Expressway/I-94 north, take Willow Road east exit. Go to Hibbard Road, turn left, go to Tower Road, turn right, and proceed as directed above.

Dorothy & John Gardner
94 Indian Hill Road, Winnetka

This second-generation garden was designed by John's mother in 1926. The original landscape garden and design are based on the principles of focus and axis. A sweeping park-like view in the front extends west to the expanse of the golf course. Five small but distinct gardens behind the house provide a good example of how to maximize the use of one acre. The second generation added a swimming pool designed as a reflecting pool and integrated into the garden by an allée of columnar maples. Gardens include a small white garden off the canopied north terrace, four parterres of roses, three parterres of vegetables and herbs, and a perennial cutting garden.

Hours: 10 a.m. to 4 p.m.

From Edens Expressway/I-94, take Lake Avenue exit if traveling north. Take Skokie Road exit to Lake Avenue if traveling south. Go east to Ridge Avenue, turn left (north), and drive .9 mile to entrance of Indian Hill Road (#100-55). *Please park in lot by gate next to paddle courts and walk a short distance to #94. No cars will be allowed to park on road.*

Highland Park

Markus Collection & Garden

484 Hillside Drive, Highland Park

Brent remembers gardening with his mother when he was just a toddler. At thirteen, he discovered his real passion: conifers. At twenty, Brent completed a coveted summer internship with the legendary Belgian landscape architects Jacques and Peter Wirtz. Brent is currently in his junior year in Cornell University's renowned landscape architecture program, concentrating in horticulture and Japanese garden design. An outstanding, extensive collection of conifers, evergreen shrubs, and Japanese maples, along with the cyclical season of foliage and flower, can transform the banal, twiggy, and sometimes lifeless northern garden into a treasure to behold. Enjoy!

Hours: 10 a.m. to 4 p.m.

From Chicago, take I-94 west towards Milwaukee. Continue on Route 41 north. Exit at Clavey Road and turn right to go east. One mile down, before driving up hill, turn left onto Hillside Drive. Continue straight, past road on left, and turn into cul-de-sac on left. Number 484 is white house with fire hydrant in front. *Please park on street.*

From northern suburbs, take Route 41 south towards Chicago. Exit at Clavey Road/ Skokie Boulevard. Turn right onto Skokie Bulevard and immediate right onto Clavey Road. Proceed as directed above.

From western suburbs, take I-294 toll road to Lake Cook Road. Turn to go east. After 4 miles, turn left (north) onto Skokie Valley Road and go .5 mile. Turn right onto Clavey Road (east) and proceed as directed above.

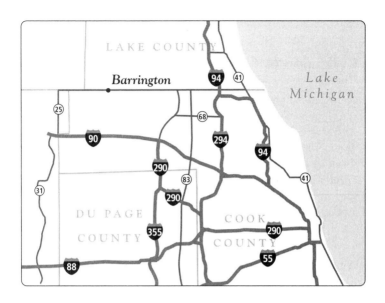

Saturday, June 28

LAKE COUNTY

BARRINGTON

The Gardens at Wandering Tree—
The "Glorée & Tryumfant" Garden Railway

125 Arrowhead Lane, Barrington

Thirty-five years ago, my husband, Harvey, and I purchased a ten-acre property known as Wandering Tree. Nestled beside a three-acre pond frequented by waterfowl, the gardens of Wandering Tree are varied. There are rose gardens, a woodland garden featuring a 400-year-old oak tree, a pleached allée of twenty-four crab apple trees, a Japanese-style garden with a bridge and stream, an herbaceous border, a sunken formal vegetable potager, dooryard rose gardens, and, perhaps most importantly, the "Glorée and Tryumfant" Garden Railway. This internationally recognized prototypical garden railway consists of 6,000 square feet of miniature waterfalls, bridges, trestles, streams, city and country vignettes, and miniature plant material of every description, as well as eleven different half-inch scale operating toy trains. Our company, Huff and Puff Industries Ltd., designs and installs garden railways nationwide.

Hours: 10 a.m. to 4 p.m.

From Chicago, take Kennedy Expressway to I-90. Follow signs to Rockford. Exit at Route 53 north and follow to end at Lake Cook Road. Turn left onto Route 12, about .5 mile. Turn right and follow Route 12 north to Miller Road. Turn left and go to Arrowhead Lane. Turn right into #125, identified by 2 locomotive mailboxes.

From North Shore, take Lake Cook Road or Route 22 west to Route 12/Lake Zurich. Turn right onto Route 12 and proceed as directed above.

Proceeds shared with the Interlochen Center for the Arts

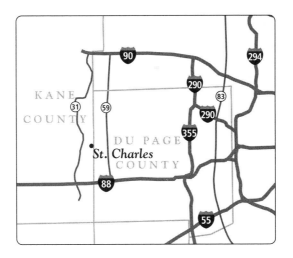

Saturday, July 12

KANE COUNTY

ST. CHARLES
Charles & Patricia Bell
39W582 Deer Run Drive, St. Charles

In a semi-rural area west of Chicago, amid the tall oak trees and open vistas, we have established a series of gardens on two acres featuring numerous sun- and shade-tolerant perennials. Colors and textures are combined to accent and highlight how our collection of more than 400 varieties of daylilies can interact with other sun-loving plants. Several hundred varieties of perennials, decorative grasses, and flowering shrubs provide a constantly changing view in the gardens during the growing season. In the shade gardens, spring brings Virginia bluebells, bleeding hearts, primroses, brunnera, epimedium, and other shade lovers, giving way to our hosta collection, astilbes, and ferns to provide various shades of green and variegated leaf patterns throughout the summer and fall. Various annuals are used throughout the gardens and in containers for constant color. A garden is a personal expression that is meant to be shared with others—that's our gardening principle.

Hours: 10 a.m. to 4 p.m.

From I-90, take Randall Road to Bolcum Road (about 9 miles) and turn right. Continue to Denker Road and turn right. Turn left onto first street, Deer Run Drive, and continue to first house on right.

From I-88, take Farnsworth Road exit, travel north about 5 miles to Fabyan Parkway, and turn left. Travel about 3.5 miles, turn right onto Randall Road, then turn left onto Bolcum Road (about 3 miles north of Route 64). Proceed as directed above. *Please park along street.*

Proceeds shared with the Morton Arboretum

The Haggas Garden
38W612 Greenview Court, St. Charles

Situated next to a golf course, the Haggas Garden takes advantage of the sense of dramatic proportions afforded by the spacious vistas surrounding them. Gardening is a team effort, with all the design, planting, and maintenance performed by the homeowners. A large backyard garden provides an outlet for their passion for collecting unusual plant material and is managed by intertwining paths that allow visitors to casually stroll and enjoy the many species of perennials and shrubs.

Hours: 10 a.m. to 2 p.m.

From downtown St. Charles, go west on Route 64/Main Street to Randall Road. Turn right and head north .4 mile to traffic light at Dean Street. Turn left and head west 1.2 miles to Burr Road. Turn right, go north for 1.2 miles to Fairway Drive, and turn left. This is the Blackhawk Golf Course homesites neighborhood. Make first right onto East Lakeview Circle. Go to second cul-de-sac on right, Greenview Court. Haggas house is first on right, a brick 2-story colonial with white columns and gray shutters. *Please park on street, not in driveway.*

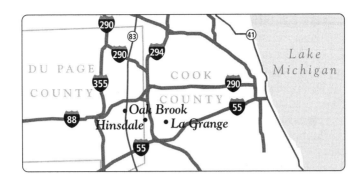

Saturday, July 19

COOK COUNTY

HINSDALE

Musso Garden

242 East Third Street, Hinsdale

The Mussos' 1800 Victorian-style house sits on the corner of a three-quarter-acre lot in the village of Hinsdale. On the west side of the house is a brick path that winds through a bermed garden bordered on one side by a Victorian-style child's playhouse and on the other by large trees and bushes, which give the garden privacy and provide a sense of serenity. Meandering through one of the rose-covered arches, the path opens onto a large brick patio with iron furniture and planters surrounding a trickling three-tiered fountain. As you walk past the coach house, you enter the oldest section of the garden. Four flagstone squares house antique roses, clematis, perennials, and a variety of vegetables and annuals. Along the backyard and east side there is a row of apple trees and mature bushes, which houses many birdhouses and forms a backdrop for the perennial garden that runs the length of the property. Stone and iron benches offer a retreat on a hot summer day.

Hours: 10 a.m. to 4 p.m.

From I-294, take Ogden Avenue west. After 2 traffic lights, turn left onto York Road (Shell gas station and Dunkin' Donuts). Follow past "S" curve and over train tracks to 4-way stop sign. Turn left onto Third Street and go 2 blocks. Garden is at southwest corner of Third and Elm Street, at a 2-story gray house with burgundy, white, and green trim. *Please park on north side of Third or Elm Street.*

The Gardens of Kellie & Barry O'Brien

527 West Maple Street, Hinsdale

This three-quarter-acre garden reflects the lifestyle and personality of Kellie O'Brien and her husband, Barry. Fifteen years ago, they transformed their 1950s ranch home into a stately Tudor, which created the background for the continuous perennial gardens weaving throughout their property. The sunny front borders are a combination of unusual evergreens and perennials. In the spring, thousands of daffodils and tulips announce the beginning of a new season. Hydrangeas, roses, and buddleias all add to the ongoing changes from early spring to late fall. Special attention to combining different textures is evident in the grouping of these plants. Walking through the hosta walk to the back 2,000-foot bluestone patio, you will pass an English fishpond, rose-covered balustrades, and many groupings of container gardens. This is where the O'Briens host many family celebrations and spend hours with their five grandchildren, introducing them to the world of plants. The back gardens are mainly shade gardens with huge mature hostas, astilbes, hydrangeas, and a variety of unusual shade plants. The shed and vegetable garden are a reflection of Kellie's farm background. The swing under the mulberry tree is where quiet moments are spent at the end of the day looking through the "magic window" created by an opening in the trees facing west. The garden has speakers throughout to further enhance this peacefulness that a gardens brings.

Hours: 10 a.m. to 4 p.m.

Garden is between Madison and Monroe, 1 block north of Chicago Avenue or 4 blocks south of Ogden Avenue. House is a red brick Tudor on north side of Maple. *Please park on street.*

Proceeds shared with Illinois Citizens for Life

LA GRANGE

Catherine & Francis Donovan

320 South Waiola, La Grange

An English-style garden surrounds our Victorian house built in 1890. Through a tall hedge, you enter the Parlor Garden with its thyme lawn and herbaceous border. A sunny corridor dotted with alpine troughs leads you to the pond with surrounding shade garden. Across the terrace is a floral alleé. The gardener's service area and small vegetable garden are to the left. An open lawn, enclosed by mixed borders, leads to the Circle Garden, a symphony of perennials, annuals, and roses.

Hours: 10 a.m. to 4 p.m.

From I-294, take Ogden Avenue exit east. At third traffic light, turn right onto Brainard. At third stop sign, turn left onto Maple. Travel 2 blocks to Waiola and turn right. It is third house on right. *Please park on street.*

Proceeds shared with the Heifer Project International

Oak Brook
Susan & Ken Beard
3711 Madison Street, Oak Brook

We have lived and gardened on these three acres in Oak Brook for thirty-three years. Each year we tackle a new project in the garden, trying to make a private oasis for our family and grandchildren. Three years ago we added a nineteen-foot bridge, which made the flow of the garden more interesting. Two years ago, an arbor with an eight-foot opening was also completed in an effort to keep the deer out. Last year we continued to add more flagstone paths in the woods and we built a pond and added some fish. Most of the property is in various degrees of shade, which lends itself to hostas and many other woodland plants (ferns, epimediums, corydalis, etc.) that border paths lined with flagstone. I am a hosta collector, with 300 plus varieties and climbing. The garden has been designed to play down the old swimming pool, which was here when we moved in, and to give views with focal points from every room in the house and during every season of the year.

Hours: 10 a.m. to 4 p.m.

Take I-294 to Ogden Avenue. Go west towards Hinsdale and pass York Road to next traffic light, which is Madison Street. Go right about .6 mile across from far end of Brownswood Cemetery. Garden is at rough-cedar-and-stone 2-story house on right side of street. *Please park on east side of street (same side as house).*

Shady Oaks—Joe & Barbara McGoldrick
3118 White Oak Lane, Oak Brook

This garden, on two acres, features sixty-five majestic oaks and evergreens of every variety. Shade-loving perennials thrive through the filtered sunlight of the sweeping limbs on the grand oaks. Ponds, waterfalls, paths, and hidden treats abound. Paths lead you from the shade of the oaks to an expansive green lawn, which extends to a 100-foot sunny berm of annuals and perennials stretching across the back of the garden. The natural flowing designs of the garden express the personal style of its owner, Joe McGoldrick, who has been creating landscape designs and gardens for forty-five years. Both front and back gardens are a wonderful blend of the art of man and the art of nature…a delight to the senses and a true sanctuary for man and bird.

Hours: 10 a.m. to 4 p.m.

Take I-294 to Ogden Avenue. Go west to Cass Avenue and turn right (north). Proceed north to 31st Street (Oak Brook Road) and turn left (west). Proceed west to Meyers Road (next traffic light) and turn left (south). Go to first street on right, White Oak Lane, turn right, and go to end of street to 2 brick columns at driveway. *Please park on street and walk down driveway.*

Sunday, July 27
DU PAGE COUNTY

WEST CHICAGO
The Ball Horticultural Trial Garden
622 Town Road, West Chicago

The Ball Horticultural Trial Gardens have been the site for the evaluation and display of the newest annuals and perennials for the Ball Seed Company since the early 1930s. This is a rare opportunity for garden enthusiasts to stroll the colorful six-acre gardens usually reserved for the wholesale customers of the ninety-eight-year-old Ball Horticultural Company, world leader in the breeding, production, distribution, and marketing of floricultural products. As guests wander the grounds, they will see more than 3,000 varieties of flowering plants in the Parkway Garden, Anna's Garden, the Circle Garden, and the new Simply Beautiful Garden. Thousands of containers and hanging baskets fill the Sun Container Garden and the Shade House, while experimental varieties can be viewed in the All-America Selections Evaluation Garden. Guests may want to allow one to two hours or more to visit these exceptional gardens.

Hours: 10 a.m. to 4 p.m.

Entrance to parking is just off Roosevelt Road/Route 38 in West Chicago. The driveway that enters parking area is marked by small sign that reads "Pan-American Seed." A small greenhouse and 2 flower beds are visible from road.

From the east, continue west on Roosevelt Road past Route 59. Entrance will be .2 mile beyond Town Road, first driveway west of Town Road to north.

From the west, continue east on Roosevelt Road past intersections of Washington/ Fabyan Parkway. Railroad tracks cross road .5 mile east of Fabyan intersection and entrance to gardens is another .2 mile east of tracks. Turn left into drive.

Proceeds shared with the University of Illinois Extension

LAKE COUNTY

HIGHLAND PARK
Magic Garden
2219 Egandale Road, Highland Park

Stroll through the enchanted grounds of our Tudor-style house. Along with an extraordinary view of the lake, tranquility is reflected throughout three acres of trees, gardens, and terraces designed by Jens Jensen seventy-three years ago and updated by Douglas Hoerr Landscape Design Architects. Meander through the newly revised West Garden and Woodland Garden, then enjoy the colorful container gardens, view of the lake, Jens Jensen Sculpture Terrace, the East Rose Garden, and the Pool Terrace. Feel transported inside a Monet painting as you enter our magic garden. Using lush, informally planted pink, lavender, and blue flowers within curvilinear boxwood parterres, decorative wrought-iron arbors, and inviting gravel paths, Mr. Hoerr has created a garden room that evokes peace and serenity. Anchored on each end by a rippling sculpture fountain and rare myrtle topiaries, our romantic garden has become a place for butterflies by day and a perfect spot for late night dining with family and friends.

Hours: 10 a.m. to 2 p.m.

Take Route 41 to Central Avenue east in Highland Park. Turn left onto Sheridan Road and go to Park Avenue. Turn right and go to stop sign and Egandale Road. Turn left and go to top of hill. First house on right is #2219. *Please park on street.*

LAKE FOREST
Camp Rosemary
930 Rosemary Road, Lake Forest

This garden was designed by Rose Standish Nichols in the 1920s and is made up of wonderful garden rooms partitioned by pines, yews, and boxwood hedges. A sweeping lawn and luscious container plantings at the front steps are the first hints of delightful discoveries inside: a charming box-edged parterre, a thyme garden, and an urn brimming with roses, perennials, and annuals set against an ancient yew hedge affectionately called "the couch." Other areas include a chapel-like white garden with two reflecting pools and a vine-and-rose entwined pergola garden with three exuberant borders surrounding a small pool. During the spring of 1998, work began in earnest on the walled garden, which now graces the area surrounding the pool house. Elegant wide grass steps, paired rose borders, a linden allée, intricately patterned knot gardens, and four well-planted perennial borders are all key elements of this new landscape. In contrast to the softer colors of the perennial beds near the pergola, these borders reflect a stronger palette of red, orange, violet, and blue. Some wonderful burgundy and silver foliage plants complement the whole scheme. Beyond the walled garden is a lush wooded ravine. A meandering path traces the ravine's edge beginning at the grass labyrinth and ending in the small glade, which overlooks the ravine. From this vantage point, a statue of Diana, the huntress, watches over the whole garden.

Hours: 10 a.m. to 4 p.m.

From Route 41, take Deerpath Road exit east (right). Proceed through town, over railroad tracks to stop sign at Sheridan Road. Turn right. Go .5 mile, past Lake Forest College, past blinking yellow light, and past Rosemary Road on right. Go half block to Rosemary Road on left. Turn left (east). Number 930 is in middle of block on left. *Please park in front driveway area and on south side of Rosemary Road.*

Carr Garden

1055 Woodbine Place, Lake Forest

Our garden was designed as a series of rooms to be lived in and to serve specific purposes: morning coffee, grilling, dining, and entertaining. We wanted to develop unique views out of each window of the house while at the same time creating an integrated private and serene space. This is a green garden punctuated by roses and hydrangeas and blooming containers. As such, it is a study in structure and the play of light and shadows that changes with the hours of the day.

Hours: 10 a.m. to 4 p.m.

Take Route 41 north, to Deerpath Road in Lake Forest. Turn right (east) to Greenbay Road. Turn left and go 1 block to Westminster, turn right. Go through town, past Sheridan Road, and continue to Woodbine Place. Turn left and go .1 mile to #1055. *Please park on one side of street only, as indicated by signs.*

Old Mill Farm

499 West Old Mill Road, Lake Forest

Once a working dairy farm siring championship bulls, this property consisted of a 1929 English Tudor-style house and several outbuildings eventually demolished by the original owner when selling a large portion of the property. Jens Jensen designed the original master plan for the entire property. The current owners purchased the property from the original owner's estate for their family residence, dreaming of restoring the property and home. Collaborating with John Mariani, Sara Furlan, and Jim Osborne of Mariani Landscape, they've created a truly magical garden. The Old Mill Farm focuses on the potager garden of boxwood partitions filled spring to fall with bulbs and annuals for flower arranging and herbs and vegetables for cooking. Next to this garden is a berry patch and, unusual for this northern climate, a bed of Italian figs. Two perennial borders are adjacent to the potager garden. One border focuses on perennials with annuals added for seasonal color. The other border is a butterfly garden surrounded by yew hedges. Future gardens are in the beginning stages, including an orchard, a woodland garden, and a prairie restoration.

Hours: 10 a.m. to 4 p.m.

From Route 41 north, take Route 22 West/Half Day Road. Turn right onto Route 43/Waukegan Road and go about .5 mile to first street on right, Old Mill Road. Turn right and go east to end of street. House is last drive on right. *Please park along north side street.*

Mettawa

Mettawa Manor

25779 St. Mary's Road, Mettawa

The house and grounds were built in 1927 as a family compound. The current owners, only the second in the manor's rich history, have been working for the past ten years to refurbish some garden areas and create new ones. The centerpiece of the garden is a newly built walled English-style garden with forty-foot perennial borders on either side of a sunken lawn that leads to a spring walk and rose room centered on an old fountain. Outside the east gate is a golden garden and an orchard/meadow underplanted with 20,000 narcissi and bordered by a fenced potager/cutting garden and a circular herb garden. The eighty-acre property has two ponds, a woodland garden, an eight-acre prairie, and a parkland of specimen trees, and is surrounded by a newly reclaimed oak-hickory forest.

Hours: 10 a.m. to 4 p.m.

Take Edens Expressway/I-94 to Tri-State Tollway/I-294. Exit at Route 60 west/Town Line Road, follow 1 mile to St. Mary's Road, and turn left just past horse stables to Open Days signs on left side of St. Mary's Road marking driveway entrance.

Public Gardens
COOK COUNTY

CHICAGO
Garfield Park Conservatory
300 North Central Park Avenue, Chicago (312) 746-5100

Opened in 1908, the conservatory is one of the largest gardens under glass in the world. It was the vision of landscape architect Jens Jensen, who based its form on the domed haystacks that dotted the Midwest. The conservatory's eight exhibit houses feature plants from around the world, as well as an indoor Children's Garden.

Hours: year round, daily, 9 a.m. to 5 p.m.

Admission: free

From I-290, take Eisenhower Expressway exit at Independence/Exit 26A and go north. Turn right onto Washington Boulevard, go east to North Central Park Avenue, and turn left.

Grandmother's Garden
Fullerton Avenue (2400 N) and Stockton Drive (50 W), Chicago (312) 747-0740

Wide, undulating, island beds of annuals, perennials, and grasses are set off by broad expanses of lawn weaving the gardens together. These lovely, freeform beds are a fine counterpoint for the formal plantings at the Lincoln Park Conservatory across the street.

Hours: year round, daily, dawn to dusk

Admission: free

Take Fullerton Avenue to Stockton Drive. Garden is located on west side of Stockton Drive, south of Fullerton, near entrance to Lincoln Park Zoo.

The Lincoln Garden
425 East McFetridge Drive, Chicago (312) 747-0698

Set amid a broad expanse of lawn in Lincoln Park adjacent to the Chicago Historical Society, these gardens are at the foot of a handsome sculpture of Abraham Lincoln (1897). The six raised beds, thirty by 360 feet, contain eighty varieties of perennials. Annuals are added to provide seasonal color and interest. The gardens remain standing in winter, with the perennials and ornamental grasses giving form and color to the landscape.

Hours: year round, daily, dawn to dusk

Admission: free

North State Parkway at North Avenue (1600 North) just east of Chicago Historical Society.

Lincoln Park Conservatory
2391 North Stockton Drive, Chicago (312) 742-7736

Lincoln Park Conservatory has provided a botanical haven in the city for over a century. It was designed by well-known Victorian era architect Joseph L. Silsbee to showcase exotic plants and grow flowers for use in Chicago's parks. Today the conservatory houses palm, fern, and orchid collections, and produces four annual flower shows.

Hours: year round, daily, 9 a.m. to 5 p.m.

Admission: free

From Lake Shore Drive, take Fullerton Avenue exit and travel 2 blocks west.

From I-94, take Fullerton Avenue exit and travel 2 miles east. Conservatory is located on southeast corner of Fullerton Avenue and Stockton Drive.

Michigan Avenue Streetscape
Chicago (847) 733-0140

Stretching thirty city blocks, these island beds fill Michigan Avenue with big, bold, beautiful seasonal plantings. Tulips underplanted with grape hyacinth herald spring. Masses of annuals, perennials, and grasses celebrate summer. Kale, pansies, and chrysanthemums, added to the fall-blooming perennials and grasses, announce fall, creating a stunning effect.

Hours: year round, daily, dawn to dusk

Admission: free

From north, take Lake Shore Drive south to Michigan Avenue exit. Central median planters extend from Roosevelt Road north to Oak Street.

EVANSTON

The Shakespeare Garden
Northwestern University, Garrett Place at Sheridan Road, Evanston (847) 864-0655

Designed by Jens Jensen in 1915 and surrounded by the original hawthorn hedges planted in 1920, the garden is romantic, secluded, and especially beautiful in June and July when its eight flower beds are filled with roses, lilies, pansies, artemisia, herbs, campanula, forget-me-nots, and daisies, all evocative of Shakespeare's poetry.

Hours: year round, daily, dawn to dusk

Admission: free

From the north or south, enter Evanston along Sheridan Road and proceed to Garrett Place (2200 North). Park on Garrett Place (about mid-campus), east of Sheridan. Garden is reached by bluestone walk on east side of Howe Chapel (on north side of street). Enter along this walk; garden is not visible from Sheridan or Garrett.

Chicago Botanic Garden
1000 Lake Cook Road, Glencoe (847) 835-5440 www.chicagobotanic.org

The garden covers 385 acres and features twenty-three specialty gardens, including a waterfall garden, English walled garden, three-island Japanese garden, prairies, lagoons, and Enabling Garden, which shows strategies that make gardening accessible to everyone. Nine islands on seventy-five acres of waterways and six miles of shoreline distinguish this "garden on the water."

> Hours: year round, daily, 8 a.m. to dusk; closed Christmas
> *Admission:* $7.75 for parking
> *Located .5 mile east of Edens Expressway/Route 41* at Lake Cook Road.

Lake Forest Open Lands Association
272 Deerpath, Lake Forest (847) 234-3880 www.lfola.org

Mellody Farm Preserve is a fifty-acre nature preserve with restored prairies, savanna, and wetlands. It is also the site of the Lockhart Family Nature Center, a restored historic gatehouse, and surrounding landscape of the J. Ogden Armor estate circa 1909. Vestiges of the original estate landscape designed by Ossian Simmonds and Jens Jensen are still evident today.

> Hours: year round, daily, dawn to dusk
> *Admission:* free
> *From Tri-State Tollway/I-294 and I-94,* exit at Route 60 and proceed east to Waukegan Road north to Deerpath west into nature center parking lot. Located on southwest corner of Waukegan and Deerpath.

Anderson Gardens
340 Spring Creek Road, Rockford (815) 229-9390 www.andersongardens.org

Anderson Gardens contains an authentic Japanese pond strolling garden, guest house, teahouse, gazebo, and four waterfalls, as well as lanterns, bridges, a stone pagoda, water basins, and gates. A Japanese garden provides a place for meditation and contemplation.

> *Hours:* May through October, weekdays, 10 a.m. to 5 p.m., Saturday, 10 a.m. to 4 p.m., Sunday, 12 to 4 p.m.
> *Admission:* $5 adults, $4 senior citizens, $3 students, children under 5 free
> *From the east,* take I-90 west to Business 20/East State Street exit. Go west (right) on Business 20 and turn north (right) onto Mulford Road. Turn west (left) onto Spring Creek Road and go 3 miles to entrance at Parkview Avenue. Turn right into parking lot.
> *From the north,* take I-90 east to Riverside Boulevard exit and go west (right) to Mulford Road. Turn south (left), then turn west (left) onto Spring Creek Road and go 3 miles.

Klehm Arboretum & Botanic Garden

2701 Clifton Avenue, Rockford (888) 419-0782 www.klehm.org

Klehm Arboretum & Botanic Garden has over 150 acres of magnificent trees and plants. Explore this "living museum" every season—majestic colors of fall, hundreds of blooming crab apples in spring, butterfly gardens in summer, and snow-covered evergreens in winter. The Botanical Education Center has changing exhibits and a gift shop.

Hours: Memorial Day through Labor Day, daily, 9 a.m. to 8 p.m.; rest of year, 9 a.m. to 4 p.m.

Admission: $2 adults, children under 16 free

Off I-90/State Road 20, exit west; to Main Street/State Road 2, exit north; 2 miles to Clifton Avenue, exit west; .5 block to 2701 Clifton Avenue.

DU PAGE COUNTY

LISLE

The Morton Arboretum

4100 Illinois Route 53, Lisle (630) 968-0074 www.mortonarb.org

The Morton Arboretum is a 1,700-acre outdoor museum of woodlands, wetlands, gardens, and a restored native prairie. Established in 1922, its mission is to collect trees, shrubs, and other plants from around the world and to display them in naturally beautiful landscapes for people to study and enjoy. Tours offered daily, family activities on weekends.

Hours: year round, daily, 7 a.m to 5 p.m.

Admission: $7 per car

Located at I-88 and Illinois Route 53, 25 miles west of Chicago.

MAINE

The McLaughlin Garden, South Paris.
Photo by Claire Andorka.

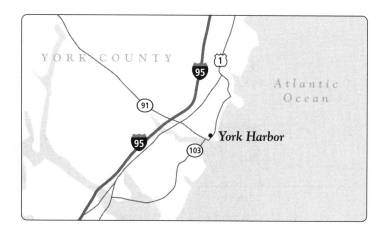

Saturday, July 12
YORK COUNTY

YORK
Braveboat Harbor Farm—Calvin & Cynthia Hosmer
110 Raynes Neck Road, York

This garden has been evolving over the last fifty years. It surrounds and complements a Georgian-style stone house. There are formal and informal borders, a vegetable garden, orchards, and collections of various flowering trees and shrubs. Apples and pears are espaliered on the house and along the walls of the formal front garden. Water features include a goldfish pond in an old septic tank, a farm pond with rustic bridge, and the Atlantic Ocean. This treasure is protected by a sculpted arborvitae hedge on the northwest, a mature stand of hickory on the northeast, and an extensive screen of old lilacs on the south. New projects include expanding the collection of magnolias and rhododendrons, introducing hydrangeas, espaliering a pear fence, and making a woodland walk.

Hours: 10 a.m. to 4 p.m.

Located off Route 103S and Braveboat Harbor Road to end of Raynes Neck Road. *Please park in field below house.*

Proceeds shared with the York Land Trust

Godfrey Pond Garden
22 Godfrey Pond Road, York

To reach the garden, you have two choices. You can approach through a short passageway at our front door and arrive at the intimate section nestled against a rock ledge and surrounded by forest. Then you come to a gate and a view of the sea. Down a slope, daylilies flourish and an area surrounded by roses with a bench or two invites a quiet pause. For another experience, walk a wooded pathway with the sound of the sea urging you on. Arriving at the bottom of the slope leading to the upper garden, the sight of the daylilies and roses comes as a delicious surprise. At the top of the slope, the back garden awaits with its quite different atmosphere.

The ocean and Godfrey Pond on two sides with marine damp and winds, the forest with all the wildlife looking for fancy food, and a dedicated commitment to organic gardening present challenges galore.

Hours: 10 a.m. to 4 p.m.

Take I-95 to York exit. Turn right onto Route 1 south and make next left onto Route 1A. Go through York Village (1.3 miles) to Route 103. Turn right and go 1 mile to Brave Boat Harbor Road. Turn left. Keep bearing right. Soon, after a small red house with picket fence, turn left onto Pepperell Way. Take next hard left onto dirt road just before gray house. Sign post reads "Sparhawk, Winebaum." Go to end (.3 mile). *Please park at bottom or top of driveway.*

Proceeds shared with the York Land Trust

Johnson Garden
16 Pepperell Way, York

This garden has an informal setting of both shade and sunny gardens. The shade garden consists of many varieties of hosta, astilbe, seeded geraniums, and ground covers, plus added patches of color. The sunny garden is a happy garden, with the woodland in the background featuring a graveyard dating back to 1871-1873. A variety of both day- and hybrid lilies, grasses, catmint, and annuals are grown for an ever-blooming effect throughout the summer.

Hours: 10 a.m. to 4 p.m.

Take I-95 north to York exit. Go to traffic light and turn right onto Route 1 south. At next light, turn left onto Route 1A. Go to Route 103 and turn right. Travel about 1 mile to Brave Boat Harbor Road on left. The second road off Brave Boat Harbor Road is Pepperell Way. Our house is at #16, third house on left. *Please park on street.*

Proceeds shared with the York Land Trust

Radochia Gardens & Neighbors
28 Kings Road, York

You are welcomed to adjacent gardens that draw you to the rocky Maine coast. Sculptured sumac, native hickory, and a tapestry of fir help define over an acre of flowers, trees, ornamental grasses, and shrubs. Take a leisurely stroll through the garden pathways featuring perennial plantings and specimen trees. Enjoy the vista of wildflowers with the ocean as a backdrop. Meander through a field of motion where native plantings extend the surf. Adjacent gardens feature more than one acre of various horticultural specimens and spectacular ocean views.

Hours: 10 a.m. to 4 p.m.

Take I-95 north to Exit 4. Turn right onto Route 1 south to first traffic light. Turn left onto Route 1A/York Street and follow about 1.4 miles. Turn right onto Route 103 West/Lilac Lane and go 1 mile. Turn left onto Brave Boat Harbor Road. Take fourth left onto Raynes Neck Road and go .3 mile. Turn left onto Godfrey Cove Road and go .3 mile. Turn left onto Locke Lane and immediately right onto Kings Road. Follow to end, bearing left at fork. *Please park on street.*

Proceeds shared with the York Land Trust

Sea Spray—Georgia & Dan McGurl
34 Sea Breeze Lane, York

Blessed with a long and mostly rural sea view, we have attempted to blend old with new. Mature trees and shrubbery have been combined with many new gardens surrounding a newly constructed Cape Cod-style farmhouse. The rambling connective architecture affords many opportunities for different styles of gardens—pocket, terrace, and meadow—as well as a woodland retreat in progress.

Hours: 10 a.m. to 4 p.m.

From Route 1A in York, take Route 103 to Brave Boat Harbor Road (1 mile). Turn left and take fourth left, Rayne's Neck Road (.25 mile). Take first left, Godfrey's Cove Road (.5 mile). Go to second left, Sea Breeze Lane (.75 mile). Go to end of lane and through gate.

Proceeds shared with the York Land Trust

Public Gardens
OXFORD COUNTY

SOUTH PARIS
The McLaughlin Garden & Horticultural Center
97 Main Street, South Paris (207) 743-8820 www.mclaughlingarden.org

For sixty years, gardeners and garden lovers have been welcome to enter the gate of the McLaughlin Garden. Bernard McLaughlin began the garden in 1936, gardening in his spare time until retiring in 1967. From that point until his recent death, he devoted his full energies to the garden, collecting plant material from everywhere. Bernard was a quiet mentor to countless gardeners, sharing his wisdom and promoting gardening at every opportunity. Since 1997, the garden has been stewarded by the McLaughlin Foundation.

Hours: May through October, daily, 8 a.m. to 7 p.m.; gift shop, daily, 10 a.m. to 5 p.m.; tea room, June through August, Wednesday through Saturday, 11 a.m. to 4 p.m.

Admission: free

Located at junction of Western Avenue and Route 26 in South Paris, .8 mile north of Oxford Hills Comprehensive High School. Parking available along Western Avenue.

Massachusetts

OPEN DAYS:

May 3
June 7
June 26

Captain Daniel Draper House, Westwood

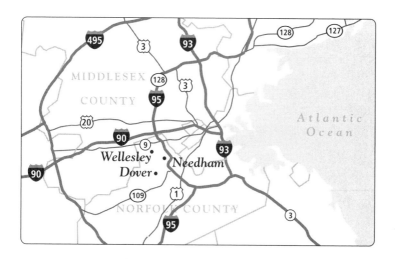

Saturday, May 3
NORFOLK COUNTY

DOVER

Kevin J. Doyle & Michael Radoslovich—Cairn Croft
81 Wilsondale Street, Dover

My garden is a personal garden. The cairns mark its location and the croft is "a special place within." My design intention for the garden is to have guests enter and quickly forget from where they've come. It is a place of unspeakable joy. Cairn Croft also exhibits a variety of outdoor sculpture in many mediums that enhance the garden experience. Cairn Croft has been featured in *Fine Gardening* and *Horticulture* magazines, and *The Victorian Garden*.

Hours: 10 a.m. to 4 p.m.

From Route 128, take Exit 16B/Dedham/Route 109. Travel 1 mile or less on Route 109 west and take second right onto Summer Street. Travel 1 mile to end. Turn left onto Westfield Street. Travel 300 yards; turn left onto Wilsondale Street. Travel .2 mile. Watch for cairns on left at #81. *Please park beyond house on opposite side of street.*

The Halligan Garden
27 Dover Road, Dover

Surrounded as we are, by the Charles River, a vernal pool, and an oak forest, Kevin Doyle has landscaped for us a series of garden events. A welcoming small woodland path leads to a formal secret garden surrounded by Siberian spruce, azaleas, rhododendrons, and a plethora of spring bulbs. The front entrance captures the essence of the forest that surrounds us with three stunning clumps of paper bark birch. The boxwood-lined front walk is a subtle juxtaposition of formality. The front entrance is evergreen to express a warmth through our long winter. Finally, a point of view garden with an Asian flair provides interest from within the house throughout the year. We are a work in progress and our focus continues to be to enhance the beauty of our woodland setting.

Hours: 10 a.m. to 4 p.m.

Take Route 128 to Route 16 west. Go through Wellesley into South Natick. Go to Natick Center at traffic light and turn left onto Pleasant Street. Dover Road is third street on left; #27 is .25 mile on left. You cannot see house from road. *Proceed down driveway and park in designated area on right of driveway. Please note that all gardens open on this date are very close together. Maps will be available at all gardens during the Open Day.*

NEEDHAM
Ellen Lathi's Garden
119 Locust Lane, Needham

The woodland surrounding our home inspired the gardens that wind through the forest, around the bog, and through a sunny area toward the house. Here, spring-flowering shrubs and trees, summer annuals and perennials, fall-blooming ornamental grasses, and winter evergreens all celebrate the individuality of our New England seasons. The gardens, spread over two acres and designed in collaboration with Kevin Doyle, are connected by a series of steppingstone and mulched paths with transitions punctuated by lichen-covered natural stone. Destinations we particularly enjoy include a gathering area in the woods, a natural bog and creek, and a ropes course. Within this plot of land that we love, where change is the only constant, native woodland and designed landscape are celebrated together.

Hours: 9 a.m. to 5 p.m.

Take Route 128 to Exit 21/Newton/Wellesley/Route 16. Turn right off ramp and follow Route 16W towards Wellesley just over 3 miles to where 5 streets meet in Wellesley Square. Take most extreme left turn onto Grove Street and go 1.8 miles to end. Turn right onto Charles River Street. Go .2 mile to first street on right, Locust Lane. Turn right (white rocks at mouth of street) and go .2 mile to second house from end, #119. *Please park on street. Please note that all gardens open on this date are very close together. Maps will be available at all gardens during the Open Day.*

Taylor Garden
372 Warren Street, Needham

Every inch of space is part of the design of this four-season garden located in a densely populated suburban neighborhood. Perennials, annuals, wildflowers, tropicals, and bulbs are artfully woven together into a bold tapestry of color, shape, and size. Visitors coming down the multilevel path are treated to many elements of surprise and curiosity, including lush and unusual container plantings and brilliant late-season color combinations. There are no fences or barriers to separate this garden from its close neighbors. Of special interest are a very shady rock garden under a deck, distinct sitting areas, a grove of eight different Japanese maples, small water features, a grist-wheel stone, and a newly created greenhouse in a former garage.

Hours: 10 a.m. to 4 p.m.

From Route 128, take Exit 17/Needham/Natick/Route 135. At end of exit ramp, turn towards Needham. Go 1.4 miles through 2 traffic lights to hospital sign on left. Turn at sign and go 1 block to a stop sign. Turn left and go .4 mile to garden on left. *Please park on closest side street, Laurel Drive.*

Kelly Wingo's Garden
47 Mayo Avenue, Needham

My bungalow was the inspiration to create a garden that unifies the architecture and the outside space. Stone paths lead the eye through the early season plantings combining the coolness of stone with the warmth of spring bulbs and budding shrubs and trees. As the growing season progresses, the paths become secondary to an abundant summer garden filled with the exotic and the familiar. Stone, a fountain, containers, and plants work together to complement and enhance the house and garden.

Hours: 10 a.m. to 4 p.m.

Take Route 128 towards Needham. Take Exit 18/Great Plain Avenue/ West Roxbury. Follow signs to Needham/Great Plain Avenue. Go about 1.5 miles and turn left onto Mayo Avenue. Number 47 is on right. *Please park on street. Note that all gardens open on this date are very close together. Maps will be available at all gardens during the Open Day.*

WELLESLEY
Hunnewell Garden
845 Washington Street, Wellesley

Four generations of the Hunnewell family have had a hand in this estate garden, which includes a formal azalea garden and pinetum. Greenhouses produce delicate camellias, exotic orchids, flowers, and fruit. The highlight of your visit is bound to be the whimsical yet monumental clipped evergreens, which adorn the sloping shores of Lake Waban.

Hours: 10 a.m. to 4 p.m.

From Massachusetts Turnpike/I-90 west, take Exit 16. Follow signs to Route 16 west/ Washington Street. Follow about 5 miles, passing through Wellesley Hills, to center of Wellesley. Follow Route 16/South Natick/Holliston. Next traffic light marks entrance to Wellesley College. Proceed 6 miles to #845. *Follow parking instructions.*

WESTWOOD
Captain Daniel Draper House
360 Dover Road, Westwood

The Captain Daniel Draper House, once part of a family compound of farmhouses, sits on one acre. The homestead features old stone walls, a cobblestone entry court, a pool sunken in the foundation of an old barn, and majestic elms. Off the entry court are a formal garden, which overlooks the pool, and a courtyard shaded by an ancient crab apple. The pool features a diving rock that is softened by sweeping cedars and surrounded by plantings, rock gardens, a brick terrace, and bluestone coping. The six-foot round window in the pool house overlooks a portion of a large wooded garden highlighted by a frog pond with a waterfall, stone Chinese lanterns, and a pond house retreat. These gardens were designed by Kevin Doyle.

Hours: 10 a.m. to 4 p.m.

Take Exit 16B off Route 128/I-95/Route 109. Go about 1 mile on Route 109 west. Turn right onto Dover Road. The house is a white colonial on left and sits atop a stone wall. *Please park on either side of street. Note that all gardens open on this date are very close together. Maps will be available at all gardens during the Open Day.*

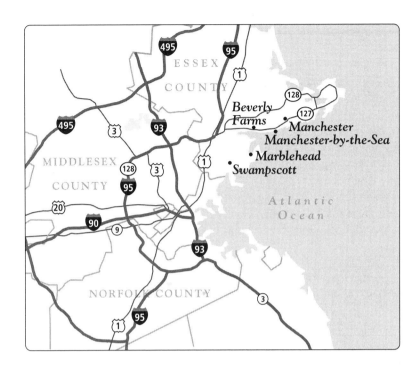

Saturday, June 7

ESSEX COUNTY

BEVERLY FARMS

Sea Meadow

675 Hale Street, Beverly Farms

Sea Meadow is an informal family place for all ages. Our rambling shingled house looks south-east across a sloping lawn, meadows, a pond with wildfowl, wetlands, and woods to the ocean. A terrace with an ancient wisteria vine, roses, bulbs, and a large *Cornus kousa* connects the house to an herb garden, a bed of heather, perennials, wildflowers, a vegetable garden, and blooming trees and shrubs. An intriguing rock garden under a thirty-foot glacial rock face has a secret path leading to the gazebo. Grassy trails take you through the wetlands to the dunes. We've made inviting areas from which to enjoy the beauty of the natural site.

Hours: 9 a.m. to 5 p.m.

From Route 128, take Exit 17. Turn right onto Grapevine Road. Continue 1.3 miles, passing Chapman's Greenhouse on right. At graveyard, turn right onto Haskell Street. Go .4 mile to end of street. Turn left onto Hale Street/Route 127. Go .1 mile. Take first right between stone gateposts, #675. Cross railroad tracks. Bear left at fork. Pass pond on left; the driveway faces you. *Please park in driveway.*

Manchester
Grafton
285 Summer Street, Manchester

This garden was designed by Martha Brookes Hutcheson in 1902. The original name was "Undercliff." The garden is still as it was when it was designed and is the only one that exists in such a complete state. Originally, there were ten to fourteen gardens to look after; now there are one and a half! The lawn in front of the garden was put in when the original house was torn down in 1939. We have put in many perennials and a few shrubs into the beds. Two of the beds have tree peonies and two have roses.

Hours: 10 a.m. to 4 p.m.

Take Route 128 north from Boston to Gloucester. Take Exit 15 into Manchester. Follow signs to Route 127/Magnolia/Gloucester. Go 1 mile out of town and under railroad bridge. We are at fifth driveway on right. Follow to end. *Please park on side of driveway.*

Manchester-by-the-Sea
The Garden at 9 Friend Street—Frederick Rice
9 Friend Street, Manchester-by-the-Sea

The first garden at 9 Friend Street was laid out in 1928 for the present owner's grandfather. Frederick Rice, a floral and garden designer and lecturer, has made major changes during the past twenty years. The English cottage-style garden, ablaze with color and awash with texture, is laid out in a series of rooms furnished with an extraordinary variety of perennials, annuals, roses, vines, and deciduous and evergreen shrubs. Brick and stone patios have been constructed for outdoor living. There are two fishponds, a pavilion, and a newly renovated teahouse. Arches of espaliered pear trees were added in 2002. The garden was featured in the 1996 summer issue of *Country Home-Country Gardens* magazine and in Meredith Publishing's *Country Garden Planner*.

Hours: 10 a.m. to 4 p.m.

From Route 128 north, take Exit 15/Manchester/School Street. Turn right onto School Street at end of exit ramp. Pass Essex County Club on left and proceed through blinking traffic light. Friend Street is second right beyond Sacred Heart Catholic Church. House, #9, is gray with black shutters, on right, only house on street with a white picket fence. *Please park on Friend Street or in lot behind Sacred Heart Church.*

Proceeds shared with the Manchester Council On Aging

MARBLEHEAD
Gerald & Rose Anne Levinson
4 Park Lane, Marblehead

The horticultural materials that make up these gardens are plant treasures, choice and unusual things gathered over twenty-five years by the gardener/owner. Several years ago Ellen Cool was asked to professionally redesign the property and to sort out the plants and put them into better pictorial relationships. She reshaped the landscape by changing grades and adding beds, stone walls, paths, and a bluestone entryway. By moving our mature plants into new contexts and adding 200 or so new and special varieties, she has provided compositional beauty to the plant groupings, honoring their relationships in a painterly way within a cohesive landscape setting.

Hours: 10 a.m. to 4 p.m.

Take Route 114 east to traffic light at West Shore Drive and turn left. After passing Tower School on right, take second left onto Park Lane. Number 4 is last house on left.

The Parable—Ellen Cool's Garden
19 Circle Street, Marblehead

In the oldest part of Marblehead, alongside a 1720 house of historic interest, there is a garden gate, which leads into a highly developed and very personal landscape. Here there are examples of the buildings, structures, tools, materials, and books which, together with the gardens, comprise the setting for a landscape designer's life and work. Many unusual early-, late-, and long-blooming plants combine with artifacts of stone and wood to make satisfying compositions from April until November. In early June, there will be many rock garden plants in bloom. Ellen has created landscapes for a number of adjoining and nearby properties and a map is available for a walking tour of those that can be viewed from the street.

Hours: 10 a.m. to 4 p.m.

From the south, take Route 1A north to Route 129 east (it becomes Atlantic Avenue in Marblehead). Just past Mobil gas station on left, turn right onto Washington Street and follow to Old Town House, then turn right onto State Street, to Marblehead Harbor, then turn left onto Front Street. Circle Street will be third and fourth left.

From north or west, take Route 114 east to end at Old Town House. Proceed as directed above. *Look for parking on Front Street, as parking on Circle Street is very limited.* The walk by the water is, in any case, very pleasant. Number 19 is halfway up from water on right.

Proceeds shared with Trustees of Reservation

Gardens of Donald & Beverly Seamans

10 Harbor View, Marblehead

A walk through this garden is full of surprises. Discover bronze sculptures of animals, birds, and children nestled in natural settings or as fountains recirculating water in the pool. Entering the path from the driveway that leads to the house is a small rock garden. To the right is a vegetable and cutting garden. To the left is a grassy glade bordered by pachysandra and rhododendrons. A three-panel decorative fence forms a backdrop for a stone bench where a bronze child sits reading her book. Beside the house are pools with a mermaid fountain flowing into a small upper pool, which flows into a lower pool with water and goldfish. Two bronze children pour buckets of recirculating water on either end. Over this pool is a bridge which leads to two gardens. Follow a rocky path to the right and find a daylily garden, clematis, a dwarf Japanese cut-leaf maple, a shade garden containing ferns and hosta, and a variety of heathers and junipers on a low ledge. Go straight after the bridge to view the harbor. Note the semi-circular flower garden backed by *Rosa rugosa*. Beyond is a natural field where viburnum, witch hazel, blueberry bushes, and wildflowers grow. A gazebo sits on a rock terrace with thyme, lavender, and daisies, the perfect place to stop and rest.

Hours: 9 a.m. to 5 p.m.

From Route 128 east, take Route 114 east to end (in Marblehead). Turn right onto Route 129 for 1 block. At traffic light, turn left onto Atlantic Avenue. Go past big church on left and turn right onto Chestnut Street (at hardware store). At top of hill, turn right onto Harbor View. House is #10, on water side of street.

SWAMPSCOTT

Wilkinson Garden—Blythswood

29 Little's Point Road, Swampscott

Two families, Little and Proctor (now Wilkinson), have owned Blythswood from its inception in 1847 to the present. Arthur Little, a well-known Boston architect, named and styled his summerhouse after an English country home and that aspect is still reflected in the gardens, lawns, shrubs, and trees contained within the six and one half acres of grounds. The site rises from a rocky headland on Massachusetts Bay to a ridge dominated by the main house, then slopes gently westward down a long tree-lined gravel driveway to the old stable and farm areas. Among the current plantings are a rose garden, a peony that came from China in 1829, and fifty-two species of trees. Simplicity reflects a change from many groundskeepers to one part-time head gardener and assistant, who care for the formal beds, lawns, and urns.

Hours: 10 a.m. to 4 p.m.

From Swampscott, with ocean on right, take Puritan Road 1 mile. Little's Point Road is on right. Look for "Marion Court Junior College and Blythswood" sign; it is a shared driveway.

From Marblehead, take Route 129/Atlantic Avenue and turn left onto Puritan Road. Little's Point Road is 3 blocks on left. *Please do not park on grass.*

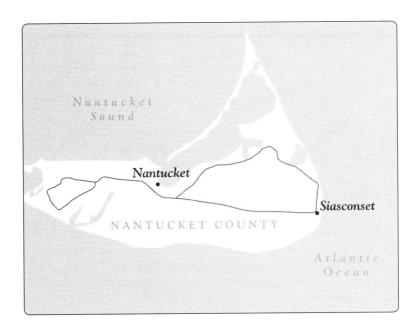

Thursday, June 26

NANTUCKET COUNTY

NANTUCKET
Blueberry Hill—Douglass & Caroline Ellis
8 Quaise Pastures Road, Nantucket

An oak forest and tupelo grove protect the house and garden from ocean winds. The naturalistic landscape designed by Lucinda Young contrasts rolling serene meadow views of West Poplis Harbor with an enclosed garden set in a small building envelope on a conservation restriction, consisting of heaths, heathers, and a crab apple espalier. A vegetable garden and chicken yard are hidden from view.

Hours: 10 a.m. to 4 p.m.

Located 3.3 miles on Poplis Road from Milestone Road turnoff. Turn left after mailbox #209 onto Quaise Pastures Road. Hardtop road turns to gravel. *Please park at circle before gate (except wheelchairs).* We are #8. Walk through gate and bear left up hill.

Proceeds shared with the Nantucket Preservation Trust

Dr. & Mrs. John W. Espy
4 New Dollar Lane, Nantucket

This is an unusual "in-town" garden because of a large lawn with spreading elm trees. The house is 200 years old and has a converted stable in the garden. The formal terraced garden features a sixty-year-old *grandiflora* magnolia, a waterlily pond, roses, and perennials.

Hours: 10 a.m. to 4 p.m.

Located just off monument on Main Street. At monument, turn onto Milk Street, then take first left. It is a white house with green door, third on left.

Proceeds shared with the Nantucket Historical Association

Inishfree—Coleman & Susan Burke
37 Gardner Road, Nantucket

The challenge for this garden was to preserve the panoramic view of Nantucket Harbor while enjoying unusual plantings in the foreground. Native plants along the coastal dunes' horizon surround the ha-ha filled with exotic plants and ornamental grasses. The effect allows one to enjoy many sight lines through the columns of the house's porch, over and through the garden to the freshness of blue water and sailboats beyond.

Hours: 10 a.m. to 4 p.m.

From Nantucket, proceed to rotary; go left on Milestone Road towards Siasconset. Take second left (Polpis Road). Go about 1 mile, pass Moor's End Farm on left. Turn left at end of cornfield onto Gardner Road. Go .7 mile to end and turn right onto Burke property. It is first house on left past gate.

Proceeds shared with the Nantucket Garden Club

Kate's Folly
3 Grant Avenue, Nantucket

This hidden garden encircling a mimosa tree and reached by a short pathway down the cliff is Kate's Folly's special secret. Now in its third incarnation, we have tried to create a tranquil, low-maintenance setting that discourages the deer yet remains in keeping with the formality of the old elements of the garden. Overlooking Nantucket Sound and Nantucket Harbor, the house is surrounded by hydrangeas, perennial beds, and kitchen and cottage gardens.

Hours: 10 a.m. to 4 p.m.

From Nantucket, take Cliff Road .3 mile to first right, Cabot Lane. Follow to end and turn left onto Grant Avenue. Kate's Folly is second house on right. *Do not park on Cabot Lane.*

Proceeds shared with the Nantucket Conservation Foundation

Nindethana
24 Almanack Pond Road, Nantucket

Tucked between the windswept Cranberry Bog and the enchanted Hidden Forest, we have created a private world. The classical perennial garden, conceived as an outdoor room off the guest wing of our house, is defined by open lattice fencing and an arbor walk wrapped with roses. The sunken lawn doubles as a croquet court and serpentine paths wind through the plantings. Beyond the moon gates of the garden sits an octagonal pool house overlooking a dark, stone-edged pool circled with grasses and lush bamboo. The most unusual element in the landscape is the long reflecting pond, which mirrors the back of the house and is home to hundreds of Japanese koi, herons, turtles, and ducks—a perfect ecological balance.

Hours: 10 a.m. to 2 p.m.

From Main Street in town, take Lower Orange Street to rotary. Nantucket Looms will be on corner. Go around the circle and turn right onto Milestone Road. Take second left onto Polpis Road. Island Lumber will be on right. Drive 4.3 miles to Almanack Pond Road and turn right. Continue on dirt road for .3 mile past Cranberry Bog on left. Turn left at large white gates (#24) and drive up small hill. *Please park along driveway.*

Proceeds shared with Cambridge College—Stacey Milgrim Scholarship Fund

Townhouse Garden
12 India Street, Nantucket

This is a perennial garden at the rear of a brick townhouse built in 1828. The garden is in the English style with brick paths and a fountain at the far end. It is enclosed by evergreen hedges and incorporates a conservatory built in Darlington, North Umberland, which was added in 1997.

Hours: 10 a.m. to 4 p.m.

Located 2 blocks down Centre Street from Pacific National Bank on Main Street. Turn left at India Street and #12 is third house from corner of India and Centre.

Proceeds shared with the Nantucket Historical Association

Constance Umberger
Eel Point Road, Nantucket

This informal garden has evolved in stages over the years from a flat, treeless, grassless barn-yard surrounding a house—the former horse barn. The challenges of sun, wind, deer, and rabbits have resulted in a garden of six enclosed rooms within an overall enclosure of fencing, hedging, and stone walls. The rooms, which are planned to give year-round interest and to provide places for outdoor sitting and dining, include a cottage garden; a pool garden with massed spring-flowering bulbs, trees, and shrubs; the Green Room, with box globes and other topiary; and the New Garden, with long double perennial borders. There are two pergolas and a small pool with frogs, turtles, and fish.

Hours: 10 a.m. to 2 p.m.

From either Cliff Road or Madaket Road, turn onto Eel Point Road. Take first sand road on right, where there will be a stop sign on a bike path, 3 or 4 mailboxes, and several name signs. Turn into second driveway on right, a long, straight driveway with post-and-rail fencing. Turn into lower house drive at bottom of hill on right. *Please park in field.*

Proceeds shared with the Royal Oak Foundation

Whitney Garden
19 Pleasant Street, Nantucket

This Federal-style brick house and garden were built in 1829 by Jared Coffin. The owner has been restoring the intricate patterns of boxwood that outline beds of old roses. Within the walled garden is an ornamental iron gazebo surrounded by hostas, lilies, rose of Sharon, *Hibiscus syriacus*, and white oak-leaf hydrangea.

Hours: 10 a.m. to 4 p.m.

Go up Main Street and turn left at Hadwyn House Museum onto Pleasant Street. Go to large bridge house on right. Entrance to garden is on Mill Street.

SIASCONSET
Hedged About—Charlotte & Macdonald Mathey
Polpis Road, Siasconset

Hedged About is a two-and-one-half-acre property with five different garden areas. First is the perennial flower border seen from the road, then an herb garden, a fenced area for holding plants and a covered area for blueberries, a hosta garden, and a completely invisible shrub garden of about half an acre with gazebo, fountain, decorative garden shed, and curving grass paths. The flower border was much enlarged since 1976 when we bought the house. A path through it was added at that time and it was completely replanted with the help of horticulturist Geraldine Weinstein. The placement of plants in the border is the work of the owner. The flower border, herb garden, and hosta beds were put in and designed by the owners with some labor provided by family and local garden crews. The "Nook" or secret garden was designed by Nantucket landscape designer Lucinda Young.

Hours: 10 a.m. to 4 p.m.

From Siasconset, 6 miles from Nantucket Rotary on Milestone Road, go towards Sankaty Head on Polpis Road/Sankaty Road about .25 mile. Hedged About is on left. Flower garden is easily seen from hedge at end of driveway. House has green trim and upper enclosed porch. *Please park along road by front hedge.*

Public Gardens

ESSEX COUNTY

BEVERLY

The Sedgwick Gardens at Long Hill

572 Essex Street, Beverly (978) 524-1871 www.thetrustees.org

Long Hill was first purchased by noted editor (1909-1938) of *Atlantic Monthly*, Ellery Sedgwick, and his first wife, Mabel Cabot Sedgwick, accomplished horticulturist and author of *The Garden Month by Month*. Today, the five acres are laid out in a series of distinct garden areas, each accented by a tremendous diversity of garden ornaments, structures, and statuary.

Hours: year round, daily, dawn to dusk. Guided tours for groups of eight or more.

Admission: free, $5 per person for groups.

From Route 128, take Exit 18 to Route 22/Essex Street north and proceed 1.3 miles. Bear left at fork and continue .2 mile to brick gateposts and entrance drive on left.

MIDDLESEX COUNTY

CAMBRIDGE

Mount Auburn Cemetery

580 Mount Auburn Street, Cambridge (617) 547-7105

Mount Auburn Cemetery, founded in 1831, is America's first landscaped cemetery, with 174 acres and more than 5,000 native and exotic trees identified and tagged. Many important and famous people are buried here. A fascinating place to visit and wonderful for bird watching.

Hours: year round, daily, 8 a.m. to 5 p.m. (7 p.m. during summer)

Admission: free

Entrance is on Mount Auburn Street near border of Cambridge and Watertown, about 1.5 miles west of Harvard Square, just west of Mount Auburn Hospital and Freshpond Parkway. Cemetery is easily reached by bus from Harvard Square (#71 or #73 bus).

FRAMINGHAM

Garden in the Woods of the New England Wildflower Society

180 Hemenway Road, Framingham (508) 877-7630 www.newfs.org

Garden in the Woods, New England's premier wildflower showcase, displays the largest landscaped collection of native plants in the Northeast. Forty-five acres with woodland trails offer vistas of wildflowers, shrubs, and trees. More than 1,700 varieties of plants, including more than 200 rare and endangered species, grow in protective cultivation.

Hours: April 15 through June 15, daily, with extended hours in May to 7 p.m.; June 16 through October 31, Tuesday through Sunday, 9 a.m. to 5 p.m.

Admission: $7 adults, $5 senior citizens, $3 children 6 to 16 years, children under 6 free

From Route 128, take Route 20 west; go 8 miles to Raymond Road (second left after traffic lights in South Sudbury); 1.3 miles to Hemenway Road.

From Massachusetts Turnpike/I-90, take Exit 12 to Route 9 east. Go 2.4 miles to Edgell Road (Route 9 overpass), then 2.1 miles to lights. Turn right onto Water Street and left onto Hemenway Road. Follow garden signs.

JAMAICA PLAIN

Arnold Arboretum of Harvard University

125 The Arborway, Jamaica Plain (617) 524-1718 www.arboretum.harvard.edu

The 265-acre Arnold Arboretum displays North America's premier collection of more than 13,000 hardy trees, shrubs, and vines. The grounds were planted and designed by the arboretum's first director, Charles Sprague Sargent, and America's first landscape architect, Frederick Law Olmsted. Highlights include crab apple, conifer, lilac, rhododendron, and bonsai collections.

Hours: year round, daily, dawn to dusk

Admission: free

From Storrow Drive, take Fenway/Park Drive exit. Follow signs to Riverway, which becomes Jamaicaway and then Arborway/Centre Street.

From I-95/Route 128, exit onto Route 9 east. Follow Route 9 for 7 miles to Riverway/Centre Street.

From Southeast Expressway/I-93, take Exit 11/Granite Avenue/Ashmont onto Route 203. Follow past Franklin Park. This site is also accessible by public transportation.

WALTHAM

Lyman Estate, The Vale

185 Lyman Street, Waltham (781) 891-4882

The Lyman Estate is one of the finest examples in the United States of a country property laid out according to the principles of eighteenth-century English naturalistic design. The greenhouses were built from 1800 to 1930, and contain century-old camellias and grapevines, as well as tropical and subtropical plants.

Hours: year round, daily, dawn to dusk. Greenhouses are open year round, Monday through Saturday, 9:30 a.m. to 4 p.m.

Admission: free

From Route 128, take Exit 26/Route 20 east to Waltham/Boston. Follow Route 20 (it becomes Main Street) through center of Waltham about 1.7 miles. At Kentucky Fried Chicken, turn left onto Lyman Street. Follow .5 mile to a rotary and bear immediately right into estate driveway (check for SPNEA sign).

WELLESLEY

Massachusetts Horticultural Society Elm Bank Reservation

900 Washington Street, Wellesley (617) 933-4900 www.masshort.org

The Massachusetts Horticultural Society's Elm Bank Reservation is filled with secret gardens. Thirty-six acres encompass educational, horticultural, and historic gardens such as the All-American Selections trial garden, Weezie's Garden for Children, the Noanett Garden Club's Daffodil and Grass Garden, the Tree House Garden, and the Italianate Garden.

Hours: 8 a.m. to 6 p.m.

Admission: free

From Route 16 west in Wellesley, you will come to a traffic light (5-way intersection). Bear left to continue on Route 16 for 1.7 miles. The Elm Bank Reservation will be on left, marked by a green sign.

MICHIGAN

Dr. Alice R. McCarthy Garden, Birmingham.
Photo by Bridge Communications, Inc.

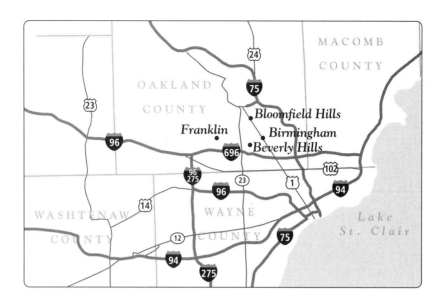

Sunday, July 13
OAKLAND COUNTY

BEVERLY HILLS
Yvonne's Garden
21800 Normandale, Beverly Hills

My garden provides a serene setting for family gatherings. The garden has many Asian influences, including a bronze temple bell, Japanese lanterns, and beautiful evergreens—cedar of Lebanon, umbrella pine, and Silberlock fir to name a few. Two water features are highlighted by river birch, katsura, and a granite bridge that crosses a dry bed. A wall of hemlock provides a feeling of seclusion as one walks along the path that weaves through a shade garden featuring ginger, ferns, hostas, grasses, daylilies, Chinese orchids, Japanese maples, dogwood, hydrangea, and tree peonies. A grandchildren's garden can also be found, which contains a glider and rocks for climbing and sitting.

Hours: 10 a.m. to 4 p.m.

Take Lahser Road south. Normandale is between 12 and 13 Mile Roads, east off Lahser. Turn left 3 streets south of 13 Mile Road. Bear to left and it is fourth house on left. *Please park on street.*

Proceeds shared with the Franklin Garden Club

BIRMINGHAM
The Dr. Alice R. McCarthy Garden
1450 Pilgrim Road, Birmingham

There were no gardens on this beautiful property in 1968; however, the one-acre site had magnificent trees—please note the Norway maple (this tree is old enough to draw Social Security). Now the garden has my dwarf conifer collection plus ten Alberta spruces ten to fifteen feet tall. There are nine garden areas with many small flowering trees and shrubs and two 100-foot perennial gardens nine feet deep with a five-foot path between them. I have moved my rose garden to a sunnier area—and added more older roses. I have added as many tree peonies as sun and space will allow! These shrubs are easy and the blooms are magnificent. I will have photos of these peonies for you, since bloom time is very early here. The clematis are a challenge, but I like a challenge! I think of the individual gardens as something like English gardens I have visited, with room-like settings. I have designed the gardens myself and they reflect my interest in style, art, and horticulture. Sculptures by several nationally known artists are in the gardens. The garden was featured on HGTV's *Secret Gardens* in 2001. Come and enjoy!

Hours: 10 a.m. to 4 p.m.

From downtown Birmingham, travel north on Woodward Avenue (M1) to Quarton Road (about 1 to 2 miles from downtown Birmingham). Turn left and go about .5 mile to Pilgrim Road just past Manressa Retreat. Turn left. Property is third house on left.

From I-75, take Big Beaver Road exit. Go west (Big Beaver will turn into Quarton Road at Woodward Avenue). Go .5 mile past Woodward and turn left onto Pilgrim Road. Property is third house on left. *Please park on street.*

BLOOMFIELD HILLS
Virginia Fox
1371 Pembroke Drive, Bloomfield Hills

This garden has been developing for more than thirty years. The wildflower garden, under the elevated branches of mature evergreens, includes many varieties of trillium, ferns, and other native Michigan wildflowers. Mature spruce, fir, pines, Japanese maples, tulip trees, and sour gum provide the framework for a new shrub border, hostas, and a large vegetable garden. The goal of this gardener is to create a rural, naturalized landscape in the middle of an urban area.

Hours: 10 a.m. to 4 p.m.

Take Long Lake Road/18 Mile Road west from Woodward about .75 mile. Turn south (left) onto Pembroke Drive. It is fourth house on right, #1371, with a long driveway. *Please park along street.*

Judy & Jim's Garden
3916 Cottontail Lane, Bloomfield Hills

This spectacularly diverse three-quarter-acre property contains a woodland garden, sun garden, and a two-tiered, 10,000-gallon water garden with streams and waterfalls. More than 300 varieties of hosta, New Zealand hostas, plants from other parts of the world, unusual and rare specimen evergreens and shrubs, wildflowers, numerous varieties of fragrant flowers, ferns, grasses, and an interesting integration of textures, shapes, and colors complement the curved lines of the beds. The visually stimulating garden rooms are augmented with garden art, sculpture, birdhouses, a unique children's playhouse and garden shed, and the constant sound of the waterfalls.

Hours: 10 a.m. to 4 p.m.

Located between Lahser and Telegraph Roads north of Maple Road/Fifteen Mile Road. Travel east on Maple Road from Telegraph Road to second traffic light. Turn left onto Gilbert Lake Road. At third street on left, turn left onto Cottontail Lane. Garden is first driveway on right. *Please park on street.*

Franklin
Hickory Hill
26705 Irving Road, Franklin

Designed around our historic 1894 Greek Revival-style farmhouse, our gardens at Hickory Hill capture the imagination in all seasons. Our three-and-one-quarter-acre property features a spring garden, an iris and peony border, a rose garden, a brilliantly colored midsummer perennial bed, and a treasured sunken white garden complete with flowing fountain, wisteria arbor, and black stone paths. Further afield from our house are an organic raised-bed vegetable garden, a meadow for our beehives, a small wood, and large pond with a developing bog garden. Near our back porch, a classic herb garden provides fragrance and culinary herbs for the kitchen. Boxwood hedges, a 1930 Lord & Burnham greenhouse, old stone walks, and stairwells charm us to keep up the hard work. In the planning stage: a children's garden honoring our grandchild, Maxine Rose.

Hours: 10 a.m. to 4 p.m.

From the corner of Telegraph Road and Maple/Fifteen Mile Road, go west about 2 miles to Franklin Road. Turn south, pass Cider Mill, cross Fourteen Mile Road (flashing traffic light), continuing past gas station to Wellington Road. Turn west and go to fourth road, Irving Road. Turn right. Hickory Hill is second house on left, #26705.

Proceeds shared with the Franklin Garden Club

Public Gardens

OAKLAND COUNTY

BLOOMFIELD HILLS

Congregational Church of Birmingham

1000 Cranbrook Road, Bloomfield Hills (248) 644-8065

Within a nine-acre property we have created the most interesting group of gardens, blooming from early spring with bulbs, to asters in the fall. We have award-winning displays of tree and herbaceous peonies. Included are five kinds of irises, *Lilium* beds, several hosta beds, daylily beds, and a memorial garden. Rose beds complement specimen trees and shrubs.

Hours: year round, daily, dawn to dusk

Admission: free

Take Woodward Avenue north to Cranbrook Road.

Cranbrook House & Gardens

Lone Pine Road, Bloomfield Hills (248) 645-3147

Stroll through the forty acres of gardens surrounding historic Cranbrook House, the 1908 Arts & Crafts-style manor house of founders George and Ellen Scripps Booth. The formal gardens and terraces are enhanced by sculptures, fountains, paths, lakes, and streams. Tended and maintained by devoted volunteers, the gardens are exquisite.

Hours: May through Labor Day, Monday through Saturday, 10 a.m. to 5 p.m., Sunday, 11 a.m. to 5 p.m.; September, daily, 11 a.m. to 3 p.m.; October, weekends only, 11 a.m. to 3 p.m.

Admission: $5 adults, $4 senior citizens, children under 5 free

Lone Pine Road is north of Quarton Road about 16 miles, east of Telegraph/Route 24, and west of Woodward Avenue/M-1.

NEW HAMPSHIRE

Peter & Theodora Berg's Garden, Walpole.
Photo by Gordon Hayward.

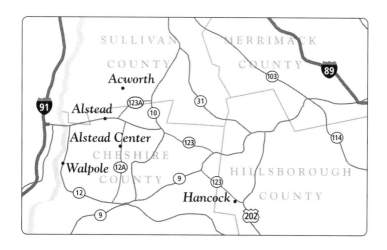

Saturday, July 19

CHESHIRE COUNTY

ALSTEAD

Mountain View—Gordon & Helene Moodie

97 Bennett Road, Alstead

Mountain View Garden is four landscaped acres surrounding a 1795 house built on the brow of a hill overlooking a spectacular view of the Green Mountains of Vermont. A series of gardens begun in the 1930s and added to over the years has flowers in bloom from April until late October. Some of the perennials, shrubs, and trees date back to the 1930s and most of the annuals are raised from seed under lights in the basement by the Moodies. A beautiful half-acre pond was designed and added in 1980. The entire garden is almost exclusively planted and maintained by the Moodies.

Hours: 10 a.m. to 4 p.m.

From Keene, come up Main Street to town circle. Go left around circle to first street on right, Court Street (courthouse is on left). Follow north to a traffic light (gas station and convenience store on right). Route 12A forks to right. Go 12.5 miles on Route 12A to Alstead Center. There will be an old stone-walled cemetery on left and a gravel road (Pratt Road) angling to left around cemetery and a small white house. Follow Pratt Road past cemetery and up steep hill to Bennett Road. Turn right and go .4 mile to end.

From Alstead, Route 12A joins Route 123 in Alstead. Take Routes 12A/123 east out of Alstead. After 1.5 miles, Route 12A forks to right (sign reads Surry/Keene). Go right on Route 12A and drive 2.3 miles to gravel road on right, Pratt Road. Turn right and proceed as directed above.

Proceeds shared with the Alstead Conservation Commission

Alstead Center
Bill & Judy Moran's Garden
282 Pratt Road, Alstead Center

The vision of our garden flows from the wonderful natural setting of the original farm homestead with its rolling hills, open fields, ledge outcroppings, mixed hardwood and pine woods, and mountain views. Utilizing this landscape as the background, we have added a large pond with a small feeder pond and created a series of planting areas branching out from the house into the fields. These areas feature flowering trees, shrubs, and perennials. Old stone foundations and border walls have been reworked into freestanding fieldstone walls and terraces, which serve as a special focus, tying together the total design.

Hours: 10 a.m. to 4 p.m.

From Keene, follow Court Street north to a traffic light (gas station and convenience store on right). Route 12A forks to right. Go 12.5 miles on Route 12A to Alstead Center. There will be an old stone-walled cemetery on left and a gravel road (Pratt Road) angling to left around the cemetery and a small white house. Follow Pratt Road for 1.6 miles to Moran's garden. *Signs direct you to parking on right before garden entrance.*

From Alstead, Route 12A joins Route 123 in Alstead. Take Routes 12A/123 east out of Alstead. After 1.5 miles, Route 12A forks to right (sign will read Surry/Keene). Go right on Route 12A and drive 2.3 miles to gravel road on right, Pratt Road. Turn right and proceed as directed above.

Proceeds shared with the Alstead Conservation Commission

Walpole
Peter & Theodora Berg's Garden
Rice Mountain Lane, Walpole

Gardening at the top of a windswept mountain on exposed bedrock has been quite a challenge, which has been met by master dry-stone waller Dan Snow and landscape and garden designer Gordon Hayward. Their combined talents, relating the construction of a "medieval" manor house by the homeowners to the site, hold many wonders. There is a grotto resting on the bedrock overlooking a pond; an "old" barn foundation with a small stream flowing in, out, and through it; assorted perennial beds and borders; a dwarf conifer garden; a spring garden; and everywhere, from the pond to the top of the tower, is the magnificent view.

Hours: 10 a.m. to 4 p.m.

Follow Route 123/12N together for 2.7 miles. Leave Route 12 and stay on Route 123 for .8 mile to Valley Road. Follow Valley Road for 3 miles; Rice Mountain Lane is on left. Go up hill and follow signs. *Parking area will be marked at top of mountain.*

Proceeds shared with the Monadnock Garden Club

HANCOCK

Schaefer Gardens

84 Norway Hill Road, Hancock

The gardens began with the purchase of my house in 1993 and are the result of collaboration with local landscape gardeners George Lohmiller, Steve Morrison, and, most recently, G. Kristian Fenderson. The informal gardens feature an extensive collection of specimen trees, deciduous shrubs, broad-leaved evergreens, and conifers. In addition, ornamental grasses, ground covers, and herbaceous perennials have been used and, most recently, several beds devoted to annuals for cutting and seasonal color. Above the driveway is a woodland garden with dogwoods, azaleas, boxwood, and specimen trees and shrubs. To the north of the pool house is a memorial garden commemorating beloved pets. It combines elements of a sunny rock garden with shady woodland plants and water feature gardens below. There are also views of Crotched and Pack Monadnock mountains.

Hours: 10 a.m. to 4 p.m.

From Peterborough at intersection of Routes 101 and 202, go north on Route 202 for 7 miles. Take first left after blinking traffic light onto Norway Hill Road. Proceed up hill 1 mile to #84; house is on right set back from road. *Please park along driveway or marked grassy area.*

Proceeds shared with the Monadnock Garden Club

ACWORTH

The Gardens on Grout Hill

Grout Hill Road, Acworth

The gardens on Grout Hill were developed over a period of thirty years from an abandoned farm and house dating from the 1790s by owners G. Kristian Fenderson and Alston Barrett. The gardens and other planted areas are several acres in extent. They serve as a laboratory for Kristian's landscape design business and also showcase the owners' personal favorites. The garden features many mature examples of rare and unusual woody and herbaceous plants in a variety of environments. Seasonal annuals and containers also form a large part of the summer display. Azaleas, rhododendrons, viburnums, conifers, magnolias, beech trees, and old roses are just a few of the areas of emphasis.

Hours: 10 a.m. to 4 p.m.

From the south and east (Keene/Marlow), take Route 10 north to Route 123A west/ south left about 3 miles. Bear left following Route 123A along river for less than .5 mile. At first crossroad, turn right onto Grout Hill Road. Cross wooden bridge, go up hill passing Russell Road on right and Ball Road on left. *Please park in first driveway on left after small red Grout Hill Schoolhouse.*

From Alstead, at Kimec's station (east end of Alstead village) bear left and follow Route 123A east/north along Cold River to South Acworth Village. Continue east on Route 123A for 2.25 miles. About .75 mile after passing Echo Valley Road on left, turn left onto Grout Hill Road and proceed as directed above.

Public Gardens

SULLIVAN COUNTY

NEWBURY

The Fells at the John Hay National Wildlife Refuge

Route 103A, Newbury (603) 763-4789

These gardens, developed from 1914 to 1940 as a showplace country estate, had
fallen into decline. Work by Garden Conservancy staff, current managers, and
Friends of the John Hay National Wildlife Refuge has revived the historic design

A PROJECT OF
THE GARDEN
CONSERVANCY

of formal naturalized plantings, terraced lawns, and native New Hampshire granite walls. The
rock garden, in which Clarence Hay experimented with alpines for over forty years, is in its
eighth year of rehabilitation.

Hours: year round, daily, dawn to dusk. House tours available on weekends. Call ahead
for special events and educational programs.

Admission: $4 grounds, $5 house and grounds

From the south and east, take I-89 north to Exit 9/Route 103 and go west to Newbury.
Take Route 102A north for 2.2 miles. The Fells is on left.

From the north, take I-89 south to Exit 12/Route 11. Turn right at end of exit ramp and
make an immediate left onto Route 102A south. Travel 5.6 miles to The Fells on right.
Please park in lot and walk down driveway to gardens.

New Jersey

Garden of Dr. & Mrs. George E. Staehle, Short Hills
Photo by Stephanie Werskey

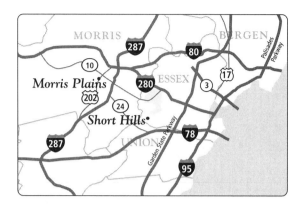

Saturday, May 17

ESSEX COUNTY

SHORT HILLS

Garden of Dr. & Mrs. George E. Staehle
83 Old Hollow Road, Short Hills

Our garden is in an old quarry. Over the years we have cleared and planted it ourselves, after a local landscaper told us it was impossible and to "let it stay wild." We started about forty years ago with azaleas, rhododendrons, and wildflowers, then went on to hostas, hellebores, daylilies, geraniums, primulas, and other perennials. We continue to collect and plant experimentally.

Hours: 10 a.m. to 2 p.m.

From Route 24 west, take Hobart Gap Road exit. Turn right at traffic light onto Hobart Gap Road. At blinking traffic light, road name changes to White Oak Ridge Road. At next light (1 mile), turn right onto Parsonage Hill Road. Continue to "T" junction. Turn left onto Old Short Hills Road and go about .5 mile to second street on right, Old Hollow Road. Garden is at #83, fifth house on right. *Please park along street.*

Winter's Garden
28 Dryden Terrace, Short Hills

This garden is densely packed with conifers ranging from miniature to dwarf, intermediate to full size. Ground covers, perennials, shrubs, and deciduous trees, including dozens of Japanese maples, are incorporated. Weathered limestone is extensively integrated throughout for contrast with the plantings. The arrangements include many rare and unusual specimens. The maturity of the rare specimens makes this garden unique.

Hours: 10 a.m. to 4 p.m.

From Route 24 east, take Exit 8. Go to second traffic light and turn left. Continue about 6 blocks and turn left onto Dryden Terrace.

From Route 24 west, take Exit 9/Hobart Avenue. Go to first light and turn right onto Hobart Avenue. Go about 6 blocks to Dryden Terrace. Dryden Terrace is off White Oak Ridge Road between Parsonage Hill Road and Route 24. *Please park on street.*

MORRIS COUNTY

Morris Plains
Watnong Gardens
2379 Watnong Terrace, Morris Plains

Watnong Gardens is the former Watnong Nursery made famous by Don and Hazel Smith. The garden now consists of two and one half acres of collections, including conifers, shrubs, hostas, ferns, perennials, and a water garden. Special plants are added each year. A train, complete with four railroad cars, was made into six- and eight-foot-long troughs, all handcrafted by the owner and planted with mini-plants and alpines.

Hours: 10 a.m. to 4 p.m.

From I-80 west, take Exit 43 to I-287 south. Take to Exit 39B/Route 10 west. Go about 3 miles west to third traffic light, Powdermill Road. Take "jug handle" turn and head east on Route 10. After passing Mountain Club Garden Homes, go slow. Watnong Terrace angles off to right and parallels Route 10 like a service road. It is .7 mile from "jug handle" turn. *Please park on street.*

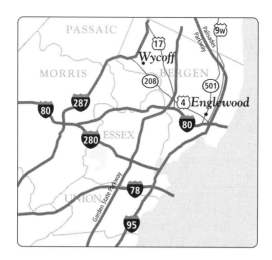

Sunday, May 18

BERGEN COUNTY

ENGLEWOOD

Peggy & Walter Jones

401 Morrow Road, Englewood

This rolling hillside encompasses a variety of gardens, ranging from a formal rose garden to a wild woodland garden where the Japanese primrose and shooting stars dance with the helle-bores. Other highlights include a rock garden, a living wall, a small enclosed courtyard with wonderful climbing hydrangeas, and an elliptical herb garden in the center of the back lawn. Come and discover a wealth of unique trees, shrubs, and perennials. Find the split-leaf beech in the expansive front lawn. In the rear of the garden, look for the old moss-covered stone steps, which lead to the outdoor fireplace nestled under a canopy of large oaks. Look to the left and you will see the sorrel tree.

Hours: 10 a.m. to 4 p.m.

From I-95/I-80 east (local lanes), exit at Broad Avenue/Englewood. Follow Broad Avenue north until it ends at a traffic light at Palisades Avenue. Turn left, then make a quick right at light onto Lydecker Street. Follow to 4-way stop. Turn right onto Booth Avenue. Head uphill and turn left onto first road, Morrow Road. Go to top of hill. House, #401, is on right.

From Palisades Interstate Parkway, take Exit 1/Englewood/Palisades Avenue. Turn right onto Palisades and go to fifth light. Turn right onto Lydecker Street and proceed as directed above.

WYCKOFF
Tall Trees—Garden of Janet Schulz
16 Colonial Drive, Wyckoff

My creation, Tall Trees, is a wonderful woodland garden featuring shade-loving perennials, bulbs, vines, and shrubs. There is an extensive collection of hostas as well as trough gardens, homemade arbors, and garden statuary. Places to sit have been created so that the garden features can be enjoyed from many areas. Almost all of the plants are labeled. Many of the clematis are growing in other shrubs, which produces an extended season of interest in plants that would have bloomed at another time. An avid plant collector, I am always searching for, and trying to find, plants that may do well in my garden. Plants must be strong to succeed here at Tall Trees, for I do not believe in growing plants that require a lot of spraying or staking.

Hours: 10 a.m. to 4 p.m.

From George Washington Bridge, take Route 4 west to Route 208 north/Oakland about 7.5 miles to Ewing Avenue. Go down exit ramp and turn right onto Ewing. Go to traffic light and turn right onto Franklin Avenue. Go through 2 lights to first street on right, Godwin Drive, and turn right. First left is Colonial Drive. Garden is at #16 on right.

From I-287, take Route 208 south. Exit onto Ewing Avenue. Turn left at stop sign and go to light. Turn right onto Franklin Avenue. Proceed as directed above.

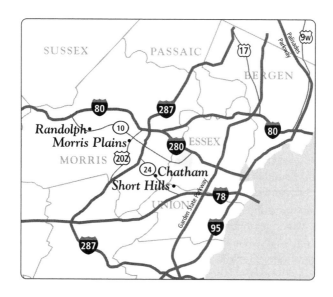

Saturday, June 7
ESSEX COUNTY

SHORT HILLS
Winter's Garden
28 Dryden Terrace, Short Hills

This garden is densely packed with conifers ranging from miniature to dwarf, intermediate to full size. Ground covers, perennials, shrubs, and deciduous trees, including dozens of Japanese maples, are incorporated. Weathered limestone is extensively integrated throughout for contrast with the plantings. The arrangements include many rare and unusual specimens. The maturity of the rare specimens makes this garden unique.

Hours: 10 a.m. to 4 p.m.

From Route 24 east, take Exit 8. Go to second traffic light and turn left. Continue about 6 blocks and turn left onto Dryden Terrace.

From Route 24 west, take Exit 9/Hobart Avenue. Go to first light and turn right onto Hobart Avenue. Go about 6 blocks to Dryden Terrace. Dryden Terrace is off White Oak Ridge Road between Parsonage Hill Road and Route 24. *Please park on street.*

MORRIS COUNTY

CHATHAM
Jack Lagos
23 Pine Street, Chatham

I have been developing this one-acre property, which backs onto a lovely wood, for twenty-five years. The first garden and island perennial border is now one among many. A 100-year-old barn is backdrop for shade-loving plants and on its sunny sides lie an herb garden and another perennial border. Ten graceful clematis vines climb beautifully designed lattice fencing, which defines the dwarf conifer collection. A woodland garden, my latest project, lies beneath a very large white oak and features a natural rock fountain.

Hours: 10 a.m. to 4 p.m.

From Garden State Parkway or New Jersey Turnpike/I-95, take I-78 west to Route 24 west. Take Chatham exit (immediately after Short Hills Mall). Follow signs to Route 124 west/Main Street and, at fifth traffic light, turn left onto Lafayette Avenue. Go all the way to top of hill and, when Lafayette bends to right, turn right onto Pine Street. Number 23 is fourth house on left.

From I-287, exit onto Route 24 east. Continue to The Mall at Short Hills exit. At end of exit ramp, turn right onto River Road. At first light, bear right and continue straight (River Road becomes Watching Avenue) to fifth light. Turn left onto Lafayette Avenue. Proceed as directed above. *Please park on street.*

Morris Plains
Watnong Gardens
2379 Watnong Terrace, Morris Plains

Watnong Gardens is the former Watnong Nursery made famous by Don and Hazel Smith. The garden now consists of two and one half acres of collections, including conifers, shrubs, hostas, ferns, perennials, and a water garden. Special plants are added each year. A train, complete with four railroad cars, was made into six- and eight-foot-long troughs, all handcrafted by the owner and planted with mini-plants and alpines.

Hours: 10 a.m. to 4 p.m.

From I-80 west, take Exit 43 to I-287 south. Take to Exit 39B/Route 10 west. Go about 3 miles west to third traffic light, Powdermill Road. Take "jug handle" turn and head east on Route 10. After passing Mountain Club Garden Homes, go slow. Watnong Terrace angles off to right and parallels Route 10 like a service road. It is .7 mile from "jug handle" turn. *Please park on street.*

Randolph
Jones Garden
123 Mountainside Drive, Randolph

Our garden covers about one half of our one-acre propery. After thirty-two years, the garden has evolved from a collection of more than 500 different specimens to a more designed setting. I have created sunny borders by the pool, which are inspired by Piet Oudolf's books. The backyard shade garden features many plants with interesting foliage characteristics: variegation, color, texture, structure. Other features include a small bog garden and a deer-resistant border by the drive.

Hours: 10 a.m. to 4 p.m.

From I-287, take Exit 39 to Route 10 west for 5 miles to Franklin Road (traffic light, Exxon gas station on right). Proceed through light, taking Shongum exit onto Franklin Road (south), which becomes Openaki Road. One mile from Route 10, turn right onto Mountainside Drive. We are on left, .3 mile from Openaki, at #123. *Please park on street.*

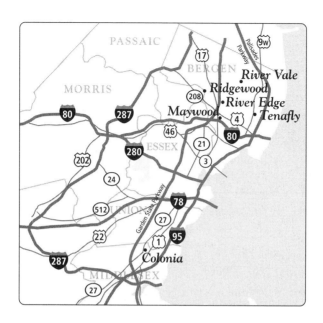

Saturday, June 21

BERGEN COUNTY

Maywood
Dail & Tony's Garden
66 West Magnolia Avenue, Maywood

Ten or so years ago, Tony and I began gardening under the two maple trees that canopy our quite small backyard. Early on, a bluestone path developed, now enticing the visitor beneath a copper arch we created ourselves, alongside another copper piece we built to support tomato plants, beyond to a dwarf weeping crab apple and the rest of the shade beds. The garden has evolved over the years, reflecting our growing fascination with "winter interest," as well as with texture plays both in and out of season. Sedges tuck up to gentians and campanulas, veronica tumbles under a caryopteris. The lavender *Phlox subulata* is later a verdant mat under a lavender callicarpa. Whimsy is all about—an original art piece by Jeanne Wheaton of New Jersey is a focal point in the sun garden and a couple of old candelabra floor lamps set with candles light the way to the three-whiskey barrel water garden, somewhat obscured by mature ficus, schefflera, and draceana houseplants out summering. Come be transported—so small a piece of land, so large the garden.

Hours: 10 a.m. to 4 p.m.

From George Washington Bridge, take Route 4 west to Forest Avenue and take north. Turn left at traffic light and go back over Route 4. Road becomes Maywood Avenue at Spring Valley Avenue. Continue south for 1 mile and turn right onto West Magnolia Avenue. Ours is thirteenth house on the left, second up from corner of Rampo Avenue.

From Route 208, take Route 4 east to Forest Avenue. Exit to right and, at light, turn left. Proceed as directed above. *Please park on street.*

RIDGEWOOD
The Zusy/Ortiz Garden
299 West Ridgewood Avenue, Ridgewood

First came the perennials and bulbs, hundreds of them, driven up in a truck from my Washington, D.C., home. They were plopped into newly worked soil to create a perimeter garden at our just-bought 1870 Italianate Victorian. Then came the removal of dozens of trees hugging the house. Untouched for years, they had caused structural damage and made the place look like Sleeping Beauty's castle in the ninety-ninth year. Three dying birches finally succumbed and were taken out, providing the impetus for a garden out front. One semi-circle begat another; soon there were four. My pot-bound plantings on front steps and in hanging baskets, inspired by years in London, now had friends. Soon there were more containers, including a Victorian urn and a planter hung where a window should've been but wasn't at the back door. Busy landscaping was tamed bit by bit—goodbye, low-growing juniper and cotoneaster. Then it was time to deal with Vietnam. That was the jungle on both sides of my front walk. Sweeps of grass now lie in an area once covered by pachysandra, vinca, lily of the valley, hosta, weeds, and two dozen bushes—azaleas and yews, which were recycled to become foundation plantings around the house. There was also the 300-pound rhododenron. It was moved to the border, where it keeps company with another specimen nearly as tall as the house. The lily of the valley and vinca were placed here and there. The hostas were whacked to bits and replanted along the side of the house in our rhody-inspired Secret Garden, a woodland Thoughtful Spot. Nooks and crannies can always be found for sticking in one more perennial offspring or offering from a nursery or friend. Harvested seeds and bulbs are dispersed from one place to another. There's always a container to pot up. For someone who has never gardened in one spot for more than three years at a stretch, it has been a joy and a journey to see what could be accomplished here in four. Please stop by for a look-see over tea sandwiches, cookies and drinks on the lemonade porch. If you are a crowd, please give warning with an e-mail to gardencook52@aol.com.

Hours: 10 a.m. to 4 p.m.

From Route 17, take Ridgewood Avenue exit and follow directly into village. Staying on East Ridgewood Avenue, pass duck pond and go through commercial area all the way up to train station. Turn right onto North Broad Street and continue 1 block to Franklin Avenue. Turn left, going under railroad bridge, and follow curving road to traffic light. Turning right, you are now on West Ridgewood Avenue; continue, passing West Side Presbyterian Church on left and Women's Club on right. Go up hill to North Murray. Our house, #299, is yellow with white trim and black shutters and stands at corner of West Ridgewood and North Murray. (If you go past Ridge School, you've gone too far.)

River Edge
Anthony "Bud" & Virginia Korteweg
800 Summit Avenue, River Edge

Edgecroft is a unique three-acre terraced property laid out in 1910 by Italian artisans, with 100 cararra marble stairs to a swimming pool with a Venetian bridge surrounded by a stone-columned pergola draped in roses, wisteria, and honeysuckle. The property has five garden rooms: a gated brick courtyard entrance with rare *Cryptomeria* 'Lobbii', rhododendrons, azaleas, and *Magnolia virginiana*; a centerpiece tiered bronze angel fountain; a Victorian perennial garden with David Austin antique roses and over fifty perennials; a formal garden with crape myrtles, azaleas, a fountain with a copy of Verrochio's fifteenth-century bronze cupid with dolphin; a series of three koi ponds interspersed with nine waterfalls cascading down terraces edged by aged pines, golden larches, flowering cherry trees, dogwoods, *Styrax japonicum*, hydrangeas, wild strawberries, and creeping roses. Look for bronze water statuary, stone benches, and stone statuary throughout the grounds. An all-white Bridal Room is in progress: white birches and dogwoods, Japanese tree lilacs, rhododendrons, hydrangeas, azaleas, buddleia, and creeping cushion white roses will provide the backdrop for white perennials and annuals of the season.

Hours: 10 a.m. to 4 p.m.

From George Washington Bridge, take Route 4 west to Route 17 north. Take Midland Avenue/River Edge exit. Go east about 2 miles to "T" junction and turn right onto Kinderkamack Road. Travel south to first traffic light. Turn right onto Lincoln Avenue up a cobblestone hill. The walled property on right is Edgecroft. Turn right onto Summit Avenue. Number 800 is immediately on right.

From I-80 or Garden State Parkway, get on Route 17 north and proceed as directed above. *Please park along street and enter through open gates.*

Proceeds shared with Beautification of River's Edge

River Vale
Cupid's Garden—Audrey Linstrom Maihack
690 Edward Street, River Vale

With a background of conifers, pines, tall trees, and flowering shrubs, the sun and shade garden at my home is my artistic version of nature's best. It is adorned with rocks, shells, ponds, and driftwood and blended with ground covers, paths, vine-covered trellises, potted tropicals, and bonsai. Spring is color: bulbs, wisteria, azaleas, dogwoods, a weeping cherry, and Scotch broom. Later, iris, peonies, dianthus, roses, and lilacs make way for foxgloves and assorted perennials, as well as water plants, daylilies, hostas, ferns, and herbs. Fall color starts the retreat to the potting shed and cedar greenhouse, my winter garden. Outside, under the watchful eye of cupid, hawks and doves, as well as many other birds, frogs, rabbits, chipmunks, "Woody" the chuck, raccoons, and Mr. Skunk, all visit the fish in the ponds.

Hours: 10 a.m. to 4 p.m.

From Garden State Parkway north, take Exit 172, last exit in New Jersey. Turn right onto Grand Avenue east. Pass Kinderkamack Road (railroad tracks) and go over hill to a "T" (about 3 miles). Turn right onto South Middletown Road, which becomes River Vale Road, for .5 mile to right on Thurnau Drive (first right after Forcellati Nursery).

First right is Edward Street. Ours is first house on right.

From Palisades Interstate Parkway, take Exit 6W. Travel west on Orangeburg Road to fourth traffic light and turn left onto Blue Hill Road at end of reservoir. Go 1.4 miles to a stop sign. Turn left onto River Vale Road and proceed as directed above. *Please park on street.*

Tenafly
Linda Singer
170 Tekening Drive, Tenafly

I designed this romantic garden to include bluestone walks and patios, fieldstone sitting walls, rose-and-vine-covered arbors and trellises, stone ornaments, a swimming pool, and a small vegetable garden enclosed by a white picket fence. There are perennial and mixed borders. A cottage garden is of special interest for a wide variety of flowering shrubs. The greatest challenge is thwarting the legions of moles, voles, field mice, and rabbits that love the garden as much as I do.

Hours: 10 a.m. to 4 p.m.

From Palisades Interstate Parkway, take Exit 1/Englewood/Palisades Avenue. Turn right at first traffic light onto Sylvan Avenue/Route 9W, drive north about 3 miles, and turn left at light onto East Clinton Avenue. Drive .5 mile and turn right onto Ridge Road. Drive 1 block and turn right onto Berkeley Drive. Drive 1 block and turn left onto Highwood Road. Drive 2 blocks and turn right onto Tekening Drive. House is third on right. A sign with #170 is high on a tree. *Please park on street.*

Proceeds shared with Tenafly Nature Center and PFLAG of Bergen County

MIDDLESEX COUNTY

Colonia
Babbling Brook
335 New Dover Road, Colonia

Babbling Brook is located on three and one half acres adjacent to the Colonia Country Club. This garden has been in the same family for fifty years. It includes a brook, two ponds, specimen trees, an orchid greenhouse, waterfall with fishpond, perennial borders, wild garden, and indoor and outdoor pools that give this property a uniqueness. All this while sitting majestically on a hill enjoying the expansiveness of the fairways beyond.

Hours: 10 a.m. to 2 p.m.

From Garden State Parkway, take Exit 131. At end of exit ramp, turn left onto Route 27 north. Go through traffic light. Go .25 mile to overpass. Under overpass, turn left, go to a stop sign, and turn right onto New Dover Road. Go 1,000 feet. Brick house is on left, on golf course. *Please park in driveway.*

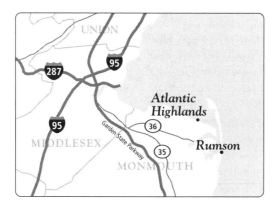

Sunday, June 22

MONMOUTH COUNTY

ATLANTIC HIGHLANDS

Mrs. Sverre Sorensen

1 Hill Road, Atlantic Highlands

Nestled in the hills (the highest coastal point from Maine to Florida) overlooking Sandy Hook Bay to New York City is a mature, natural woodland garden created by the owner and her late husband, Sev. Years ago plants were started by cuttings and seeds (many by daughter Sandy Sorensen Henning). Today, charming paths flanked with brunnera, epimediums, and phlox wind in and about rhododendrons, azaleas, skimmias, laurel, and dogwood—all with spectacular vistas of the ocean beyond.

Hours: 10 a.m. to 4 p.m.

Take Garden State Parkway south to Exit 114. Turn left at end of ramp and right onto Nutswamp Road. Turn left onto Neversink River Road across Route 35, onto Locust Point Road. Do not go over Oceanic Bridge to Rumson. Go straight through intersection with Red Country Store entrance on right, bear right downhill, through traffic light at Route 36, up Grand Avenue, under Stone Bridge, and turn right onto Ocean Boulevard/Scenic Drive. Turn at second right onto Hill Road to # 1, first driveway on right. Look for high stone walls and gravel driveway. *Please park along street.*

Rumson
Beliza Ann Furman
8 Woods End Road, Rumson

Over the past ten years, my late husband, Sam, and I replaced horticultural cliches with our interpretation of a real garden. The focal point is the pond-like swimming pool and waterfall, which are surrounded by several planted areas. In spring, bulbs, azaleas, viburnums, lilacs, astilbes, and rhododendrons stand out. In summer, assorted lilies, spirea, crape myrtle, hydrangea, old roses, and gazillions of perennials fill in the gaps. We are in bloom from February to November. Behind the pool, climbing roses and wisteria standards enhance a columned pergola and seating area. A formal parterre features a stone dining set, standard 'Fairy' roses, and assorted annuals.

Hours: 10 a.m. to 4 p.m.

From Garden State Parkway, take Exit 109. Coming from north, turn left (east) onto Newman Springs Road, from south, bear right. Go through 5 traffic lights to end. Turn right onto Broad Street/Route 35. Go to next light and turn left onto White Road. Go to end. Turn left onto Branch Avenue. At blinking light, turn right onto Rumson Road. Continue straight to a sign "Rumson, Settled 1665." Second left is Woods End Road. Our house is third on left. *Please park on street, not in driveway.*

King & Leigh Sorensen
7 North Ward Avenue, Rumson

The house is a former windmill adjacent to a river. The landscape design includes a raised perennial bed with shrubs and flowering trees in the background. The garden was featured in the January 1983 issue of *House Beautiful*. There are espaliered apple trees near King's vegetable garden, which features five varieties of lettuce. Leigh has a collection of bonsai and King raises honeybees. Many ornamental grasses are incorporated into the gardens, which flood at times of extreme high tides.

Hours: 10 a.m. to 2 p.m.

From Garden State Parkway, take Exit 109. Turn left onto Newman Springs Road and after 1.5 miles turn left onto Broad Street. After .75 mile turn right onto Harding Place and continue east 5 miles (road name changes to Ridge, then Hartchorne). At end, turn left onto North Ward Avenue. Our driveway is a continuation of North Ward Avenue. The house, #7, is marked on an oar in a grass garden.

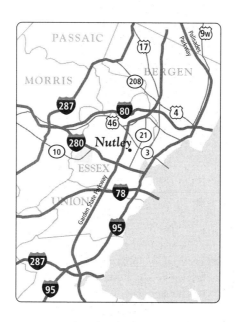

Saturday, August 16

ESSEX COUNTY

NUTLEY

Graeme Hardie

210 Rutgers Place, Nutley

New Jersey? When you step into my garden, you are transported to a world far from what most imagine is a "typical" New Jersey garden. I call it my "jungle." This is a forty by sixty-foot walled contemporary garden, designed by Richard Hartlage. For its size, it is richly planted in perennials and tropicals—a mix that works to great effect. My garden is one of texture and contrasting leaf form and color. Good use has been made of level changes, affording the garden the experience of, at one point, having an overview of the garden and the next, walking under and surrounded by it. The garden boasts bold sculpture, terraces, and a well-hidden hot tub. It was featured in *Traditional Home* magazine in September 2000.

Hours: 10 a.m. to 4 p.m.

Take Route 3 east, from Lincoln Tunnel, or Exit 16 off New Jersey Turnpike/I-95, or Exit 153 off Garden State Parkway, head west on Route 3, and proceed to Main Avenue/Nutley/Passaic exit. At end of exit ramp, turn left and proceed through 2 traffic lights (3 lights if coming from east). Fourth street to left is Rutgers Place, just past a small bridge. Come up Rutgers Place to top of hill; when road flattens, you're at #210 on left side of street.

Silas Mountsier

205 Rutgers Place, Nutley

With the help of Seattle landscape gardener Richard Hartlage, my garden has grown in the last few years from one half acre to one acre. I like drifts of plants and the interplay of strong lines of contrasting leaf texture and color gives this mostly shade garden a strong, almost architected, form. But, too, my garden has many nooks and crannies, each with its own surprise to delight the eye. Sculpted objects abound in my garden and complement the rich botanical mix. My garden brings me joy and has for over fifty years; I find it hard to believe it's mine—truly a long-held dream come true.

Hours: 10 a.m. to 4 p.m.

Take Route 3 east from Lincoln Tunnel, or Exit 16 off New Jersey Turnpike/I-95, or Exit 153 off Garden State Parkway, head west on Route 3, and proceed to Main Avenue/Nutley/Passaic exit. At end of exit ramp, turn left and proceed through 2 traffic lights (3 lights if coming from east). Fourth street to left is Rutgers Place, just past a small bridge. Come up Rutgers Place to top of hill; when road flattens, you're at #205, on right side of street.

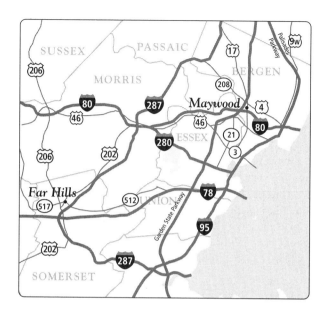

Saturday, September 6

BERGEN COUNTY

MAYWOOD

Dail & Tony's Garden

66 West Magnolia Avenue, Maywood

Ten or so years ago, Tony and I began gardening under the two maple trees that canopy our quite small backyard. Early on, a bluestone path developed, now enticing the visitor beneath a copper arch we created ourselves, alongside another copper piece we built to support tomato plants, beyond to a dwarf weeping crab apple and the rest of the shade beds. The garden has evolved over the years, reflecting our growing fascination with "winter interest," as well as with texture plays both in and out of season. Sedges tuck up to gentians and campanulas, veronica tumbles under a caryopteris. The lavender *Phlox subulata* is later a verdant mat under a lavender callicarpa. Whimsy is all about—an original art piece by Jeanne Wheaton of New Jersey is a focal point in the sun garden and a couple of old candelabra floor lamps set with candles light the way to the three-whiskey barrel water garden, somewhat obscured by mature ficus, schefflera, and draceana houseplants out summering. Come be transported—so small a piece of land, so large the garden.

Hours: 10 a.m. to 4 p.m.

From George Washington Bridge, take Route 4 west to Forest Avenue and take north. Turn left at traffic light and go back over Route 4. Road becomes Maywood Avenue at Spring Valley Avenue. Continue south for 1 mile and turn right onto West Magnolia Avenue. Ours is thirteenth house on the left, second up from corner of Rampo Avenue. From Route 208, take Route 4 east to Forest Avenue. Exit to right and, at light, turn left. Proceed as directed above. *Please park on street.*

Far Hills

Kennelston Cottage

48 Post Kennel Road, Far Hills

Several gardens surround the early 1900s main residence, reflecting the English Tudor architecture of the house and the European tradition of creating garden rooms. Organized along axial lines, the gardens form enclosures within walls, fences, or plant masses, each for a different function and each with its own ambiance, enhanced by a rich planting palette. There is a courtyard garden with a reflecting pool, a potager, a shrub garden with its millstone, a sunken garden set within an old stone foundation, a conservatory terrace garden, and a pool garden. Further away, there are less formal lines of a bird garden and a shade garden. The property also features an English greenhouse by Alitex and a small nursery garden near the barn complex and, at the main entrance, an early colonial gatehouse surrounded by an old-fashioned cottage garden. Evolving over the past seven years, the gardens were designed by B. W. Bosenberg & Company of Far Hills and Ania Bass of Peapack.

Hours: 10 a.m. to 4 p.m.

From I-287, take Exit 26/Liberty Corner/Mt. Airy Road/Bernardsville and go 200 yards to traffic light. Turn left onto Whitenack Road and continue 2 miles to end at Route 202. Turn right onto Route 202 north and go 200 yards to Douglass Avenue. Turn left and continue uphill for 1.3 miles to "T" intersection at stop sign. Turn right onto Post Kennel Road and proceed to third driveway on right, #48, bordered by a stone wall and a beige-and-green gatehouse. *Follow signs for parking.*

Public Gardens

BERGEN COUNTY

RIDGEWOOD

The James Rose Center

506 East Ridgewood Avenue, Ridgewood (201) 446-6017 www.jamesrosecenter.org

James Rose was a pioneer of applying modern design principles to landscape architecture in the 1930s. Built in 1953, his house and garden were designed to change over time and now reflect more than forty years of evolution. It is a unique environment of interwoven spaces formed by structure, plants, and water to create a strong fusion between house and garden.

Hours: April through October, first and third Saturday, 10 a.m. to 4 p.m., by appointment only

From George Washington Bridge, take Route 4 west to Route 17 northto Ridgewood Avenue/Ridgewood exit. Follow East Ridgewood Avenue towards Ridgewood. House is on corner of East Ridgewood Avenue and Southern Parkway.

TENAFLY

Davis Johnson Park & Gardens

137 Engle Street, Tenafly (201) 569-7275

Featuring an award-winning rose garden recognized by the American Rose Society, this seven-and-one-half-acre park has many floral beds, paths, and benches. Our gazebo is a favorite place for wedding ceremonies and photos. This former estate has several mature beech trees.

Hours: year round, daily, dawn to dusk

Admission: free

Take Route 9W to East Clinton Avenue. Go west downhill to first traffic light (Engle Street). Turn left. Park entrance is on right, .25 mile from Clinton Avenue.

ESSEX COUNTY

BLOOMFIELD

Oakeside-Bloomfield Cultural Center

240 Belleville Avenue, Bloomfield (973) 429-0960

A three-acre garden, Oakeside is on the state and national registers of historic places. The grounds are currently undergoing restoration. A formal rose garden (1913) and large kitchen garden (1922) were designed by Vitale, Brinckerhoff, and Geiffert. A naturalistic water garden and terrace garden near the solarium date from about 1929.

Hours: year round, daily, dawn to dusk, except during private events; groups by appointment

Admission: free

From Garden State Parkway south, take Exit 148. Stay straight on J.F.K. Drive to end, then turn left and make quick right back onto J.F.K. Drive. At first traffic light, turn right onto Belleville Avenue. Take second entrance on right for parking.

From Garden State Parkway north, take Exit 149. Turn right off exit ramp onto J.F.K. Drive. Proceed as directed above.

Durand-Hedden House & Garden
523 Ridgewood Road, Maplewood (973) 763-7712

The Durand-Hedden House sits on two picturesque acres that include a sloping meadow edged with trees, shrubs, annuals, and perennial beds. It boasts one of the largest herb collections in the Northeast, with many species and cultivated varieties of thyme, sage, and mint.

Hours: year round, daily, dawn to dusk

Admission: free

From I-78 west and Route 24 west, take Exit 50B/Millburn/Maplewood. At top of exit ramp, turn right onto Vauxhall Road. Continue to intersection of Millburn Avenue at third traffic light. Cross Millburn onto Ridgewood Road. Go 1 mile, past blinking light. House is first on left after Durand Road and opposite Jefferson School.

MONTCLAIR
Van Vleck House & Gardens
21 Van Vleck Street, Montclair (973) 744-0837 www.vanvleck.org

Begun at the turn of the century, these gardens have been developed by several generations of a family of committed horticulturists. The plan is largely formal, responding to the Mediterranean style of the house. The extensive collection of rhododendrons and azaleas, including several named for family members, is renowned. Also of note are the many mature plant specimens.

Hours: May 1 through October 31, daily, 10 a.m. to 5 p.m., June through October, Thursdays until dusk

Admission: $3 suggested donation

From Garden State Parkway north, take Exit 148/Bloomfield Avenue. Stay in left lane of exit ramp through first traffic light and take "jug-handle" under Garden State Parkway back to Bloomfield Avenue; turn right (west) at light. Proceed on Bloomfield Avenue for 2.5 miles through Bloomfield, Glen Ridge, and Montclair town centers. Turn right onto North Mountain Avenue (Montclair Art Museum is on left). Proceed through 1 light (Claremont Avenue) and take next left onto Van Vleck Street; Van Vleck House & Gardens is on left.

From Garden State Parkway south, take Exit 148/Bloomfield Avenue. Follow service road (paralleling the GSP) through 1 stop sign and 2 lights. Turn right (west) at third light onto Bloomfield Avenue. Proceed as directed above.

From New York City, take Lincoln Tunnel to Route 3 west. Exit at Grove Street, Montclair. Turn left at top of exit ramp onto Grove Street and proceed 3.9 miles to Claremont Avenue. Turn right onto Claremont Avenue and proceed .9 mile to fifth light.

The Presby Memorial Iris Garden
474 Upper Mountain Avenue, Upper Montclair (973) 783-5974

The Presby Memorial Iris Garden is the world's largest display garden of irises, with over 100,000 blooms throughout the season (three weeks). The collection of more than 2,000 varieties in thirty beds, mostly tall bearded iris, also contains miniature dwarf bearded, Louisiana, Siberian, Japanese, remontant, and historic irises. A display bed demonstrates the varied landscapes in which irises can grow.

Hours: Tall bearded iris display, May 17 through June 7, dawn to dusk

Admission: free

Upper Mountain Avenue is bounded by Route 46 on the north, Route 23 to the west, Bloomfield Avenue, Montclair, on the south and is easily reached from Route 3, I-80, I-280, I-287, and Garden State Parkway. Please call for directions.

MERCER COUNTY

PRINCETON
Historic Morven
55 Stockton Street, Princeton (609) 683-4495 www.historicmorven.org

Home to a signer of the Declaration of Independence and five New Jersey governors, the Morven landscape is a composite of 200 years of American history. Its gardens interpret three periods in Morven's history: a nineteenth-century picturesque entrance lawn, an eighteenth-century horse chestnut walk, and an early twentieth-century Colonial Revival garden.

Hours: May through October; call for information about hours and garden tours

Admission: $2 suggested donation

From Somerville Circle, Route 202, and I-287, take Route 206 south about 17 miles into Princeton. Road (called Bayard Road in Princeton) ends at traffic light, with Nassau Street/Route 27 to left and Stockton Street (continuation of Route 206) to right. Turn right onto Stockton. Morven's driveway is second on right just past Princeton Borough Hall and Police Station.

MORRIS COUNTY

BOONTON
The Emilie K. Hammond Wildflower Trail
McCaffrey Lane, Boonton (973) 326-7600

This 463-acre park of hilly terrain and granite boulders includes mountain trails that wind their way through a forest of white oaks, maples, beeches, and hemlocks, and a series of niches provides specific microclimates suitable for more than 250 different wildflowers and shrubs native to the eastern U.S.

Hours: year round, daily, 8 a.m. to dusk

Admission: free

From I-80 west, take Route 46/Denville exit. Take Route 46 east to Mountain Lakes exit. Turn left onto the Boulevard. Bear left onto Powerville Road. Take first left onto McCaffrey Lane.

MORRISTOWN

Acorn Hall
68 Morris Avenue, Morristown (973) 267-3465

Acorn Hall, the headquarters of the Morris County Historical Society, is a Victorian Italianate mansion (circa 1853-1860). The gardens have been restored by the Home Garden Club of Morristown to be reflective of the 1853-1888 period. Features include spring-flowering trees, shrubs, and bulbs; more than thirty varieties of authentic Victorian roses; an herb garden and traditional knot garden; and a fern garden.

Hours: year round, daily, dawn to dusk

Admission: free

From I-287 south, take Exit 37/Route 24 east/Springfield to first exit (2A) and follow signs to Morristown. Follow Columbia Road to end traffic light (in front of Governor Morris Hotel). Turn left at light into second driveway on right.

From I-287 north, take Exit 36A onto Morris Avenue. Take first right fork onto Columbia Turnpike and make an immediate left at light. Turn left into second driveway on right.

Delbarton—St. Mary's Abbey School
Mendham Road, Morristown (973) 538-3231 www.delbarton.org

Delbarton, the largest estate of Morris County's Gilded Age, is now a private boys' school run by Benedictine monks and occupies more than 380 acres of the original four thousand. A splendid Italian garden with a pergola and statuary flanks the west side of Old Main, the imposing old residence.

Hours: year round, weekdays, 9 a.m. to 5 p.m., weekends, 9 a.m. to dusk

Admission: free

From I-287, take Exit 35/Route 124/Madison Avenue. Bear right at end of exit ramp onto Route 124 west/South Street. Proceed straight to Morristown Green. Follow signs for Route 510 west/Washington Street. This becomes Route 24/Mendham Road. Delbarton is on left, 2.5 miles from Morristown Green.

Morris Township
Frelinghuysen Arboretum
53 East Hanover Avenue, Morris Township (973) 326-7600

The 127-acre Frelinghuysen Arboretum displays a wide range of native and exotic plants in home demonstration gardens of perennials, annuals, plants for shade, ferns, vegetables, and roses. Collections include peonies, dogwoods, crab apples, cherries, and a pinetum.

Hours: year round, daily, 8 a.m. to dusk; closed Thanksgiving, Christmas, and New Year's Day

Admission: free

From I-287 north, take Exit 36A. Proceed to Whippany Road. At second traffic light, turn left onto East Hanover Avenue. Entrance is on right.

From I-287 south, take Exit 36. Turn right onto Ridgedale Avenue. Turn right at first light onto East Hanover Avenue. Entrance is on left.

Ringwood

New Jersey State Botanical Garden at Skylands

Morris Road, Ringwood (973) 962-9534 www.njbg.org

This 96-acre Historical Landmark Garden is surrounded by 4,084 acres of woodland with hiking and biking trails. The garden includes a forty-four-room Tudor-style manor house, generally open on the first Sunday of the month, an arboretum, formal gardens, lilac garden, crab apple allée, water gardens, statuary, wildflower area, rhododendron garden, and heath and heather garden.

Hours: year round, daily, 8 a.m. to 8 p.m.

Admission: $3

From Route 208 and Skyline Drive, turn right at end of Skyline Drive onto Route 511. Take second right onto Sloatsburg Road. Pass Hewitt School and Carletondale Road. Turn right onto Morris Road; Skylands is 1.5 miles up Morris Road.

From I-287, take Exit 57, then follow the signs to Skyline Drive and proceed as directed above.

From New York State Thruway/I-87 and Route 17, take thruway to Exit 15A/Route 17, then take Route 17 to Route 72 west, which becomes Sloatsburg Road in New Jersey. Take Sloatsburg Road past Ringwood Manor; Morris Road is on left and proceed as directed above.

Bedminster

The Upper Raritan Watershed Association

2121 Larger Cross Road, Bedminster (908) 234-1852 www.urwa.org

The Upper Raritan Watershed Association has established a garden on Fairview Farm Wildlife Preserve to promote the conservation of birds and butterflies, to provide environmental and horticultural education, and to foster an appreciation of nature. The garden offers food, water, protective cover, and a sheltered place for reproduction.

Hours: year round, daily, dawn to dusk

Admission: free

From I-287, take Bedminster exit to Route 202/206 north. Go 5 traffic lights from exit ramp, bearing left on Route 206 towards Chester. Turn left onto Pottersville Road. Go .8 mile and turn left onto Larger Cross Road. Go .5 mile to URWA's stone pillars on right.

Bernardsville
The Cross Estate Garden
Leddell Road, Bernardsville (973) 539-2016 www.nps.gov\morr

Tucked away along the headwaters of the Passaic River, the Cross Estate Gardens go back to the early years of this century when wealthy people built grand country mansions as summer retreats in the "Mountain Colony" located in Bernardsville. Its gardens and buildings provide a glimpse of a lifestyle that is now but a memory.

Hours: year round, daily, 8 a.m. to 6 p.m.

From I-287 south, take Harter Road Exit. Turn left at stop sign onto Harter Road and then left at stop sign onto Route 202/Mount Kemble Avenue south. Go .9 mile and turn right traffic light onto Tempe Wick Road and go 2 miles (past entrance to Jockey Hollow). Turn left onto Leddell Road at waterfall and go 1.1 miles. Turn left onto long driveway at sign "New Jersey Brigade Area—Cross Estate Gardens."

Take I-287 north, to Route 202/North Maple Avenue/Jockey Hollow exit. Turn right at traffic light onto Route 202 north/Mount Kemble Avenue. Go 1.7 miles and turn left at light onto Tempe Wick Road. Proceed as directed above.

East Millstone
Colonial Park Arboretum, Fragrance & Sensory Garden, Perennial Garden & Rudolf W. van der Goot Rose Garden
156 Mettlers Road, East Millstone (732) 873-2459, TTY (732) 873-0327, or use NJ Relay Service @711

The 144-acre arboretum contains labeled specimens of flowering trees and shrubs, evergreens, and shade trees that grow well in central New Jersey. The five-acre perennial garden contains beds of flowering bulbs, perennials, annuals, trees, and shrubs that provide year-round interest. The rose garden offers a formal display of more than 3,000 roses of 285 varieties The Rose Garden is the Fragrance & Sensory Garden is designed especially for those with visual impairment or physical handicaps.

Hours: year round, daily, 8 a.m. to dusk, Wednesday, noon to dusk. Guided tours can be arranged for groups on weekdays for a small fee

Admission: free, but donations are appreciated

From I-287, take Exit 12. At end of exit ramp, turn left onto Weston Canal Road. After 2 miles, turn left before bridge (do not cross the canal). Continue along Weston Canal Road, which becomes Weston Road. Make first right onto Mettlers Road. Continue ahead to Colonial Park. Arboretum is first right (lot F) and second right (lot A). Perennial Garden is first right (lot F) and the Rose Garden and Fragrance & Sensory Garden are second right (lot A).

From Route 206 south, proceed to Dukes Parkway "jug handle" (sign says "Manville/Somerville"). Follow Dukes Parkway to end and turn right onto Main Street. Go through center of Manville (Route 533) towards Millstone. Turn left onto Route 623/Wilhousky Street. Go over a small bridge and turn right onto Weston Canal Road. Proceed as directed above.

FAR HILLS
Leonard J. Buck Garden
11 Layton Road, Far Hills (908) 234-2677

The Leonard J. Buck Garden is a nationally known rock garden, developed by its namesake in the 1930s. It lies in a woodland stream valley where natural rock outcroppings have been uncovered. There are extensive collections of pink and white dogwoods, azaleas, rhododendrons, wildflowers, ferns, alpines, and rock-loving plants.

Hours: March through November, weekdays, 10 a.m. to 4 p.m., Saturday, 10 a.m. to 5 p.m., Sunday, 12 to 5 p.m.; December through February, weekdays, 10 a.m. to 4 p.m. Closed on major holidays.

Admission: $1 suggested donation

From I-287 north, take Exit 22B; from I-287 south, take Exit 22. At end of exit ramp, take Route 202/206 north, staying right to continue north on 202. Follow signs to Far Hills and Morristown. At Far Hills train station, turn right before tracks onto Liberty Corner/Far Hills Road. Travel .9 mile to Layton Road and turn right. Garden is on left.

UNION COUNTY

SUMMIT
Reeves-Reed Arboretum
165 Hobart Avenue, Summit (908) 273-8787 www.reeves-reedarboretum.org

A twelve-and-one-half-acre former country estate, the arboretum is a historic site and nature conservancy with a focus on horticultural and environmental education for children and adults. There are azalea, rose, rock, and herb gardens, thousands of April-blooming daffodils, and a perennial border that flowers April through October. Naturalistic areas provide wildlife habitat.

Hours: year round, daily, dawn to dusk

Admission: free

From New Jersey Turnpike/I-95, take Exit 14/Newark Airport onto I-78 west. After several miles, take Exit 48/Springfield/Millburn onto Route 24 west. Take Hobart Avenue exit, go left over highway, and continue straight past traffic light. Up hill on left will be sign for arboretum.

WESTFIELD
Mindowaskin Park
11 Kimball Circle, Westfield (908) 233-8110

Mindowaskin Park was established in 1918. A large lake, fountains, waterways, winding paths, hardwood trees, a bird sanctuary, new playground equipment, flowering gardens, and a large gazebo offer opportunities for walking and watching, ice skating, model boat sailing, performances, art shows, picnics, and relaxation.

Hours: year round, daily, 7 a.m. to 10 p.m.

Admission: free

From Garden State Parkway, take Exit 137 and head towards Westfield on North Avenue. After 3.1 miles, turn right onto Elmer Street and right again onto East Broad Street. Mindowaskin Park is within 1 block on left.

NEW YORK

The Captain John House Garden, Palisades.
Photo by Erin Dempsey.

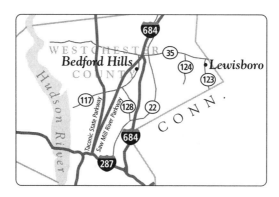

Saturday, April 19
WESTCHESTER COUNTY

BEDFORD HILLS
Phillis Warden
531 Bedford Center Road, Bedford Hills

This garden of many facets includes perennial borders, two water gardens, a formal vegetable garden, a wildflower garden, a fern garden, a marsh garden, a tree platform overlooking the marshlands, a woodland walk, and a formal croquet court. The garden extends over seven acres.

Hours: 10 a.m. to 4 p.m.

From Bedford Village, take Route 22 towards Katonah to intersection at Bedford Cross. Garden is on left. *Please park at Rippowam School and walk to 531 Bedford Center Road.*

Proceeds shared with the Native Plant Center of Westchester Community College

LEWISBORO
The White Garden
199 Elmwood Road, Lewisboro

The hardwood forest and native plants provide a "sacred grove" setting for the Greek Revival-style house. The gardens, designed by Patrick Chassé, are classically inspired near the house, including a nymphaeum, pergola garden, labyrinth, and theater court. Last year an Oriental garden reached by a bridge was added. More exotic surprises are hidden in separate garden rooms. Sculptures and water features enrich the gardens. In spring, 100,000 daffodils bloom.

Hours: 10 a.m. to 4 p.m.

From Merritt Parkway/Route 15, take Exit 38 and follow Route 123 north through New Canaan to New York State line. "Town of Lewisboro" and "Village of Vista" are first signs encountered. Go past Vista Fire Department about .25 mile. Just after shingled Episcopal church on right, Route 123 will bear left and Elmwood Road will bear right. Go about another .25 mile just over a hill. At beginning of a gray stockade fence on right is driveway at #199.

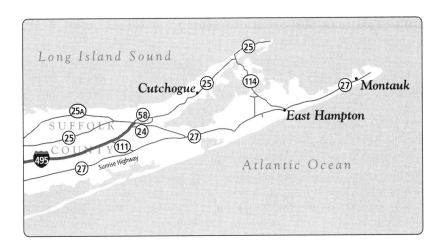

Saturday, May 3
SUFFOLK COUNTY

CUTCHOGUE
Manfred & Roberta Lee
26850 Main Road, Route 25, Cutchogue

Located in the village of Cutchogue, these two and one-half acres of gardens complement the Victorian house and outbuildings. Four large tulip trees punctuate the front lawn. Deep perennial gardens surround the property. Mature azaleas, rhododendrons, roses, hydrangeas, and lilacs are spread throughout the garden. There are unusual conifers and Japanese maples as well as golden chain trees.

Hours: 10 a.m. to 4 p.m.

From Long Island Expressway/I-495, take Exit 73/Route 58. Take Route 58, which leads into Route 25. Continue to Cutchogue. We are 5 houses past North Fork Country Club on right (south) side of Route 25. *Please park on street.*

EAST HAMPTON
Mrs. Donald Bruckmann
105 Lily Pond Lane, East Hampton

This seaside location emphasizes traditional and informal plantings of herbaceous borders, woodland, meadow, and rose gardens. Two ponds are surrounded by iris, asters, and other sun-loving plants. An ocean terrace and adjacent dune combine beach vegetation with bright annuals for an interesting contrast of the cultivated and naturalistic.

Hours: 10 a.m. to 2 p.m.

From Montauk Highway/Route 27, proceed to East Hampton. At traffic light at head of pond, turn right onto Ocean Avenue. Take third right onto Lily Pond Lane. Go .5 mile to driveway (#105) on left (ocean side) marked with brick posts and a white gate. *Please park along Lily Pond Lane.*

Margaret Kerr & Robert Richenburg
1006 Springs Fireplace Road, East Hampton

The garden, designed by Kerr, surrounds their house and studios on two acres that extend down to the wetlands of Accabonac Harbor. Kerr's brick rug sculptures, inspired by tribal Middle Eastern carpets, are placed throughout the garden. One, a brick prayer rug, lies in a contemplative glade below the studios. Kerr collects plants grown in the Middle Ages in a courtyard around a fountain and lily pool highlighted with espaliered pear trees. In the spring, drifts of thousands of daffodils bloom in the fields around the house and are left unmowed until late fall. Native grasses and wildflowers make islands of meadow during the summer.

Hours: 10 a.m. to 2 p.m.

From Montauk Highway/Route 27, turn left at traffic light in East Hampton. Pass town pond. Continue .9 mile past next light, taking an immediate left onto North Main Street. Pass windmill on right. Go .3 mile, bearing right at fork onto Springs Fireplace Road. Go 5 miles. Driveway is marked by mailbox #1006. *Please park along Springs Fireplace Road and walk down dirt road to second house on left.*

Proceeds shared with Bridge Gardens Trust and the Horticultural Alliance of Hamptons

MONTAUK

Richard Kahn & Elaine Peterson
224 West Lake Drive, Montauk

Stately old oaks and maples frame our three-acre property on Lake Montauk. The gardens meander around a romantic brick-and-shingle Tudor-style house built in 1930. A diversity of species reveals itself in collections of hosta, heath and heather, conifers, broadleaf evergreens, alpines, spring bulbs, and iris. An upper garden contains herbs, a potager, and various flowering shrubs and trees, beyond which is a meadow with a mowed labyrinth. All plants are chosen for their ability to withstand the persistent challenges of heavy wind and salt spray. Year-round residents, we design and maintain the gardens ourselves, with deference to the ecology of the lake.

Hours: 10 a.m. to 4 p.m.

From Montauk Highway/Route 27 go past village of Montauk .8 mile. Turn left onto West Lake Drive (signs for Montauk Harbor/Route 77/Montauk Downs). Garden, #224, is 1.2 miles on right. *Please park along road, not on grass.*

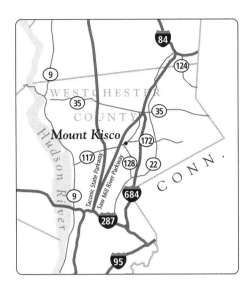

Sunday, May 4
WESTCHESTER COUNTY

MOUNT KISCO
Judy & Michael Steinhardt
433 Croton Lake Road, Mount Kisco

The Steinhardts' love of plants is evident throughout this 55-acre estate. More than 2,000 species of trees, shrubs, and perennials have been incorporated into the gardens. Landscape designer Jerome Rocherolle has created a naturalistic setting with walkways, stream beds, bridges, and ponds where plants can be appreciated and nurtured. There are diverse orchards, a mature perennial bed, and a newly developed alpine and wall garden. Much of the plant material is labeled for the viewer's benefit. Look for extensive use of ferns, moss (a moss bridge), more than 200 cultivars of Japanese maples, and hundreds of varieties of *Hemerocallis*. Wildlife and not-so-wildlife include exotic waterfowl, miniature horses, and more.

Hours: 10 a.m. to 4 p.m.

From Saw Mill River Parkway, take Kisco Avenue exit (1 exit beyond Mount Kisco). Turn right at end of exit ramp and, after a few hundred feet, turn right onto Croton Lake Road. Number 433 is 1.8 miles to mailbox on left. *Please park where directed.*

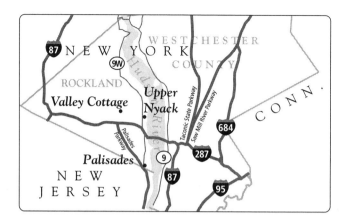

Saturday, May 10
ROCKLAND COUNTY

PALISADES

The Captain John House Garden

20 Washington Spring Road, Snedens Landing, Palisades

This is a small cottage-style garden with a (too) large diversity of plant material, including petasites, hakonechloa, many yellow-foliaged plants, a rose pergola, and a young triple hedge of peegee hydrangeas, yews, and azaleas. It features interestingly steep topography with a stream that empties into the Hudson River. The garden was featured in the July 1999 issue of *House & Garden* magazine.

Hours: 10 a.m. to 4 p.m.

From Palisades Interstate Parkway, take Exit 4. From traffic light at end of exit ramp, proceed north on Route 9W about 1 mile. At first light, where Oak Tree Road and Washington Spring Road cross, turn right onto Washington Spring Road. Follow it down to 2 dead end signs. Bear left. The 3-story white house is at bottom of hill on left. *Please park on street and enter garden through driveway.*

Judy Tomkins Gardens
75 Washington Spring Road, Snedens, Palisades Landing

As a designer, I have become aware of the striking difference in the topography of the land and how important it is for me to learn and observe, depending on where I am, just how the site emerges in its natural perfection—in other words, "the genius of the place"—I feel strongly that gardens should be walked through each day as each day changes and brings delight or sorrow with each of these changes. With this in mind, I am opening two properties that I designed, each different due to the change of land and views. My house is near eighteenth century, looking over the Hudson River. It is nestled by gardens with a garden path approaching the house. For the past few years I have collected somewhat rare trees for the property, primarily for the enjoyment of my grandchildren. There are young examples of cedar of Lebanon, *Franklinia*, Carolina bell, pink styrax, dove tree, yellowhorn, Chinese elm, *Stewartia*, and variegated aralia. The second house included with admission to my garden is primarily Victorian with an apple orchard, wildflower and courtyard garden, and a cliffside with a maze of paths leading to different plateaus overlooking the Hudson River.

Hours: 10 a.m. to 4 p.m.

From Palisades Parkway, take Exit 4. From traffic light at end of exit ramp, proceed north on Route 9W about 1 mile. At first light, where Oak Tree Road and Washington Spring Road cross, turn right. *Please park at church on right and walk down to house, #75.*

Upper Nyack
Cornuscopia
314 North Broadway, Upper Nyack

My garden evolved over the forty-plus years I have gardened here. After 1981, when I retired, I began to expand and landscape this corner property to create more privacy, seasonal and especially winter vistas, and shady refuges, bordered by undulating mixed borders. A hemlock hedge to the west and copious (more than twenty) dogwoods planted by birds were transplanted to define the boundaries. A stone path connects the house to the terrace and, combined with grass paths, leads to different garden areas planted with shrubs and perennials suited to their locations, whether sunny or shady, moist or dry. Many rhododendrons, azaleas, dogwoods, and spring bulbs will bloom at the open time.

Hours: 2 to 6 p.m.

From Westchester, take New York State Thruway/I-87 west, cross Tappan Zee Bridge, and take Exit 11. From exit ramp, go on High Avenue, cross Route 9W at first traffic light, and turn left onto Midland Avenue at second light. Go north past Nyack Hospital and light at Fifth Avenue to Highmount Avenue. Turn right. Number 314 is at corner of Highmount and Broadway. *Please park on Highmount and enter at garden gate.*

From Rockland, take New York State Thruway/I-87 east to last exit before Tappan Zee Bridge (Exit 11) and turn left at first light onto Route 59. Turn left onto Route 9W at second light, right onto Highland Avenue, and, at light, left onto Midland. Proceed as directed above.

From New York City, take Palisades Interstate Parkway to Exit 4/Route 9W, continue to light at High Avenue, turn right, left onto Midland at next light, and proceed as directed above.

Proceeds shared with the Historical Society of the Nyacks

South Cottage—The Moorings
507 North Broadway, Upper Nyack

Passing through a high brick wall, one enters a park-like area of lawn and specimen trees dotted with animal sculptures setting off a circular mixed border. Through the inner gate are hydrangeas and tree peonies. From here we see the Hudson River. Approaching the house a shaded hosta, fern, hellebore, and wildflower area leads to the "wedding circle." High above a bird and butterfly sanctuary is a large deck holding a collection of coleus and houseplants. A path leads down through an Oriental garden to reach the river.

Hours: 10 a.m. to 4 p.m.

Garden about 2 miles north of Tappan Zee Bridge on Hudson River. From New York State Thruway/I-87, take Exit 10. Stay in left lane on exit ramp. Take next left. Stay to extreme right, hugging chain link fence. Follow arrow to South Nyack. At second full stop sign, go right 1 short block to Broadway. Go left on Broadway 1.8 miles to 507 North Broadway (you will go through village of Nyack). Garden behind high brick wall. *Please park on Broadway.*

Proceeds shared with the Historical Society of the Nyacks

Valley Cottage
Hiroshi & Maria Nakazawa
450 King's Highway, Valley Cottage

When we first moved into our home, a seventeenth-century farmhouse, the landscape included a stream that had suffered years of neglect. The bank of the stream had been eroded by flooding until it was a crumbling cliff that threatened to undermine the foundation of our house. By working with native materials such as stone and wood, we were able to build up the bank into terraces that lead gracefully down to the stream. There is also a spring-fed pond, which serves at the focal point for our garden. In this way, we were able to minimize the weaknesses of the landscape and allow the strong points to emerge. We invite you to stroll down a gentle slope shaded by beech trees to the garden path, which winds along the stream and opens by the pond. The garden is accented by an eclectic mix of Oriental- and European-style statuary, a bridge, and a small log chalet. There is a variety of perennial plants, ranging from tall grasses near the pond to cactus on the terraces.

Hours: 10 a.m. to 4 p.m.

From New York State Thruway/I-87 north, take Exit 12/Nyack and turn right onto Route 303. Turn left at second traffic light onto Lake Road. Turn right at first light onto King's Highway. Proceed north about .5 mile and look for our house on left, which is #450.

From New York State Thruway/I-87 south, take Exit 12/West Nyack, turn left at first light, and left again onto Route 303. Turn left at third light and proceed as directed above.

Proceeds shared with Keep Rockland Beautiful

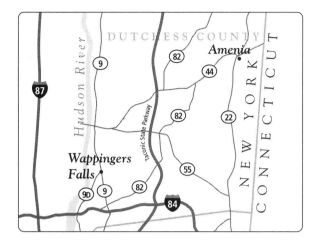

Sunday, May 18

DUTCHESS COUNTY

AMENIA
Broccoli Hall—Maxine Paetro
23 Flint Hill Road, Amenia

Visitors to Broccoli Hall describe this English-style cottage garden as "incredible," "inspirational," "magical"—and they come back again and again. Starting in 1986 with an acre and a half of bare earth, Maxine Paetro collaborated with horticulturist Tim Steinhoff to create a series of enchanting garden rooms. Broccoli Hall offers an apple tunnel, a brick courtyard, a lavish display of spring bulbs blooming with crab apples in May, an extensive border of iris, peonies, and old shrub roses flowering in June, a tree house with long views, and a secret woodland garden. Photos of Broccoli Hall can be seen at www.broccolihall.com. This garden will also featured in the early spring 2003 issue of *Country Garden* magazine.

Hours: 10 a.m. to 4 p.m.

From Route 22 north, go towards Amenia. Go west on Route 44 to Route 83 north/ Smithfield Road. Go 2.5 miles to dirt road on right, Flint Hill Road. Turn right. House (#23) is first on left. *Please park on Flint Hill Road. Be careful of ditches.*

Proceeds shared with the Amenia Free Library

WAPPINGERS FALLS
Anne Spiegel
73 Maloney Road, Wappingers Falls

This dramatic natural rock garden is planted on a series of stepped ledges and cliff. It includes screes, sand beds, lime beds, and a large collection of troughs. One end of the garden was newly rebuilt after the tornado in 2000, the other end has been extended another 50 feet in a series of stone-walled raised beds. A never-watered garden (inadequate well) is open, sunny, and windy; plants from Turkey, the Great Basin, and our western mountains are a specialty. There is continuing experimentation with xerophytes and drought-tolerant plants.

Hours: 10 a.m. to 4 p.m.

From the Taconic State Parkway north, take first exit for Route 82 north and turn right. Go 1 mile to left at Emans Road. Continue to stop sign and turn left. At end of road, turn right onto Noxon Road. Go about 2.2 miles to Maloney Road on left, then 1.5 miles to garden on left. *Please follow parking signs and drive past house only when exiting.*

From Taconic Parkway south, take Arthursburg Road exit. Go 3.2 miles to Maloney Road on left and proceed as directed above.

Proceeds shared with the North American Rock Garden Society

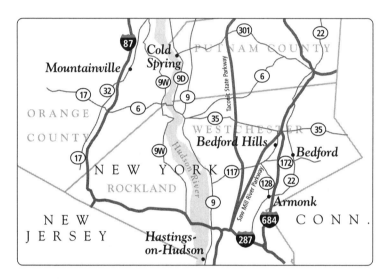

ORANGE COUNTY

MOUNTAINVILLE

Cedar House—Garden of Margaret Johns & Peter Stern
Otterkill Road at Anders Lane, Mountainville

Mixed perennial borders, "enhanced" meadows, informal flower beds, specimen trees, berries, lilacs, tree peonies, old clipped boxwood, espaliered fruit trees, and a white wisteria-draped pergola are connected by stone walls, trellises, and grass paths. The garden overlooks 200 acres of orchard, farmland, and dogwood-rich forest, as well as the Hudson Highlands to the east and the Moodna Valley to the west.

Hours: 10 a.m. to 6 p.m.

From New York State Thruway/I-87 north, take Exit 16/Harriman/Monroe. Turn right onto Route 32. Travel north 10 miles to green metal bridge. Cross bridge and immediately turn left onto Orrs Mill Road. Take third left onto Otterkill Road. Follow .6 mile to Anders Lane (driveway is on right). Go up driveway to house.

From Hudson Valley and Connecticut, travel west on I-84 across Newburgh-Beacon Bridge. Take Exit 10 south. Travel south on Route 32 for 7 miles. Before crossing green metal bridge, turn right onto Orrs Mills Road. Proceed as directed above.

Proceeds shared with Cornwall Garden Club

WESTCHESTER COUNTY

ARMONK

Cobamong Pond

15 Middle Patent Road, Armonk

This is one of the great woodland gardens of the world—a twelve-acre pond is surrounded by twelve acres of naturalistic woodlands with an abundance of flowering shrubs that have been enhanced for almost forty years. It is featured in the book *The Beckoning Path*, with eighty color photographs. The garden has an abundance of rhododendrons, flowering trees, shrubs, and Japanese maples. The garden was also developed to emphasize New England fall color, which is at its most dramatic in October.

Hours: 10 a.m. to 4 p.m.

From I-684 south, take Exit 4/Route 172. Turn left (east) and continue to end. Turn right (south) at Shell gas station onto Route 22. Go 2.2 miles, then turn left onto Middle Patent Road. Take second driveway on right, marked by 4 mailboxes. House, #15, is at end of a long driveway.

From I-684 north, take Exit 3N and go north on Route 22 for 4 miles, then turn right onto Middle Patent Road and proceed as directed above. *Please park along driveway near house.*

Proceeds shared with the Mount Kisco Day Care Center

BEDFORD

Penelope & John Maynard

210 Hook Road, Bedford

We created a garden among rock ledges and oak woods on the steep shoulder of Mount Aspetong. The site is fragmented; thus, the garden areas are designed to flow from one to another, linked together by a ribbon of stone walls. The greatest challenge has been to create some flat, restful spaces. The wide variety of plants must meet one criterion—to prove themselves in dry woodland conditions.

Hours: 10 a.m. to 4 p.m.

From I-684, take Exit 4. Turn east onto Route 172. Go 1.5 miles to Route 22. Turn left and drive through Bedford. Just beyond Bedford Oak Tree, 2.1 miles from Routes 172 and 22, turn right onto Hook Road. Garden (#210) is almost at top of hill. *Please park along road.*

BEDFORD HILLS
Phillis Warden
531 Bedford Center Road, Bedford Hills

This garden of many facets includes perennial borders, two water gardens, a formal vegetable garden, a wildflower garden, a fern garden, a marsh garden, a tree platform overlooking the marshlands, a woodland walk, and a formal croquet court. The garden extends over seven acres.

Hours: 10 a.m. to 4 p.m.

From Bedford Village, take Route 22 towards Katonah to the intersection at Bedford Cross. Garden is on left. Please park at Rippowam School and walk to 531 Bedford Center Road.

Proceeds shared with Native Plant Center of Westchester Community College

HASTINGS-ON-HUDSON
Midge & Dave Riggs
112 Lefurgy Avenue, Hastings-on-Hudson

The house is nestled into a rock ledge with natural outcroppings and niches all planted with choice alpines and rock plants covering one-third acre. A recirculating waterfall built into the ledge is edged with ferns, primroses, creeping phlox, and campanulas planted in the chinks nearby. Alpine plants are nestled in holes drilled into the rocks in the tufa bed. Our great interest in western American plants prompted construction of sand beds to ensure perfect drainage; penstemons, townsendias, acantholimons, oxytropis, and eriogonums grow in them.

Hours: 10 a.m. to 4 p.m.

From Saw Mill River Parkway, turn west onto Farragut Parkway. Go .9 mile to Mount Hope Boulevard. Go up hill .5 mile to Lefurgy Avenue; turn left. Go to Edgewood and turn right, then turn right onto Sunset Road. *Please park on Sunset Road and walk to right down private road.*

Proceeds shared with the North American Rock Garden Society

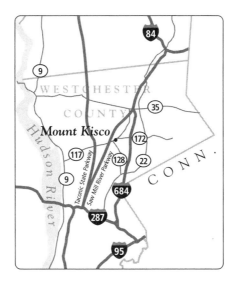

Saturday, May 24
WESTCHESTER COUNTY

MOUNT KISCO
Rocky Hills—The Gardens of Henriette Suhr

95 Old Roaring Brook Road, Mount Kisco

Rocky Hills is an appropriate name for this property with hills, rocks of all sizes, and a lovely brook. The garden was started by the owner and her late husband over forty years ago. The azalea and rhododendron plantings number in the thousands. There is an extensive tree peony collection, woodland garden, fern garden, wildflower garden, lots of bulbs, and irises of all descriptions. An interesting group of evergreens is planted among rocks. This is a most varied garden in all seasons.

A PROJECT OF
THE GARDEN
CONSERVANCY

Hours: 2 to 6 p.m.

From Saw Mill River Parkway, travel north to Exit 33/Reader's Digest Road. At traffic light, turn left, then make a sharp right onto Old Roaring Brook Road. Rocky Hills, #95, is 1 mile on right.

From Merritt Parkway/Route 15, travel to I-287 west. Exit I-287 at Saw Mill River Parkway north. Proceed as directed above. *Please park along Old Roaring Brook Road or Lawrence Farms Crossways as directed.*

Proceeds shared with Friends of Lasdon

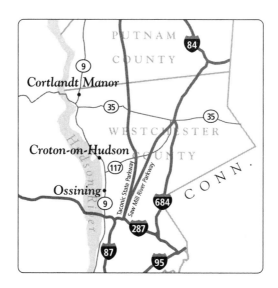

Sunday, June 1
WESTCHESTER COUNTY

CORTLANDT MANOR
Vivian & Ed Merrin
2547 Maple Avenue, Cortlandt Manor

Overlooking a small lake, this garden has unfolded over a rocky wooded site over the last fifteen years, under the guidance of designer Patrick Chassé. New additions include a large variety of azaleas, a tempered glass-enclosed lookout over the lake, and a wooden lotus bridge for perfect lotus viewing on a private pond. Mixed borders line garden rooms that flow among the landforms. Native plants form the framework for a collection that embraces many unusual and rare plants, as well as a large tree peony garden. Several water gardens enhance the site, and greenhouses and a formal kitchen garden provide additional plants, both ornamental and edible. A new parking and entrance garden has been planted. This garden was featured in *House & Garden's* 100th anniversary issue, October 2001. A woodland walk is a new 2003 addition.

Hours: 10 a.m. to 2 p.m.

From Taconic State Parkway, take Route 202 exit. Turn left (west) towards Peekskill. Go 2.5 miles, then turn left at traffic light onto Croton Avenue, just past Cortland Farm Market. Go 1.2 miles to blinking light/stop sign and turn right onto Furnace Dock Road. Go .8 mile to blinking light/stop sign and turn left onto Maple Avenue. Go .9 mile to private road on right. Go .2 mile to #2547 on left. *Please park at house.*

CROTON-ON-HUDSON
The Gardens of Dianna & Howard Smith
30 Fox Run Road, Croton-on-Hudson

Enter this park-like two-acre property overlooking the Croton Reservoir and follow the paths through undulating woodland gardens to sunny cultivated islands of perennial beds, a hillside grass garden, terraced rock gardens, and a koi pond. Emphasis has been placed on discovering (through trial and error, mostly) and utilizing a huge variety of deer-resistant plants, while creating a haven for birds, frogs, beneficial insects, and other native wild creatures. (Dianna Smith produces a series on gardens and the environment for cable television called SCAPES.)

Hours: 10 a.m. to 4 p.m.

From Taconic State Parkway, take Underhill Road exit towards Croton-on-Hudson. Turn right onto Route 129. Drive 1.9 miles to Fox Run Road, which is first left after crossing over reservoir's Hunterbrook Bridge.

From Route 9/9A, take Route 129 for 3.5 miles through Croton-on-Hudson, past sign for town of Cortlandt and Croton Gorge Park, towards Yorktown. Fox Run Road is last street on right side after passing "Camp Discovery" mailbox (also on right). *Please park along Fox Run Road or in cul-de-sac. Enter path to gardens from driveway.*

OSSINING
Paul & Sarah Matlock
26 Piping Rock Drive, Ossining

The garden is done in a cottage style on a suburban plot. It is planted for progression of bloom. There are brimming perennial borders, walls, terraces, and walks with numerous thymes and alpines, little secret places, vegetable gardens, and a trough/gravel garden. We have a collection of old-fashioned daylilies and many old roses, especially climbers. Many unusual plants are started from seed. The garden was built by the owners over twenty years ago and is maintained by them.

Hours: 10 a.m. to 4 p.m.

From I-684 east, take either Route 134 or 133 into heart of Ossining (134 merges with 133). Turn right onto Route 9. At far end of town (about 2 miles), turn right onto Piping Rock Drive, which is opposite green sign for Cambridge House. Garden is about 5 houses up on right.

From Route 9 in Tarrytown, proceed north, passing through Ossining. Proceed as directed above.

From Route 9 in Peekskill, proceed on Route 9 south. After passing through Croton, keep right when Route 9A leaves to left. Go through 1 traffic light and turn left onto Piping Rock Drive, which is opposite green sign for Cambridge House. Garden is about 5 houses up on right.

Proceeds shared with the Taconic Gardeners Club

Saturday, June 7

COLUMBIA COUNTY

COPAKE FALLS

Margaret Roach

99 Valley View Road, Copake Falls

This thirteen-year-old homemade garden reflects my obsession with plants, particularly those with good foliage or of interest to wildlife. Sixty species of birds visit annually. Informal mixed borders, frog-filled water gardens, a paved garden, and a bluestem meadow cover my two-and-one-half-acre hillside, a former orchard dotted with simple, Victorian-era farm buildings and house, surrounded by Taconic State Park land. Expansion continues and this year visitors are welcome to walk next door to see the beginnings of a landscape I started in 2002 around a new, modern guest house. Even I am shocked at the stark contrast between the two places, the new one featuring a large, enclosed gravel courtyard with formal lines.

Hours: 10 a.m. to 4 p.m.

Off Route 22 (5 miles south of Hillsdale, 13 miles north of Millerton), take Route 344 towards Taconic State Park signs. Bear right after park entrance and blue store, over metal bridge and past camp. After High Valley Road intersection on left, continue right another 100 feet to green barn and house on left *(park on that side only, please).*

GERMANTOWN
An Artist's Garden
Block Factory Road, Germantown

My gardens began as subject matter for my art and have become the form of art, in them-selves. They are conceived as outdoor rooms, places in which to sit and experience an inner reality, for instance: the Zen Bed/Fairy Grove/Pine Circle/Overlook/Stone Circles—and many more. Then, of course, there are the Iris Beds/Lily Beds/Rose Garden/Conifer Garden/etc., developed for their specimens to paint. As with all forms of art, the gardens are built to be seen, so please come.

Hours: 10 a.m. to 4 p.m.

From Rhinebeck and points south, take Route 9G north through traffic lights of Germantown. After about 3 miles (just before bridge), turn right onto Block Factory Road (whole road is less than 1 mile long). At bottom of hill, turn into a dirt driveway. There is a fence with an owl seated on top; there are signs for "DuBack" and "Three Rock Pond." Follow signs .75 mile through woodland.

From New York State Thruway/I-87, take Exit 19/Kingston-Rhinecliff Bridge. Cross bridge, follow Route 199 to Route 9G, and proceed north as directed above.

From Albany, take New York State Thruway/I-87 south to Hudson/Catskill Region exit. Follow signs to Rip Van Winkle Bridge. Cross bridge and head south on Route 9G for 2 to 3 miles. Turn left onto Block Factory Road. Proceed as directed above.

Tailings—Robert Montgomery
404 White Birch Road, Germantown

The gardens at Tailings comprise a series of bulb, perennial, and rose plantings closely inte-grated with the natural landscape and joined to each other by woodland paths. Axial cuts have been made through the woods to offer views in all directions and to complement the architecture. These culminate in a prospect of the Hudson River and the entire Catskill Mountain range.

Hours: 10 a.m. to 2 p.m.

From Germantown, take Route 9G north from traffic light to intersection with Route 10; turn right. Go .25 mile to White Birch Road and turn left. Go 1 mile to Tailings' driveway on right; look for #404 on mailbox. *Please park at top of driveway.*

Proceeds shared with Friends of Hudson/O.S.I.

LINLITHGO

Mark A. Mcdonald—Runningwater

67 Wire Road, Linlithgo

The sound and motion of a rocky creek lend rhythm to the Japanese spirit of this intimate, multi-level, eighteen-year-old garden. Rising above the lower creekside beds that feature "weeping" trees and shrubs, the naturalized steep walls of a curving ravine ultimately open to reveal a sudden view of distant Catskill peaks. A weathered fence dotted with architectural fragments and a baffle of evergreens define the roadside border of the upper garden, affording privacy and furnishing a backdrop for compact trees, mature shrubs, and perennial beds. This is essentially a shade garden hugging a precipitous hillside that relies on combinations and contrasts of shapes, foliage, and texture. Notable structures include a sculptor's lead-coated gate opening to expose a wisteria arbor, a rustic garden shed, and steps, walls, and terraces crafted from local stone. Runningwater was featured in *Martha Stewart Living*, August 2001, and was inspired by Frank Lloyd Wright's "Fallingwater" and Russell Wright's "Dragon Rock."

Hours: 10 a.m. to 4 p.m.

From Route 9, take Route 31 north from Blue Stores 1.5 miles to Wire Road. Turn left and go about 3 miles to #67 on left.

From Route 9G, go south 4 miles from Rip Van Winkle Bridge or 5 miles north from Germantown to Route 10 (green Linlithgo sign). Go east into village and bear right at red brick church onto Wire Road. Go 500 yards across bridge to #67 on right.

Proceeds shared with Friends of Hudson/O.S.I.

LIVINGSTON

Starr Ockenga & Donald Forst

786 Church Road, Livingston

Country gardens, which have evolved over the last decade, surround barn-like buildings. A fence, potting shed, and teahouse enclose the main garden; terraced on three levels by stone walls, it contains structural plantings of boxwood, arborvitae, top-grafted 'Palibin' lilacs, and Japanese maples. A studio/greenhouse features its own enclosed gardens, where stone stairways lead from a kitchen garden and a gold garden to a 100-foot-long mixed border. Other gardens include a white garden, gray borders, and flowering tree and conifer collections. The garden complex is fenced, including a cattle guard at the entrance, to thwart the deer. Trails, leading to ponds with natural plantings, are mown through the surrounding pastures. The hilltop site provides dramatic views of the Catskill Mountains and Berkshire Hills.

Hours: 10 a.m. to 2 p.m.

From Taconic State Parkway, take Route 82 exit and go northwest (towards Hudson and Rip Van Winkle Bridge) 1.9 miles to Willow Brook Road. (It is first road on left after Taconic Orchards farm stand.) Turn left and follow .7 mile to end. Turn left onto Church Road. Turn into second driveway on right, where there are 2 posts and a green metal farm gate. Mailbox reads "786." Follow driveway to end. *Please park as directed.*

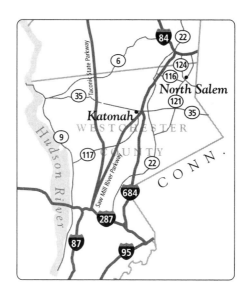

Sunday, June 8

WESTCHESTER COUNTY

KATONAH

Cross River House

129 Maple Avenue, Katonah

Cross River House's gardens are situated on seventeen acres overlooking the Cross River Reservoir in northern Westchester County. The gardens unfold through woodland paths filled with ferns, wildflowers, and large rhododendrons. From the paths, you enter the first of the garden rooms. The hosta or shade garden is surrounded by trellises covered in clematis and wisteria. From the hosta garden, you enter the perennial garden. Low fencing and stone-work separate the border from a white azalea allée and a small crescent shade area under the magnolias.

Hours: 10 a.m. to 2 p.m.

From Bedford Village, take Route 22 north out of Bedford about 3.3. miles. At sign for Caramoor and Pound Ridge, get off Route 22. Maple Avenue is a dirt road straight ahead. Once on Maple Avenue, we are .5 mile on right, #129.

From I-684 north, take Exit 6/Route 35/Cross River/Katonah. Turn right at end of ramp onto Route 35 east. Take next right onto Route 22 south. Go 1.8 miles. Turn left at intersection in curve onto Maple Avenue (a dirt road), go .5 mile, and the garden is on the right, #129. *Please park along Maple Avenue on either side of the white gates.*

Susan & Carmine L. Labriola
80 Cherry Street, Katonah

Stone walls, interesting pathways, arbors of clematis and wisteria, boxwood and holly hedges, antique garden statuary and sculpture wave their way through groupings of four-season interest supported by Old-World evergreen plantings. Early spring features hostas, peonies, and iris among flowering fruit trees, giving way to mass plantings of lilies, rudbeckia, and echinacea. In summer we delight in grazing from berry beds, organic vegetable gardens, and herb beds. Many interesting specimen trees are highlighted, as well as interesting changes of grades and elevated plantings throughout our sloping property. A secluded pool with stone waterfalls, a rain garden, wetland plantings and several secret gardens are quietly tucked in.

Hours: 10 a.m. to 4 p.m.

From the south, take Saw Mill Parkway north to I-684 to Exit 6/Route 35/Katonah/ Cross River. At light off exit ramp, turn left and go west through 3 more lights (about 1 mile). Turn left onto Cherry Street and go to eighth house on left with #80 on a stone wall pier. *Please park on street.*

North Salem
Artemis Farm—Carol & Jesse Goldberg
22 Wallace Road, North Salem

Five years ago, I dismantled a barn on our farm and spent a winter designing a new garden for the site. I created a furnished Victorian garden room featuring many unusual garden antiques that complement our mid-nineteenth-century farmhouse. The property includes a gravel courtyard trough garden, two other large border gardens with a sweeping view of the back pasture, and a kitchen garden. The front of the house, surrounded by maple trees, has primarily shade-loving plants.

Hours: 10 a.m. to 4 p.m.

From I-684, take Exit 7/Purdys. Follow Route 116 east, bearing left where it joins Route 121 north. Travel about 2 miles and turn right onto Route 116 east. Auberge Maxime Restaurant is on corner. Go .1 mile to Wallace Road and turn left. It is first house on left. Note Artemis Farm sign on tree. *Please park as directed.*

Proceeds shared with Adopt a Dog

Keeler Hill Farm

Keeler Lane, North Salem

Although the land has been farmed since 1731, it is just in the last ten years that gardens have been developed, including the perennial garden, green garden, and white garden. A friendship garden, which provides swimming pool privacy, was planted with friends' castoffs. The vegetable and fruit gardens were placed among the farm buildings. Cutting borders and a lilac walk were added in 1999.

Hours: 10 a.m. to 4 p.m.

From I-684 north, take Exit 7/Purdys. Turn right off exit ramp onto Route 116 east and go about 5 miles. Cross over Old Route 124/June Road. Route 116 will join up with Route 121 about 1 mile after June Road intersection. Bear left at that intersection. About 1 mile up road, turn right onto Keeler Lane. Continue .5 mile. On left, you will see 7 yellow barns. Turn in gate with sign on left pillar that reads "Keeler Hill Farm" and "Keeler Homestead" on right pillar. *Proceed up driveway to parking.*

Proceeds shared with North Salem Open Land Foundation

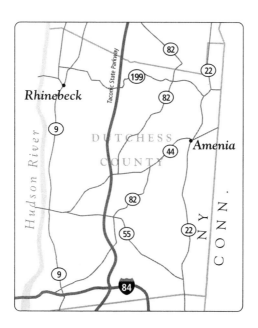

Saturday, June 14
DUTCHESS COUNTY

AMENIA
Broccoli Hall—Maxine Paetro
23 Flint Hill Road, Amenia

Visitors to Broccoli Hall describe this English-style cottage garden as "incredible," "inspirational," "magical"—and they come back again and again. Starting in 1986 with an acre and a half of bare earth, Maxine Paetro collaborated with horticulturist Tim Steinhoff to create a series of enchanting garden rooms. Broccoli Hall offers an apple tunnel, a brick courtyard, a lavish display of spring bulbs blooming with crab apples in May, an extensive border of iris, peonies, and old shrub roses flowering in June, a tree house with long views, and a secret woodland garden. Photos of Broccoli Hall can be seen at www.broccolihall.com. This garden will also featured in the early spring 2003 issue of *Country Garden* magazine.

Hours: 10 a.m. to 4 p.m.

From Route 22 north, go towards Amenia. Go west on Route 44 to Route 83 north/ Smithfield Road. Go 2.5 miles to dirt road on right, Flint Hill Road. Turn right. House (#23) is first on left. *Please park on Flint Hill Road. Be careful of ditches.*

Proceeds shared with Amenia Free Library

RHINEBECK
Cedar Heights Orchard—William & Arvia Morris
8 Crosby Lane, Rhinebeck

The garden has mixed borders for sun and shade, a pergola with many pots and vines, and a large vegetable garden near the house. Mowed paths through the fields lead to two ponds, which are extensively planted. We have made a large wild garden in the woods. There are various structures to provide focus and rest along the way. The orchard hillside faces west to views of the Catskills.

Hours: 10 a.m. to 4 p.m.

From Taconic State Parkway, take Rhinebeck/Red Hook exit and follow Route 199 west to traffic light (about 4 miles). Take Route 308 straight for 2 miles to Cedar Heights Road. Turn right and take second right onto Crosby Lane. Follow to dead end and into Cedar Heights Orchard. *Please park in barnyard and in marked areas.*

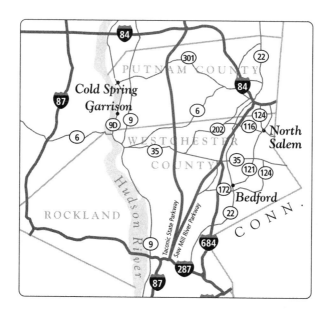

Sunday, June 15

Note: Local public gardens, Stonecrop Gardens and Manitoga, will welcome visitors on this date. Please consult their listings in the Public Garden section at the end of this chapter for directions and hours.

PUTNAM COUNTY

GARRISON

Ross Gardens

43 Snake Hill Road (Travis Corners), Garrison

This garden is a series of vignettes that flow into each other on five acres overlooking the Hudson River. The gardens are designed and maintained by the owner, Arthur Ross, and include a water garden, a moon (white) garden, meditation garden, rock garden, interesting daylilies, a fern garden, shrub garden, cutting gardens, and garden sculptures, along with a waterfall. Garden paths give easy access to many unusual flowers.

Hours: 10 a.m. to 4 p.m.

Take Route 9 to Garrison Golf Course. Turn west onto Snake Hill Road. Garden is .25 mile on left. Parking is available for 30 cars at any one time.

Proceeds shared with Philipstown Garden Club

BEDFORD
Ann Catchpole-Howell
448 Long Ridge Road, Bedford

This garden features large perennial borders. It is designed on a central axis with terraces, stone walls, and hidden steps leading to an unusual shrub garden. It was featured in Melanie Fleischmann's *American Border Gardens*.

Hours: 10 a.m. to 4 p.m.

From I-684, take Exit 4/Route 172. Take Route 172 east to Route 22, and turn left. In Bedford Village, go right, staying on Route 172 east. Go about .5 mile and turn right at Mobil gas station onto Route 104/Long Ridge Road (road to Stamford). Follow 2 miles to house, #448, on right. *Please park in meadow as directed.*

Lulu Farm
614 Croton Lake Road, Bedford

Lulu Farm is a hilltop garden in a park-like setting. This hundred-acre property contains ten acres of garden and ninety acres of field and woodland intersected by old stone walls. The gardens are: a dwarf conifer garden, terraces of mixed herbaceous and woody plants, a formal herb garden, woodland garden walk, large vegetable garden, and orchards. A pergola, arbors, and antique garden pieces are incorporated throughout the design. The landscape is characterized by diverse plantings of mature trees, some planted when the house was built at the turn of the century. There are many varieties of European beech and a number of unusual Japanese maples. Farm animals, barns, and sheds complete the picture.

Hours: 10 a.m. to 4 p.m.

From Saw Mill River Parkway, take Kisco Avenue exit (1 exit beyond Mount Kisco). Turn right off exit ramp, travel a few hundred yards, and turn right onto Croton Lake Road. Lulu Farm is about 1 mile ahead on right, #614 (mailbox with number is on left). *Please park on property as directed.*

North Salem
Jane & Bill Bird
6 Spring Hill Road, North Salem

This owner-maintained garden contains one of the nation's largest collections of clematis, including many scarce cultivars not available anywhere in the United States. In addition, the owners have developed many new clematis cultivars, which have been planted among the more than 420 clematis featured in the garden. The owner-designed property is sprinkled with multiple garden areas, including a pool garden. It is a plant collector's paradise, featuring about 100 large-flowered dahlias, roughly 100 roses, and hundreds of trumpet, Asiatic, Oriental, and species *Lilium*. Hard-to-find annuals and perennials have been started from seed by the owners, many collected during garden tours in Europe, England, and throughout the United States.

Hours: 10 a.m. to 4 p.m.

From the south, take I-684 north to Exit 7. Proceed to intersection of Routes 22 and 116. From there, proceed east 2.8 miles on Route 116/Titicus Road to Delancy Road on left. Proceed to first left turn, Spring Hill Road. We are third house on left, #6.

From the north, take I-684 south to Exit 8. Proceed as directed above.

From the east, proceed on Route 116 to Delancy Road on right. Proceed as directed above.

Proceeds shared with the Taconic Gardeners Club

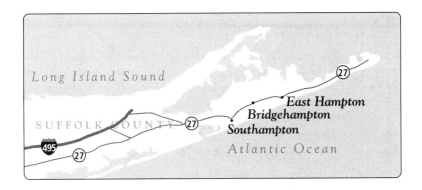

Saturday, June 21

SUFFOLK COUNTY

BRIDGEHAMPTON

Mrs. Dinwiddie Smith

158 Quimby Lane, Bridgehampton

Largely grasses with groupings of lilies, irises, sedums, and evergreens.

Hours: 10 a.m. to 2 p.m.

From *Montauk Highway/Route 27*, travel east through Bridgehampton to traffic light at Ocean Road. Turn right, continuing 1.75 miles to Quimby Lane. Turn left. Make a quick right and another left (this is still Quimby Lane). House is on left; #158 is on lamp post.

Proceeds shared with Habitat for Humanity of Peconic

EAST HAMPTON

Margaret Kerr & Robert Richenburg

1006 Springs Fireplace Road, East Hampton

The garden, designed by Kerr, surrounds their house and studios on two acres that extend down to the wetlands of Accabonac Harbor. Kerr's brick rug sculptures, inspired by tribal Middle Eastern carpets, are placed throughout the garden. One, a brick prayer rug, lies in a contemplative glade below the studios. Kerr collects plants grown in the Middle Ages in a courtyard around a fountain and lily pool highlighted with espaliered pear trees. In the spring, drifts of thousands of daffodils bloom in the fields around the house and are left unmowed until late fall. Native grasses and wildflowers make islands of meadow during the summer.

Hours: 10 a.m. to 2 p.m.

From *Montauk Highway/Route 27*, turn left at traffic light in East Hampton. Pass town pond. Continue .9 mile past next light, taking an immediate left onto North Main Street. Pass windmill on right. Go .3 mile, bearing right at fork onto Springs Fireplace Road. Go 5 miles. Driveway is marked by mailbox #1006. *Please park along Springs Fireplace Road and walk down dirt road to second house on left.*

Proceeds shared with the Horticultural Alliance of Hamptons and Bridge Gardens Trust

Carol Mercer

33 Ocean Avenue, East Hampton

An undeniable partnering of pattern, movement, and color makes this garden seem to glow and come alive. Mercer and her partner, Lisa Verderosa, have a thriving garden design business called The Secret Garden, and they have received several gold medals at New York City flower shows. The garden was a cover story in *Garden Design* magazine. It appeared in *Better Homes & Gardens, Martha Stewart Living, Victoria,* and *Design Times* magazines, and Time/Life book series' *Beds and Borders, Gardening Weekends,* and *Shade Gardening,* as well as in *The Natural Shade Garden* and *Seaside Gardening.* It was also featured in *Newsday* in 1999.

Hours: 10 a.m. to 4 p.m.

From Montauk Highway/Route 27, proceed east through Water Mill, Bridgehampton, and Wainscott to East Hampton. At traffic light at head of pond, turn right onto Ocean Avenue. House, #33, is fourth on left. White stone driveway is marked by a small gray sign. *Please park as directed.*

Proceeds shared with East End Hospice

SOUTHAMPTON

Kim White & Kurt Wolfgruber—Secret Garden

699 Hill Street, Southampton

Secret Garden is designed and maintained by the owners on weekends. At the middle of the drive, the garden opens to a series of rooms surrounded by evergreens and hedges. An 1866 carriage house sits in the center of the property and is surrounded by perennial island borders filled with flowers. A water garden is at the rear of the house and an herb garden with low boxwood edging lies in front of the living room window. A white garden and perennial beds enclose the pool area. A clipped boxwood path leads to the front door. This is a most varied garden in all seasons.

Hours: 10 a.m. to 4 p.m.

From Route 27, take Southampton College exit. Turn right 1 block to a stop sign. Turn left onto Montauk Highway, which becomes Hill Street. Look for blinking traffic light. Go to Lee Avenue on right side only. Garden is directly across from Lee Avenue. *Please park on Lee Avenue.*

Proceeds shared with the Southampton Fresh Air Home

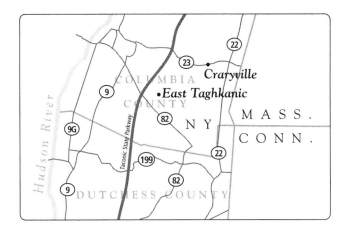

Sunday, June 22

COLUMBIA COUNTY

CRARYVILLE

Susan Anthony & Richard Galef

158 Maiers Road, Craryville

With a view of the Berkshires to the east, the garden has large, exuberant perennial borders, a bog bed with unusual plants and grasses, a flowering shrub border, and pondside beds planted with perennials, evergreens, and specimen trees. A long rock ledge has been exposed and is a backdrop to the lawn and to a large woodland grove that is planted with shade-loving plants and shrubs, a wide variety of small flowering trees, and a number of maple varieties. The grove is terraced with stone walls and crisscrossed with stone paths. Stone walls and terraces also surround the house and a gravel courtyard. And, where there once was a swamp filled with dead trees, a beautiful five-acre naturally landscaped lake has been created.

Hours: 10 a.m. to 4 p.m.

From Taconic State Parkway, exit east at Manor Rock Road. Go 1 mile to fork and turn right onto Maiers Road. Twenty feet on left are 5 mailboxes and our driveway with a sign, "158 Maiers Road."

From junction of Routes 22 and 23 at Hillsdale, proceed west on Route 23 exactly 4 miles to County Route 11/Beauty Award Highway. Go south 2.2 miles to Craryville Road. Turn right and go .8 mile to fork. Bear right onto Manor Rock Road and proceed 1.5 miles to Maiers Road fork. Keep left for about 20 feet. Our driveway is just past 5 mailboxes. *Please park on Maiers Road and walk in.*

EAST TAGHKANIC
Grant & Alice Platt
41 Tibbet Lane, East Taghkanic

Nestled in the woods at the end of a country lane, this garden takes advantage of a widely varied landscape to create a series of informal gardens that attempt to exploit the beauty of the natural setting. The site contains a series of woodland paths, which wanders over bridges across a creek and past the remains of old stone walls and natural rock formations. Included in the gardens are sunny herbaceous borders, a rock garden with varied alpine plants, a shade garden, and a park-like hillside garden including a pergola. Out of sight but just over a rise is a path that leads to a swimming pond.

Hours: 10 a.m. to 4 p.m.

From Taconic State Parkway north, pass Route 82 Ancram/Hudson exit and go 1.6 miles. Turn right (east) onto Post Hill Road (coming from north, turn left). Go .8 mile to a silo at Nostrand Road. Turn left and go .3 mile to Route 27 (no sign). Turn left onto Route 27 and go 1 mile to Taconic Parkway underpass. Continue .5 mile to Tibbet Lane. *Turn left and proceed to indicated parking area.*

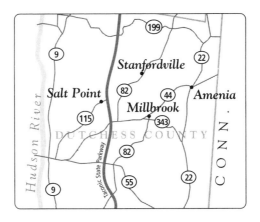

Sunday, July 6
DUTCHESS COUNTY

AMENIA
Jade Hill—Paul Arcario & Don Walker
13 Lake Amenia Road, Amenia

Jade Hill is a hillside stroll garden with a varied collection of exotic plant material. A partial list includes dwarf yellow-stripe bamboo, fountain bamboo, lotus, magnolias, Japanese maples, and conifers. Trees, shrubs, and perennials have been planted to form a tapestry of color and texture. Features include a walk-through bamboo grove and goldfish ponds. An Oriental viewing pavilion cantilevered over a ledge overlooks a gold-themed garden. The rose garden has more than fifty varieties of hardy shrub roses.

Hours: 10 a.m. to 4 p.m.

From traffic light in Amenia at intersection of Routes 22, 44, and 343, take Route 44 west. Make first left after 55 mph sign onto Lake Amenia Road. A gated driveway is after fifth house on right. *Please park on Lake Amenia Road.*

MILLBROOK
Far A-Field—John Whitworth
500 Overlook Road, Millbrook

The garden at Far A-Field, most of all, is a collection of ornamental trees planted over the last 25 years in extensive lawns surrounding a small brick Adamesque house built in 1931, which was enlarged in the early 1990s to add a conservatory and library. Protective woods giving the garden privacy and quiet contain another collection of trees, mainly deciduous hardwoods indigenous to Dutchess County. There is a yellow-blossom/silver-foliage garden, a shade garden of large-leaved, mostly white-blossoming plants, a collection of large conifers, a hidden hot colors garden, and the principal border in the garden—a long, curving, richly planted double border in a green/gray/pastel palette accented with wine-colored foliage plants. Up the hill from the front entrance of the house is a small Oriental garden. As you walk back to your car along the drive, there is a small dwarf conifer garden planted in moss beneath native gray birches.

Hours: 10 a.m. to 4 p.m.

From traffic light at intersection of Routes 44, 82, and 343 in Millbrook, travel east on Route 343 towards Dover Plains, passing Millbrook Golf and Tennis Club and a cemetery on left. Then, almost immediately, turn right onto Altamont Road/Route 96. Follow for just under 2 miles, passing Hoxie Road on left, then take next left onto Overlook Road. Proceed up hill only a short distance to gravel driveway on left marked #500. *Please park as posted.*

Proceeds shared with Saint Peter's Episcopal Church, Lithgow

SALT POINT

Ely Garden
28 Allen Road, Salt Point

Our contemporary gardens have evolved within the original nineteenth-century setting of the house, barn, and woods. These elements are set amid a rolling terrain, which runs down to a five-acre pond surrounded by both native and invasive plants. Between the house and barn we placed large, deep, robust beds, which are bordered by a pergola on one side and an Italianate upper garden on the other. There is also a long spring border leading from the house to the pond.

Hours: 10 a.m. to 4 p.m.

From Taconic State Parkway, take Salt Point Turnpike/Route 115 exit. Go west 1.75 miles into town of Salt Point. Turn right onto County Route 18. Bear right at fork onto Allen Road. House is first on right. There is a 5-foot-tall white fence along road in front of property. *Please enter south gates and park in field.*

STANFORDVILLE

Zibby & Jim Tozer
840 Hunns Lake Road, Stanfordville

The gardens at Uplands Farm are surrounded by rolling hills, horse paddocks with grazing miniature horses, Nubian goats, Belted Galloway cows, grand old trees, and a lush meadow of rye. Among the gardens, the Romantic Garden, with its forget-me-nots, bleeding hearts, blue trapezoidal loveseats by Madison Cox, and blue Moorish gate, is of special interest. The Wedding Folly, built in 1998 for the wedding of Katie Tozer and Jamey Roddy, was inspired by the teahouse at Kykuit and has latticed walls and pagoda lanterns. The images of the fanciful juniper animal topiaries are mirrored in the long reflecting pool. Nearby there are large arches, covered with William Baffen roses, which create a path to a meadow. The playhouse has its own charming garden. The main garden is a seventy-foot-long herbaceous border filled with flowering perennials and grasses. Other gardens dot the property.

Hours: 10 a.m. to 2 p.m.

From Taconic State Parkway, take Millbrook/Poughkeepsie exit. Turn right at end of exit ramp onto Route 44. Go about .2 mile. Turn left onto Route 82and go about 8 miles. At "Y" intersection at Stissing National Bank, bear right onto Route 65. Go 2 miles, passing Hunns Lake on left. Main house is third house past lake on right. *Please park where indicated.*

Proceeds shared with Wilderstein Preservation

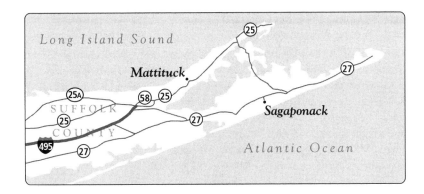

Saturday, July 12
SUFFOLK COUNTY

MATTITUCK
Maurice Isaac & Ellen Coster Isaac
4835 Oregon Road, Mattituck

This early 1900s country farmhouse has been designed with two major borders incorporating extensive plantings of unusual combinations of bulbs, perennials, trees, shrubs, and annuals. A pond well-stocked with koi and water plants adds a beautiful and soothing touch. A path leads to a swimming pool and plantings, as well as an old restored barn adjacent to an arbor planted with wisteria, clematis, and several vines offering tranquility, shade, and a view of the extensive nearby farm fields.

Hours: 10 a.m. to 4 p.m.

From Long Island Expressway/I-495, take Exit 73/Route 58 and follow to Route 25. Go through Mattituck past Love Lane to Wickham Avenue. Turn left and go past railroad tracks and traffic light. Stay straight on Wickham; it will turn into Grand Avenue. Take Grand about .25 mile to East Mill Road. Turn right, keeping to left; and this will turn into Oregon Road. *Look for signs for parking.*

Dennis Schrader & Bill Smith
1200 East Mill Road, Mattituck

Set in the heart of the North Fork wineries, the two-plus-acre garden surrounds a restored 1850 farmhouse. The gardens are encircled by fourteen acres of fields. The decks, porches, and terraces are filled with container plantings. There are many perennial and mixed shrub borders, vegetable, herb, and dwarf fruit tree plantings, a formal knot garden, and a woodland shade area. The garden has rustic arbors, trellises, stone walls, a garden pavilion, many sitting areas, and a natural clay pond with a stream and bridge. There are other ponds for waterlilies and papyrus. Many of the plantings contain tropicals, subtropicals, tender perennials, and annuals. Dennis is coauthor of the book *Hot Plants for Cool Climates: Gardening with Tropical Plants in Temperate Zones.*

> *Hours:* 10 a.m. to 4 p.m.
>
> *From Long Island Expressway/I-495,* take Exit 73/Route 58 and follow to Route 25. Go through town of Mattituck past Love Lane to Wickham Avenue. Turn left and go past railroad tracks and traffic light. Stay straight on Wickham and it will turn into Grand Avenue. Take Grand about .25 mile to East Mill Road. Turn left and look for #1200. *Please park along street.*
>
> *Proceeds shared with the Horticultural Alliance of Hamptons*

SAGAPONACK
Susan & Louis Meisel
81 Wilkes Lane, Sagaponack

Our property encompasses more than 100 specimen trees, with a focus on special beeches. Susan uses the flower color of several hundred perennials as if it were paint on canvas to create the visual effects I enjoy seeing.

> *Hours:* 10 a.m. to 2 p.m.
>
> *From Montauk Highway/Route 27,* go to intersection at Sagg Main Street. Turn south. Go past red schoolhouse on right and general store. Turn left onto Hedges Lane. Go .5 mile and take next left onto Wilkes Lane. House (#81) is second house on right. *Please park along road.*

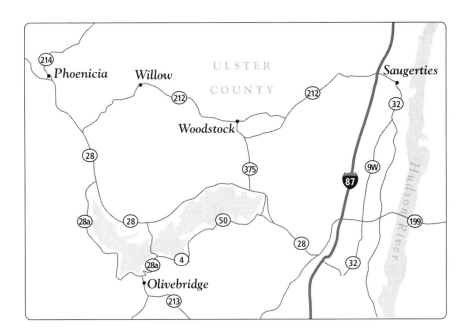

ULSTER COUNTY

OLIVEBRIDGE

James Dinsmore Garden

11 Tongore Kill Road, Olivebridge

The garden is best described as having a formal structure with hedges, paths, arbor, even trees, laid out in a symmetrical and geometric design, which is softened by loose, exuberant plantings. There are four main perennial gardens, each with its own design and color scheme. There is also a long shrubbery, which ends with a stone Chinese pagoda, a latticework "temple," pyramids, arch, terraces, and a dry stone creek. All in all, the gardens extend over six acres.

Hours: 10 a.m. to 4 p.m.

From New York State Thruway/I-87, take Exit 18/New Paltz. Turn left at traffic light after toll. Follow signs to Route 32 north (right turn). Go about 7 miles to left turn to High Falls on Route 213 west. Go about 4 miles to second light and turn right (this will still be Route 213, as well as Route 209 north). Go about 1 mile, turning left at Route 213 sign. Stay on Route 213 for about 7 miles to sign pointing left for Krumville. Turn left (Route 2A). Go 1 mile and turn right onto Weber Lane. Go .3 mile and turn left onto Tongore Kill Road. Property is first driveway on left with gate. *Please park on street outside gate.*

PHOENICIA
The Garden of Jane & Alfred Peavy
140 Waterworks Road, Phoenicia

Our one-acre garden was called "Trails End" when we bought it some thirty years ago. Since then we have dropped the name and the pretense and have devoted the ensuing years to developing it with extensive stonework and many unusual plants. We have an excellent collection of rhododendrons, Japanese maples, and conifers situated on a terraced hillside. Our garden offers both contemplative seclusion and sunny openness surrounded by views of the beautiful Catskill Mountains.

Hours: 10 a.m. to 4 p.m.

From Kingston, take Route 28 west 25 miles and turn right onto Main Street in Phoenicia. Proceed .25 mile on Main Street/Old Route 28 to Waterworks Road on left. Go up hill to #140, a brown house with a brown board fence at end of road.

From west, take Route 28 east and turn left onto Main Street in Phoenicia. Proceed as directed above.

From Woodstock, take Wittenberg Road to Mount Tremper and proceed straight at stop sign for 3 miles. Just past Terrace Farm Garden Center, turn onto Waterworks Road. *Please park in snowplow turnaround outside our gate.*

SAUGERTIES
The Donald Elder & Richard Suma Garden
31 Adams Road, Saugerties

This is an artist's garden, diversely influenced by the randomness of the English cottage garden, the formality of the clipped-bordered garden, and the subtlety of the studied views of the Japanese garden. An Asian-style screened pavilion provides a restful retreat and mountain views. Nestled in the woods, this unique garden incorporates the elements of water and stone as well as indigenous and exotic plants. Gravel paths link the garden together to form a balanced and tranquil place.

Hours: 10 a.m. to 4 p.m.

From the south, take New York State Thruway/I-87 to Exit 19/Kingston. Stay right as you pay toll and follow signs to Route 28 west. Go 6 miles to Woodstock. Turn right onto Route 375/Woodstock and go 2 miles to Route 212. Turn right and go 2 miles to driveway on left. Look for Adams Road, turn left, and go up dirt driveway to end, #31.

From north, follow signs to Route 212 west/Woodstock. Go 6.5 miles to Adams Road on right. Turn right and go up dirt driveway to end, #31.

WILLOW
Suzanne Pierot's "Garden by the Stream"
33 Hickory Road, Willow

My shade garden rambles over twelve wooded acres, with a mountain stream that provides an environment for more that 20, 000 hostas (124 varieties) and hundreds of astilbes (twenty-five varieties) in pink, white, and lavender that mingle with twenty-five varieties of ivy in the ground and in hanging baskets. A striking feature is the quantity of stone. When I started building the garden fifteen years ago, I found that under the thin layer of soil there was nothing but glacial rocks. What I thought of as a handicap became a focal point of the garden. Small rocks became the edge of a multitude of raised beds and terraced pools. Bigger flat ones became steppingstones in winding paths, and the giant ones gave me what is now my river-of-stone staircase that leads down the hillside to the lower gardens next to the stream. Be sure to wear low heel shoes. Ask to see before and after photos.

Hours: 10 a.m. to 4 p.m.

From the south, take New York State Thruway/I-87 to Exit 19/Kingston onto Route 28 west towards Pine Hill. Turn right at traffic light onto Route 375 to end (2.9 miles). Turn left onto Route 212 into village of Woodstock. Go through Woodstock on Route 212 to Bearsville. Turn right (remaining on Route 212 for 7.3 miles). Turn right onto Grog Kill Road. Go .3 mile to first paved road (no sign) and turn left. Continue .4 mile and turn left onto Four Wheel Drive. Go .2 mile and turn left onto Hickory Road. Go .1 mile to dead end. Gate has a sign that reads "Pierot." Enter gate and turn right down hill to main house. *Drop off passengers and return to area outside gate to park cars.*

From the north, take New York State Thruway/I-87 to Exit 20/Saugerties/Woodstock. Turn left after toll. Turn right onto Route 212 into village of Woodstock. Proceed as directed above.

WOODSTOCK
Joanne & Richard Anthony
136 Cooper Lake Road, Woodstock

The dream began when my grandparents bought an old farmhouse in 1929. In the following years, terraces, walkways, gardens, and a beautiful pergola were built. They have been lovingly restored, maintained, and extended since we moved here in 1985. The long perennial beds parallel a large open lawn. Hidden behind the pergola is a secret herb garden and three-tier fishpond. A 200-year-old stone smokehouse and summer kitchen serves as a pool house and is surrounded by a silver-and-pink garden. With the addition of deer fences, the fun of caring for this large garden is just beginning.

Hours: 10 a.m. to 4 p.m.

From Woodstock, follow Route 212 west to Bearsville (about 2 miles). Cross bridge just after Bear complex and take right fork onto Wittenberg Road. About 100 yards further, road forks again. Take right fork and continue up hill on Cooper Lake Road. Number 136 is seventh on right.

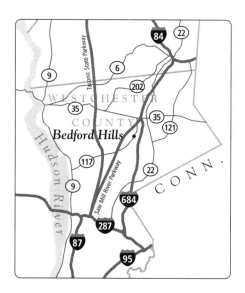

Sunday, July 20
WESTCHESTER COUNTY

BEDFORD HILLS
Phillis Warden
531 Bedford Center Road, Bedford Hills

This garden of many facets includes perennial borders, two water gardens, a formal vegetable garden, a wildflower garden, a fern garden, a marsh garden, a tree platform overlooking the marshlands, a woodland walk, and a formal croquet court. The garden extends over seven acres.

Hours: 10 a.m. to 4 p.m.

From Bedford Village, take Route 22 towards Katonah to the intersection at Bedford Cross. The garden is on the left. *Please park at Rippowam School and walk to 531 Bedford Center Road.*

Proceeds shared with Native Plant Center of Westchester Community College

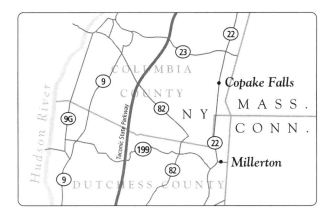

Saturday, September 6

COLUMBIA COUNTY

COPAKE FALLS

Margaret Roach

99 Valley View Road, Copake Falls

This thirteen-year-old homemade garden reflects my obsession with plants, particularly those with good foliage or of interest to wildlife. Sixty species of birds visit annually. Informal mixed borders, frog-filled water gardens, a paved garden and a bluestem meadow cover my two-and-one-half-acre hillside, a former orchard dotted with simple, Victorian-era farm buildings and house, surrounded by Taconic State Park land. Expansion continues and this year visitors are welcome to walk next door to see the beginnings of a landscape I started in 2002 around a new, modern guest house. Even I am shocked at the stark contrast between the two places, the new one featuring a large, enclosed gravel courtyard with formal lines.

Hours: 10 a.m. to 4 p.m.

Off Route 22 (5 miles south of Hillsdale, 13 miles north of Millerton) take Route 344 toward Taconic State Park signs. Bear right after park entrance and blue store, over metal bridge and past camp. After High Valley Road intersection on left, continue right another 100 feet to green barn and house on left. *Please park on that side only.*

MILLERTON
Helen Bodian's Garden
Carson Road, Millerton

In these four gardens, connected by grass paths, we try to use unusual plant varieties. First, along the north side of the house is a large rock garden sheltering small perennials and alpine plants. From there, a path leads to an ornamental vegetable garden also containing cutting flowers and herbs. Across the road are shrub borders and a square garden composed mainly of summer perennials. And next to those is a walled, late summer garden planted with hot-colored annuals and tropicals. Growing in pots set on top of its walls is a comprehensive collection of tender salvias.

Hours: 2 to 6 p.m.

From Taconic State Parkway, take Route 44/Millbrook exit. Turn right towards Millbrook and stay on Route 44 for less than a mile. First real left turn is Route 82 north. Turn left and continue north for about half an hour until you reach traffic light in Pine Plains. Turn right onto Route 199 east. Continue to Route 22. Turn left (north) and go straight through light in Millerton (intersection of Routes 22 and 44). Continue on Route 22 for 4 more miles. On right, you will see a sign for Columbia County. On left will be Carson Road. Turn onto Carson Road and go uphill for 1 mile. On left are a tennis court and metal barn. On right is a white farmhouse with a modern addition. *Please park along road or in field next to barn.*

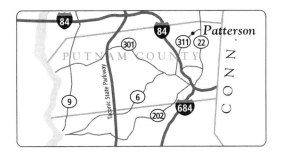

Saturday, September 13
PUTNAM COUNTY

PATTERSON
The Farmstead Garden
590 Birch Hill Road, Patterson

This garden, located on historic Quaker Hill, was planned as a rural landscape in keeping with its 1740 farmstead beginnings. A master plan was commissioned by the owners in 1985 to combine the site's woodlands, wetlands, house gardens, and agricultural fields into a harmonious native plant landscape while preserving the property's horticultural heritage. An heirloom apple orchard greets you as you enter the fieldstone entrance. The driveway is the old stagecoach road, which connected Pawling, New York, with Danbury, Connecticut. Native wildflower meadows now grace the upper and lower fields after decades of haying. A grove of more than eighty mature blueberry bushes tells the story of the acid soil and summers of picking and tasting. The original vegetable garden is anchored by an old majestic quince and the kitchen herb garden is filled with flowering thyme, catnip, and lavender, with a border of germander. A two-acre wetland can be traversed to experience plant and aquatic wildlife. The roadside sloping fields have been mowed to create welcoming paths and sculptural grasslands.

Hours: 12 to 6 p.m.

Take I-684 to Pawling exit. At intersection of Route 311, turn right onto South Quaker Hill Road. At first stop sign (2.5 miles), turn right onto Birch Hill Road. Follow road to #590. Garden is on left.

From Connecticut, take Route 37 through Sherman and continue to Wakeman Road. Akin Hall Library is on right and Hill Farm on left. Turn left and continue south. This road becomes Birch Hill Road. *Please park on road.*

Proceeds shared with The Battery Conservancy

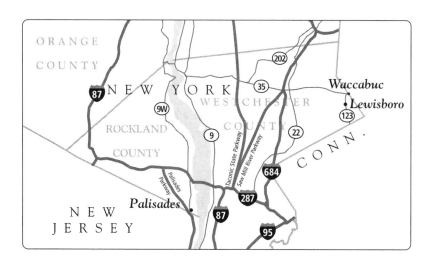

Sunday, September 14
ROCKLAND COUNTY

PALISADES

The Captain John House Garden
20 *Washington Spring Road, Snedens Landing, Palisades*

This is a small cottage-style garden with a (too) large diversity of plant material, including petasites, hakonechloa, many yellow-foliaged plants, a rose pergola, and a young triple hedge of peegee hydrangeas, yews, and azaleas. It features interestingly steep topography with a stream that empties into the Hudson River. The garden was featured in the July 1999 issue of House & Garden magazine.

Hours: 10 a.m. to 4 p.m.

From Palisades Interstate Parkway, take Exit 4. From traffic light at end of exit ramp, proceed north on Route 9W about 1 mile. At first light, where Oak Tree Road and Washington Spring Road cross, turn right onto Washington Spring Road. Follow it down to 2 dead end signs. Bear left. The 3-story white house is at bottom of hill on left. *Please park on street and enter garden through driveway.*

Judy Tomkins Gardens
75 *Washington Spring Road, Snedens Landing, Palisades*

As a designer, I have become aware of the striking difference in the topography of the land and how important it is for me to learn and observe, depending on where I am, just how the site emerges in its natural perfection—in other words, "the genius of the place"—I feel strongly that gardens should be walked through each day as each day changes and brings delight or sorrow with each of these changes. With this in mind, I am opening two properties that I designed, each different due to the change of land and views. My house is near eighteenth century, looking over the Hudson River. It is nestled by gardens with a garden path approaching the house. For the past few years I have collected somewhat rare trees for the property, primarily for the enjoyment of my grandchildren. There are young examples of cedar of Lebanon, Franklinia, Carolina bell, pink styrax, dove tree, yellowhorn, Chinese elm, Stewartia, and variegated aralia. The second house included with admission to my garden is primarily Victorian with an apple orchard, wildflower and courtyard garden, and a cliffside with a maze of paths leading to different plateaus overlooking the Hudson River.

Hours: 10 a.m. to 4 p.m.

From Palisades Interstate Parkway, take Exit 4. From traffic light at end of exit ramp, proceed north on Route 9W about 1 mile. At first light, where Oak Tree Road and Washington Spring Road cross, turn right. *Please park at church on right and walk down to house, #75.*

WESTCHESTER COUNTY

LEWISBORO

The White Garden

199 Elmwood Road, Lewisboro

The hardwood forest and native plants provide a "sacred grove" setting for the Greek Revival-style house. The gardens, designed by Patrick Chassé, are classically inspired near the house, including a nymphaeum, pergola garden, labyrinth, and theater court. Last year an Oriental garden reached by a bridge was added. More exotic surprises are hidden in separate garden rooms. Sculptures and water features enrich the gardens. In spring, 100,000 daffodils bloom.

Hours: 10 a.m. to 4 p.m.

From Merritt Parkway/Route 15, take Exit 38 and follow Route 123 north through New Canaan to New York State line. Town of Lewisboro and village of Vista are first signs encountered. Go past Vista Fire Department about .25 mile. Just after shingled Episcopal church on right, Route 123 will bear left and Elmwood Road will bear right. Go about another .25 mile just over a hill. At beginning of a gray stockade fence on right is driveway at #199.

WACCABUC

James & Susan Henry

36 Mead Street, Waccabuc

A nineteenth-century farm is the setting for perennial gardens, specimen trees, a walled garden, cordoned apple trees, a vegetable garden, berries and fruits, a pond in a meadow, and a vineyard producing red and white wines.

Hours: 10 a.m. to 5 p.m.

From I-684, take Exit 6/Route 35/Cross River/Katonah. Follow Route 35 east for 5 miles. After a long hill, look for Mead Street on left. Take .25 mile to #36 on left. Turn left into driveway, then left into parking area.

From Connecticut, Mead Street is 4 miles from traffic light at Routes 35 and 123. *Please park in field behind vineyard.*

Proceeds shared with the South Salem Fire Department

Public Gardens

BRONX COUNTY

Bronx

The New York Botanical Garden

200 Street & Kazimiroff Boulevard, Bronx (718) 817-8616 www.nybg.org

The New York Botanical Garden is one of the foremost public gardens in America, with some of the most beautiful natural terrain of any botanical garden in the world. Within this grand 250-acre setting, forty-eight gardens and special plantings offer stunning seasonal displays, from rainbows of tulips and azaleas in the spring to the rich tapestries of fall foliage.

Hours: April through October, Tuesday through Sunday, and Monday holidays, 10 a.m. to 6 p.m.; November through March, 10 a.m. to 4 p.m.; closed Thanksgiving and Christmas

Admission: Please call for rates or check the website

From Westchester County, take Cross County Parkway/I-287 to Bronx River Parkway south. Take Exit 7W/Fordham Road and continue on Kazimiroff Boulevard to Conservatory Gate on right.

From Connecticut, take I-95 to Pelham Parkway west. Go 3 miles. Across from Bronx Zoo entrance, bear right onto Kazimiroff Boulevard to Conservatory Gate entrance on right.

From New Jersey, take George Washington Bridge to Henry Hudson Parkway north to Mosholu Parkway exit. Continue on Mosholu to Kazimiroff Boulevard, turn right, and continue to Conservatory Gate on right.

Wave Hill

679 West 252nd Street, Bronx (718) 549-3200 www.wavehill.org

Often called "the most beautiful place in New York," Wave Hill is a 28-acre public garden in a spectacular setting overlooking the Hudson River and Palisades. Formerly a private estate, Wave Hill features several gardens, greenhouses, historic buildings, lawns, and woodlands, and also offers programs in horticulture, environmental education, land management, landscaping history, and the visual, performing, and literary arts. All programs focus on fostering relationships between people and nature.

Hours: October 15 through April 14, Tuesday through Sunday, 9 a.m. to 4:30 p.m.; April 15 through October 14, Tuesday through Sunday, 9 a.m. to 5:30 p.m.

Admission: free on Tuesday all day and Saturday until noon, otherwise, $4 adults, $2 senior citizens/students, children under 6 free

From the West Side and New Jersey, take Henry Hudson Parkway to Exit 21/246-250th Street. Continue north to 252nd Street. Turn left at overpass and left again. Turn right at 249th Street to Wave Hill Gate.

From Westchester, take Henry Hudson Parkway south to Exit 22/254th Street. Turn left at stop sign and left again at traffic light. Turn right onto 249th Street to Wave Hill Gate.

Brooklyn

Brooklyn Botanic Garden

900 Washington Avenue, Brooklyn (718) 623-7200 www.bbg.org

Brooklyn Botanic Garden is a living museum of plants blooming in one of the largest cities in the world. Highlights on our 52 acres include the Japanese Hill-and-Pond Garden, the Fragrance Garden designed for the visually impaired, the children's Discovery Garden, and the Steinhardt Conservatory, displaying tropical, desert, and temperate plants.

Hours: April through September, Tuesday through Friday, 8 a.m. to 6 p.m., weekends 10 a.m. to 6 p.m.; October through March, Tuesday through Friday, 8 a.m. to 4:30 p.m., weekends, 10 a.m. to 4:30 p.m. Closed Thanksgiving, Christmas, and New Year's Day.

Admission: $3 adults 16 and over, $3 children under 16 free, $1.50 seniors/students, seniors free on Friday.

From Brooklyn-Queens Expressway, take Kent Avenue exit. Follow service road (Park Avenue) alongside and then under expressway for 5 blocks. Turn left onto Washington Avenue and continue for 1.75 miles.

By subway, take Q local or Q express train to Prospect Park station or the 2 or 3 train to Eastern Parkway.

Hudson

Olana State Historic Site

Route 9G, Hudson (518) 828-0135 www.olana.org

The flower garden at Olana was designed in the nineteeth century "mingled garden" style recommended by Andrew Jackson Downing. It is a 165-foot-long and twenty-foot-wide garden curving along the base of a rustic stone wall supporting the carriage drive to the main house. It has a center path and ornamental gates at each end. The flowers are a mix of annuals, perennials, vines, and shrubs laid out in an irregular pattern to create a riot of color. Landscape and garden tours are available in season; self-guided tours are welcome whenever the grounds are open.

Hours: year round, daily, 8:30 a.m. to sunset.

Admission: $3 adults, $2 seniors citizens, $1 children 5 to 12

From New York State Thruway/I-87, take Exit 21/Catskill. Follow Route 23 east to Rip Van Winkle Bridge, cross bridge, and go south on Route 9G for 1 mile. Entrance is on left.

From Taconic State Parkway, take Route 82/Ancram/Hudson exit. Follow signs for Hudson and Rip Van Winkle Bridge (Route 82 to Route 23 west). At bridge intersection, do not cross bridge; take Route 9G south. Entrance is 1 mile on left.

AMENIA

Wethersfield

214 Pugsley Hill Road, Amenia (845) 373-8037

Ten acres of formal classical-style and outer gardens surround Chauncey D. Stillman's Georgian-style brick home. The original garden around the perimeter of the house was created in 1940 by Bryan J. Lynch. Evelyn N. Poehler oversaw the maintenance of the garden from 1952 on and designed the formal gardens over a twenty-year period.

Hours: June through September, Wednesday, Friday, and Saturday, 12 to 5 p.m.

Admission: free

From Route 44 east of Millbrook, take Route 86 and turn right onto Pugsley Hill Road. Follow signs for 1.3 miles to estate entrance on left.

ANNANDALE-ON-HUDSON

Montgomery Place

River Road, Annandale-on-Hudson (845) 758-5461 www.hudsonvalley.org

This 200-year-old estate enjoys a picturesque landscape, as extolled by Andrew Jackson Downing. Included are ancient trees and vistas of the Hudson River and Catskill Mountains. The early twentieth-century garden includes a wide variety of plants, many unusual. There are also hiking trails, and waterfalls.

Hours: April 1 through October 31, Wednesday through Sunday; November, weekends only; the first 2 weekends in December, 10 a.m. to 5 p.m.; closed the last 2 weeks of December through March

Admission: $3 grounds only, $6 house and grounds

From New York State Thruway/I-87, take Exit 19/Kingston onto Route 209/199 east across Kingston-Rhinecliff Bridge. Turn left onto Route 9G and proceed 3 miles, then turn left onto Annandale Road, bearing left onto River Road to estate entrance.

HYDE PARK

Vanderbilt National Historic Site: Italian Gardens

511 Albany Post Road, Route 9, Hyde Park (845) 229-6432 www.marist.edu/fwva

This three-level formal garden covers three acres. The rose garden has more than 1,200 plants. The perennial garden, along the cherry walk, includes several hundred perennials, and thousands of annuals are planted each year in the upper beds.

Hours: year round, daily, dawn to dusk; group tours available by appointment

Admission: free, but donations are appreciated

Located on Route 9, on left side of road, just north of Hyde Park Post Office.

MILLBROOK
Innisfree Garden
Tyrrel Road, Millbrook (845) 677-5286

Innisfree reflects an Eastern design technique called a cup garden, which draws attention to something rare or beautiful by establishing the suggestion of enclosure around it. A cup garden may be an enclosed meadow, a lotus pool, a waterfall, or a single dramatic rock covered with lichens and sedums. Visitors to Innisfree stroll from one 3-dimensional garden picture to another.

Hours: May 1 through October 20, Wednesday through Friday, 10 a.m. to 4 p.m., weekends and holidays, 11 a.m. to 5 p.m. Closed Monday and Tuesday, except holidays.

Admission: $3, Wednesday through Friday; $4, weekends and legal holidays; children under 6 free

Innisfree is on Tyrrel Road, 1 mile from Route 44 and 1.75 miles from Taconic State Parkway overpass on Route 44.

Mary Flagler Cary Arboretum/Institute of Ecosystem Studies/ New York Botanical Garden
181 Sharon Turnpike/Route 44A, Millbrook (845) 677-5359 www.ecostudies.org

The three-acre perennial garden features ecological demonstration beds. The fern glen is a two-acre display of native plants in natural communities. The greenhouse, open year round, is a tropical plant paradise and includes an "Economic Botany Trail." There are also nature trails, a picnic area, and an Ecology Shop with a plant room.

Hours: year round, Monday through Saturday, 9 a.m. to 4 p.m., Sunday, 1 to 4 p.m. Closed major holidays. Grounds open until 6 p.m., May through September. Greenhouse closes at 3:30 p.m.

From Taconic State Parkway, take Route 44 east for 2 miles. Turn onto Route 44A. Gifford House Visitor and Education Center is 1 mile along Route 44A on left.

From Massachusetts and Connecticut, take Route 22 to Route 44. Where Route 44 takes a sharp left to village of Millbrook, continue straight on Sharon Turnpike/Route 44A. Gifford House Visitor and Education Center is on right, just before Route 44A rejoins Route 44.

POUGHKEEPSIE
Springside Landscape Restoration
Academy Street, Poughkeepsie (845) 454-2060

Springside is the only unaltered documented work of Andrew Jackson Downing, one of the most influential landscape architects in American history. Once the summer home of Matthew Vassar (founder of Vassar College), the site was an "ornamental farm." Although unrestored, the landscape bears Downing's undeniable influence, illustrating the principles of the beautiful and the picturesque.

Hours: year round, daily, dawn to dusk

Admission: free

From Taconic State Parkway, take Poughkeepsie/Route 44 exit and proceed on Route 44 west through Poughkeepsie until just before Mid-Hudson Bridge. Stay in right lane for Route 9 south/Wappingers Falls and proceed on Route 9 for 1 mile to Academy Street exit. At bottom of the exit ramp, turn left. Proceed to first entrance on right at bottom of hill.

Vassar College Arboretum & Shakespeare Garden
124 Raymond Avenue, Poughkeepsie (845) 437-5686

First planted in 1918, the Shakespeare Garden has brick walks, statuary, knot beds, rose beds, heath and heather beds, and twelve raised-brick beds containing herbs and cottage garden plantings. A hemlock hedge encloses the garden. There is also an arboretum with 220 species of native and non-native trees and shrubs.

Hours: year round, daily, dawn to dusk

Admission: free

From Route 44/55 in Poughkeepsie, turn onto Raymond Avenue to Main Gate, about 3 blocks.

NASSAU COUNTY

MILL NECK
The John P. Humes Japanese Stroll Garden
Corner of Oyster Bay Road & Dogwood Lane, Mill Neck (516) 676-4486

A PROJECT OF
THE GARDEN
CONSERVANCY

A four-acre gem of landscape design, the garden provides a retreat for passive recreation and contemplation. The views, textures, and balance of elements in the garden follow Japanese aesthetic principles, encouraging a contemplative experience. The garden suggests a mountain setting beside a sea, where gravel paths represent streams forming pools of cascades, eventually flowing into the ocean, represented by a pond.

Hours: April 29 through October 22, weekdays, 11:30 a.m. to 4:30 p.m.; private tours and tea ceremony can be arranged during week

Admission: $5 adults, children under 12 free

From Long Island Expressway/I-495 east, take Exit 39/Glen Cove Road north to Route 25A/Northern Boulevard, turn right onto Route 25A, and pass C.W. Post University. At next traffic light turn left onto Route 107. Go to Chicken Valley Road and turn right. Go past Planting Fields Arboretum, continue straight through a blinking light, and garden is .5 mile on right. You will see a terra cotta-colored wall. Turn right at end of wall onto Dogwood Lane to parking lot on immediate right.

From Long Island Expressway/I-495 west, take Exit 41N. Take Route 106 to Route 25A/Northern Bouelvard/West. Turn right at second light onto Wolver Hollow Road. Go to second stop sign, turn right onto Chicken Valley Road, and proceed as directed above.

OLD WESTBURY
Old Westbury Gardens
71 Old Westbury Road, Old Westbury (516) 333-0048 www.oldwestburygardens.org

North America's most beautiful English-style country estate, its 160 acres include a walled garden, a sunken parterre rose garden, boxwood garden, thatched cottage garden, woodlands, ponds, lawns, statuary, and follies. A magnificent 1906 mansion contains fine English antiques and decorative arts. Old Westbury Gardens is on the National Register of Historic Places.

Hours: Late April through October, Wednesday through Monday, 10 a.m. to 5 p.m.; Sundays in November, 10 a.m. to 5 p.m. Holiday Celebration December 6 through 16, 11 a.m. to 4 p.m.

Admission: $10 adults, $8 senior citizens, $5 children 6 to 12

From Long Island Expressway/I-495, take Exit 39/Glen Cove Road south. Stay on service road of Long Island Expressway. At third traffic light, turn right onto Old Westbury Road. Entrance to Old Westbury Gardens is .25 mile on left.

ORANGE COUNTY

WEST POINT
Anna B. Warner Memorial Garden
Constitution Island at the U.S. Military Academy, West Point (845) 446-8676 www.constitutionisland.org

This is an old-fashioned perennial and annual border garden lining a fifty-yard path, planted in nineteenth-century style with flowers described by Anna Warner in her book *Gardening by Myself* written in 1872. Cared for by dedicated volunteers, this garden received the Burlington House Award.

Hours: Mid-June through October. Tours to Constitution Island are available on Wednesday and Thursday, mid-June through September. Reservations required.

Admission: $10 adults, $9 senior citizens and students, children under 4 free; present this book and admission will be reduced to $5

From the south, take Route 9W or Palisades Interstate Parkway to Bear Mountain Bridge Circle. Go 2 miles north on Route 9W, then take Route 218 through Highland Falls to West Point. After Hotel Thayer, take first right (Williams Road) downhill. Cross railroad tracks. Park north of South Dock.

From the north, take Route 9W south. Take first sign to West Point. Drive through West Point on Thayer Road. After road goes under stone bridge, take first left (Williams Road) downhill. Proceed as directed above.

COLD SPRING

Stonecrop Gardens

81 Stone Crop Lane, Cold Spring (845) 265-2000 www.stonecropgardens.org

At its windswept elevation of 1,100 feet above sea level in the Hudson Highlands, Stonecrop enjoys a Zone 5 climate. The display gardens cover an area of about twelve acres and include a diverse collection of gardens and plants: woodland and water gardens, a grass garden, raised alpine stone beds, a cliff rock garden, perennial beds, and an enclosed English-style flower garden. Additional features include a conservatory, display alpine house, and pit house with an extensive collection of choice dwarf bulbs.

Hours: Open Days on April 27, May 18, June 15, July 13, and September 21. Otherwise, open by appointment only, April through October, Tuesday, Wednesday, Friday, and first and third Saturday of each month, 10 a.m. to 4 p.m.

Admission: $5

From Taconic State Parkway, take Route 301/Cold Spring exit. Travel 3.5 miles to Stonecrop's entrance on right. A street sign reading "Stonecrop Gardens" marks driveway.

From Route 9, take Route 301 east for 2.4 miles. Our driveway will be on left marked by a street sign reading "Stonecrop Gardens."

GARRISON

Manitoga/The Russel Wright Design Center

589 Route 9D, Garrison (845) 424-3812 www.russelwrightcenter.org

A premier example of naturalistic landscape design, Russel Wright's woodland garden invites active participation in the two and one half miles of trails. This is a landscape not just to be seen but to be experienced, with feature highlights that Russel Wright wanted you to notice. The seventy-five-acre site, including Wright's house, is listed on the National Register of Historic Places. Please note that Dragon Rock, Russel Wright's house, is open to the public by reservation only during scheduled tours and will not be accessible on the Open Day event.

Hours: Open Day on June 15, 10 a.m. to 2 p.m.; otherwise, year round, weekdays, 9 a.m. to 4 p.m.; April through October, also weekends and holidays, 10 a.m. to 6 p.m.

Admission: $5 suggested donation

Located on Route 9D, 2.5 miles north of Bear Mountain Bridge and 2 miles south of intersection of Routes 403 and 9D.

BAYPORT

Meadow Croft, The John E. Roosevelt Estate

138 Bayport Avenue, Bayport (631) 472-9395

This nature preserve of seventy-five acres of woods and tidal wetlands was the summer home of John E. Roosevelt, a first cousin of President Theodore Roosevelt. The privet-and-lattice-enclosed kitchen garden adjacent to the Colonial Revival home contains plant material that would have been available in 1910, the year to which the house is restored. Included are twenty-four varieties of heirloom roses, heirloom vegetables, annuals, and more than fifty varieties of perennials.

Hours: third Sunday in June through third Sunday in October, Sunday, 12 to 5 p.m., with tours at 1 p.m. and 3 p.m.; closed weekends of July 4th, Labor Day, and Columbus Day

Admission: free

From Sunrise Highway/Route 27, take Lakeland-Ocean Avenue/Route 93 exit south about 2 miles to Main Street. Turn left and immediately bear right onto South Main Street/Middle Road. Continue for .5 mile and turn left at estate entrance.

BRIDGEHAMPTON

Bridge Gardens Trust

36 Mitchell Lane, Bridgehampton (631) 537-7440 www.bridgegardens.org

The gardens on these five acres include a formal knot surrounded by herbal beds, perennial mounds, topiaries, specimen trees, expansive lawns, aquatic plantings, woodland walks, a bamboo "room," lavender parterre, and hundreds of roses. A 750-foot-long double row of privet hedge encloses a pavilion-like garden house (not open to the public).

Hours: late May through late September, Wednesday, and Saturday, 2 to 5 p.m.

Admission: $10 adults, $9 senior citizens

From Montauk Highway/Route 27, go to Bridgehampton. At blinking traffic light at western edge of village, turn left onto Butter Lane. Go .25 mile and under railroad bridge; turn left immediately onto Mitchell Lane. Bridge Gardens, #36, is first driveway on left. Please park along Mitchell Lane with flow of traffic.

East Hampton
LongHouse Reserve
133 Hands Creek Road, East Hampton (631) 329-3568 www.longhouse.org

Sixteen acres of gardens are punctuated with contemporary sculpture. Landscape features include a pond, numerous allées and walks, a dune garden, and 1,000-foot-long hemlock hedge. There are collections of bamboo and grasses, 200 varieties of daffodils with more than 1 million blooms, and numerous irises, conifers, and broadleaf evergreens.

Hours: Open Days on May 3 and June 21, 10 a.m. to 2 p.m.; otherwise, open late April through mid-September, Wednesday and Saturday, from 2 to 5 p.m.

Admission: $10 adults, $8 senior citizens

From East Hampton Village, turn onto Newtown Lane from intersection at Main Street. Go to Cooper Street, turn right, and go to end. Turn left onto Cedar Street and bear right at fork onto Hands Creek Road. Go .7 mile to #133.

Sagaponack
Madoo Conservancy
618 Main Street, Sagaponack (631) 537-8200 www.madoo.org

This two-acre garden is a virtual compendium of major garden styles, including an Oriental bridge, box-edged potager, Renaissance-perspective rose walk, knot garden, laburnum arbor, hermit's hut, grass garden, and an exedra, as well as an Italianate courtyard and a user-friendly maze. It is noted for its innovative pruning techniques and striking colors. The Quincunx beds are notable. Rare trees and plants abound.

Hours: May through September, Wednesday and Saturday, 1 to 5 p.m.; tours of 10 or more may be arranged at other times

Admission: $10

From Long Island Expressway/I-495, take Exit 70 and follow signs to Montauk. Sagaponack is on Route 27, 1 mile east of Bridgehampton. Turn right at traffic light (first light east of Bridgehampton on Route 27). Madoo Conservancy is a little over 1 mile from highway and is 3 driveways after post office on right.

ULSTER COUNTY

Woodstock
Bowen House—Roseland Cottage
556 Route 169, Woodstock (860) 928-4074 www.spnea.org

The gardens were laid out in 1850 as part of the landscape of Henry Bowen's summer "cottage" built in 1846. Boxwoods border the twenty-one beds of annuals and perennials, forming a parterre garden. Landscape designer Andrew Jackson Downing's theories inspired the design of the ribbon and carpet-bedding plantings. Noteworthy trees and shrubs include a tulip tree, Japanese maple, Chinese wisteria, and old-fashioned roses.

Hours: year round, daily, dawn to dusk

Admission: free

From I-395, take Exit 97/Route 44 west for 1 mile. Go west on Route 171 for 3 miles and north on Route 169 for 1 mile. House is on left.

CROTON-ON-HUDSON

Van Cortlandt Manor

South Riverside Avenue, Croton-on-Hudson (914) 271-8981 www.hudsonvalley.org

This restored Federal period manor complex includes a border of period ornamentals of interest throughout the growing season, a large tulip display, a vegetable garden, an orchard, and narcissi naturalized at the woodland's edge. An extensive culinary and medicinal herb garden is also noteworthy.

Hours: April through October, daily, except Tuesday, 10 a.m. to 5 p.m.; November, weekends only

Admission: $4 for grounds

Take Route 9 to Croton Point Avenue. Go east on Croton Point Avenue to first traffic light. Turn right at light onto South Riverside Avenue. Van Cortlandt Manor is at end of road, past Shop Rite shopping center.

KATONAH

Caramoor Gardens

Girdle Ridge Road, Katonah (914) 232-1253 www.caramoor.com

Located throughout the 100 acres are the Sunken Garden, Spanish Courtyard, Butterfly Garden, Sense Circle for the visually impaired, Cutting Garden, Medieval Mount, Woodland Garden, Cedar Walk, and numerous antique containers planted in creative ways.

Hours: May through October, Wednesday through Sunday, 1 to 4 p.m. Group tours by appointment; call to reserve.

Admission: $7

Girdle Ridge Road is off Route 22. Enter through Main Gate.

Lasdon Park, Arboretum & Veterans Memorials

2610 Amawalk Road/Route 35, Katonah (914) 232-3141 www.westchestergov.com/parks/ locationpage/lasdonsanctuary.htm

A 243-acre property consisting of a twenty-two-acre arboretum and formal azalea garden, the park has woodlands with paths and open grass meadows. Focal points are the Azalea Garden, Historic Tree Trail, Lilac Collection, Magnolia Grove, Dwarf Conifer Collection, a collection of over sixty varieties of dogwood from around the world, and the Chinese Culture Garden.

Hours: year round, daily, 8 a.m. to 4 p.m.

Admission: free

Entrance is on Route 35, 2.5 miles west of intersection of Routes 100 and 35.

Muscoot Farm
Route 100, Katonah (914) 232-7118

Muscoot is a Westchester country gentleman's farm circa 1880-1950. The herb garden on the property is cared for by the Muscoot Naturalist. The garden displays beds with tea, dye, fragrance, and cooking herbs to be used for programs and workshops.

Hours: year round, daily, 10 a.m. to 4 p.m.

Admission: free, but donations appreciated

From I-684, take Exit 6/Route 35/Katonah/Cross River and go west on Route 35 for 1.3 miles. Turn left (south) onto Route 100. Muscoot Farm is on right after 1.5 miles.

NORTH SALEM

Hammond Museum Japanese Stroll Garden
Deveau Road, North Salem (914) 669-5033 www.hammondmuseum.org

A three-and-one-half-acre garden with thirteen different landscapes, the Japanese Garden is a living collection. The stroll garden contains a pond and waterfall, a garden of the Rakan, a red maple terrace, a Zen garden, and many species of trees and flowers, including cherry, katsura, quince, azalea, peony, and iris. The café serves lunch on the terrace.

Hours: May through October, Wednesday through Saturday, 12 to 4 p.m.

Admission: $4 adults, $3 seniors citizens/students, children under 12 free

From I-684, take Exit 8/Hardscrabble Road. Turn right off exit ramp and continue 4 miles to end. Turn right onto June Road. Take second left onto Deveau Road. Garden and museum are at the top of Deveau Road.

OSSINING

The Wildflower Island at Teatown Lake Reservation
1600 Spring Valley Road, Ossining (914) 762-2912 www.teatown.org

The island is a woodland garden of more than 200 species of native flowers. Several hundred pink lady's slippers make a spectacular display in May. In late summer, the sunny shores of the island are ablaze with cardinal flowers, lobelia, ironweed, and other bright, moisture-loving flowers. Visitors are guided along narrow paths by experienced volunteers.

Hours: Open Day on May 18; 10 a.m. to 2 p.m.; otherwise, open May through September, Tuesday through Sunday, 9 a.m. to 5 p.m., Sunday, 1 to 5 p.m. Wildflower Island tours: April and June, weekend, 2 p.m.; May, Saturday, 10 a.m. and 2 p.m., Wednesday, 7 p.m.; July through September, Saturday, 10 a.m.

Admission: $3

Take Major Deegan Expressway to New York State Thruway/I-87 north to Exit 9/ Tarrytown (last exit before Tappan Zee Bridge). Take Route 9 north to Ossining. Watch for Route 133 on right. At third traffic light after Route 133, turn right onto Cedar Lane. Cedar Lane will become Spring Valley Road. Teatown is on left, 3.8 miles from Route 9.

POCANTICO HILLS
Kykuit, The Rockefeller Estate
Pocantico Hills (914) 631-9491 www.hudsonvalley.org

The extraordinary early twentieth-century gardens at Kykuit, The Rockefeller Estate, were designed by William Welles Bosworth. Included are a formal walled garden, woodland gardens, a rose garden, fountains, and spectacular Hudson River views. Important twentieth-century sculptures were added by Governor Nelson Rockefeller, including works by Alexander Calder, Henry Moore, Pablo Picasso, Louise Nevelson, David Smith, and many others.

Hours: May through October, daily, except Tuesdays, 10 a.m. to 3 p.m., no reservations needed

Admission: $20 adults, $19 senior citizens, $17 children

All tours begin at historic Philipsburg Manor, located on Route 9 in village of Sleepy Hollow.

PURCHASE
The Donald M. Kendall Sculpture Gardens at PepsiCo
700 Anderson Hill Road, Purchase (914) 253-2000

One hundred and twelve acres of landscape designed by Russell Page surround the world headquarters of PepsiCo, Inc. Spacious lawns and shrubs, plantings of trees, and small gardens provide settings for 45 sculptures by renowned twentieth-century artists.

Hours: year round, daily, dawn to dusk

Admission: free

From I-84, take I-684 south to the Westchester Airport exit. Take Route 120 south to Anderson Hill Road to PepsiCo on the right.

From Merritt Parkway/Route 15 south (which becomes Hutchinson River Parkway), take Exit 28/Lincoln Avenue/Port Chester. Turn left onto Lincoln Avenue and proceed 1 mile to PepsiCo on right.

TARRYTOWN
Lyndhurst
635 South Broadway/Route 9, Tarrytown (914) 631-4481 www.lyndhurst.org

The grounds at Lyndhurst are an outstanding example of nineteenth-century landscape design. Elements include a sweeping lawn accented with shrubs and specimen trees, a curving entrance drive revealing "surprise" views, and the angular repetition of the Gothic roofline in the evergreens. The rose garden and fernery are later Victorian additions.

Hours: mid-April through October, Tuesday through Sunday, 10 a.m. to 4:15 p.m.; November through mid-April, weekends only, 10 a.m. to 3:30 p.m.

Admission: $4

From New York State Thruway/I-87, take Exit 9/Tarrytown/Route 9. Turn left at end of exit ramp onto Route 119 and continue to traffic light at Route 9/Broadway. Turn left and proceed .5 mile to Lyndhurst gates on right.

Valhalla
The Lady Bird Johnson Demonstration Garden—
The Native Plant Center
75 Grasslands Road, Valhalla (914) 785-7870

This two-acre garden on the campus of Westchester Community College contains only native American plants indigenous to the northeastern United States. The perennial and shrub beds are designed to show how these genera can be used in the home landscape. The garden is designed for summer and fall color but is interesting all year. No pesticides or fertilizers are used.

Hours: Open Day on September 14, 12 to 4 p.m., guided tours will be available. Otherwise open year round, daily, dawn to dusk

Admission: free

From northern Westchester, take Taconic State Parkway south to Sprain Brook Parkway, to Eastview exit. Turn left onto Route 100. Enter Westchester Community College at East Grasslands Gate and bear right at fork. Follow to parking lot 1 on right. Path through woods on far right of lot leads to garden.

From southern Westchester, take Sprain Brook Parkway to Eastview exit. Turn right onto Route 100. Proceed as directed above.

From I-287, take Exit 4/Route 100A and go north .5 mile to entrance to Westchester Community College on right. At end of entrance road, turn right and follow to parking lot 1. Proceed as directed above.

NORTH CAROLINA

Knowe Manor, Asheville.

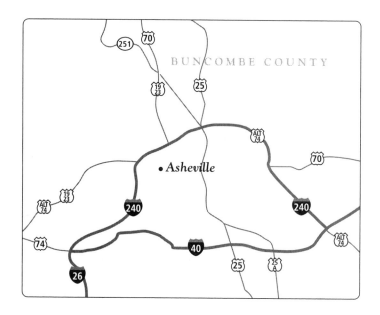

Saturday, July 12

BUNCOMBE COUNTY

ASHEVILLE

Garry-Doll Garden

67 Cutlers Green, Asheville

This is a seven-year-old perennial garden and a work in progress. The owners brought in ten truckloads of fill to create a large berm. New beds are being designed and refined to reflect the owners' love of flowers. "Exuberant chaos" describes this collection of plants selected to offer blooms from February to November.

Hours: 10 a.m. to 4 p.m.

From I-40 east, take Exit 55. Turn left off exit ramp. Turn left at traffic light onto Route 70. Go about 50 yards and make first right onto Moffitt Branch Road. Take first left onto Moffitt Road just before church. You will see "Eastmoor-by-the-River" sign. At Eastmoor entrance, bear left at stop sign. Follow Eastmoor Drive .4 mile and turn left onto Cutlers Green; street sign is on corner of my property. Number 67 is first house on left on corner of Cutlers Green and Eastmoor Drive. House has light-gray siding, a red mailbox and door. *Please park in driveway or in cul-de-sac.*

Knowe Manor

1010 Oteen Church Road, Asheville

Our garden covers four acres of a sixteen-acre tract, once the center of the Whitson family farm. It is an informally planted hillside stroll garden with paths wandering through a variety of settings and exposures. Starting from the propagation house, walk through mature woods underplanted with native shrubs and wildflowers to the 1926 farmhouse overlooking sunny herbaceous borders, a meadow, and pond. From here, explore walks to a dwarf conifer collection, shady woodland plantings, and mixed deciduous shrub and perennial borders. The paths are punctuated with spots for rest, reflection, and whimsy. The original impulse for the garden was our mutual love of plants' individual peculiarities and taxonomic relationships. These interests led to our collections of Asian maples (about thirty species and 100 cultivars) and other North American-Asian cognates. This Open Day extends our garden's place in many celebrations—of births and marriages, and of solstice, equinox, and cross quarter days.

Hours: 10 a.m. to 4 p.m.

From Asheville, take I-240 east to Exit 7 to Highway 70 east. Go 1.8 miles on Highway 70 east and turn right onto Oteen Church Road at traffic light (opposite VA Hospital's main entrance on left). Go .4 mile to dead end. Enter at gate marked #1010. *Park near greenhouse or along end of Oteen Church Road.*

The Richmond Hill Inn

87 Richmond Hill Drive, Asheville

Shortly after the historic Richmond Hill Mansion opened in 1989 as an inn, the Michel family began working with landscape designer Chip Callaway from Greensboro, North Carolina, to create a world-class Victorian landscape for the ten-acre estate. What evolved is a spectacular Victorian garden that is reminiscent of the year in which the mansion was built, 1889. Today, our landscape features English cottage-style gardens, spacious lawn areas, a croquet court, monuments, a mountain brook, and a waterfall. The crown jewel of the gardens is the Parterre Garden, a simple, geometrically landscaped garden.

Hours: 10 a.m. to 4 p.m.

Richmond Hill is located 3 miles northwest of downtown Asheville. From Route 19/23, take Highway 251/UNC-Asheville exit and follow signs.

Sanders' Garden
11 Glenn Cable, Asheville

Our hillside garden is a reflection of the mountainous area we live in. The emphasis is on native trees, grasses, shrubs, and perennials. Year-round interest is created by the staggered bloom time of the plants and the winter seed heads and berries. A windswept iron tree surrounding a patio provides a resting place for birds that wish to use a miniature pond for bathing and drinking.

Hours: 10 a.m. to 4 p.m.

From I-40, take Exit 55. Turn toward traffic light. Turn left at light onto Route 70/ Tunnel Road. Immediately get into right lane. Turn right in half of a block just past Econo Lodge onto Moffitt Branch Road. Go about 1 block and turn left onto Moffitt Road. Go 1.5 miles to end at Eastmoor (name of our area). Take right road up hill until road splits. Eastmoor continues up hill and Glenn Cable stays to right. Our house is second driveway on left, with a stone wall out front.

Public Gardens

BUNCOMBE COUNTY

ASHEVILLE

Biltmore Estate

1 North Pack Square, Asheville (800) 543-2961 www.biltmore.com

Frederick Law Olmsted, designer of New York's Central Park, created the stunning backdrop for George W. Vanderbilt's chateau. The seventy-five acres of landscaped gardens, grounds, and park are as spectacular as the house itself. From manicured grounds to forests and fields, the landscape was shaped by Olmsted's naturalistic vision.

Hours: year round, daily, 9 a.m. to 5 p.m.; closed Thanksgiving and Christmas

Admission: $34 adults, $25.50 students 10 to 15, children under 10 free

From I-40, take Exit 50 or 50B, then follow signs.

The Botanical Gardens at Asheville

151 W. T. Weaver Boulevard, Asheville (828) 252-5190 botgardens@main.nc.us

The Botanical Gardens at Asheville are a ten-acre preserve dedicated to the display and study of plants native to the southern Appalachians. The gardens are located adjacent to the University of North Carolina at Asheville.

Hours: year round, daily, dawn to dusk

Admission: free

From Route 19/23, take UNC-Asheville exit. Turn right onto Broadway and turn left at second traffic light onto W.T. Weaver Boulevard. Entrance is first driveway on left.

The North Carolina Arboretum

100 Frederick Law Olmsted Way, Asheville (828) 665-2492 www.ncarboretum.org

Visiting the arboretum is the perfect way to experience the natural beauty of western North Carolina. There are miles of nature trails, cultivated gardens that reflect the unique culture and craft of the southern Appalachian Mountains, a state of the art greenhouse complex and the National Native Azalea Repository.

Hours: April through October, daily, 8 a.m to 9 p.m.; November through March, 8 a.m. to 7 p.m.; closed Christmas

Admission: free

From Blue Ridge Parkway, exit at mile marker 393, where there are signs for Arboretum/Highway 191/I-26. On ramp, entrance to arboretum is on left, before Highway 191.

From I-40, merge right onto I-26 east. Take Exit 2/Blue Ridge Parkway/Brevard Road/Highway 191 and turn left (south) onto Highway 191. Proceed 2.1 miles (past Biltmore Square mall). Highway 191 merges from 4 to 2 lanes. Look for brown signs for Blue Ridge Parkway and the arboretum. Turn right at traffic light and entrance will be ahead on right.

From Asheville, take I-240, which merges into I-26 east. Proceed as directed above.

Hillsborough

Montrose

320 St. Mary's Road, Hillsborough (919) 732-7787

Montrose is a sixty-one-acre property listed on the National Register of Historic A PROJECT OF THE GARDEN CONSERVANCY Places with gardens begun in the nineteenth century. The grounds contain several nineteenth-century buildings, a rock garden, scree garden, several acres of woodland plantings, and large areas of sunny gardens with unique color and planting schemes. Mass plantings of bulbs, including rain lilies, cyclamen, galanthus, and crocus species, bloom throughout the year. Unusual trees, shrubs, trellises, fences, and arbors provide structure in winter and large urns planted with spectacular color combinations brighten the summer gardens.

Hours: year round, guided tours by appointment, Tuesday and Thursday, 10 a.m., Saturday, 10 a.m. and 2 p.m. Tours for larger groups may be arranged at other times. Two open garden days a year, May 17, 2003, and a fall date to be announced.

Admission: $10

From I-85, take Exit 164 and go north into Hillsborough. Turn right onto East King Street. At stop sign, bear left and up hill onto St. Mary's Road (not a sharp left). Pass St. Matthew's Church on right and Cameron Park Elementary School. Montrose is just past school on right. There are large red brick gate posts with a plaque on right that reads "Montrose 320." Please park at school.

From I-40, take Exit 261. Go north towards Hillsborough and pass under I-85. Proceed as directed above.

owner
tour

July 15

10:00 a.m.

OHIO

OPEN DAY:

June 8

The Gardens at Pau Hana Farm, Granville.

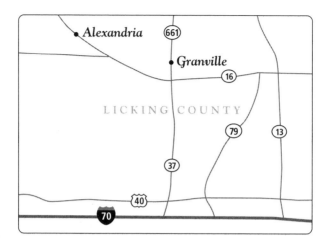

Sunday, June 8
LICKING COUNTY

Alexandria
Spring Hill Farm
4235 Morse Road, Alexandria

Although Spring Hill Farm dates back to the early 1800s, the gardens are relatively new. There are a variety of borders, a sprawling hillside planting with meandering paths, and the walled garden built with wide gravel areas defined by a home-grown line of boulders and backed by a fifty-foot-long retaining wall. Barns, a massive silo, corn fields, woods and a pond maintain the country casual setting. My interest in wildflowers, natives, and drought-resistant plants is taking precedence. A small portion of fields has been converted to a restored prairie.

Hours: 10 a.m. to 4 p.m.

From I-70, exit onto Route 37 to Granville. Go about 10 miles and turn left (west) onto Route 161/37. After passing Racoon Valley Golf Course (on left), turn left onto Morse Road. Travel .7 mile to #4235 on left. Look for a white rail fence close to road.

From Route 16 from Columbus, travel towards Granville, turn left onto Route 161/37, and proceed as directed above.

From the Columbus outerbelt/I-270, go east and take Exit 30 to Route 161 east towards New Albany. Continue on Route 161 for about 19 miles, then turn right onto Morse Road and proceed as directed above. If you pass Racoon Valley Golf Club on Route 161, you have missed turn. *Please park on south or west side of pole barn, close to road.*

Proceeds shared with the Granville Land Conservancy and Licking Land Trust

Granville
Maplewood
865 Newark Granville Road, Granville

Welcome to Maplewood. The Keegans' garden is in its third year, designed as if it has always been there. Honoring the ground on which it is planted, the Keegans attempt to grow a garden befitting the Maplewood Homestead, settled and built by one of Granville's founding fathers, Spencer Wright in 1812. The garden's formal structure is softened by freeform growth of many varieties of plants propagated from collected seeds and cuttings grown in a small year-round glasshouse.

Hours: 10 a.m. to 4 p.m.

Located 25 miles east of Columbus. From Routes 16, 161, 37, and 661 travel into Granville village to Broadway. Drive east on Broadway past Granville Inn on left and Buxton Inn on right. Continue east past Granville golf course on left and St. Edward's Church on left. Maplewood is immediately next on left. *Please park in St. Edward's Church parking lot and enter through center gate.*

The Gardens at Pau Hana Farm
2640 North Street, Granville

Our gardens are at their best in the spring with rhododendrons, daffodils, flowering crabs, and wisteria coloring the landscape. There are nine distinct gardens in our rural farm setting. Near the farmhouse is a shady Victorian wedding garden, enhanced by one of several unique Italian statuary. Other gardens include a raised-bed organic vegetable garden enclosed by a picket fence, a four-acre pond ruffled with rhododendrons, a daffodil walk through the woods featuring more than 50,000 spring bulbs, and a natural wildflower meadow. A collection of unusual plants, shrubs, and trees complements the farm's rolling terrain. Our personal collection of antique Fords will be on display for visitors to enjoy.

Hours: 1 to 6 p.m.

From I-70 east, proceed to Route 37 north to Broadway, which is in center of Granville. Turn right onto Broadway to Route 661 north/Pearl Street. Go 2.2 miles. House is at bottom of second hill on right.

Proceeds shared with the Granville Land Conservancy and Granville Junior Gardeners

The Reiner Ross Garden
215 West Broadway, Granville

The Victorian-style Elizur Abbott House, circa 1855, supports a classic English-style village garden with many formal elements throughout. The house inspired us to build gardens that were created by how they are to be viewed and for functionality. Inspiring plantings include a moon garden framed by clipped privet, a romantic allée garden filled with foxgloves, love-in-a-mist, and boxwood, and a container garden display filled with color-supporting tropicals and perennials. There is also a shade garden with more than sixty varieties of hosta. Vintage cold frames built from a salvaged 1953 glasshouse help to support new annuals and perennials each season. Come and enjoy!

Hours: 10 a.m. to 4 p.m.

From Route 16, 161, or 37, travel into Granville to Broadway. From center of village, take Broadway west past Mulberry Street about 2 blocks. We are third house on left after Mulberry, #215. *Please park on street.*

Proceeds shared with the Licking Land Trust

Reynolds English Cottage Garden
129 Shepardson Court, Granville

My English-style cottage garden was created out of a love of gardening, flowers, color, and architecture. The gardens flow from an entrance of old-fashioned roses, boxwood, and herbs— surrounded by a white picket fence integrated with a gazebo—into grass walks lined with stone-edged perennial borders, through flagstone walks and patios, into formal raised gardens and perennial borders backed by a serpentine stone wall. A winding brick path through fox-glove, astilbe, helleborus, and boxwood leading to a Victorian-style garden house nestled between the hillside and trees caught the eye of *Country Homes* magazine, resulting in a feature article. Share this "creation from the heart" with its owner.

Hours: 10 a.m. to 2 p.m.

From I-70, take Route 37 north 12 miles to Granville. Go downtown to traffic light at Broadway and Main, turn left (west), and go 4 blocks to Shepardson Court. Turn left again to #129, a Victorian house with white picket fence. *Please park on street.*

Proceeds shared with the Granville Garden Club Junior Gardeners

Public Gardens

LICKING COUNTY

NEWARK
Dawes Arboretum
7770 Jacksontown Road S.E., Newark (740) 323-2355 or (800) 44-DAWES

Established in 1929, The Dawes Arboretum is dedicated to education in horticulture, natural history, and arboretum history. It includes nearly 2,000 acres of horticultural collections, gardens, natural acres, a Japanese garden, and collections of hollies, crab apples, rare trees, and rhododendrons. A four-and-one-half-mile auto tour and eleven miles of trails provide easy access.

Hours: year round, daily, dawn to dusk; visitor center open Monday through Saturday, 8 a.m. to 5 p.m.; Sunday and holidays, 1 to 5 p.m.; closed Thanksgiving, Christmas, and New Year's Day.

Admission: free

Located 30 miles east of Columbus and 5 miles south of Newark on Route 13, north of I-70, off Exit 132.

OREGON

OPEN DAYS:

April 12
May 31
June 14
June 22
July 20

Alan & Sharon McKee Garden, Salem.
Photo by Chris Greenwood.

Saturday, April 12

MARION COUNTY

SALEM

Richard & Deanna Iltis

3402 Biegler Lane South, Salem

We began building the house and garden in 1973, both taking inspiration from existing land forms, plants, and wildlife on the gently sloping ridge-top site. The woodland garden section is nestled among basalt boulders under a canopy of native oak, dogwood, and wild currant. April is a fine time to view favorite collections of ferns, ginger, trillium, erythronium, hellebore, and more. Whimsical, home-crafted art adds to a woodland celebration of the beauty and variety of spring renewal

Hours: 10 a.m. to 4 p.m.

Follow directions to Rockhaven garden. Turn right onto Madrona and take first left onto Biegler Lane, proceeding to dead end. *Parking is limited on street. Additional parking is available at neighborhood swimming pool on east side of Biegler Lane.*

Proceeds shared with the Salem Hardy Plant Society

Rockhaven
3630 Sunridge Drive South, Salem

My half-acre garden, established in 1969, is a woodland paradise under a canopy of old Douglas fir and Garry oaks. In addition, I have planted vine maples, Canadian hemlock, and other small trees. A quarry rock wall with a small waterfall to attract birds winds along the east side. Accenting the terrain are mossy boulders. Rhododendrons and many erythroniums and trilliums are in bloom.

Hours: 10 a.m. to 4 p.m.

Take I-5 to Exit 253/Mission Street and head west. At 25th Street, turn left and continue south to Madrona (across from Salem airport). Turn right and go west across town, crossing Commercial and Liberty Streets. Continue to crest of hill. Turn left onto Sunridge, keeping left. House is last on block on left side. *Please park on street.*

Proceeds shared with the Salem Hardy Plant Society

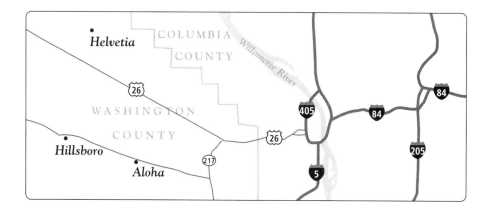

Saturday, May 31
WASHINGTON COUNTY

ALOHA
The Garden of Vickie Braman
6377 S.W. Broad Oak Drive, Aloha

Color, texture, and fragrance abound in this ten-year-old garden of a landscape designer and plant collector. Visitors will find lush mixed borders surrounding the house and outer edges of the landscape. Overflowing perennial beds are reminiscent of a country cottage garden. The cottage charm is enhanced by a rustic willow bench and willow arbors laden with climbing vines and roses. A stone terrace and raised beds contain herbs and edible flowers. The multi-level deck offers colorful containers and the sound of bubbling water. Bits of garden art, some created by the gardener, are positioned throughout.

Hours: 10 a.m. to 4 p.m.

From Portland, go west on Highway 26 to 185th Street exit. Turn south onto 185th and go about 4 miles. Just past Farmington Road, turn left onto Broad Oak Boulevard, then left onto Broad Oak Drive. Take second left, which is still Broad Oak Drive. House is straight back.

Proceeds shared with the Pregnancy Resource Centers of Greater Portland

Guinther Garden
19885 S.W. JayLee Street, Aloha

Rustic structures and garden art punctuate this multi-level one-acre suburban garden, and a splashing stream tumbles downhill through the center. Tied together by meandering paths, the garden is primarily a woodland garden containing an impressive variety of evergreen and deciduous trees and shrubs. However, there are also perennial beds surrounding a central lawn. In twelve years, the garden has reached a maturity that provides a sense of shaded tranquility.

Hours: 10 a.m. to 4 p.m.

At 198th Avenue and Tualatin Valley Highway, turn south onto 198th. Cross railroad tracks and continue 1 mile to JayLee Street. It is next street after guardrails where 198th crosses Butternut Creek. Turn right. Garden is first house on right.

From Braman Garden, return to Farmington Road and turn left. Go .8 mile to 198th and turn right. Go .9 mile to second yellow street intersection sign. That sign indicates JayLee. Turn left. Garden is at first house on right. *Parking is available on both sides of street.*

Proceeds shared with the Boys & Girls Clubs of Portland

HELVETIA

Elizabeth Furse Garden

22485 N.W. Yungen Road, Helvetia

This twenty-year-old "work in progress" is an exuberant country garden. Old English roses and hydrangeas are the dominant plants, with cottage garden flowers like phlox and penstemon throughout the beds. Three small ponds have fish and waterlilies, each with its own fountain. The garden is divided into a number of separate spaces; the rear garden is predominantly shade, while the front is sunny. Set in a 100-acre property with large trees and vineyards, the garden is a peaceful place, with many birds attracted by the water and the surrounding forests. Oregon's famous climate helps keep the garden blooming year round, but its best times are May and September.

Hours: 10 a.m. to 4 p.m.

From Portland, take Highway 26 west about 13 miles to Exit 61, turn right onto Helvetia Road and go about 3 miles to Bishop Road (a dirt road). Pass Helvetia Tavern on left. Turn right (there is a big sign for Helvetia Winery and Vineyards). Continue to Yungen Road and turn right. Pass signs for Helvetia Winery to end of Yungen. *Please park on road and walk into garden.*

Proceeds shared with the Community Action Organization of Washington County

Goodwin Gardens

11617 N.W. Helvetia Road, Helvetia

Our garden is set amid twenty acres of sloping pastureland with sweeping views of the Coast Range and Tualatin Valley. It is one and a half acres in size, limited only by what our backs and knees can maintain. Designed around flowing walkways and anchored by big rocks and trees, it includes unique owner-built metal and wood arbors and trellises. Japanese wisteria provides a magnificent springtime display on a two-story, thirty-foot-long arbor. Our large bonsai collection was begun over forty years ago. An overall exuberance of bloom and variety of perennials, shrubs, and grasses speak of our gardening passion.

Hours: 10 a.m. to 4 p.m.

Go west from Portland on Highway 26, take Exit 61, and turn right (north) onto Helvetia Road. Follow 3.9 miles to marked driveway on left. Helvetia makes a sharp left turn (west) at Meier Road. There is a sign marking both roads. *Please park on site.*

Proceeds shared with the Hillsboro Public Libraries

Cartwheels—The Garden of Laura M. Crockett
525 N. E. Edison Street, Hillsboro

The creative outlet for a passionate garden design studio, in the midst of a quiet rural town where green lawns prevail, this garden stands alone. As an expression of living the life you love without fear of horrifying one's neighbors, this garden utilizes every inch of space for personal enjoyment, beginning with the entry courtyard, which radiates energy and tantalizes curious passers-by to enter and enjoy. The garden is experienced through structurally defined transitions offering a wide variety of garden vignettes and evoking a strong sense of style throughout.

Hours: 10 a.m. to 4 p.m.

From Highway 26 west, take Jackson School Road exit and turn left (south). Go to Evergreen Road and turn right (west) onto Evergreen Road. Travel 2 miles to Jackson School Road and turn left (south). Follow to a "Y" and veer left, coming to an immediate 4-way stop sign at crossroads of 5th and Grant. Turn left (east) onto Grant Street. Travel 1 block to 6th Street and turn right (south). Travel 1 block to Edison Street and turn right (west). Garden is on right. *Please park along street or in church parking lot across street.*

Hilltop—The Virginia Larson Garden
1905 S.E. Oak Street, Hillsboro

A half-acre country garden surrounding an 1860s house, it has been gardened for 25 years. Old walnut trees, shrubs, specimen trees, and perennials (some heirloom) provide seasonal interest spring through fall. There is also an herb garden and unusual garden sculptures. This garden was featured in 1996 in *Better Homes & Gardens* magazine.

Hours: 10 a.m. to 4 p.m.

Take Highway 26 west and exit at 185th. Turn left and go to Highway 8. Turn right and continue to Hillsboro. Stay in right lane; go to Oak Street (third traffic light after passing Shute Park). Turn right and go to 18th Street (stop sign); cross 18th and go down short hill to S.E. 20th. House is red and sits on hill. *Please park on street and walk up to house and garden. Limited parking at house for handicapped access.*

Proceeds shared with the Aloha Garden Club

Saturday, June 14
MARION COUNTY

SALEM
Keith & Madge Bauer
575 Superior Street South, Salem

Our garden reflects an uneasy truce between a husband who admires lawn and box hedges and a wife fond of invasive plants, which she euphemistically calls "weavers." Friendly and open, the site offers the challenges of slope and old trees and the benefits of view and varied growing conditions.

Hours: 10 a.m. to 4 p.m.

Take I-5 to Exit 253. Go west on Mission Street to High Street. Turn left and go past Bush's Pasture Park to Lincoln Street. Turn right and go up hill to dead end at John Street. Turn left and go 3 blocks to Superior. Turn right. House is off north alley. Please park on street.

Savicki Garden

388 Maple Hill Drive N.W., Salem

This two-and-one-half-acre natural garden overlooks the Willamette Valley and is composed of island beds and mixed borders, an orchard, a vegetable garden, and a delightful woodland garden nestled into the edge of an acre of mixed wood. Meandering paths join various parts of the garden. Special features include drought-tolerant plants, a water element, hornbeam hedge, kiwi arbor, and majestic native deciduous trees (*Quercus garryana, Acer macrophyllum*, and *Sambucus caerula*) as well as a huge madrone (*Arbutus menziesii*).

> *Hours:* 10 a.m. to 4 p.m.

> *The McKees and the Savickis are close neighbors (0.1 mile apart).* Follow directions to McKees' garden. Maple Hill Drive N.W. is on right, just before left bend to McKees'. Turn right onto Maple Hill. We are first house on left. Coming from McKees', turn right, then left onto Maple Hill. *Please park on street.*

Alan & Sharon McKee

4327 Andrea Drive N.W., Salem

We began our garden the year after building our house in 1991 and the projects have never stopped. My husband is a grass seed farmer and I am a graphic designer. What I think is interesting about our combined efforts lies in our backgrounds. Alan has knowledge of plants, mechanics, and chemistry, whereas my contributions are in color, shape, and detail. We have hundreds of feet of basalt wall that we built ourselves and even collected the stone from a nearby quarry. We are located in the Eola Hills of West Salem and have a beautiful view of the valley and river below. Our eleven acres also include a small vineyard on a terraced south-facing slope. We maintain the garden ourselves and enjoy sharing it.

> *Hours:* 10 a.m. to 4 p.m.

> *From I-5*, head west though Salem on Highway 22, crossing Willamette River into West Salem. Continue west on Highway 22 approximately 6 miles, pass John Deere dealership, turn right onto 50th Street and proceed up hill, turning right onto Andrea Drive (first right). Travel up hill; on left you will see our vineyard and our driveway is just beyond, #4327.

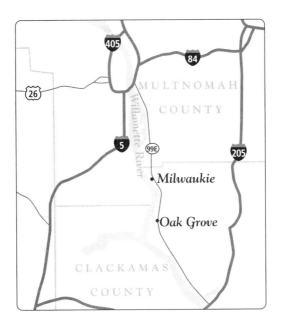

Sunday, June 22

CLACKAMAS COUNTY

OAK GROVE
Cerf-Treyve Garden
15115 S.E.Woodland Way, Oak Grove

Our garden is an example of the age of elegance in garden design. Converted from a farm in the 1920s to a home designed by Jamieson Parker and a garden by a "Miss Lord," the property originally included what is now the Freer-Maker Garden. A stable, garage, servants' quarters, and a small orchard remain intact. The garden, however, has waxed and waned with multiple owners of the past. It is still home to many old specimen trees: a copper beech, madrona, sequoia, *Prunus*, pin oak, and many magnolias. The circular driveway has large old flowering cherries of several varieties. Our St. Francis Garden is an allée of boxwood leading to a Grecian-style pergola. The rose garden has changed shape several times and the espaliered fruit trees have aged gracefully. Restoration of the garden is in the planning stages.

Hours: 10 a.m. to 4 p.m.

From Sellwood Bridge traveling south, take Highway 99E/McLoughlin Boulevard to Oak Grove Boulevard. Turn right, go 1 block to Woodland Way, and turn left.

From I-205 traveling north, take Oregon City exit and proceed to Oak Grove Boulevard. Turn left, go 1 block to Woodland Way, and turn left. *Please park on street and walk through iron gates.*

The Kalbfleisch/Matteucci Garden
15315 S.E. Woodland Way, Oak Grove

Our two-acre garden has a small creek bordered by old Douglas firs, cedars, and a 150-foot-tall cherry tree. It is mostly a woodland garden with natural and artificial scree beds in both dry and wet environments on the slopes of the creek. A moss garden and gravel garden have matured nicely. We have been interested in woodland plants particularly and have a fair collection of different species of terrestrial orchids, peonies, magnolias, rhododendrons, trilliums, hardy aroids, and ferns.

Hours: 10 a.m. to 4 p.m.

Travel south from Portland on Highway 99E/McLoughlin Boulevard east towards Oregon City about 6 miles from where Ross Island Bridge crosses McLoughlin. Turn right onto Oak Grove Boulevard at traffic light near Fred Meyer store. Proceed .2 mile to Woodland Way and turn left. House is last on right.

Paradise Creek
15125 S.E. Woodland Way, Oak Grove

The minute you approach the property and peek through the gateway entrance, you'll know why we named the one and one-quarter acres Paradise Creek. Over the past three years, we have devoted numerous hours to saving the property from the invasion of ivy and blackberry bushes that had been growing freely for 28 years. A spring-fed creek was uncovered and we hauled in 100 tons of rock and boulders to landscape the creek, build a waterfall, and elevate the area. Hundreds of different plants and trees were planted along the winding paths, at the viewing decks, along the footbridges, and by the gazebo we built. As you walk up the steps through the bamboo *tori* (gateway), you'll enter the grassy, park-like setting, which features a 110-year-old sycamore tree, 175-foot firs, madrona, holly, laurel, cedar, and copper beech trees. This year we have added an 18-foot *palapa* (thatched hut).

Hours: 10 a.m. to 4 p.m.

From Portland, go south on Highway 99E/McLoughlin Boulevard. From Milwaukie, go 2 miles (Fred Meyers on left, Jack in the Box on right). Turn right onto Oak Grove Boulevard. Go 2 short blocks and turn left at Woodland Way, first street after fire station, to #15121.

From I-205, take Exit 9/Oregon City/Gladstone. Go north 3.7 miles on Route 99E to Oak Grove Boulevard. Proceed as directed above.

Proceeds shared with the Susan G. Komen Breast Cancer Foundation

Quercus Terra
15014 S.E. Woodland Way, Oak Grove

Dick Groener toiled for over forty years creating a "Northwest garden." We are told that he often worked by lantern at night constructing rock terraces and garden paths. So, with the "bones" in place, we began Dave & Bob's gardening adventure in 1998. Initially we thinned the trees and shrubs and envisioned a more "naturalized" garden. Five individual gardens seem to be evolving: a formal entry garden where the sunshine supports our vegetable garden, a pond/bog garden fed by year-around "seeps," a mature rhododendron/camellia garden at the center of the property, a native oak grove, and a new courtyard garden of tropical plants. This is a "work in progress."

Hours: 10 a.m. to 4 p.m.

Take Highway 99E/McLoughklin Boulevard, go west on Oak Grove Boulevard and south on Woodland Way. *Please park in front of hedge along street.*

Survival of the Fittest
15017 S.E. Woodland Way, Oak Grove

The three-quarter-acre garden began life as part of an extensive Lord and Schryver garden, but seventy-five years of neglect left only a few giant rhododendrons, two broken fishponds, and several magnificent trees planted near the borders. During the last ten years, we have designed and implemented a garden to complement the English-inspired banqueting house built in the 1920s. We use exotic plants as well as old standbys, with special emphasis on texture, form, color, and fragrance to create informal backdrops for a variety of garden features. We don't pamper our plantings and the best win out. Our garden has been featured in national and international house and garden publications.

Hours: 10 a.m. to 4 p.m.

From downtown Portland, take Burnside Bridge east. After crossing Willamette River, turn right at first traffic light and go south on Martin Luther King Boulevard. Head south through Milwaukie. Martin Luther King Boulevard turns into McLoughlin Boulevard. Pass B-52 bomber airplane on right. Second light past bomber is Oak Grove Boulevard. Turn right. Fred Meyer will be on left. Go west 1 short block and 1 long block. Pass fire station on left. Next street after fire station is Woodland Way. Turn left. We are halfway down dead end on right. *Please park on street.*

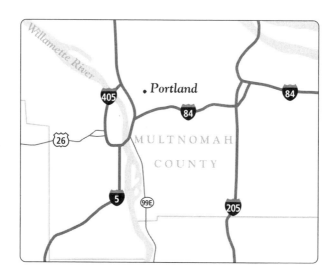

Sunday, July 20
MULTNOMAH COUNTY

PORTLAND
Bates-McDonald Garden
11626 S.W. Military Lane, Portland

This property was acquired in 2002 by Susan and John Bates. The garden had been developed over 60 years by Lady Anne Kerr McDonald and her husband, Sir James McDonald. The 1.75 acres encompass a grand upper parkland plus paths that wind down the hill. The hillside garden is left more natural with natives. There are many magnolias, peonies, roses, rhododendrons, fuschias, and azaleas, plus several unusual varieties of trees and shrubs in the upper garden. Some of the interesting trees are a trochodendron behind the living room, *Cunninghamia lanceolata* on the north path, and the *Magnolia wilsonii* with pendulous flowers on the south border. The azara shrub/tree on the north path is of interest, as is the *Actinidia kolomikta* below the ponderosa pine. Also near the *Actinidia* are several *Rosa mutabilis* that have wonderful colors. The wisteria at the east edge of the lawn has been trained as a standard. To the south of the house is the Chilean garden. The palm tree and the hibiscus survive our Zone 8 winters. There is also a *Taxodium distichum*, the swamp cypress. At the edge of the Chilean garden, on the side of the house, large *Lagerstroemia* and *Punica* (pomegranata) are espaliered.

Hours: 10 a.m. to 4 p.m.

From Highway 43, 2 miles north of Lake Oswego, turn east onto Military Road. Turn immediately right onto Military Lane. We are third house on left. *Please park on street.*

High Hatch—Garden of Susan Stevenson

11648 S.W. Military Lane, Portland

The High Hatch house was built in 1911 by a prominent Portland architect, William Whidden, for himself. The garden surrounding the stately stucco house was very formal. In 1986, I purchased the house and have created new garden spaces in this beautiful property overlooking the Willamette River and Mount Hood. A small contemplative white garden is situated left of the driveway. Beyond waits a large rockery area with many rare species. A hybrid tea rose garden surrounds the entrance. The garden below has a bulb border with many unusual varieties, a formal lawn area around a pool with 85-year-old Irish yews, crab apples, persimmon, rhododendrons, camellias, weeping cherries, and cryptomeria.

Hours: 10 a.m. to 4 p.m.

Travel south of Portland on Highway 43. At 3 traffic lights past Sellwood Bridge, turn left toward Willamette River on Military Road. Take an immediate right onto Military Lane and Stevenson garden is fourth property on left.

O'Bannon's Garden

0203 S.W. Palater Road, Portland

Using different plant groupings, I have created a woodland setting in the front half of our junior acre and a sunny garden in the back, incorporating perennials, trees, shrubs, and vegetables. Boulders provide seating and frame a stairway; large rocks form a path through a bog garden. An arbor of peeled logs supports different vines; a Zen garden provides a quiet retreat area. Two fountains and numerous birds attracted to the garden add sound on each side of the house. Low rock walls from rocks we collected in Oregon define some borders, including a mass planting of heathers. Mature rhododendrons mix with a multitude of unusual varieties throughout the different garden environments.

Hours: 10 a.m. to 4 p.m.

Take I-5 to Terwilliger Boulevard/Lewis & Clark College exit. Follow east for 2 miles to roundabout by law school. Garden is off north side of roundabout at 0203 S.W. Palater Road. Park at Lewis & Clark Law School across from garden or at main campus east of roundabout and walk back 1 block.

Proceeds shared with Lewis & Clark College

Alice & Wayne Plummer Garden

10535 S.W. 11th Drive, Portland

We began building our western-style garden in 1971. Basic Japanese themes have emerged: clusters of stones and plants, pruned Japanese pines, vine maple groves, and paths integrate the individual garden spaces and levels. These spaces continually extend the aesthetics of the rooms in our home and professional office.

Hours: 10 a.m. to 4 p.m.

Take I-5 south to Exit 297/Burlingame. Turn right and turn right again onto Terwilliger Boulevard at next traffic light. Go 1.3 miles to Riverdale High School and turn right onto Boones Ferry Road. Go 1.9 miles to Arnold Street (turns only to right). Watch for Garden Conservancy signs from this point. Right turn onto next street, 11th Drive. Proceed .3 mile past dead end sign at Kari Lane; next residence on left is #10535. *There are 3 disabled spaces at top of driveway, about .25 mile. Otherwise, please park on both sides of street.*

Wat Pho? Pan-Asian Garden

149 S.W. Ridge Drive, Portland

Wat Pho? is a lighthearted nod to Asian-style garden design. A blend of Asian elements, mainly Thai, create a lush tropical oasis in its suburban setting. The garden visitor enters through a pair of teak gate doors to wind up a bordered path to a Shuzou-style pebbled court-yard. Continuing, the wanderer will enter a river-rock path lined with large Asian pots leading to the greenhouse styled with Thai ornamentation. It is home to a Japanese guardian in the form of a large clay oven. A formal elevated pond draws the eye up to a bright perennial garden with large ornate Burmese jardinières. At this writing, the foundation is being laid for a forced perspective water feature emanating from an elevated Thai-style spirit house.

Hours: 10 a.m. to 4 p.m.

From I-5, south of downtown Portland, take the Terwilliger exit, following signs to Lewis & Clark College. Crossing back over freeway, go to fourth light. Take a hard left up 2nd Avenue. (If you reach the college you've gone too far). First right is Ridge Drive. Garden is on upper corner of 2nd and Ridge at #149. *Please park on street.*

Public Gardens

MARION COUNTY

SALEM

Bush's Pasture Park

600 Mission Street S.E., Salem (503) 838-0527

Originally the home of Asakel Bush, pioneer banker and newspaperman, the park now boasts a delicious mix of open spaces, walking paths, perennial and annual gardens, and a Victorian greenhouse. Native Garry oaks tower over the main axis of the park, while a spectacular well-labeled collection of unusual flowering shrubs and trees surrounds the house and rose gardens. The latter date from the 1950s and include extensive older hybrid tea plantings as well as the Fartar Old Rose Collection, the finest collection of old roses on public property in the Northwest.

> *Hours:* year round, daily, dawn to dusk
> *Admission:* free
> *From I-5*, take Exit 253/Mission Street and head west over overpass to High Street. Turn left and take first left (opposite Bush Street) to parking lot. This park in a neighbor of Historic Deepwood Gardens.

Historic Deepwood Estate

1116 Mission Street, S.E., Salem (503) 363-1825 www.oregonlink.com\deepwood

The English-style gardens of Historic Deepwood Estate were created from 1929 to 1936 by Lord and Schryver. The estate consists of a series of beautifully designed garden rooms: Great Room, Spring Garden, Tea House Garden, 1905 Gazebo, Scroll Garden, Shade Garden, Secret and Border Gardens.

> *Hours:* year round, daily, dawn to dusk
> *Admission:* free
> *From I-5*, take Exit 253/Mission Street and continue west over overpass. Turn left onto 12th Street then take next right onto Lee Street. Parking lot is at that corner and well marked. Park is adjacent to Bush's Pasture Park.

Willamette University—Martha Springer Botanical Garden

900 State Street, Salem (503) 838-0527 www.willamette.edu/dept/plant/grounds/botanical

Three special gardens have been created amidst the beautifully landscaped sixty-one-acre campus, which spans the Mill Race along with more than 1,000 trees and several sculptures. The Springer Botanical Garden has twelve acres, including a butterfly garden, herb garden, alpine rock garden, theme borders, and an Oregon native area.

> *Hours:* year round, daily, dawn to dusk
> *Admission:* free
> *From I-5*, take Exit 253/Mission Street and go west. As you approach overpass, bear right, then left following the signs to Willamette University. After crossing 12th Street, take first right opening into a parking lot. Garden is north of Sparks Gym.

The Oregon Garden

879 West Main Street, Silverton (877) 674-2733 www.oregongarden.org

The Oregon Garden is a world-class botanical display garden in the making. Special gardens include the Conifer Garden, Northwest Garden, Oak Grove (which features a collection of 150-year-old Oregon white oaks), Children's Garden, Rediscovery Forest, Amazing Water Garden, Jackson & Perkins Rose Garden, and the wetlands. It is the home of the Gordon House, the only Frank Lloyd Wright-designed house open to the public.

Hours: March through October, daily, 9 a.m. to 6 p.m.; November through February, daily, 9 a.m. to 3 p.m.; closed Thanksgiving, Christmas, and New Year's Day

Admission: $7 adults, $6 senior citizens/students, $3 children 8 to 13, under 8 free

From I-5, follow signs to Silverton and the Oregon Garden.

MULTNOMAH COUNTY

Portland

The Berry Botanic Garden

11505 S.W. Summerville Avenue, Portland (503) 636-4112 www.berrybot.org

Guide yourself through this six-acre historic garden, created by renowned plantswoman Rae Selling Berry. Explore the curving herb lawn, 150-tree rhododendron forest, a secluded and shady fern garden, our water garden, a native plant trail, the sunny quarter-acre rock garden, and moist border areas featuring species primroses.

Hours: by appointment only

Admission: $5 nonmembers

From I-5, take Exit 297/Terwilliger Boulevard/Lewis & Clark College and follow signs for Lewis & Clark. Turn right onto Terwilliger and cross freeway. Drive through small business district. Keep left at forks at Boones Ferry and at Terwilliger Boulevard/Lake Oswego, onto Palatine Hill Road. Pass college and turn right onto Military Road. Summerville Avenue is about .5 mile on left. Follow to end and go down left driveway with arrow that reads "Botanic Garden."

Portland Classical Chinese Garden

239 N.W. Everett Street, Portland (503) 228-8131 www.portlandchinesegarden.org

Discover Portland's newest garden, the Garden of Awakening Orchids. The largest Suzhon-style urban garden outside of China is waiting for you to explore an infinite number of views that unfold from each vantage point. Pavilions, a teahouse, rugged rocks, and serpentine walkways reflect in the lake. This is an ever-changing poetic landscape to revive your spirit.

Hours: November 1 through March 31, daily, 10 a.m. to 5 p.m.; April 1 through October 31, daily, 9 a.m. to 6 p.m.

Admission: $6 adults, $5 senior citizens and students, children under 5 free

From I-405, take Everett Street exit east and go to Third and Everett.

Crystal Springs Rhododendron Garden
S.E. 28th Avenue, Portland (503) 771-8386

This is a unique seven-acre garden with 2,000 rhododendrons and azaleas, 145 different tree species, and numerous companion plants. Trees add color and structural interest in winter. A lake surrounds the garden, attracting waterfowl to nest.

Hours: year round, daily, dawn to dusk

Admission: Labor Day through February, free; March through Labor Day, $3, children under 12 are free

A 10-minute drive from city center, nearly surrounded by Eastmoreland Golf Course and across street from Reed College. One block north of Woodstock Boulevard.

Elk Rock, The Garden at the Bishop's Close
7405 S.W. Newton Place, Portland (503) 636-5613

Begun in 1912 by an avid plantsman, this 6.5-acre English-style garden is a treasure trove of rare and unusual plants. A delightful rock garden, woodland garden and fishpond, and cascade garden are all features of this garden, which was innovative in its blending of new plant introductions from around the world with Northwest natives. A renowned collection of *Magnolia* species provides spectacular interest March through June.

Hours: year round, daily, 8 a.m. to 5 p.m.; closed some holidays

Admission: free

Take Route 43 south from downtown Portland to S.W. Military Road (traffic light) about 1.5 miles south of Sellwood Bridge. Turn left, then immediately right onto S.W. Military Lane. Garden is at end of lane. Parking is limited and guests are asked to park in upper lot only on weekdays. No buses.

Hoyt Arboretum
4000 S.W. Fairview Boulevard, Portland (503) 228-8733 www.hoytarboretum.org

Hoyt Arboretum is a treasured living museum close to the city center, with trails, majestic groves, and sunny clearings. Home to 1,100 species of trees and woody shrubs, it provides a living classroom to students from pre-school through college. Twelve miles of trails are a favorite place for walkers, joggers, and people who appreciate the world of plants.

Hours: year round, daily, 6 a.m. to 10 p.m.

Admission: free

From downtown Portland, take Route 26 to Washington Park/Oregon Zoo exit and follow signs to Hoyt Arboretum. TriMet bus #63 stops directly in front of visitor center and Max Light Rail station is nearby at zoo.

Japanese Garden Society of Oregon
Portland (503) 223-1321 www.japanesegarden.com

The Japanese Garden is nestled in the scenic west hills of Portland. It encompasses 5.5 acres and is composed of five garden styles: Tea Garden, Strolling Pond Garden, Natural Garden, Karesansui Dry Meditation Garden, and Flat Garden.

Hours: April 1 through Sept 30, Tuesday through Sunday, 10 a.m. to 7 p.m., Monday, 12 to 7 p.m.; October 1 through March 31, Tuesday through Sunday, 10 a.m. to 4 p.m.,

Monday, 12 to 4 p.m.

Admission: $6 adults, $5 senior citizens, $4 students, children under 6 free

From Route 26 west, take 200 exit and follow road past the 200, Forestry Center, and Vietnam Memorial. Turn right onto Kingston, follow 1.6 miles, and continue left on Kingston to garden's parking lot on left across from Rose Garden Tennis Courts.

Leach Botanical Garden

6704 S.E. 122nd Avenue, Portland (503) 823-9503

The fifteen-acre garden with four and one-half acres in cultivation is located in a riparian drainage with a dense overhead canopy of evergreen and deciduous specimens; as a result, the major plant collections are adapted to shade. The garden's focus is on Pacific Northwest native species and historic collections displayed with like genera.

Hours: year round, Tuesday through Saturday, 9 a.m. to 4 p.m., Sunday, 1 to 4 p.m.

Admission: free

Located 4 blocks south of 122nd Avenue and Foster Road S.E. We are 3 miles east of Foster Road exit.

Lewis & Clark College

0615 S.W. Palatine Hill Road, Portland (503) 768-7000 www.lclark.edu

The 65-acre Lloyd Frank estate, once maintained by 28 gardeners, is now a bustling college campus. Expanses of lawn, pools, and watercourses built in the 1920s still lead the eye down the formal terraces to a large hidden rose garden. Splendid Japanese lace-leaf maples and stately Atlas cedars accent these terraces. From the first terrace, Mount Hood is framed by the trees. On the rest of the campus are spring-flowering shrubs, native dogwoods, and unusual trees such as sassafras, Spanish fir, Mexican umbrella pine, and dawn redwood.

Hours: year round, daily, dawn to dusk

Admission: free

Take I-5 to Exit 297/Terwilliger Boulevard. Follow signs to Lewis & Clark College.

St. Paul
Cecil & Molly Smith Garden

14635 S.W. Bull Mountain Road, St. Paul (503) 590-2505

This mature woodland garden was the inspiration of Cecil Smith, whose love of rhododendrons combined in a most felicitous way with his love of native plants and selected exotics. The garden features superior forms of both species and hybrid rhododendrons complemented by choice trees, shrubs, wildflowers, and bulbs.

Hours: March 3 through May 24, Saturday, 10 a.m. to 3:30 p.m., or by appointment

Admission: $3 for non-ARS members

Located 3.5 miles south of Newberg. Take Route 219 to Champoeg Road and turn right. Continue straight ahead onto Ray Bell Road for .8 mile to #5060.

From I-5, take Exit 278, turn west onto Ehlen Road, and continue straight ahead (Ehlen changes to Yergen, then to McKay). This reaches a "T" intersection with Route 219. Turn right. Turn left onto Champoeg Road. Continue straight ahead onto Ray Bell Road for .8 mile to #5060.

PENNSYLVANIA

OPEN DAYS:

June 8
June 28

Hortulus Farm, Wrightstown.
Photo by Laura Palmer.

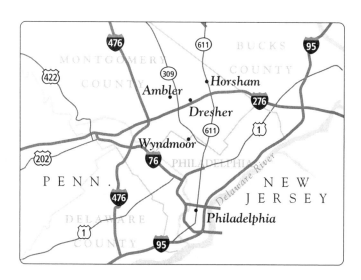

Sunday, June 8
MONTGOMERY COUNTY

AMBLER

Cynthia & Morris Cheston
560 Lewis Lane, Ambler

We have been very fortunate to have gardened here for the last thirty-two years, watched over by a pair of 200-year-old sycamore trees. From the windows of our 1845 house and adjoining eighteenth-century cottage, there is a sweeping vista of a colorful three-tiered perennial garden framed by a 'Blue Princess' holly hedge culminating at a swimming pool. A meadow garden with grasses and wildflowers contrasts wonderfully with the formal structure of our garden. Don't miss the remains of a huge copper beech (virus victim), which is gradually being overtaken by recently planted beeches and a shade garden underneath. At the top of this old soldier, a pair of Canada geese often nest in the spring! Chickens, ducks, a donkey, and horse add a colorful and melodious note to this pastoral scene.

Hours: 11 a.m. to 4 p.m.

From Philadelphia, take Schuykill Expressway east to I-476 north and follow to end. Take Plymouth Road exit just before toll to end of exit ramp. Turn right. Travel .25 mile to dead end at traffic light. Go left onto Butler Pike. Follow to fourth light (2 to 3 miles). There are Exxon and Sunoco gas stations and Broad Axe Tavern at intersection. Go left onto Route 73/Skippack Pike. Go .75 mile to Lewis Lane on right just after Shady Grove School. Go right and follow .5 mile to #560. Driveway is on right just after curve, marked by a post-and-rail fence.

From New York and New Jersey, take Pennsylvania Turnpike/I-276 to Exit 26/Fort Washington/Ambler. Proceed through toll straight ahead to stop sign. Turn right onto Pennsylvania Avenue and follow until road dead ends at a light. Turn left, go over a railroad bridge, and make an immediate right through a parking lot with Maria's Cantina on right and Rich's Deli on left. Turn right at intersection at end of parking lot onto Morris Road. Travel 1.5 miles to light at Butler Pike. Cross over Butler Pike and proceed to Lewis Lane, about .5 mile on left. House is .3 mile on left.

DRESHER

Tollhouse Garden

1515 Jarrettown Road, Dresher

The 1700s tollhouse provides the historical setting for an eclectic mix of garden styles. From the cacti and succulent plants of the "ruins" to the lush setting overlooking the pond, this garden is actually a combination of many smaller gardens linked by the use of color and texture. With only a small glimpse visible from the road, one would not realize the assortment these small gardens have in store, including a variety of mixed borders of woody and herbaceous plants. Nestled next to the patio, the 'Duchess of Albany' clematis encircles the gazebo to the sound of a nearby waterfall and pond filled with fish, frogs, and a turtle. A natural creek running through the property divides the garden into two separate landscapes. Cross the footbridge and enter a woodland garden that includes a variety of shade-loving plants. This garden provides a perfect haven from the hubbub of every day life.

Hours: 11 a.m. to 4 p.m.

This house is located at corner of Jarrettown Road and Limekiln Pike/Route 152. It is across street from Jarrettown Inn. *Please park along our side of Jarrettown Road.*

Proceeds shared with Longstreth Childrens Park

HORSHAM

Brickman's Garden

445 Cloverly Lane, Horsham

Earlier travels to Japan inspired elements of design throughout our house and garden. Our windows provided the framework from which we created a design that could be viewed from the inside out and throughout all seasons. This contemporary-style house on one and one half acres allowed us enough space to explore new ideas as well as implement more traditional ideas of garden design. A challenge was to create privacy and beauty in a suburban setting along a busy state road. Through our love of plants, we were able to not only expand our gardens, but also have the opportunity to start a collection of interesting and beautiful specimens. There are many special areas to this garden. A Zen-style pathway leads to the front door. Through a gateway the sound of water can be heard from the two patio ponds. A footbridge across the wetlands with ornamental grassess leads to the willow and perennial meadow.

Hours: 11 a.m. to 4 p.m.

From Limekiln Pike/Route 152 and Jarrettown Road, go east on Jarrettown to traffic light and turn left onto Welsh Road/Route 63. Cloverly Lane is second street on right. House is on corner of Cloverly and Welsh Road. *Please park on Cloverly Lane.*

Proceeds shared with Longstreth Children's Park

Wyndmoor
English Village
633 East Gravers Lane, Wyndmoor

The garden at the "English Village" is a work in progress. We purchased these extraordinary, Elizabethan-style farm buildings on four and one half acres of a former estate in 2000 and rehabilitated the garage and a sixteenth-century English-style cottage as a residence. Installation of a formal parterre garden in the courtyard began in 2002. Low boxwood hedges define spaces between axial paths that converge at a central fountain. A perennial bed is located along the east wall, while plant containers and hanging baskets liven the living room terrace. Outside of the court are another perennial bed, new space-defining hedges, a future croquet lawn, and a chicken house in a converted tile-roofed corncrib. The large east lawn accommodates a vegetable garden and the remnants of an orchard, which is being replanted. The former lawn west of the house is being allowed to revert to meadow.

Hours: 11 a.m. to 4 p.m.

From the Pennsylvania Turnpike/I-276, take Exit 25/Norristown or, from I-476, take the Plymouth Meeting exit and follow signs to Germantown Avenue east. Follow Germantown Avenue for approximately 5 miles. Turn left onto Northwestern Avenue at traffic light and take next right onto Stenton Avenue. Bear left, then right through complex intersection at Bethlehem Pike. Turn left onto Gravers Lane at second light. Cross Ardmore Avenue. English Village is about two thirds down block on left.

From Center City and south, take I-76 to Lincoln Drive exit. Follow several miles to end. Turn right onto Allens Lane to dead end at Germantown Avenue and turn left. Go up hill and into Chestnut Hill's retail district. Turn right onto Gravers Lane. Cross Stenton and proceed as directed above. *Please park on Gravers Lane and walk in.*

Proceeds shared with the Wissahickon Garden Club

PHILADELPHIA COUNTY

Philadelphia
Cleve Gate
8870 Towanda Street, Philadelphia

The property is entered by a long driveway into a courtyard. To the right of the house is a walled swimming pool and a folly surrounded by flower beds. At the back of the house off the kitchen is an herb garden and a brick terrace on an oval-shaped lawn surrounded by mature oaks, beeches, and flowering trees. To the left is an acre of land in the process of being reclaimed from every invasive plant known in our area. We are installing a meadow and wooded area with local trees, bushes, and flowers. We have built walkways and retaining walls, all done with stone dug up on the property.

Hours: 11 a.m. to 4 p.m.

From Pennsylvania Turnpike, take Exit 25/Norristown; from I-476, take Plymouth Meeting exit and follow signs to Germantown Avenue east. Follow Germantown Avenue east to Northwestern Avenue. Turn left at traffic light and take next right onto Stenton Avenue. Go the second light and stay right, merging onto Bethlehem Pike. Go .4 mile to light at Chestnut Hill Avenue. Turn right and go .8 mile to dead end at Towanda Street. Number 8870 is .2 mile on right. *Please park on street.*

Peter Hedrick's Garden
8018 Germantown Avenue, Philadelphia

In 1992, the new owners of this circa 1816 Federal-style house realized they had an enormous job ahead of them renovating it and the accompanying decrepit gardens. But they saw the potential and value in creating a garden to complement this lovely home in Philadelphia's historic Chestnut Hill district. By year three, this French-inspired, semiformal, "secret" garden took form. The gardens are marked by axial brick paths, boxwood parterres, topiary, arching holly, and pleached hornbeams. Blue themes dominate in spring; in summer, lush tropicals (cycads, palms, banana, colocasia, citrus) abound. This garden has enjoyed visitors from across the country and has been published in several journals, including *Classic American Homes*. In July 2000, it was voted "America's Best Garden" by *Good Morning America* in a contest of nearly 500 entries.

Hours: 11 a.m. to 4 p.m.

Located in Philadelphia's historic Chestnut Hill district near Morris Arboretum (in northwest section). Walking distance from several stations which originate from Center City Philadelphia (15-minute ride). House is on Chestnut Hill's main shopping street, Germantown Avenue.

Proceeds shared with the Chestnut Hill Garden District Fund

Old Orchard
716 West Mount Airy Avenue, Philadelphia

This gracious stone house was built in 1931 in the style of a country farmhouse. The property was landscaped by Frederick Peck thirty-five years ago. As the trees and shrubs matured, they destroyed the feeling of light and space of the original design, so the present owners decided it was time for a major restoration. One of the primary redesign objectives was to open up the garden to use the entire two acres, to save and reuse as many of the old plants as possible, and, because the owners are the gardeners, make the property as low-maintenance as possible. First, the many large mature trees and shrubs were moved to the perimeters of the property. Next, the perennial garden was transformed from the Williamsburg style of four fifteen-foot squares into an open space with curving walks and manageable beds. In this process the owners moved 400 perennials from the old garden and then back into the garden you see today. Two years ago, the old pond was redesigned and rebuilt, and now features waterfalls and bog gardens. The U-shaped driveway in the front of the house is highlighted by a continuous bed of pachysandra under an allée of crab apple trees. The overgrown foundation planting has been replaced by drifts of astilbe and fern and the old box hedge has been cut back to be more in scale with the house. The garden is at its best in late spring, but is designed to offer attractions in every season of the year. Today you see a six-year-old garden designed to flow from one space to another, using stone, brick, texture, shape, and color to achieve harmony and balance.

Hours: 11 a.m. to 4 p.m.

Take Pennsylvania Turnpike/I-276 to Exit 25/Norristown. Exit onto Germantown Pike east and continue about 6 miles through Chestnut Hill to Lincoln Drive (thirteenth traffic light). Turn right. After first light, next street is Mount Airy Avenue. Turn right and continue 4 blocks to #716 on left. Please park on street.

Proceeds shared with the Morris Arboretum

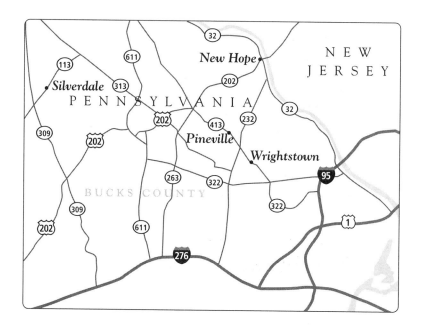

Saturday, June 28
BUCKS COUNTY

NEW HOPE

Kevin Hasney's Garden

65 Covered Bridge Road, New Hope

The one acre of the property's three acres located in front of the house is unfenced, so everything must be deer-resistant. Behind the house is a large lawn, pond, and rock garden with dwarf conifers, which screens the swimming pool beyond. Further back are newer plantings that are forming various outdoor rooms and paths. The emphasis is on plants with year-round appeal that can be used to form screens and hedges.

Hours: 10 a.m. to 4 p.m.

From New Hope, take Route 32 south 1 mile and turn right onto Aquetong Road. Second left on Aquetong is Covered Bridge Road (across from a church). Our house is after covered bridge.

From points south, take Route 32 north to left onto Aquetong Road. *Please park on grass along road or in driveway.*

Jericho Mountain Orchards
Buckmanville Road, New Hope

This is a delightful terraced country garden surrounding a seventeenth-century stone-and-timber farmhouse on extensive acreage. Many varieties of old garden roses and climbers ramble over eighteenth-century walls, barns, trellises, and tuteurs, leading to lovely perennial borders and formally parterred beds. There are also charming shade, pond, and stream gardens, as well as a sizeable nineteenth-century apple orchard.

Hours: 10 a.m. to 4 p.m.

From New Hope, take Route 232 south about 3 miles to Street Road. Turn left, then take first right onto Buckmanville Road. Jericho Mountain Orchards will be about .5 mile down on right.

From Hortulus Farm (see next page), turn left out of drive onto Thompson Mill Road. Continue to stop sign, then turn left onto Pineville Road. Buckmanville Road will be about .5 mile down on right. Turn right and continue .5 mile to orchards on right.

Proceeds shared with the Riverside Symphonia

Pineville
Emilie & Walter Cullerton—Oxford Gardens
4607 Smith Road, Pineville

A barn, a rill, and a springhouse set the stage for a collection of over 500 hostas on this three-acre property of woods and pasture. Throughout various gardens, the hostas are kept company by a multitude of shade-loving companion perennials, as well as some sun-lovers. Scattered about is a budding conifer collection and uncommon shrubs and trees.

Hours: 10 a.m. to 4 p.m.

From New Hope, take Route 232 south for 4.7 miles. Turn right onto Pine Lane and proceed .7 miles to the "T" intersection with Route 413 (Pineville Post Office). Turn right (north) onto Route 413/Durham Road. Proceed .4 mile to Geerlings Wholesale Florist. Please park in Geerlings and a shuttle will take you to Oxford Gardens.

Silverdale
Carol A. Pierce
839 Callowhill Road, Silverdale

This is a series of vignette gardens set on one and one-third acres designed to flow from one to another. Perennials and flowering shrubs combine to attract birds and butterflies. Featured is a beach theme garden packed with ornamental grasses, boulders, and perennials for a burst of color. There are two water gardens, one of traditional design to be viewed from the home's breakfast area, and a second of contemporary design built into the entranceway deck, accenting the home's summer living space.

Hours: 12 to 6 p.m.

From I-276, take Fort Washington Exit. Take Route 309 north to Route 113 exit. Turn right. At fifth traffic light, turn right onto Callowhill Road; #839 is 1 mile on left.

From Doylestown, go north on Route 313 through Dublin. Turn left onto Route 113. Travel to first light and turn left onto Callowhill Road; #839 is 1 mile on left. *Please park on right, next to detached garage.*

WRIGHTSTOWN
Hortulus Farm
60 Thompson Mill Road, Wrightstown

Our garden appears as an integral part of the Pennsylvania landscape, as befits an eighteenth-century farmstead with barns and a healthy population of animals. We are lucky enough to be nestled in our own little valley, quite far off the road and unusual for a house of this age. Our 100 acres try to respect the integrity of the farm's historical significance and the natural landscape, with the occasional whimsical or formal statement thrown in. There are lots of woods and pasture, lots of shrubs and naturalized perennial plantings in the stream and woodland gardens, yet also formal borders, follies, gazebos, and sizeable herb and vegetable gardens. All is anchored by the formal simplicity of classic Bucks County architecture.

Hours: 10 a.m. to 4 p.m.

From New Hope, take Windy Bush Road/Route 232 south about 5 miles. At "Wrightstown Township" sign on right, turn immediately left onto Pineville Road. Go about 1 mile to right onto Thompson Mill Road. Continue over bridge through series of steep, winding, uphill turns and up into a clearing and straightaway. *Proceed to #60 for parking.*

From Philadelphia, take I-95 north towards Trenton about 40 miles to Exit 31/New Hope. Turn left at end of exit ramp onto Taylorsville Road. Go north 3 miles to Wood Hill Road, and turn left. Go about 2.7 miles to first stop sign. Turn right onto Eagle Road, go .3 mile and make first left onto Pineville Road. Proceed as directed above.

Public Gardens

CHESTER COUNTY

CHADDS FORD

Brandywine Conservancy

Route 1, Chadds Ford (610) 388-2700

Begun in 1974, the gardens feature indigenous and some naturalized plants of the greater Brandywine region displayed in natural settings. The gardens use wildflowers, trees, and shrubs in landscaped areas. Plants are selected to provide a succession of bloom from early spring through the first killing frost.

Hours: year round, daily, dawn to dusk

Admission: free

From I-95, take Route 141 exit north to Route 52 north. Follow Route 52 until it intersects with Route 1. Turn right onto Route 1 north. Travel 2 miles to the conservancy.

KENNETT SQUARE

Longwood Gardens

Route 1, Kennett Square (610) 388-1000 www.longwoodgardens.org

One of the world's premier horticultural displays, Longwood offers 1,050 acres of gardens, woodlands, and meadows; twenty outdoor gardens; twenty indoor gardens within four acres of greenhouses; 11,000 types of plants; spectacular fountains; extensive educational programs; and 800 events each year.

Hours: year round, daily, 9 a.m. to 5 p.m.; frequently open later for seasonal displays

Admission: $12 adults ($8 on Tuesdays), $6 students 16-20, $2 children 6 to 15, children under 6 free

Located on Route 1, three miles northeast of Kennett Square and 12 miles north of Wilmington, Delaware.

SWARTHMORE
Scott Arboretum of Swarthmore College
500 College Avenue, Swarthmore (610) 328-8025 www.scottarboretum.org

The Scott Arboretum is a green oasis uniquely situated on the Swarthmore College campus. More than 300 acres create the college landscape and provide a display of the best ornamental plants recommended for Delaware Valley gardens. There are more than 3,000 different kinds of plants grown on the campus. Major plant collections include flowering cherries, crab apples, hydrangeas, lilacs, magnolias, rhododendrons, tree peonies, viburnums, wisteria, and witch hazels. Special gardens include the Rose Garden, Fragrance Garden, Teaching Garden, Entrance Garden, and Winter Garden.

Hours: year round, daily, dawn to dusk

Admission: free

From I-95 take Exit 7/I-476 north/Plymouth Meeting. Take I-476 to Exit 3/Media/Swarthmore. Turn right onto Baltimore Pike to follow signs for Swarthmore. Stay in right lane for .25 mile and turn right onto Route 320 south. Go to second traffic light turn right onto College Avenue.

WAYNE
Chanticleer
786 Church Road, Wayne (610) 687-4163 www.chanticleergarden.org

This thirty-acre pleasure garden was formerly the home of the Rosengarten family. Emphasis is on ornamental plants, particularly herbaceous perennials. The garden is a dynamic mix of formal and naturalistic areas, collections of flowering trees and shrubs, ponds, meadows, wildflower gardens, and a garden of shade-loving Asian herbaceous plants.

Hours: April 1 through October 31, Wednesday through Saturday, 10 a.m. to 5 p.m.

Admission: $5

Take I-76 West to I-476. Turn south onto I-476 towards Chester. Take Exit 5 towards Villanova. Turn right at intersection of Route 30 and 320 south. Turn right at next traffic light onto Conestoga Road. Turn left at second light onto Church Road. Go .5 mile to Chanticleer.

MEADOWBROOK

Meadowbrook Farm & Greenhouse

1633 Washington Lane, Meadowbrook (215) 887-5900

This beautiful garden is the life work of J. Liddon Pennock. Designed as a series of outdoor rooms, each garden is unique and comfortable, with the emphasis on design. The public display garden leads to the greenhouse, where plants and garden gifts of all types are available.

Hours: tours for groups of 15 to 40 people of house and private gardens by appointment only; call for reservations and tour fee; otherwise, public portion, open year round, Monday through Saturday, 10 a.m. to 5 p.m.

Admission: free

From I-76, take Route 611 south and turn left onto Route 63. After about 1.5 miles, turn right onto Washington Lane. Meadowbrook Farm sign is located about .75 mile on left.

PHILADELPHIA

Fairmount Park Horticulture Center & Arboretum

Belmont Avenue & North Horticultural Drive, Philadelphia (215) 685-0096

The arboretum covers twenty-two acres and boasts an assortment of trees, many of which have been labeled with both common and botanical names. The display house is the first greenhouse you enter from the lobby. Its permanent display includes palm and fig trees, oleander, and bougainvillea. The next greenhouse contains a magnificent collection of cacti and succulents. There are also many statues and perennial gardens on these grounds.

Hours: year round, daily, 9 a.m. to 3 p.m.

Admission: free

From I-76/I-276, take Exit 35/Montgomery Drive. Turn left at traffic light onto Montgomery Drive and travel 1 block, turning left onto Horticultural Drive. Drive through front gates on left; the building is on right.

Historic Bartram's Garden

54th Street & Lindbergh Boulevard, Philadelphia (215) 729-5281 www.bartramsgarden.org

Historic Bartram's Garden is America's oldest living botanical garden, founded in 1728 by John Bartram, America's first great botanist, naturalist, and plant explorer. The forty-five-acre site on the banks of the Schuylkill River includes the furnished Bartram house and other unique eighteenth-century farm buildings, a botanical garden, historic trees, a fifteen-acre wildflower meadow, a water garden, a wetland, a parkland, and a museum shop.

Hours: March through December, Tuesday through Sunday, 10 a.m. to 4 p.m.; January and February, group tours by reservation

Admission: free

Located less than 15 minutes from Center City Philadelphia and convenient to I-76 and I-95. Please visit website for direction.

Morris Arboretum of the University of Pennsylvania

100 Northwestern Avenue, Philadelphia (215) 247-5777

Morris Arboretum is an historic Victorian garden and educational institution dedicated to understanding the relationships between people and plants. Its living collection contains about 2,532 taxa and more than 14,000 accessioned and labeled plants from the temperate northern hemisphere, parts of Asia, Europe, and North America.

Hours: April through October, weekdays, 10 a.m. to 4 p.m., weekends, 10 a.m. to 5 p.m.; November through March, daily, 10 a.m. to 4 p.m.

Admission: $8 adults, $6 senior citizens/children 8 to 13, $3 children 6 to 12, children under 3 free

Take I-76/Schuylkill Expressway to Blue Route/I-476 north. Take Exit 8/Plymouth Meeting and follow signs for Germantown Pike east. Continue on Germantown Pike 4 miles and turn left onto Northwestern Avenue. Arboretum entrance is .25 mile on right.

Tennessee

Kitty P. Taylor garden, Collierville.

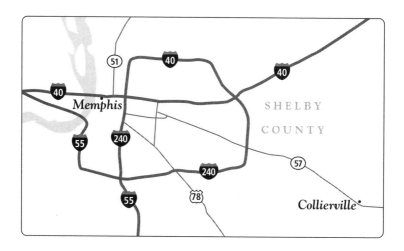

Saturday, May 17
SHELBY COUNTY

COLLIERVILLE
Kitty P. Taylor
1600 Quinn Road, Collierville

My garden is a country garden that looks out on fields and horses. It includes a sun garden, which has long double borders filled with perennials. A rock garden is across from the sun garden, which consists of many spring-blooming plants in May. The back garden is a large woodland garden with mature azaleas and shade-loving perennials. It is accessed by walks and crisscrossed with bark paths. There is a dry creek bed down one side. The whole concept is an informal, relaxed garden.

Hours: 10 a.m. to 2 p.m.

In Collierville, turn right off Poplar Avenue/Highway 57 to Highway 72 towards Corinth, MS. There are 2 gas stations at corners, Texaco and Chevron. Go about 2 miles on Highway 72 past Nonconnah Expressway 385, which dead ends into Highway 72. Turn right imediately past expressway onto Shelby Drive. Take first left onto Quinn Road. Go .25 mile to #1600, Ash-Ne Farm. Turn left into a long gravel drive. *Please park along drive, leaving room for cars to get by.*

Proceeds shared with St. Andrew's Episcopal Church, Heifer Fund

MEMPHIS
Hughes Garden
2948 Iroquois Road, Memphis

Our garden is located in an older section of Memphis. The house is English Tudor-style using "clinker" brick. Both the house and garden were completely renovated in 2000. I love collecting antique garden pieces, ranging from old terra cotta columns to ornate iron gates. My landscape architect was directed to utilize these collections in my garden. There are three garden rooms in our small space; all flow together through the placements of my garden art. One room is the intimate swimming pool area with a fountain and fireplace. Another is my personal garden with a tiny bluestone terrace bordered with antique terra cotta blocks. The third is our front entry court with cobbled driveway, metal urns, and stone planter boxes. Throughout the entire garden, I sprinkle annuals and hardy perennials for color during our long, hot summers.

Hours: 10 a.m. to 2 p.m.

From I-240 Loop, exit at Poplar Avenue west. Travel west 4.5 miles to Highland Street. Turn left and go to Central Avenue (about .25 mile), Turn right (west) and go to West Chickasaw Parkway (about 1.5 miles). Turn right and go to stop sign at Iroquois Road. Turn left and go through 1 stop sign; house will be on right, #2948. *Please park on street.*

Proceeds shared with the Memphis Botanic Garden

Alex & Karen Wellford's Garden

199 Ridgefield Road, Memphis

This is a small urban garden consisting of many "rooms" on two levels. It is a garden with lots of invitations to sit around a fountain filled with goldfish, under an arbor of roses, beneath an umbrella, or off a hidden path near the fig tree. The garden is a riot of hydrangeas, lilies, roses, blooming shrubs, and perennials. Our garden is a shared adventure, which combines our love of England and its gardens with the flavor of the South and New Orleans.

Hours: 10 a.m. to 4 p.m.

From I-240, take Poplar Avenue west. Ridgefield Road is south off Poplar Avenue between Goodlett Avenue and Highland Avenue. House is second on right after turning onto Ridgefield Road. *Please park on street.*

Proceeds shared with the Little Garden Club of Memphis

Gina & John White's Garden

6639 Green Shadows Lane, Memphis

This small formal garden has been created to blend traditional English hedges, and evergreen shrubs with foliage and flowers cultivated for floral design. White Lady Banks roses combined with 'Ramona' clematis drape the house's rear French doors, while a hedge of 'Iceberg' roses frames the pool. A stone path leads to the rose-covered entrance of the perennial garden, a lively palette of peonies, phlox, hydrangeas, and Griffith Buck roses. The owners' favorite cutting garden of yellow, orange, and apricot hybrid tea roses borders the driveway.

Hours: 10 a.m. to 4 p.m.

From Poplar/I-240 interchange, go east on Poplar .9 mile. Turn right (south) onto Massey Road at traffic light. Turn left (east) onto Poplar Pike at light. Turn right (south) onto Kirby Road (not Kirby Parkway). Turn left onto Green Shadows Lane. Number 6639 will be on right. *Please park along street.*

Proceeds shared with the Little Garden Club of Memphis

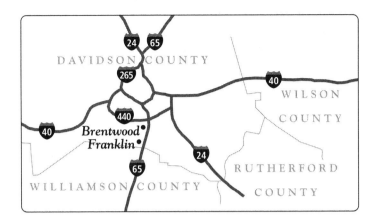

Sunday, June 1
DAVIDSON COUNTY

Brentwood
Reynolds Garden
1360 Holly Tree Gap Road, Brentwood

Mille Fleurs is a five-acre hillside setting, with three acres cultivated and the balance at the rear in mature hillside forest. The garden wraps around the brick ranch cottage and has nine garden rooms to stroll through. A 200-foot mixed border is the highlight in the front and finishes beside a custom-built garden house. The focal point in the rear is the 9,000-gallon koi pond fed by a meandering stream with multiple waterfalls and a stone bridge. The 650 varieties of trees, shrubs, roses, perennials, ornamental grasses, and ground covers are arranged for many views. A raised-bed vegetable garden and dwarf fruit trees are a bit further up the hill. The garden is complete with horse barn and two resident trail horses. Still further up the hill are a sunny wildflower meadow and pavilion with seating to enjoy the wonderful view of surrounding hills. For more adventurous visitors, the steep forest at the rear of the property is home to over thirty varieties of native wildflowers.

Hours: 1 to 5 p.m.

From intersection of Hillsboro Road and Old Hickory Boulevard, travel east on Old Hickory Boulevard 4.4 miles. Turn right onto Franklin Road. Travel 5 miles and turn right onto Holly Tree Gap Road. Go .2 mile to #360 on right.

Proceeds shared with Cheekwood

FRANKLIN

Callicott Garden—Back of Beyond

1733 Old Hillsboro Road, Franklin

Back of Beyond is a horticultural hodgepodge, which depends on virtually no hardscape, thus allowing the gardener and Mother Nature continually to alter and enhance the view from within the residence. The evolution of this property over thirty-six years from family farm with panoramic views to specific views has been achieved by the design of turf areas surrounded by mature trees and a layering of plant material, including evergreen hedges and flowering shrubs, perennials, and ground covers. Axes and water features complete the scene.

Hours: 1 to 5 p.m.

From intersection of Old Hickory Boulevard and Hillsboro Road, travel west on Hillsboro Road 3.2 miles. Turn right onto Old Hillsboro Road. Go 5.2 miles to #1733 on left.

Proceeds shared with Cheekwood

Hewitt Garden

3052 Old Hillsboro Road, Franklin

What was once a barren hillside has been transformed into a garden with more than 1,000 varieties of plants. Entering the property, one crosses an arched bridge leading to a pond and waterfalls, which are havens for waterlilies and lotus. The area is graced by specimen Japanese maples, a European beech, and many other species of plants. Lush shade gardens abound under the canopy of maple, poplar, linden, and gingko trees that surrounds the back of the house. The latest addition to the garden is a natural pool and spa. The garden also contains extensive collections of conifers, Japanese maples, and new varieties of perennials. A cedar pavilion provides shelter and a fire pit provides warmth in different seasons. Foliage colors and textures are the key elements to this garden.

Hours: 1 to 5 p.m.

From intersection of Old Hickory Boulevard and Hillsboro Road, travel west on Hillsboro Road 3.2 miles. Turn right onto Old Hillsboro Road. Go 8.8 miles to #3052 on right.

Proceeds shared with Cheekwood

Stewart Garden
814 Sneed Road West, Franklin

Reminiscent of early pioneer days in Tennessee, the Stewarts' ten-year-old log home sits nestled in a valley near the Harpeth River in northern Williamson County. Visitors will enter by way of a field where rows of mint, artemisia, feverfew, and Chinese lanterns are being grown for use in dried and fresh arrangements. Crossing a bridge from the field brings visitors to the back of the house, where most of the two-acre garden is located. A Williamsburg-style garden with raised beds and an arbor enclosed in a cedar rail fence is home to more herbs for drying, along with annuals such as sunflowers and celosia. One predominant feature that ties the many perennial, herb, wildflower, and hosta gardens together is the rock walls the owner has built to level beds and divert water.

Hours: 1 to 5 p.m.

From intersection of Old Hickory Boulevard and Hillsboro Road, go west on Hillsboro Road for 2.4 miles. Turn right onto Sneed Road and go 2.8 miles to #814 on right.

Proceeds shared with Cheekwood

Public Gardens

DAVIDSON COUNTY

NASHVILLE

Cheekwood
1200 Forrest Park Drive, Nashville (615) 356-8000 www.cheekwood.org

At Cheekwood, you'll find collections of dogwoods, wildflowers, herbs, iris, roses, peonies, magnolias, daylilies, ferns, hydrangeas, and much more. Specialty gardens include the Color Garden, showcasing gardening as a year-round activity, water gardens, the Japanese Garden, and the Trial Garden, where annuals are tested for performance in the mid-South. The perennial gardens are at their peak in June and July. The original Bryant Fleming-designed gardens around the Cheek mansion, which now houses the Museum of Art, are fully restored to their former elegance, with lovely vistas, boxwood gardens, Italianate water features, and spectacular stonework.

Hours: year round, Monday through Saturday, 9:30 a.m. to 4:30 p.m., Sunday, 11 a.m. to 4:30 p.m.

Admission: $10 adults, $7 senior citizens, $5 children 6 to 17, children under 6 free

From I-65, take I-440 west to Exit 1/West End Avenue. Travel west 5.1 miles to Belle Meade Boulevard and turn left. Go 2.8 miles to Page Road, turn right, go .2 mile, and turn left onto Forrest Park Drive. Follow .2 mile to Cheekwood entrance.

MEMPHIS

The Dixon Gallery & Gardens

4339 Park Avenue, Memphis (901) 761-2409

The Dixon Gardens were carefully carved out of seventeen acres of native Tennessee woodlands and landscaped in the manner of an English park with open vistas and formal gardens. Within the garden are a two-acre woodland garden, perennial borders, and a recently renovated cutting garden that was part of the 1997-98 garden expansion plan that also included new horticultural buildings, production greenhouses, and an exquisite conservatory.

Hours: year round, Tuesday through Saturday, 10 a.m. to 5 p.m., Sunday, 1 to 5 p.m.; Monday, garden only open

Admission: $5 adults, $4 senior citizens, $3 students, $1 children 5 to 11; Monday, admission half price

Located in East Memphis at 4339 Park Avenue, between Getwell and Perkins, across from Audubon Park. It is about 9 miles from downtown Memphis and only about a 10-minute drive from Memphis International Airport via I-240 east. Motorists should take the Getwell North exit to Park Avenue, turn right, and proceed about 4 blocks to museum.

The Memphis Botanic Garden, Home of the Goldsmith Civic Garden Center

750 Cherry Road, Memphis (901) 685-1566

The Memphis Botanic Garden is dedicated to being an exemplary regional center for horticulture and environmental enrichment. The MBG is the garden showcase of the mid-South. It has 22 different display areas and gardens, including the Japanese Garden of Tranquility, featuring the most photographed site in Memphis—The Red Drum Bridge—the Little Garden Club Sensory Garden, and the new Tennessee Bicentennial Iris Garden. The garden is owned by the Memphis Park Commission and operated by the Memphis Botanic Garden Foundation, Inc.

Hours: March through October, Monday through Saturday, 9 a.m. to 6 p.m., Sunday, 11 a.m. to 6 p.m.; November through February, Monday through Saturday, 9 a.m. to 4:30 p.m., Sunday, 11 a.m. to 4:30 p.m.

Admission: $4 adults, $3 senior citizens/full-time students, $2 children 6 to 17, children under 6 free; Tuesday afternoon free admission

Located on Cherry Road between Park Avenue and Southern Avenue in Audubon Park and directly north of The Dixon Gallery & Gardens.

TEXAS

Richeson Garden, Dallas.

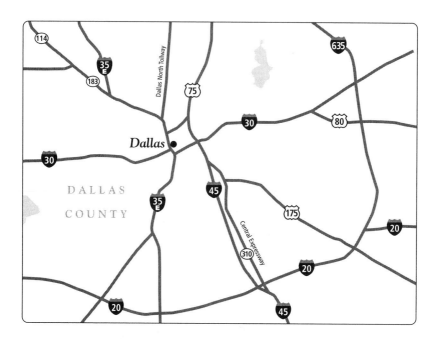

Saturday, September 13

DALLAS/COLLIN COUNTY

DALLAS

Michael Cheever's Garden

618 Valencia Street, Dallas

A charming garden of perennials, flowering shrubs, and small trees this garden reflects the owner's sixteen years of work as a botanical garden professional. Surrounding a Tudor-style cottage in an historic Old East Dallas neighborhood, the plant collection includes many Texas native plants, unusual perennials, and unique species from botanical gardens and collecting trips. A shady back garden with large pecan trees, lovely decomposed granite paths, and a patio provides a cool refuge in summer for the owner and his guests.

Hours: 10 a.m. to 4 p.m.

This garden is located about 3 miles east of downtown Dallas in the Hollywood Heights neighborhood (south of White Rock Lake and adjacent to Samuell-Grand Park). From I-30, take Winslow exit and turn north. Turn right onto East Grand at stop sign, then proceed north to Clermont Street, turn left, and go through Samuell-Grand Park. Turn left onto southbound East Grand, go 2 blocks to Valencia Street, and turn right. Garden is on north side of Valencia, 3 blocks up from East Grand.

Proceeds shared with the Texas Discovery Gardens

Judy Fender's Garden

9019 Fringewood Drive, Dallas

Visitors delight in my hidden backyard gardens, which I designed and built entirely myself. Creating a "Garden of Eden" as a place of relaxation and beauty for my enjoyment, there are three water gardens (with koi, Egg Phoenix, and other fancy goldfish), waterfalls, and a forty-six-foot-long stream. To entice birds, butterflies, and other suburban wildlife, there are over 100 roses scattered among more than 500 other varieties of native plants, perennials, and herbs. Paths wind through both the backyard and front gardens, from which all grass has been removed. This water-conserving garden is lush and full of blooms and year-round interest. A certified Wildlife Habitat and Butterfly Habitat, this garden is visited by hummingbirds and migrating monarchs in September along with many other butterfly species. Delight in the vast variety of plants in the various full-sun and shade gardens, while discovering the whimsical garden statuary, new garden murals, and other artistic touches. Sit a while at various garden nooks in these ever-changing and evolving gardens. Enjoy the butterflies, birds, anoles, plants, and whimsy you will find while exploring the garden paths.

Hours: 10 a.m. to 4 p.m.

From I-30, take Buckner Boulevard exit. Take Buckner north (past 3 traffic lights) to Ferguson Road West. Turn right. Go about .5 mile (past churches) to Lanecrest (at bottom of a slight hill) and turn left. Take first left onto Ripplewood. Make first right onto Glenmont. Make first left onto Fringewood. House is fourth on left; there is a low whimsical fence that surrounds the front gardens. Enter back gardens via driveway. *Please park on street, do not block driveways.*

From North Central Expressway/Highway 75 (in Dallas), exit at either Northwest Highway (east) or Mockingbird Lane and drive east (past White Rock Lake) to Buckner Boulevard. Take Buckner south. Pass Garland Road (at a traffic light intersection) and continue on Buckner to Ferguson Road West. Proceed as directed above.

Proceeds shared with the Dallas County Master Gardeners Association

Dave & Tracey Mason's Garden

5105 Swiss Avenue, Dallas

Our garden has been created in an Italianate style to harmonize with the house. We have created garden rooms, giving an individual significance to each one. There is a great sense of calm and serenity by the use of fountains, statuary, varying shades of green, and deep shady areas. The rooms at the back are reminiscent of a Tuscan kitchen garden with circular beds edged in rosemary containing a mixture of vegetables and herbs. There are also a grape arbor, espaliered apple trees, Italian cypress, and a rose-covered pool house.

Hours: 10 a.m. to 4 p.m.

Take I-75 south to the Knox/Henderson exit. Turn left at traffic light and continue on Henderson, past Gaston, to Greenville Avenue. Turn right and go (Greenville becomes Munger) to light at Munger and Live Oak. Proceed through intersection and take first right onto Swiss Avenue. Number 5105 is third house on right. House is beige brick with olive green trim. *Please park on right side of street only.*

Richeson Garden
6855 Lakeshore Drive, Dallas

Flexible, adaptable, evolving, and user-friendly, our garden is a melange of native and adapted plants, sculpture, and wildlife. We try to ensure that all the critters have an appropriate habitat and in return they bring us new plant additions to enrich the garden. Vegetables, herbs, fruit trees, and bushes feed us and our wild friends. Sculpture can be seen throughout and also has a dedicated space in the dry pond that is part of the back garden. There are garden work areas as well as those for gatherings with friends and places for moments of quiet reflection.

Hours: 10 a.m. to 4 p.m.

Located on north side of street between Copperfield and Wendover, 1 block west of intersection where Lakewood Boulevard crosses Lakeshore. Located approximately 1.5 miles south of Mockingbird and 1 mile east of Abrams.

Peter & Julie Schaar
3515 Haynie Avenue, Dallas

The garden of Peter and Julie Schaar is an inner city garden on a small lot. It is a mixed planting of roses, trees, shrubs, palms, woody lilies, perennials, bulbs, and containers, which includes a wide variety of native and adapted plants. The Schaars maintain their garden organically, using no sprays, fungicides, or insecticides, and fertilize only with manure, compost, and other organic products. The garden is watered only occasionally, usually five to eight times per year. The front yard is an informal design inspired by cottage gardens in order to conform to the cottage house. The backyard is a paved subtropical Mexican courtyard exhibiting strong evergreen structure and exuberantly planted beds. Palms, cycads, yuccas, and other woody lilies, southern magnolia, pecan, and crape myrtle make the small space appear larger and contribute dramatic form and texture. Cestrum, cassia, oleander, roses, gardenias, and camellias display bright color and heavy fragrance, as do several flowering vines. Mexican oregano, rosemary, lemon verbena, and shrub basil provide brushy herbs for cooking and fragrance, as do a number of long-blooming salvias. The garden is in bloom twelve months of the year, although the evergreen structure gives it a lively appearance even in the intervals of scant bloom. The Schaars welcome you to their garden and hope you have an enjoyable visit. They ask only that you refrain from smoking and ask for starts of any plants that interest you.

Hours: 10 a.m. to 4 p.m.

From the intersection of Hillcrest and Lovers Lane, drive south on Hillcrest to SMU Campus (4 to 5 blocks). Turn right onto Haynie Avenue, Schaar garden is in second block, between Dickens and Thackery, at #3515. *Please park on street or in driveway.*

Sewell Garden
9508 Chiswell Road, Dallas

Our yard has a unique shape—wide at the front, narrowing toward the back, with a narrow, finger-like extension going to our alley. Our gardens are fantastic. I have lived here for almost twenty-two years and I am impressed. If I had to describe our yard in one word, it would be "variety," from front to back. There are numbers of different beds with fountains and walkways, each with a different appearance. With myraid native plants, this Xeriscape award-winning yard was chosen by Dallas Water Utilities to kick off their 2002 water-conservation campaign. Come join us...words can't describe what your eyes will see.

Hours: 10 a.m. to 4 p.m.

From North Central Expressway/Highway 75, go east on Northwest Highway 3.5 miles to Audelia Road. Turn left, go .4 mile to Chiswell Road and turn left. Go to #9508 (on left at corner of Chiswell Road and Parkford Lane). *Please park on Chiswell Road or Parkford Lane.*

Doyle Terry & Donna Ohland-Terry
6001 Revere Place, Dallas

As a result of our love for the Texas Hill Country and Santa Fe, we were inspired to create a homestead ambiance in our surroundings with native plants in an older urban setting here in Dallas. The sway of the upright verbena and Mexican feathergrass dances with birds and butterflies in total harmony with nature. Grasses, perennials, and succulents were carefully chosen to accentuate a native and drought-tolerant environment. The large stones and rocks lend an aura of permanence and coherence to the garden, as does the long stone wall across the front. The rustic backdrop of antiques and vintage vessels harmonizes with the natural beauty of the garden to create a calm and soothing effect. The garden invites you to come in and wander along the granite-and-flagstone path to a small pond with the serenity of water cascading over the natural stone. The majestic pecan tree casts sun and shade throughout the day; many niches draw you in to sit and take in your lush surroundings. Myriad native plants forms a rich tapestry as you leisurely stroll around the garden. Come and visit a magnificent garden habitat.

Hours: 10 a.m. to 4 p.m.

From North Central Expressway/Highway 75, take Mockingbird Lane exit. Exit east to Skillman Avenue (about 5 traffic lights). Turn right (south); go 7 blocks to Revere Place. Turn right (west) and go 1 block to corner of Revere and Concho. House is on northeast corner. *Please park along street.*

Proceeds shared with the Texas Discovery Gardens

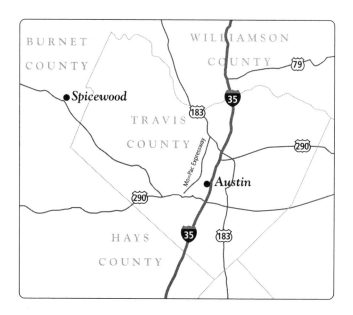

Sunday, October 5

BURNET COUNTY

SPICEWOOD

Jackson Garden

1007 Coventry Road, Spicewood

On a promontory overlooking Lake Travis, the Jackson garden is most notable for the dramatic use of large native sandstone boulders and patio spaces designed to complement the house by Dick Clark Architects. Native and deer-resistant plantings accentuate the extensive stonework and hamonize with the naturally beautiful hillside setting. The entry courtyard features a small formal water garden and a rotund, stacked stone column as a sculptural element. From there, visitors enter the east side of the garden descending a set of large natural stone steps to a shady woodland path. Cool and serene even on a hot day, this side of the house has the quiet monochromatic beauty of a Japanese garden. The experience of "East meets West" is further reinforced as a path takes visitors past several mossy stone drainage features, as well as a uniquely handcrafted stone-and-redwood potting area, before winding around to the western side of the property, where many different species of cactus, yucca, and other dry land plants have found a home in the rocky arroyo. Guests are invited to pause at spacious patios on both the east and west sides of the house to enjoy the distant views of the surrounding landscape seen from high above this bend in the river.

Hours: 11 a.m. to 6 p.m.

From Mopac Expressway South/Loop 1, take either Bee Caves Road/Route 2244 or Southwest Parkway west to village of Bee Caves. Go west on Highway 71 past intersection of Highway 620 and cross Pedernales River. Turn right 2 miles past river onto Paleface

Ranch Road (look for sign to Barton Creek Lakeside). Go about 4 miles and straight at "T" with Haney Flat Road. Go 2 miles and turn right onto CR 414 and follow signs to Windermere. Turn left alongside Spicewood Airport runway. At stop sign, turn left onto Coventry Road, which forms a loop.

Proceeds shared with the Spicewood Arts Society

TRAVIS COUNTY

AUSTIN

The Anderson Garden

2705 West 35ᵗʰ Street, Austin

Our garden was created in a Mediterranean courtyard style. We shaped this beautiful garden with very limited space. As you enter the garden from the veranda of our house, you encounter one of the breathtaking focal points, a pond and waterfall. As you meander through the maze of exquisite masonry, you will encounter spaces with their own unique beauty, encompassing several different tropical plants, including palms and cycads. The use of the plants helped us produce the feel of the Mediterranean in the heart of Austin.

Hours: 11 a.m. to 6 p.m.

From Mopac Expressway/Loop 1, exit at 35ᵗʰ Street and go west. Go through first traffic light at Exposition Boulevard and the Anderson Garden is at second house on left, sharing a circular drive with 2 other houses. Go to house on left, a Mediterranean-style house with tall Italian cypress trees and palms in front. *Please park in common drive. For additional parking, turn left onto Exposition and park on west side of street.*

Martha & Cliff Ernst

3515 Greenway Street, Austin

Our English-style garden is located on a sloping corner lot surrounding our 1933 Tudor Revival home in a tranquil central Austin neighborhood. In 1986, renowned Texas landscape architect C. Coatsworth Pinkney designed curving beds bordering old limestone walls that surround the property. After a major remodeling and addition to the house in 1999, landscape architect Marie Carmel assisted us in adding a series of garden rooms. Many elements of the garden, including a white garden, purple border, and rondel lawn, were inspired by our visit to Sissinghurst Castle in Kent, England. Something is always in bloom in our garden, which is home to a large collection of antique roses, perennials, and Texas natives. Our latest addition to the garden is a charming wood garden house designed by Gregory Free.

Hours: 11 a.m. to 6 p.m.

From Mopac Expressway/Loop 1, take the 35th Street exit and go east. Go past Seton Hospital where 35th Street turns into 38th Street. Continue east on 38th Street through the light at Duval. Turn right onto Greenway Street. The house is on the southeast corner of 37th Street and Greenway Street. *Please park on street.*

The Green Residence
1 Niles Road, Austin

The contemporary-style house is surrounded by an Italianate urban garden composed of a series of contrasting spaces, surfaces, textures, water features, and plants. There is a formal courtyard of clipped hedges and a fountain, an informal gravel terrace for lounging at the pool, and a gravel courtyard for sculpture, which contains two mature pollarded sycamores and is enclosed by a crenelated limestone wall. A long, elevated pool terrace is flanked by southern magnolias. The materials used in the landscape (gravel, limestone, brick, concrete, and steel) reflect the material and style of the architecture and are used to thoroughly integrate the house and garden. A large formal lawn in back preserves the aging live oaks original to the site and is surrounded by a garden border of mature trees and shrubs chosen for their color, texture, and form. The primary plant palette is Mediterranean in origin, but is interspersed with plants that were used in early twentieth-century Texas gardens and plants newly introduced from China.

Hours: 11 a.m. to 6 p.m.

From Mopac Expressway/Loop 1, exit east onto Enfield Road and go to traffic light at West Lynn. Turn left and go to corner of Niles Road. Garden is at #1.

Nokes Family Garden
4200 Avenue F, Austin

Our house is a historic landmark in an old Austin neighborhood, "historic" being a relative term, as anything over 100 years old, such as our Victorian cottage, is considered "old" in Texas. It is situated on a double corner lot and, in the past, had a barn and chicken coop, but today the front of the house is dominated by an enormous pecan tree and a simple lawn bordered by a pink iron fence. The garden and most of the social activity take place in the back half of the yard, which is not enclosed by a privacy fence. Instead, a series of "rooms" initiates with a generous screened porch. The floor of the porch is made from old bricks found on site and set in a herringbone pattern. Then we have a gravel courtyard connected by a ramada and enclosed on one side by my studio, which is elevated on stone piers. Finally, we have a pattern garden making the final "room." Probably what people will find most interesting is the four-foot stone wall and portal made from sandstone from Lometa, Texas, and embedded with fossils, shells, petrified wood, and debris from twenty years of family life. (Think: Gaudi on a tequila high.) The whole garden is a reliquary of memories and experiences. The plants are mainly native south Texas and Mexican species and antique roses. I have more than 180 species in this relatively small space and the list keeps growing. Eventually, I hope it evolves to become a shrub garden that also provides habitat, food, and fragrance.

Hours: 11 a.m. to 6 p.m.

From I-35, exit at either 38th or 45th Street. Go to Avenue F. House is located on northwest corner of 42nd Street, near the University of Texas. *Please park on street.*

Proceeds shared with the Austin Parks Foundation

Reissig Garden
3601 Toro Canyon Road, Austin

Our garden is integrated into a hardscape that we designed to feel like an ancient Italian ruin. It features a massive eighteen-foot-high stone wall of huge arches as a backdrop to the pool and waterfall. The pool, with its black bottom, appears to be a secluded pond nestled among an array of tropical plantings. The theme drifts to a more arid feel as you leave the oasis and venture up the wide, rustic splay of stone steps that lead to the front. Along the way, you encounter a magnificent display of bougainvillea lining either side of this spectacular stairway. In the front, beautiful ornamental grasses serve as a contrast to such feature plants as Spanish daggers and blue agave. Another thirty-foot-high, vine-covered ruin wall is featured on the opposite side. A wildflower meadow, terraced with hundreds of dry stacked boulders, lurks across on the other side of a natural creek that makes its way through the middle of our property.

Hours: 11 a.m to 6 p.m.

Take Capital of Texas Highway/Loop 360 to Westlake Drive near Davenport Village shopping center. Go east on Westlake Drive and follow through Davenport Ranch subdivision. Continue about .5 mile to Toro Canyon Road on right. Turn right and proceed another .3 mile to #3601 on left. *Please park on street.*

Public Gardens

COLLIN COUNTY

MCKINNEY

The Heard Museum Texas Native Plant Display Garden

One Nature Plaza, McKinney (972) 562-5566 www.heardmuseum.org

The two-acre Texas Native Plant Display Garden is home to over 200 native species, including twenty-six trees, twenty-nine shrubs, fifteen vines, twenty grasses, and more than 100 varieties of perennial and annual wildflowers. The purpose of the garden is to educate the public about the beauty and diversity of our native plants and how they may be used in urban landscapes.

Hours: year round, Monday through Saturday, 9 a.m. to 5 p.m., Sunday, 1 to 5 p.m.; closed major holidays.

Admission: $5 adults, $3 children

From Highway 75, take Exit 38A and follow brown-and-white highway signs. Heard Museum is located 1 mile east of Highway 5 on FM 1378, southeast of McKinney.

DALLAS COUNTY

DALLAS

Dallas Nature Center

Mountain Creek Parkway, Dallas (972) 296-1955 www.dallasnaturecenter.org

The Dallas Nature Center is a 630-acre wilderness sanctuary that provides vital habitat for several endangered plants and animals, including the black-capped vireo. In addition to prairie wildflower areas, the Dallas Nature Center also features a butterfly garden landscaped with native plants.

Hours: year round, Tuesday through Sunday, dawn to dusk

Admission: $1 suggested donation

From I-20, take Mountain Creek Parkway exit. Travel south for 2.5 miles. Nature Center entrance is just south of intersection with Wheatland.

Texas Discovery Gardens, Fair Park

3601 Martin Luther King Jr. Boulevard, Dallas (214) 428-7476

Texas Discovery Gardens is the second oldest botanical institution in Texas and has seven and one half acres of gardens. Plant collections and specialized gardens include a butterfly garden, the Benny J. Simpson Texas Native Plant Collection, antique fragrant roses, perennials, and a tropical plant collection in the conservatory.

Hours: year round, daily, dawn to dusk; visitor center and conservatory open Tuesday through Saturday, 10 a.m. to 5 p.m., Sunday, 1 to 5 p.m.

Admission: free

From I-30 east, take Second Avenue exit, curve to right, and turn left at second traffic light, which is Martin Luther King Jr. Boulevard.

From *I-30 west*, take First Avenue exit, turn under freeway onto Exposition Avenue, and turn right onto Parry Avenue. Turn left at fourth light, which is Martin Luther King Jr. Boulevard.

From *I-45 south*, take Martin Luther King Jr. Boulevard exit, curve to right, and turn left at light.

TRAVIS COUNTY

Austin

Lady Bird Johnson Wildflower Center

4801 La Crosse Avenue, Austin (512) 292-4100 www.wildflower.org

Lady Bird Johnson Wildflower Center maintains a native plant botanical garden with acres of designed gardens, courtyards, and natural areas, showcasing the magnificent native plants of the Texas Hill Country in a variety of styles from naturalistic to formal. The center also has one of North America's largest rooftop rainwater collection systems.

Hours: year round, Tuesday through Sunday, 9 a.m. to 5:30 p.m.

Admission: varies depending on season

From I-35, take Exit 227/Slaughter Lane. Bear west off exit ramp and travel 6 miles west to intersection of Slaughter Lane and Mopac Expressway. Turn left onto expressway and left again onto La Crosse

Round Mountain

Westcave Preserve

24814 Hamilton Pool Road, Round Mountain (830) 825-3442 www.westcave.org

Westcave preserve is a thirty-acre natural sanctuary protected for future generations. It is a delight for wildflower enthusiasts, hikers, birders, or anyone who loves the natural beauty of the Texas Hill Country.

Hours: year round, weekends, tours by appointment only at 10 a.m., 12 p.m., 2 p.m., and 4 p.m. Weekday programs scheduled in advance.

Admission: donations welcomed

Take Highway 71 west from Austin to village of Bee Cave. Turn left onto Ranch Road 3238 (Hamilton Pool Road) and travel 14 miles, crossing Pedernales River. Look for first gate on right.

HEMPSTEAD

Peckerwood Garden

20571 FM 359, Hempstead (979) 826-3232 www.peckerwood.org

A PROJECT OF
THE GARDEN
CONSERVANCY

Peckerwood Garden is an artist's garden uniquely combining aesthetic experience and scientific exploration. It holds an unduplicated collection of plants from around the world with emphasis on plants collected in Mexico by its founder, John G. Fairey. The cultivated garden occupies about seven acres and includes a woodland garden along the banks of a creek, a higher dry garden, and a meadow garden that is being developed into an arboretum. More than 3,000 species and cultivars can be found here.

Hours: Open Days on March 15 & 16; April 5 & 6, April 19 & 20, May 3 & 4, May 17 & 18, June 21 & 22, September 20 & 21, October 4 & 5, and October 18 & 19; 1 to 5 p.m..

Admission: $6 adults, $5 senior citizens/students over 12; Sundays, $5 general admission, $10 for groups of up to 4, $15 for groups of up to 6

From Houston, take Highway 290 west past Prairie View. Before reaching Hempstead, take Exit FM359 toward Brookshire. Proceed through traffic light at intersection with Business 290. Garden is located 1.7 mile past this intersection, on right. Look for small sign. Parking will be at Yucca Do Nursery, which is located just south of garden.

INDEPENDENCE

The Antique Rose Emporium Display Gardens

10,000 Highway 50, Independence (979) 836-5548

The site of an early settler's homestead is the location of our Texas display gardens. A variety of restored buildings has given us the opportunity to incorporate roses, perennials, herbs, and native flora into many varied garden settings. The gently rolling hills of Washington County covered with the spring display of bluebonnets surround the nursery.

Hours: year round, Monday through Saturday, 9 a.m. to 5:30 p.m., Sunday, 11:30 a.m. to 5:30 p.m.

Admission: free

Located 10 miles northeast of Brenham at 10,000 Highway 50, which is .25 mile south of FM 390 and Highway 50.

From Washington, take Highway 105 to Highway 50. Turn right and proceed as directed above.

Vermont

The Gardens at Golden Apple Orchard, Charlotte.
Photo by Celia Jelley.

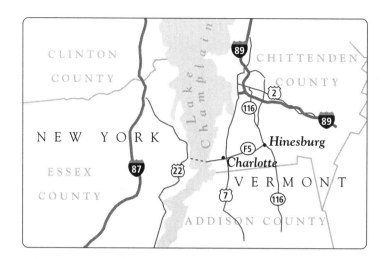

Saturday, June 21
CHITTENDEN COUNTY

CHARLOTTE
Converse Bay Farm
1028 Converse Bay Road, Charlotte

With a passion for gardening and an adept knowledge of design, the owner has created a formal yet inviting garden. This garden, developed in the 1970s, is composed of several different elements on three levels, each focusing on the view of Lake Champlain. On the upper level, the main feature is a pergola. At the next level is a parterre rose garden with an iron arbor as a backdrop. The owner's interest in developing roses that can survive Vermont winters with minimum care has dominated this garden. A ten- by sixty foot herbaceous perennial border runs parallel to the view of the lake. It has evolved from years of studying Gertrude Jekyll and is a monochromatic progression of color, with cool colors at either end, climaxing in the middle with warm tones. There is another rose garden and herb parterre with a perennial border. At the other edge of the lawn, a large lilypond is surrounded by spring blooming and shade-loving plants. To the south of the main house, where the barn is located, there is a parterre potager and peony-enclosed garden.

Hours: 10 a.m. to 4 p.m.

Take I-89 north to Vermont Exit 13. Head south on Route 7 through town of Shelburne about 5 miles to Charlotte intersection. Turn right onto Ferry Road/F-5 west. Continue straight over railroad tracks. At Lake Road intersection, turn left. Go .8 mile. Turn right onto Converse Bay Road. Go to fourth driveway on left. *Please park along driveway to barn (third drive on left).*

Proceeds shared with Shelburne Farms

The Gardens at Golden Apple Orchard

1052 Whalley Road, Charlotte

The extensive gardens are all relatively new. A formal walled garden, which surrounds the painting studio, was laid out in 1996. This garden is divided into rooms by different hedging materials, allowing for the coexistence of different planting themes. A tour from the main garden, through the orchard, to the pond and north around the house reveals mixed shrub borders, island beds of dwarf conifers, a patio garden overlooking the lake and Adirondacks beyond, and a small shade garden in the courtyard.

Hours: 10 a.m. to 4 p.m.

From traffic light on Route 7 in Charlotte, take Ferry Road/F-5 west towards lake 1.5 miles. Turn right onto Lake Road. Go 1 mile and turn left onto Whalley Road. Golden Apple Orchard is .5 mile down on left. *Please park on grass next to driveway.*

The Gardens of William & Nancy Heaslip

845 Thompson's Point Road, Charlotte

Dramatic rock ledges and stone walls create a pleasing backdrop for these gardens located in a secluded woodland setting. Enjoy the whimsical and eclectic garden ornaments placed among the plantings, small pool, and waterfall. You are welcome to tour the house which is filled with natural light and affords plentiful views of the gardens and woods from its "tree house setting."

Hours: 10 a.m. to 4 p.m.

From Route 7, go west on Ferry Road/F-5. Go .3 mile to blinking traffic light and turn left onto Greenbush Road. Travel 1.9 miles, where road bears right and becomes Thompson's Point Road, cross railroad tracks, go through intersection of Lake Road, and continue to second driveway on left (across from Black Willow Lane). *Please park along side of driveway or across street along Black Willow Lane.*

The Hidden Garden of Lewis Creek Road
693 Lewis Creek Road, Hinesburg

Carved out of woods and wetlands, this very original garden is one of the largest private gardens in Vermont. It is laid out on two levels. The upper garden surrounds the house. Curving paths wind through an extensive collection of hostas, shrubs, and perennials that leads to open lawn, a richly varied conifer garden, and a sunken walled garden. The lower garden is reached by taking the path past a stone wall and down under a canopy of mature evergreens underplanted with woodland flowers, ferns, and shrubs. Here collections of heather, ornamental grasses, damp-loving plants, conifers, and waterlilies have transformed a meadow into an abundant garden embracing a reflecting pond, trout pond, and "fishing camp," all enclosed in a canyon of woods.

Hours: 10 a.m. to 4 p.m.

Take I-89 north to Exit 12. Turn left onto Route 2A and go south 5.2 miles until road ends at Route 116. Turn left and go 2.1 miles to traffic light in Hinesburg. Continue 1 mile to intersection of Route 116 (sharp left curve) and Silver Street (straight). Go straight 2.9 miles to Lewis Creek Road. Turn left onto narrow gravel road. Driveway, #693 is .7 mile on left. *Continue up driveway to parking.*

From Route 7 light in Charlotte, go right on Church Hill Road (or, if on Ferry Road, go straight across Route 7) and continue .7 mile to stop sign. Turn right, turn onto Hinesburg Road, go .6 mile to a 4-way stop at Mount Philo Road, go 2.4 mile, to 4-way stop at Spear Street exit. Go 4.4 miles to where road ends across from Hinesburg IGA. Turn right onto Route 116 and go .2 mile to intersection (sharp left curve) with Silver Street (straight). Proceed as directed above.

Proceeds shared with the Hinesburg Land Trust

Paul Wieczoreck's Garden
2800 Lincoln Hill Road, Hinesburg

This garden is primarily a plant collection displayed in a variety of settings. A garden composed of slow-growing conifers and other unusual shrubs provides the backdrop for a sloping alpine/scree garden. The remainder of the garden is basically a woodland garden with a diversity of broadleaf evergreens (rhododendron, kalmia), more slow-growing conifers, and herbaceous plants. A large collection of native and hybrid deciduous azaleas provides the backbone for this garden with many fragrant summer-blooming varieties. The property also contains a one-acre landscape nursery with many specimens of uncommon conifers, trees, and shrubs.

Hours: 10 a.m. to 4 p.m.

Located about 5 miles south of Hinesburg Village on Route 116. Take Hollow Road east (across from Blaise's Store), go about 4 miles, passing a trailer park on left, and turn left onto Lincoln Hill Road (a dirt road). Go uphill 1.1 miles to #2800 on left. *Please park on left (south) side of Lincoln Hill Road.*

Proceeds shared with the Hinesburg Land Trust

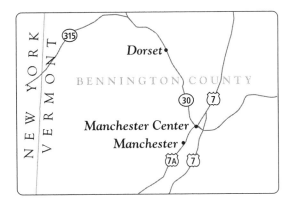

Saturday, June 28
BENNINGTON COUNTY

DORSET
Nissen Garden
564 Nichols Hill Road, Dorset

Our small country cottage sits surrounded by perennial flower beds. Designed and maintained by us (with occasional redesign by our dog, Harry), we created an informal feel and planned the plant selections to extend interest throughout the year. A small pond, stone walls, and mature trees add further structure and interest. At the rear of the house, several beds slope down the hill with their shapes defined by a small brook. Growing conditions range from moist, shady areas to full sun and allow for an extensive variety of both well-known and unusual plantings.

Hours: 10 a.m. to 4 p.m.

Located in Manchester Center at junction of Routes 11, 30, and 7A. Take Route 30 north towards Dorset. About 3.5 miles from junction and shortly after passing a small general store on left, Dorset West Road joins Route 30 from left. Take Dorset West Road 2 miles to Nichols Hill Road on left with a white house, white fence, and monument at corner. Take Nichols Hill Road about .5 mile to a sage green house on right, #564. *Some parking is available in driveway, otherwise, please park along street.*

Westerly
159 Danby Mountain Road, Dorset

Everything you see, except the large native trees, has been added by us since 1993. The garden is composed of several rooms, which deliberately shift in mood as you progress around the house. At the entryway is a green garden, with a small pool and rare and native plants. Next is a working area with fruit and nut trees, rhubarb, asparagus, grapes, elderberry and blueberry plantings, and raised beds for annuals. Then comes a circular contemplative garden planted with *Physocarpus opulifolius*, because the deer loved the *Taxus* with which we started. Finally, through a giant gateway on which are espaliered two *Larix x pendula*, comes the largest room, the south lawn. There is a view of mountains to the south, while the house is framed by raised beds. A pentagonal folly, with its own different view of mountains, is tucked into the southwest corner. One surprise (herein revealed) follows another. Note the use of bluestone and natural stone to create gardens where the soil is practically "undiggable."

Hours: 10 a.m. to 4 p.m.

Take Route 30 north from Manchester to Dorset, about 6 miles. At Dorset Inn, continue north 1.1 miles to Danby Mountain Road and turn right. Go up first pitch about 200 yards. On left is a sign for #159. Enter and turn left before first house.

MANCHESTER

Glebelands

4263 Main Street/Route 7A, Manchester

Our garden was started in the 1930s with perennials and a long allée of peonies. We later added marble defining walls, two gazebos (a Temple of Love and a Moorish-style with tassels), statues, and a tiled pool. I've incorporated a large reflecting pool with fountains at each end, antique iron (New Orleans) gates and grills, urns, and statuary from my former house. The grounds, totaling thirty acres, encompass an orchard underplanted with narcissus (a fairyland in springtime), a folly pavilion, two large ponds created by a 100-yard-long nineteenth-century marble dam (the area was a marble mill), two miles of woodland trails, brooks, and fine trees, including a *Chamaecyparis* collection I've raised from cuttings that I propagated.

Hours: 10 a.m. to 4 p.m.

Take Route 7A from Equinox Hotel in Manchester Village. Travel north for .7 mile. Orvis Company will be on right. Look for a dirt driveway within a spruce and pine grove on left. A Glebelands sign with "4263 Main Street" on it will be in middle of drive. House cannot be seen from road.

From the north, take Route 7A south past junction of Routes 11 and 30 in Manchester Center. Travel .6 mile south. Glebelands will be on right. *Please follow signs for parking.*

Proceeds shared with the Bennington Garden Club

White Tree Farm

1166 West Road, Manchester

Our garden is a quadrangle surrounded by stone walls that sits behind an early farmhouse. Three quarters of the beds are herbaceous perennial borders supplemented by annual cutting areas and a small herb patch. The house and garden are Vermont vernacular in character and could easily have been here 100 or 200 years earlier. Within the garden walls is a unique birch tree of great age and beauty that adds much charm to the garden. Beyond the garden walls are areas of interest, including an old corncrib and barn, a vegetable garden, and small pond. The grounds are particularly attractive because of the venerable native trees on the property.

Hours: 10 a.m. to 4 p.m.

Take Routes 11/30 into Manchester. At blinking traffic light turn south (left) onto Route 7A. Proceed through roundabout and take first right onto Way Lane. Follow to stop sign and turn north (right) onto West Road. Pass Brightwood Road on right. Next, pass Village Glen Road and very next driveway on right will be White Tree Farm, with white wooden gates. Number 1166 will be on gate. *Please park in driveway or on lawn.*

Edwards' Garden

67 Coventry Lane, Manchester Center

The siting of my informal garden, to run the length of the back of the house surrounding the low deck, means that, when outside, one lives in the garden, rather than looks at it. Likewise, from inside the house, the garden is constantly in view from most windows. Such scrutiny requires attentive maintenance. The garden was designed to disappear in winter, with one's attention directed past it to the woods beyond. It is a work in progress and will be extended with the remodeling of the east end of the house.

Hours: 10 a.m. to 4 p.m.

Located in northeast section of Manchester. Take Route 7A/Main Street north to Barnumville Road. Proceed .5 mile to Canterbury Road on left. Climb Canterbury until pavement ends. One hundred feet beyond end of pavement is Coventry Lane on right. House is first on left. Garden is reached around back side of garage.

Joan & Lee Fegelman's Garden

42 Coventry Lane, Manchester Center

In the spring of 1991, our gardens began as three large perennial beds on a former horse pasture. Today our gardens encompass over an acre. As you meander through the perennial garden room on wide grass pathways, you will witness a riot of color that is in various stages of bloom from spring until frost. Leaving the perennial garden through an arbor, you wander along a peony/daylily walkway, the vista opens, and, to the right, you see a pergola garden room featuring rocks, a sundial, and interesting shrubs. From there, meander on a thyme-scented stone path through the herb garden, which then flows into the grass and annual garden. The rose garden features roses that are at home in Vermont. Unusual hostas enhance the beauty of the pool area.

Hours: 10 a.m. to 4 p.m.

From Manchester Center, take Route 7A north to Barnumville Road. Go .7 mile to Canterbury Road, second left. Go .6 mile to Coventry Lane, which will be second right. House is first driveway on right.

Public Gardens

BENNINGTON COUNTY

MANCHESTER

Hildene

Manchester (802) 362-1788 www.hildene.org

Robert Todd Lincoln's Hildene was the home of Abraham Lincoln's descendants until 1975. This Georgian Revival mansion is situated among formal gardens that have been restored to their original beauty. Many of the original plantings remain and the location on a promontory in the valley provides a splendid view of the mountains on either side of Hildene's meadow-lands below. A peony festival is held in June.

Hours: mid-May through October, daily, 9:30 a.m. to 4 p.m.; tours available by appointment

Admission: $8 full tour, $4 grounds only

Located just 2 miles south of the junctions of Routes 7A and 11/30.

CHITTENDEN COUNTY

ESSEX JUNCTION

The Inn at Essex

70 Essex Way, Essex Junction (802) 878-1100 www.innatessex.com

The Inn at Essex, Vermont's only AAA four-diamond hotel, built in 1989, is also home to the Essex campus of the acclaimed New England Culinary Institute. The gardens are designed to complement the large Colonial Revival-style Federal and Georgian buildings and reflect the unique partnership of the culinary school and the inn. Two generous beds filled the annuals flank the top of the green in front of the inn and many large pots filled with flowers decorate the walkways. Behind the inn is a large tented atrium/patio with stone steps leading down to the East Lawn, a welcoming expanse bordered by eighty-foot-long hedge-lined perennial beds with a wedding gazebo at the far end. Between the patio and Butler's Restaurant is a formal herb garden for use by the chefs and their students. The herb garden has a stone wall at one end with steps leading down to an allée of green ash trees. On the other side of the patio is a partially shaded bed with a mix of woody flowering shrubs, roses, and perennial phlox complemented by flowering shrubs and other perennials and annuals. At one end of the pool is a fountain sculpted by the late Paul Aschenbach, his last work, accentuated by a semi-circle of flowering annuals.

Hours: year round, daily, 10 a.m. to 4 p.m., except during private parties

Admission: free

From I-89 south, take Exit 17/Colchester, Vermont. Turn left, then right onto Routes 2 and 7 at traffic light. Go 3 miles, then bear left onto Route 2A south, go 5 miles to Exit 10/Route 289 east/Essex Way, and turn right. Inn is .25 mile on left.

From I-89 north, take Exit 11/Richmond, Vermont. Turn right, then make an immediate right again onto Route 117 west. Go 6 miles to Exit 10/Route 289 west/Essex Way and turn left. Inn is .25 mile on left.

The Inn at Shelburne Farms

1611 Harbor Road, Shelburne (802) 985-8442 www.shelburnefarms.org

The gardens at the Inn at Shelburne Farms, originally designed by Lila Vanderbilt Webb, feature lush perennial borders inspired by the English cottage style of Gertrude Jekyll. The peak of the gardens' bloom is early June, when the 'Queen Victoria' peonies are in their glory, through July, when delphiniums bloom in front of a backdrop of tall plume poppies. Low brick walls provide the formal architectural structure to define the "rooms" within the garden and create multiple levels for the rose garden, the lily pond surrounded by Dutch and Japanese iris, and an herb garden. Continuing Lila's tradition of welcoming the community into her gardens, we invite you to visit. Shelburne Farms is a 1,400-acre working farm, a national historic site, and a nonprofit environmental education center whose mission is to cultivate a conservation ethic by teaching and demonstrating the stewardship of natural and agricultural resources.

Hours: year round, daily, 10 a.m. to 2 p.m.; garden tours available

Admission: $5

From I-89, take Exit 13 to Route 7 west at traffic light in center of Shelburne. Drive 1.6 miles to entrance of Shelburne Farms. Turn right into Welcome Center parking area before entering gates. Tickets may be purchased there.

VIRGINIA

Garden of William A. Grillo, Arlington.

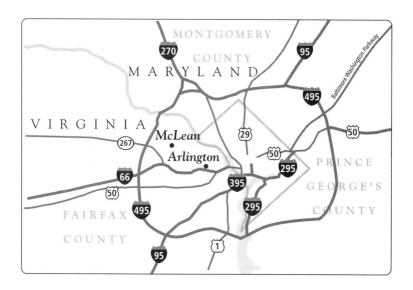

Saturday, May 17

ARLINGTON COUNTY

ARLINGTON

Palmer Aldrich Garden

3102 2nd Street North, Arlington

We're going native! Three years ago we decided to do away with the front lawn of our 1920s Tudor-style bungalow and start using more plant varieties native to the eastern United States in the garden. The northwest corner is mostly native, with ground covers under the existing oak and hickory canopy, including pachysandra, Canadian anemone, May apple, sweet woodruff, and various fern species. Walk through the garden portal to the backyard with raised beds for flowers, more woody native perennials, and even a few herbs and vegetables.

Hours: 10 a.m. to 4 p.m.

From Clarendon Metro stop between Clarendon and Wilson Boulevards, go south on North Highland Street for 11 blocks. We are on right at corner of 2nd Street North.

From Washington, D. C., go west on Route 50 past Fort Meyer. Turn right onto North Highland Street. Go north 3 blocks and we are on left on corner of North Highland and 2nd Street North.

Proceeds shared with the Virginia Native Plant Society

The Craig-Cool Garden
1039 North Daniel Street, Arlington

The original concept for this garden was developed in 1989. It is based on a desire to expand our living space with a more formal street presence to the neighborhood. Upon passing through the gates, the borders curve in and out to give a sense of mystery as to what might be around the bend. As you walk deeper into the garden, it becomes more relaxed and naturalized. The garden behind the island is the most relaxed and naturalized of all. The small pond with a trickle of water is settled into the back of the island and is not seen until after you are around the corner. The garden is planted with perennials. There are no annuals except in pots. All of the garden structures, decks, and fences were custom designed by Charlie Craig and color was custom mixed to achieve the faded look of age and weather. Thought was given to light and shade to create depth as well as plants with light or dark foliage. Winter colors and views from the interior of the house have also played a part in plant placement.

Hours: 10 a.m. to 4 p.m.

From Washington, D. C., take Route 50 west to 10th Street exit. At North Daniel Street, turn right and proceed to #1039 on right.

From I-395, take Columbia Boulevard/Washington Boulevard exit/Route 27. Go to second traffic light (a Texaco gas station on corner) at 10th Street (about 3 miles). Turn right and go to North Daniel Street. Turn left and go to #1039 on right. *Please park on street.*

Garden of William A. Grillo
606 North Edgewood Street, Arlington

Approach this shade garden over a cobblestone drive court, past the front porch covered in cypress louvered shutters. Handcrafted gates and copper pulls welcome visitors to walk down the stone path along a dry creek to the recesses of this garden. This open-air room is framed by two outbuildings and two ponds. One pond is a simple square located close to the dining pavilion; the other is centered in the flagstone patio and populated with koi swimming through the gentle current of a waterfall. A studio offers respite with different views of this tranquil setting. Ferns, astilbe, hostas, liriope, crape myrtle, oak-leaf hydrangeas, and Japanese maples fill the garden and are accentuated by a backdrop of thirty-five-foot-high bamboo and Leyland cypress. Flagstone steps arch over the dry creek to the open back porch. Several seating areas near low stone walls allow visitors to reflect and enjoy the essence of this intimate retreat.

Hours: 10 a.m. to 4 p.m.

From Washington, D.C., take Route 50 west to Pershing Drive; turn right. At intersection with Washington Boulevard, continue on Pershing. Make first right onto North Edgewood Street to second house on left.

From I-395, take Route 27/Washington Boulevard/Columbia Pike exit about 1.8 miles to Washington Boulevard. Turn left onto Pershing Drive, then make first right onto North Edgewood Street to second house on left.

Proceeds shared with the Lyon Park Citizens Association

The Weeks Garden
302 North Irving Street, Arlington

About ten years ago, our "yard," both front and back, was transformed into a "garden" with the substantial assistance of Concepts and Contours design. Gracefully curved planting areas and smaller grassy sections are joined with flagstone walks, a brick patio, and porch. The patio is our secluded summer dining room except on very hot nights. We continue to add hostas, ferns, hellebores, and other shade-loving plants under our large oaks, witch hazels, and dogwoods. Clematis are tucked into areas that get some sun. Azaleas are plentiful and bloom from April to June.

Hours: 10 a.m. to 4 p.m.

From Washington, D.C., take Route 50 west to Pershing Drive and turn right. At intersection of Pershing and Washington Boulevard, continue for a few blocks to North Irving Street (street names are in alphabetical order). Turn left and go 1.5 blocks. House is on right, in middle of block.

From I-395, take Washington Boulevard/Columbia Pike/Route 27 exit. Go about 1.8 miles on Washington. Turn left onto Pershing Drive and go a few blocks to North Irving Street. Proceed as directed above. *Please park on street.*

McLean
Ridder Garden
1219 Crest Lane, McLean

The garden slopes down to the bluffs of the Potomac River just below Little Falls. Much of the beauty of the garden derives from its views of the falls, the rapids, and an unspoiled island that is part of George Washington Park. The garden was probably started in the twenties, after farming on the rocky river bank was abandoned, so there are many mature trees, tulip poplars, oaks, and beeches, as well as old rhododendrons and azaleas. My effort has been to grow regionally appropriate flowers and vegetables and have a garden that flowers from March to November. The garden is divided between a woodland walk with wild and shade flowers and a series of parterres with perennials.

Hours: 10 a.m. to 4 p.m.

From Washington, D.C., take Canal Road to Chain Bridge. Turn left across bridge. Take first right at traffic light onto Chain Bridge Road/Route 123. At top of hill, after passing Merrywood, turn right onto Crest Lane (just before George Washington Memorial Parkway). Take third right onto small roadway. Number 1219 is a yellow house, third on right between #1260 and #1211.

From Maryland, take Beltway/I-495 south to Virginia. Take first Virginia exit onto George Washington Memorial Parkway. Exit at Chain Bridge Road/Route 123. Follow exit ramp to Route 123. Take first left onto Crest Lane. Proceed as directed above.

Proceeds shared with Potomac Conservancy

Public Gardens

ARLINGTON COUNTY

ALEXANDRIA

American Horticultural Society
at George Washington's River Farm

7931 East Boulevard Drive, Alexandria (703) 768-5700 www.ahs.org

Once part of George Washington's property, this twenty-seven-acre garden overlooking the Potomac River now serves as headquarters for the American Horticultural Society. The gardens include the Interactive Children's Gardens; George Harding Memorial Azalea Garden; Wildlife Garden; herb, perennial, and annual display beds; and a picnic area.

Hours: year round, weekdays, 8:30 a.m. to 5 p.m.; April 1 through October 31, Saturday, 9 a.m. to 1 p.m.; closed on holidays

Admission: free, but donations are appreciated

River Farm is located about 4 miles south of Old Town Alexandria, just off George Washington Memorial Parkway. Exactly .5 mile after going under Stone Bridge, turn left off parkway at Arcturus/East Boulevard/Herbert Springs exit. Turn left at stop sign. Entrance is on right.

WASHINGTON

OPEN DAYS:

May 18
May 31
June 1
June 7

Richard & Joan Kinsman Garden, Bainbridge Island.

Sunday, May 18

PIERCE COUNTY

ORTING

The Chase Garden

16015 264th Street East, Orting

A PROJECT OF
THE GARDEN
CONSERVANCY

This naturalistic style garden on four and one-half acres has been created and tended by Emmott and Ione Chase since 1960. The area surrounding the house was designed by Rex Zumwalt, evoking the simplicity of a Japanese garden by use of raked pea gravel, moss-covered boulders, and a reflecting pool. A forest of native trees is carpeted with wildflowers. There are perennial shade borders, a rock garden, and a ground cover meadow inspired by the alpine meadows of Mount Rainer.

Hours: 10 a.m. to 3 p.m. Also open by appointment only from mid-April to mid-June. Call (206) 242-4040 for more information.

From Highway 161 (Meridian), turn east onto 264th Street east, which is about 1 mile south of town of Graham. Continue for 3.5 miles. Watch for driveway directly across from road sign indicating 10 mph (with a crooked arrow).

From Seattle, go south on Highway 167. Take Puyallup/Olympia exit onto Highway 512 and take South Hill/Eatonville exit. Turn left at traffic light to access Highway 161 (Meridian). Proceed as directed above.

From Tacoma at I-5, take Highway 512 east to Eatonville exit. Turn right at light to access Highway 161 (Meridian). Proceed as directed above.

From Olympia, follow signs to Eatonville. Go north from Eatonville via Highway 161 (Meridian). Proceed as directed above.

PUYALLUP
Ernie & Julia Graham Garden
13715 Military Road East, Puyallup

Our garden is an intensely planted, organically maintained wildlife sanctuary with a beautiful view of Mount Rainier. A labyrinth of paths and focal points enables visitors to meander through several distinctive garden areas situated on varying levels of a one-acre sloped site. The garden began to seriously evolve in the early 1990s when Julia discovered that there was more to gardening than petunias. The woodland garden combines Pacific Northwest natives with strong Asian influence. It features an extensive collection of Japanese maples complemented by various conifers, unusual shrubs, perennials, and ground covers. This garden focuses on foliage color, texture, and contrast rather than flowers. Water features, intimate seating areas, and subtle art are tucked in throughout. From the woodland, paths lead to a boldly tropical poolside garden, a well-tended bonsai collection, and then a side trip to "Ernie's Garden"—an eclectic combination of vegetables, berries, herbs, flowering perennials and shrubs, and espaliered fruit trees. Finally, a cozy shade garden outside the kitchen allows relaxation amid the protection of sequoia, Douglas fir, styrax, stewartia, *Cornus kousa*, and a nearby purple and black garden. One leaves through a sixty-foot arbor with intertwined ornamental grape and other vines. The Graham Garden won second place in both the 1997 and 2000 Pacific Northwest Garden Competitions. It has been featured in *Better Homes & Gardens*, the *Seattle Times*, *Tacoma News Tribune*, and in many slide seminars at the annual Northwest Flower & Garden Show in Seattle.

Hours: 10 a.m. to 2 p.m.

From downtown Seattle, take I-5 south to I-405 north (by Southcenter Mall). Take Auburn exit heading south on Route 167/Valley Freeway. Continue south past Auburn. Exit right at Sumner/Yakima onto Route 410 go about 1 mile to Orting/Valley Avenue exit. Turn right at exit, traveling south towards Orting for about 3 miles. Not far past Todd's Nursery is a "T" intersection with Military Road East. Turn right and head up hill. Part way up hill, turn right again at a sign that reads Military Road East and proceed to #13715 on black mailbox on left. House is on right as you go up hill; garden is not visible from street. *Please park in strip along street outside fence.*

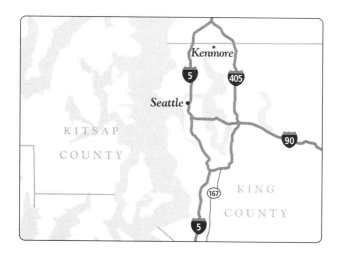

Saturday, May 31
KING COUNTY

KENMORE
The Ridge Garden
16021 76th Place N.E., Kenmore

The seven-and-one-half-acre Ridge Garden includes an Asian garden that fuses Japanese and Indonesian influences; a rhododendron garden with hundreds of woodland plants; and rock, bog, and moss gardens. Ring the Japanese temple bell, view Mount Baker, examine tiny plants in the alpine house, take a respite in the tree house, or simply stroll the half mile of paths.

Hours: 10 a.m. to 4 p.m.

From I-5 (north out of Seattle), take Exit 177 to Lake Forest Park. Continue on 205th/ Ballinger Way to Bothell Way. Turn left, then right onto 68th/Juanita Drive (second traffic light). Turn left onto 153rd/Arrowhead (third light). Turn left onto 76th Place Northeast (about .5 mile). On 76th, go .3 mile. You will see a large cedar-fenced property on left. Turn in at gates, drive to end of driveway, turn around in gravel turnaround (and garden entrance). *Please do not park in turnaround.*

From I-405 (north out of Bellevue), take Northeast 124th exit/Totem Lake. Turn left off ramp onto Northeast 124th. Turn right onto 100th Avenue Northeast. Turn left onto Simonds Road. Turn left at first light (Northeast 155th at Inglemoor High School). Go .7 mile and turn right onto 76th Place Northeast and proceed as directed above.

SEATTLE
Noel Angell & Emory Bundy
270 Dorffel Drive East, Seattle

The residence is a 1905 Craftsman-period house on the National Historic Register. From the street, the house is approached by a river rock pathway through a light woodland garden. Granite steps lead down along a granite boulder waterfall, reflecting the region's hilly topography. An upper patio in the front of the house is nestled into a dense planting of sun-loving plants. After walking through a river rock archway to the back, the gardens have a more rustic appeal, with edible berries and fruit trees.

Hours: 10 a.m. to 3 p.m.

From I-5 south, take Highway 520 to Montake exit. Travel south and east on Lake Washington Boulevard, through Arboretum. Cross Madison Street and continue on Lake Washington Boulevard. After approximately 4 blocks, pass Bush School, and turn right onto 37th East. After approximately 50 feet, 37th East curves and becomes Dorffel Drive East. Number 270 is first house on left, brown with white trim.

From I-5 north, take first Madison Street exit and travel east. At Lake Washington Boulevard, turn right and follow directions above. *Please park along street.*

The Gannon Garden
5719 Kensington Place North, Seattle

On a typical city lot, our garden houses 500 species of plants. The front garden includes a potager planted in the parking strip featuring mostly berries for browsing and a new small grape arbor. Brick pavers, pedestals, and matching urns lend a formal structure to the collection viewed from the street, which includes perennials, woody shrubs, and small garden trees planted among two brick circular paths within square borders. A narrow passage adorned with vines and shade plants leads the visitor between closely spaced houses to a larger private back garden, whose centerpiece is a 2,500-gallon koi pond. Here, formality gives way to natural stone paths and wood hardscapes encroached upon by dense plantings. Flowering plants mix with bold foliage, evoking opulence within serenity. To preview this garden, visit www.gannon.org/garden.

Hours: 10 a.m. to 4 p.m.

Take I-5 to N.E. 50th Street exit and head west, crossing freeway. Make first right turn at Latona Avenue North and drive north for 8 blocks. Turn left at N.E. 58th Street and drive 2 blocks to end of road at a "T." Turn left onto Kensington Place North. We are first house on right. Look for aforementioned grape arbor and raised vegetable beds in parking strip. *Please park on street.*

Geller-Irvine Garden
1725 26th Avenue, Seattle

I started the garden in 1981, when there were only two trees on the property. Today, the woodland cottage garden reminds me of my native New England. The placement of the main structure of trees and shrubs naturally defines the interconnected outdoor rooms. A walk through the property brings you up a steep hillside entry garden, through the woodland canopy, and onto two brick terrace gardens surrounded by perennials. The sixty- by 120-foot garden feels larger than it is due to the changing feeling and flow of the spaces.

Hours: 10 a.m. to 3 p.m.

From I-5, take Madison Street exit. Turn east onto Madison towards Lake Washington. Turn right onto 25th Avenue east (heading south). Turn left onto East John Street and proceed down hill. Take first right onto 26th Avenue and continue a couple of blocks past East Denny and East Howell. Number 1725 is on right just past East Howell. Look for a wooden staircase.

Lakeside Garden
1500 42nd Avenue East, Seattle

The gardens are a part of a family home on Lake Washington. The sandstone-paved entry garden leads through a wooden gate into a small rose garden fronting a greenhouse. Perennial gardens surround the swimming pool facing Lake Washington. There is a vegetable garden behind a brick wall east of the greenhouse.

Hours: 10 a.m. to 4 p.m.

Follow East Madison Street towards Lake Washington. Turn right onto East Lee Street in Madison Park neighborhood and continue down to 42nd Avenue East. *Park around this intersection and enter garden gate just east of intersection of East Lee and 42nd.*

Lee & John Neff
5563 South Holly Street, Seattle

Surrounding a farmhouse built in 1915, this small garden is set among holly hedges and large trees and shrubs planted between 1890 and 1940. Cedar wattle fences made by Sue Skelly frame the kitchen garden and adorn the grandchild berry bed, rock garden, and Camperdown elm tree house. There are collections of species tulips, Pacific Coast iris, and roses. Beds planted in the last nine years combine trees, shrubs, and perennials and include a five-year-old woodland garden shaded by a grove of *Idesia polycarpa*, a red and black border, and many plants selected for year-round interest.

Hours: 10 a.m. to 4 p.m.

From I-5 south, take Exit 161/Albro-Swift. At first traffic light, turn left. Cross expressway and turn right at next light. In 1 block, turn left onto Graham to Rainier Avenue South. Turn right, then left onto Holly Street. Cross Seward Park Avenue South and continue to dead end at 57th Avenue South. Turn right and you are facing our driveway, gravel with 2 large cedars marking entrance. *Please park on Holly before 57th Avenue or on west side of 57th north of Holly.*

From I-5 north, take Exit 157/Martin Luther King Way South. Go north to Othello and turn right. Go to Rainier Avenue South and turn left. Travel a short distance and turn right onto Holly. Proceed as directed above.

Phil Wood & Judy Mahoney
4314 Burke North, Seattle

This is the personal garden of Phil Wood, garden design columnist for the *Seattle Times*. It is a collector's garden filled with unusual plants as well as a family garden of intriguing spaces and structures. Paths lead from room to room, ending at a two-story pavilion.

Hours: 10 a.m. to 4 p.m.

From I-5, take north 45th Street exit and go west to Wallingford neighborhood. One block past Guild 45th Theatre, turn south onto Burke Avenue north. Garden is 1.5 blocks down on left. *Please park on street.*

Proceeds shared with the Seattle Chinese Garden Society

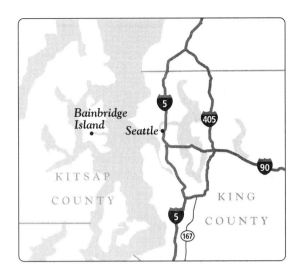

Sunday, June 1
KITSAP COUNTY

BAINBRIDGE ISLAND
Richard & Joan Kinsman
9245 Fox Cove Lane N.E., Bainbridge Island

This garden was the 2002 winner of the Pacific Northwest Garden Contest. Informal pathways wind through a garden designed to offer a variety of textures and colors that merge naturally into the woodland setting. Well-chosen groupings of shrubs, perennials, and trees provide year-round interest. The outdoor living areas offer quiet places to sit and enjoy the garden and the surrounding forest. Raised beds provide a bounty of herbs and flowers for harvesting. Garden structures, fountains, art, and living quarters blend seamlessly into the site to provide a tranquil and aesthetically pleasing environment.

Hours: 10 a.m. to 4 p.m.

From Highway 305, go west on High School Road to end. Turn right and go through 4-way stop (mini-market). Watch for sign "Battle Point Drive" (about .5 mile from stop sign). Turn left and go .5 mile to Fox Cove Lane. Garden is first house on Fox Cove Lane. Look for sign and raven totem pole. *Please park on Battle Point Drive.*

Proceeds shared with the Bainbridge Island Land Trust

Little and Lewis

1940 Wing Point Way N.E., Bainbridge Island

The garden/gallery of Little and Lewis is internationally known as one of the most photographed and published gardens in the United States. Sitting on a third of an acre in a small, quiet waterfront community, the garden is a paradise filled with exotic plants, wonderful concrete sculptures, and gently dripping water features. Little and Lewis have earned a reputation for creating beautiful, unique, and colorful concrete sculptures and water elements. Their work can be seen in private and public gardens all over the country. This is a rare opportunity to see this extraordinary garden gallery and meet these two creative gardening artists. To see a preview, visit www.littleandlewis.com

Hours: 10 a.m. to 4 p.m.

By ferry, from Coleman Dock in Seattle, take Bainbridge Island Ferry (35-minute crossing). Once off ferry, turn right at first traffic light onto Winslow Way. Go to Ferncliff and turn left. Go 2 short blocks to Wing Point Way. Turn right and go .5 mile to garden on left just after Park Avenue.

By highway, take Highway 3 to Highway 305. Once you cross Agate Passage Bridge, you are on Bainbridge Island. Travel down 2-lane highway to High School Road (McDonald's and Chevron are on corner). Turn left. Go to Ferncliff. Turn right. Go to Wing Point Way. Turn left. Go .5 mile to garden, which is on left just after Park Avenue. *Please park on street.*

Waterman Garden

6886 Wing Point Road N.E., Bainbridge Island

The expansive view of Puget Sound and Seattle takes you by surprise as you find your way through the perennial-laden meandering woodland paths on the property. You'll hear water music drifting faintly through the mature stands of rhododendrons and Douglas firs, which shade the long curved driveway. "Plantings have grown so thickly that the lavish gazebo and spacious vegetable garden, complete with its own pond, are hidden until you follow a path through the woods to emerge into sunlight, nasturtium, beans, and squash". (Valerie Easton). The garden has several animal sculptures by Betz Bernhard and Lewis and Little. You will enjoy our mature garden featured in the *Seattle Times* on August 4, 2002.

Hours: 10 a.m. to 4 p.m.

From Seattle, board Winslow Ferry. Upon docking, turn right at first traffic light (Winslow Way). Turn left onto Ferncliff. Turn right onto Wing Point Way, then turn right again onto Wing Point Road Northeast. House is located 6 driveways from corner. *Please park on street.*

Proceeds shared with the Washington Park Arboretum Foundation

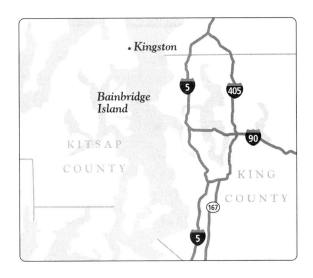

Saturday, June 7
KITSAP COUNTY

BAINBRIDGE ISLAND
Carol & Gene Johanson
14787 Henderson Road, Bainbridge Island

As you enter our property, to your left you see tall conifers hiding the house and garden beyond, and to your right a Japanese-inspired dry stream bed defined by an undulating wave of rock. The one-and-one-quarter-acre garden is located on a sweeping, sloping site overlooking Port Orchard Sound and the Olympic Mountain range. Like the water of the Puget Sound and the mountains in the distance, the garden flows with dramatic, fluid, curving lines. Gardening to scale, the beds are large, using a wide variety of trees, shrubs, and flowers to create a strong sense of texture and contrasting tonal values.

Hours: 10 a.m. to 4 p.m.

From Highway 305, go west on Hidden Cove Road. Turn right onto Henderson Road and go .5 mile to driveway on left before a large gray house. Follow gravel driveway straight ahead and down onto property. *Please park along driveway or on property. Parking cannot accommodate oversized vehicles.*

Just a Garden
1572 Fort Ward Hill Road, Bainbridge Island

My garden is relatively new, six years old. It really has no formal planning—basically I would have to say just buy and plant! A garden is very forgiving, or I should say plants are very forgiving, as they do not mind being dug up and moved, and that's what my garden is—dug up and moved! It is not easy to describe one's garden, mostly perennials, roses, a few shrubs, etc. It's a small lot with a little bit of grass—just a garden.

Hours: 10 a.m. to 2 p.m.

Take Seattle Ferry to Bainbridge Island. After disembarking, turn left at first traffic light onto Winslow Way. Go 2 blocks and turn left onto Madison Avenue and Wyatt Way intersection. Go down Wyatt, past Episcopal church, continuing downhill the bear right up hill onto Blakely Avenue. Go 1.5 miles until Blakely intersects with County Club Road. Turn right and take first right onto Fort Ward Hill Road. Go 1 mile to yellow house on left past Evergreen Road intersection.

KINGSTON
Heronswood
7530 N.E. 288th Street, Kingston

Heronswood is a world-renowned nursery and garden specializing in rare and unusual plants, located on seven acres. The ever-expanding gardens cover many different styles, from shady woodland to sunny rock garden; traditional double perennial borders to a semi-tropical vegetable garden; arbor plantings and ponds. Art in the garden includes the work of Little and Lewis, Marcia Donohue, and Mark Bulwinkle.

Hours: 9 a.m. to 3 p.m.

From Seattle-Bainbridge Ferry (ferries leave every 40 minutes from downtown Seattle terminal at Alaskan Way and Marion Street), follow exit, which becomes Highway 305 north. Go north for 7 miles. Once off island (over Agate Pass Bridge), take immediate right at first traffic light. This road heads east to village of Suquamish, where it turns sharply to left and north. From Suquamish, proceed north 8 miles to next 4-way intersection with light (Chevron gas station, new Albertson's shopping center). Proceed through light towards Hanville, 1 mile north, where N. E. 288th Street "T"s in on left. Turn left onto N. E. 288th Street. Driveway is .25 mile on left across from second set of mailboxes. Only our sign "Heronswood, by appointment" and our street address "7530" are visible from road.

Public Gardens

KING COUNTY

SEATTLE

The Dunn Gardens

Seattle (206) 362-0933 www.dunngardens.org

In 1915, the Olmsted Brothers designed a summer country place for the Arthur Dunn family on a bluff overlooking the Puget Sound. The Olmsted ideals of naturalistic groupings of trees amid broad lawns and flowering borders of shrubs and ground covers continue to be as vibrant and compelling today as they were at the turn of the century.

Hours: April through October (closed August), Thursday, 2 p.m., Friday, 10 a.m. and 2 p.m., Saturday, 10 a.m.; guided tours only

Admission: $7 adults, $5 senior citizens/students

Please call for directions.

Washington Park Arboretum

2300 Arboretum Drive East, Seattle (206) 543-8800 www.wparboretum.org

Washington Park Arboretum is a living plant museum emphasizing trees and shrubs hardy in the Pacific Northwest. Plant collections are selected and arranged to display their beauty and function in urban landscapes, to demonstrate their natural ecology and diversity, and to conserve important species and cultivated varieties for the future.

Hours: year round, daily, dawn to dusk

Admission: free

From I-5, take Exit 168-B/Bellevue/Kirkland east. Take first exit, Montlake Boulevard/UW. At traffic light, go straight onto Lake Washington Boulevard East. Follow 1 mile to stop sign with left-turn lane. Turn left onto Foster Island Road and follow signs to visitors center.

VANCOUVER

1845 Period Garden at Fort Vancouver

612 East Reserve Street, Vancouver (360) 696-7659

Fort Vancouver's 1845 Period Garden recreates the flower and vegetable gardens planted by the British Hudson's Bay Company. The original garden was the first formal garden in the Northwest. The National Park Service manages the five-acre site organically and plants only heirloom or historic varieties.

Hours: March 1 through September 30, daily, 9 a.m. to 5 p.m.; October 1 through February 28, daily, 10 a.m. to 4 p.m.; closed Thanksgiving, Christmas Eve, and Christmas Day.

Admission: free

From I-5, take Exit 1-C and follow signs to Fort Vancouver.

From I-205, follow SR14 west to I-5 north and take Exit 1-C; follow signs.

BAINBRIDGE ISLAND

Bloedel Reserve

7571 N.E. Dolphin Drive, Bainbridge Island (206) 842-7631 www.bloedelreserve.org

The Bloedel Reserve is a 150-acre former residence, now a public access garden and nature preserve. The primary purpose of the reserve is to provide people with an opportunity to enjoy nature through quiet walks in the gardens and woodlands.

Hours: year round, Wednesday through Sunday, except federal holidays. Reservations required.

Admission: $6 adults, $4 senior citizens/children 5 to 12

Reserve is located about 8 miles north of Winslow (Bainbridge Island Ferry Terminal) off Highway 305. Phone for reservations and directions.

BELLEVUE

The Bellevue Botanical Garden

12001 Main Street, Bellevue (425) 452-2750 www.bellevuebotanical.org

The Bellevue Botanical Garden comprises 36 acres of display gardens, rolling hills, woodlands, meadows, and wetlands offering an ever-changing panorama of greenery and color. A unique combination of horticulture education, scenic beauty, special events, and volunteer opportunities it has created a focus of community pride.

Hours: year round, daily, dawn to dusk

Admission: free

From I-405, exit onto N.E. Eighth east, follow to 120th, and turn right. Turn left onto Main Street. Garden is located on right at #12001.

FEDERAL WAY

Rhododendron Species Botanical Garden

Federal Way (253) 661-9377 www.rhodygarden.org

The Rhododendron Species Botanical Garden features one of the finest collections of rhododendrons in the world. Enjoy more than 10,000 rhododendrons growing in a beautiful 22-acre woodland setting with exotic and unusual companion plants. Year-round features include alpine, pond, and woodland gardens, a hardy fern collection, and a gazebo.

Hours: March through May, daily, except Thursday, 10 a.m. to 4 p.m.; June through Febuary, Saturday through Wednesday; 11 a.m. to 4 p.m.

Admission: $3.50 adults, $2.50 senior citizens and students

From I-5, take Exit 143/Federal Way/South 320th Street. Turn east onto 320th Street. At Weyerhaeuser Way South, turn right. Bear left at fork and turn left at stop sign. Take first right and follow signs for parking.

WEST VIRGINIA

Laughinghouse—The Giltinan's Garden, Charleston.

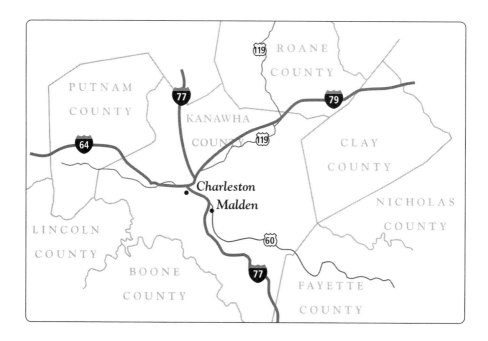

Saturday, June 7
KANAWHA COUNTY

CHARLESTON
Container Gardening with Otis Laury
1800 Roundhill Road, Charleston

After several years of gardening, I moved to an apartment. Since then, I have been gardening in containers consisting of perennials, annuals, hostas, grasses, maple trees, ponytail palms, tulips, hyacinths, daffodils, pansies, and snapdragons. There are also beautiful sculptures in the garden handcrafted by Marc Blumenstein.

Hours: 10 a.m. to 4 p.m.

From I-64, take Oakwood East exit and turn right onto South Ruffner Road. Make immediate right onto Roundhill Road. Continue up hill to apartment building at #1800. *Please park on street.*

Proceeds shared with the Kanawha Garden Club

Gardens with Views—Hillside Gardens of Charlotte & Troy Stallard

16 Fox Chase Road, Charleston

The gardens of Charlotte and Troy Stallard have a superb view and location atop a mountain with a western view of Charleston, the Kanawha River, and our beautiful state capital. Local wildflowers are combined with prairie wildflowers, little bluestem, and Indian grasses. The meadow consists of rock gardens, terraces, viewing areas, water features, and fishponds with waterfalls.

Hours: 10 a.m. to 4 p.m.

Take I-64 east to Kanawha City. Take McCorkle Avenue east to 39th Street south. Cross railroad tracks. Continue on Chappell Hollow Road to first intersection on right. Go to top of hill. Stay on Fox Chase Road and proceed to #16 at end of road. *Please park on street.*

Proceeds shared with the Kanawha Garden Club

Mr. & Mrs. Herbert E. Jones, Jr.

1508 Chafton Road, Charleston

Umberto Innocenti designed a terrace overlooking a fifteen-acre sloping woodland area with maple, walnut, beech, oak, poplar, and dogwood trees. A circular driveway was designed by Alice Ireys. A small perennial garden and a twenty-yard lap pool are on the property, which is defined by pierced brick walls.

Hours: 10 a.m. to 4 p.m.

From I-64, take Broad Street exit and go to Quarrier Street. Turn right and go 2 blocks to Dickinson Street. Turn left and cross Kanawha River Bridge. At end of bridge traffic light, turn left onto Louden Heights Road. Go about 2 miles and turn right onto Chafton Road. Garden is at last house on left. *Please park on Chafton Road.*

Proceeds shared with the Kanawha Garden Club

Laughinghouse—The Giltinans' Garden
800 Louden Heights Road, Charleston

Our gardens at Laughinghouse reflect old and new approaches. We have sited a new house in an old one-and-one-half-acre woodland, attempting a new naturalistic habitat on areas disturbed by construction. Lawns are of mixed clovers and lespedeza. Roof drains are piped to an underground cistern and rainwater is pumped to garden hydrants. Surface water from the sloping site seeps to a bog garden beside the creek that borders the property. Native trees and shrubs, wildflowers, seed-propagated deciduous rhododendrons, and mixed perennial borders attract pollinators, songbirds, and indigenous wildlife, providing safe haven for their cycles and great pleasure for the gardeners! A small pond, fed by a watershed stream, overflows to a rocky watercourse spanned by a footbridge leading to the woodland paths.

Hours: 10 a.m. to 4 p.m.

From downtown Charleston, cross Southside Bridge (Dickinson Street) toward Louden Heights. At end of bridge, turn left at traffic light and go up Louden Heights Road. Continue .7 mile to #800 on left. Just past Bougemont Road (a private drive where you may not park) are stone gate posts marking driveway at Laughinghouse. *Please park in driveway.*

Proceeds shared with the Kanawha Garden Club

MALDEN

Kanawha Salines—Garden of Mrs. Turner Ratrie
Kanawha Salines, Malden

Kanawha Salines, one of the most historic properties in the Kanawha Valley, was built by a pioneer in the exploitation of the abundant resources of salt brine beneath the earth. The original house was built in 1815 and remodeled in 1923. The owner, Mrs. Ratrie, is a direct descendent of the first salt producers and has been the garden designer since 1958. An allée of cherry trees on either side of an old brick walk leads to an enchanting white garden surrounding a rectangular pool filled with white waterlilies. There is a formal rose garden surrounded by an English boxwood hedge, an extensive vegetable garden, and a beautiful herbaceous border. The property encompasses one and one half acres.

Hours: 10 a.m. to 4 p.m.

From I-64 /I-77, take Route 60 east to Malden exit. Turn left after the underpass and proceed through town of Malden. Turn right onto a gravel road east of town. Look for a sign at gravel driveway. *Please park as directed.*

Proceeds shared with the Kanawha Garden Club

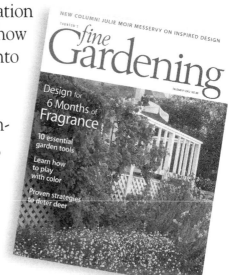

Providing Design Services for Distinctive Gardens

RODNEY ROBINSON · LANDSCAPE ARCHITECTS

707 Philadelphia Pike

Wilmington, DE 19809

tel: 302. 764. 9554

fax: 302. 764. 4628

e mail: RRLA@rrlarch.com

Photo by Jeffrey E. H

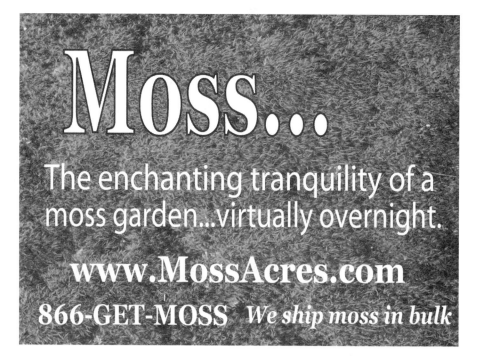

Old Westbury Gardens

Visit North America's most beautiful English-style country estate, listed on the National Register of Historic Places. Formal gardens feature classical statuary, fountains, sundials and follies within 160 acres of landscaped grounds, woodlands, lawns and lakes. Westbury House, a magnificent Charles II-style mansion built in 1906 for American financier and philanthropist John S. Phipps, his English wife, Margarita Grace Phipps and their four children, is filled with fine English antique furniture, paintings and decorative objects collected during the more than 50 years of the family's residence.

- 2.2-acre Walled Garden • Sunken parterre Rose Garden
- Boxwood Garden with reflecting pool and colonnade
- Charming Thatched Cottage and Garden • Demonstration Gardens

Open mid-April through October, 10:00 am-5:00 pm
Westbury House Gift Shop, Plant Shop, outdoor Café in the Woods

Sundays in November & Festive Holiday Celebration in December
Westbury House Gift Shop

Call **(516) 333-0048** for fees and directions or visit
www.oldwestburygardens.org
For information on Group Tours (15 or more people), dial Ext. 310

71 Old Westbury Road, Old Westbury, Long Island, New York 11568

Weekday visitors receive a FREE gift.
Bring this ad to the Gift Shop in Westbury House to receive your gift.

THE NATIONAL GARDENS SCHEME

Opening gardens of quality, character and interest throughout England and Wales with proceeds from open days supporting nursing, gardening and other charitable causes.

Gardens of England and Wales Open for Charity, the best selling annual garden visiting guide, lists some 3,500 gardens giving details of each garden s opening dates and times and a brief description. The Yellow Book , as it is popularly known, can be purchased online from ***www.ngs.org.uk***

Garden Finder, the Scheme s unique website search and mapping facility helps garden visitors plan their itineraries.

For more information about the NGS, please contact:
The National Gardens Scheme
Hatchlands Park
East Clandon
Surrey GU4 7RT
England

T 0044 1483 211535
F 0044 1483 211537
E ngs@ngs.org.uk
W www.ngs.org.uk

430

INDEX

· ·

Join the Garden Conservancy

If you have enjoyed our *Open Days Directory*, why not consider becoming a member of the Garden Conservancy? Your support will enable us to continue to preserve America's exceptional gardens and to ensure that more of these treasures are open to the public. As a member, you will receive the following valuable benefits:

- a subscription to our quarterly newsletter
- free admission to selected Garden Conservancy preservation projects
- invitations to Garden Conservancy-sponsored special events
- discounts on purchases of the *Open Days Directory* and admission coupons
- a personalized membership card and an automobile decal

With a gift of $100 or more, you will be invited to additional Conservancy activities and be acknowledged in our newsletter and annual report. A gift of $1,500 or more, will enroll you in the Society of Fellows and you will may attend garden-study tours and special events.

Please enroll me as a member of the Garden Conservancy:

❏ $35 Individual   ❏ $100 Friend   ❏ $1,500 Fellow   ❏ $10,000 Chairman's Circle
❏ $50 Family   ❏ $250 Sponsor   ❏ $2,500 President's Circle/Sustainer
❏ $50 Organization   ❏ $500 Patron   ❏ $5,000 President's Circle/Benefactor

Open Days Discount Admission Coupons
Save on admission fees with discount coupon books. They make garden visiting easier and they do not expire. Use them at any Open Day garden *(private only)*, anywhere.

Membership contribution $_____

Directories ($10.95 members, $15.95 nonmembers) $_____

Coupon Books—a $30 value ($20 members, $25 nonmembers) $_____

Add $4.50 for shipping & handling when ordering a *Directory* $_____

Add $1.50 for each additional *Directory* $_____

Total enclosed $_____

Please charge my credit card account: MasterCard ____ VISA ____

Account Number: _____ Exp. ___/___

Name _____

Address _____

City/town_____State_____Zip _____

Daytime phone _____

email _____

Please make checks payable to: *The Garden Conservancy* and send to: The Garden Conservancy, P.O. Box 219, Cold Spring, NY 10516, fax to (845) 265-5392. You may also order by calling us on our toll-free order line at (888) 842-2442 or logon to www.gardenconservancy.org.

The Garden Conservancy, Inc. is a tax-exempt organization under section 501(c)(3) of the Internal Revenue Code. Membership contributions are fully tax deductible. Purchase of *The Garden Conservancy's Open Days Directory* and/or coupon books do not constitute a charitable contribution and are not tax deductible.